For who is ignorant that the highest power of an orator consists in exciting the minds of men to anger, or to hatred, or to grief, or in recalling them from these more violent emotions to gentleness and compassion?
—Marcus Tullius Cicero

As regards appeals to the emotions, these are especially necessary in deliberative oratory. Anger has frequently to be excited or assuaged and the minds of the audience have to be swayed to fear, ambition, hatred, reconciliation. At times again it is necessary to awaken pity, whether it is required, for instance, to urge that relief should be sent to a besieged city, or we are engaged in deploring the overthrow of an allied state.
—Marcus Fabius Quintilian

Out of the marriage of reason with affect[,] there issues clarity with passion. Reason without affect would be impotent, affect without reason would be blind. The combination of affect and reason guarantees man's highest level of freedom.
—Silvan Tomkins

Affect, Emotion, and Rhetorical Persuasion in Mass Communication

This volume examines the interplay between affect theory and rhetorical persuasion in mass communication. The essays collected here draw connections between affect theory, rhetorical studies, mass communication theory, cultural studies, political science, sociology, and a host of other disciplines. Contributions from a wide range of scholars feature theoretical overviews and critical perspectives on the movement commonly referred to as "the affective turn" as well as case studies. Critical investigations of the rhetorical strategies behind the 2016 United States presidential election, public health and antiterrorism mass media campaigns, television commercials, and the digital spread of fake news, among other issues, will prove to be both timely and of enduring value. This book will be of use to advanced undergraduates, graduate students, and active researchers in communication, rhetoric, political science, social psychology, sociology, and cultural studies.

Lei Zhang is an Assistant Professor of English and Journalism at the University of Wisconsin—La Crosse, where she teaches rhetoric, journalism, and new media studies. She also serves as the faculty advisor for the student newspaper, *The Racquet*. She received her master's in Journalism from the University of North Texas and PhD in Rhetoric from Texas Woman's University.

Carlton Clark is a Lecturer in the English Department at the University of Wisconsin—La Crosse, where he teaches writing and American Literature. He earned his PhD in Rhetoric from Texas Woman's University. He has published articles in *Erfurt Electronic Studies in English, Kairos: A Journal for Teachers of Writing in Webbed Environments, Teaching English in the Two-Year College, Technological Forecasting and Social Change,* and *Kybernetes: The International Journal of Cybernetics, Systems and Management Sciences.*

Affect, Emotion, and Rhetorical Persuasion in Mass Communication

Edited by
Lei Zhang and Carlton Clark

NEW YORK AND LONDON

First published 2019
by Routledge
711 Third Avenue, New York, NY 10017

and by Routledge
2 Park Square, Milton Park, Abingdon, Oxon, OX14 4RN

Routledge is an imprint of the Taylor & Francis Group, an informa business

© 2019 Taylor & Francis

The right of the editor to be identified as the author of the editorial material, and of the authors for their individual chapters, has been asserted in accordance with sections 77 and 78 of the Copyright, Designs and Patents Act 1988.

All rights reserved. No part of this book may be reprinted or reproduced or utilised in any form or by any electronic, mechanical, or other means, now known or hereafter invented, including photocopying and recording, or in any information storage or retrieval system, without permission in writing from the publishers.

Trademark notice: Product or corporate names may be trademarks or registered trademarks, and are used only for identification and explanation without intent to infringe.

Library of Congress Cataloging-in-Publication Data
Names: Zhang, Lei, 1974 February 17– editor. |
Clark, Carlton, editor.
Title: Affect, emotion, and rhetorical persuasion in mass communication / [edited by] Lei Zhang and Carlton Clark.
Description: New York, NY: Routledge, 2019. |
Includes bibliographical references.
Identifiers: LCCN 2018019315 | ISBN 9780815374381 (hardback) |
ISBN 9780815374398 (paperback) | ISBN 9781351242370 (ebook)
Subjects: LCSH: Mass media—Psychological aspects. |
Mass media—Social aspects. | Mass media—Political aspects. |
Mass media—Influence.
Classification: LCC P96.P75 A44 2019 | DDC 302.2301/9—dc23
LC record available at https://lccn.loc.gov/2018019315

ISBN: 978-0-8153-7438-1 (hbk)
ISBN: 978-0-8153-7439-8 (pbk)
ISBN: 978-1-351-24237-0 (ebk)

Typeset in Bembo
by codeMantra

For our children, Charles Ming & Caroline Enhui Clark

Contents

List of Contributors	xii
List of Editors	xvi

**Introduction: Heartfelt Reasoning, or Why Facts
and Good Reasons Are Not Enough**   1
CARLTON CLARK AND LEI ZHANG

**PART I
Theorizing Affect and/or Emotion**   15

1 **Three Affect Paradigms: The Historical Landscape
of Emotional Inquiry**   17
KEVIN MARINELLI

2 **Bridging the Affect/Emotion Divide: A Critical
Overview of the Affective Turn**   34
PAUL STENNER

3 **We Have Never Been Rational: A Genealogy of the
Affective Turn**   56
DAVID STUBBLEFIELD

**PART II
Affect in Rhetorical and Cultural Theory**   67

4 **Affective Rhetoric: What It Is and Why It Matters**   69
SAMUEL MATEUS

5 **White Nationalism and the Rhetoric of Nostalgia**   81
MICHAEL MAYNE

x   *Contents*

6 **They Believe Their Belief: Rhetorically Engaging Culture through Affect, Ideology, and *Doxa***   93

PHIL BRATTA

7 **Governing Bodies: The Affects and Rhetorics of North Carolina's House Bill 2**   106

JULIE D. NELSON

8 **How Affect Overrides Fact: Anti-Muslim Politicized Rhetoric in the Post-Truth Era**   115

LARA LENGEL AND ADAM SMIDI

PART III
Affect in the Mass Media   131

9 **"Lee's Filling—Tastes Grant!" The Affect of Civil War Archetypes in Beer Commercials**   133

LEWIS KNIGHT AND CHAD CHISHOLM

10 **Disgusting Rhetorics: "What's the Warts That Could Happen?"**   143

JAIMEE BODTKE AND GEORGE F. (GUY) MCHENDRY, JR.

11 **Aestheticizing the Affective Politics of "If You See Something, Say Something"**   158

CHARLOTTE KENT

12 **Gratifications from Watching Movies That Make Us Cry: Facilitation of Grief, Parasocial Empathy, and the Grief-comfort Amalgam**   171

CHARLES (CHUCK) F. AUST

PART IV
Affect in 2016 U.S. Presidential Election   183

13 **The Circulation of Rage: Memes and Donald Trump's Presidential Campaign**   185

JEFFREY ST. ONGE

14 Feelings Trump Facts: Affect and the Rhetoric of
Donald Trump 195
LUCY J. MILLER

15 Affect, Aesthetics, and Attention: The Digital
Spread of Fake News Across the Political Spectrum 205
KAYLA KEENER

16 Meta-Sexist Discourses and Affective Polarization
in the 2018 U.S. Presidential Campaign 215
JAMIE CAPUZZA

Index 235

Contributors

Charles (Chuck) F. Aust is Professor in the School of Communication and Media, Kennesaw State University. Aust has published articles in *Journal of Personality and Social Psychology, Journalism & Mass Communication Quarterly, Journal of Broadcasting and Electronic Media*, and *Journal of Counseling and Values*. He published a chapter titled "Communication in Self-Help Support Groups: Positive Communication and the Al-Anon Experience" in *Positive Communication in Health and Wellness*. He also published "Face-to-face Communication Outside the Digital Realm to Foster Student Growth and Development" in *Teaching, Learning, and the Net Generation: Concepts and Tools for Reaching Digital Learners*, as well as "Factors in the Appeal of News" in *Communication and Emotion: Essays in Honor of Dolf Zillmann*. His areas of interest include media effects, media literacy, using media to grieve, and communication and positive psychology.

Phil Bratta is an Assistant Professor in the Department of English at Oklahoma State University. He has published or has forthcoming work in edited collections and journals, including *College Composition and Communication, Computers and Composition, Enculturation: A Journal of Rhetoric, Writing, and Culture, Visual Culture and Gender*, and *The Journal of American Culture*. Phil also has been involved with a number of (art) activist projects: Public Action for Today (PACT), The Cradle Project, One Million Bones, and #midwesthungeris.

Jaimee Bodtke received her B.A. from Creighton University in 2017, majoring in Communication Studies. Bodtke's research explores rhetorics of sexual assault and public health. She currently works at Trinity Services, Inc.

Jamie Capuzza (PhD, The Ohio State University) is the chair of the Department of Communication at the University of Mount Union. Her work has appeared in academic journals such as Communication Quarterly, The International Journal of Transgenderism, The Newspaper Research Journal, and Communication Education. Her book, coedited with Dr. Leland Spencer, *Transgender Communication Studies:*

Histories, Trends, and Trajectories, won the National Communication Association LBGTQ Division's Top Book award in 2017 and the Applied Communication Division's Distinguished Edited Book award in 2016 as well as the Organization for the Study of Communication, Language and Gender Top Edited Book award in 2016. Capuzza was named Gender Scholar of the Year in 2018 by the Southern States Communication Association.

Chad Chisholm is a Professor of English and Media Communication at Southern Wesleyan University where he specializes in composition, rhetoric, and language. Chisholm has published in journals as diverse as *Connecticut Review, The South Carolina Review, Mallorn: The Journal of the J.R.R. Tolkien Society, Intercollegiate Review,* and *The Mississippi Encyclopedia.*

Kayla Keener is a PhD student in the Cultural Studies Department at George Mason University. She is interested in the formation and performance of identities and subjectivities within a neoliberal political economy. She focuses on contemporaneous modes of digitally mediated labor, including sites of informal, (non)waged, and affective labor.

Charlotte Kent, PhD, is the Assistant Professor of Visual Culture in the Department of Art and Design at Montclair State University. Her past research examined the rhetorics that substantiate diverse art writings, which created art viewing identities. That has developed into a current project considering changing notions of the self as reflected in artist's works responding to a data-driven culture. She serves on the board of directors for the National Arts Club in New York City.

Lewis Knight is a journalism Professor and the coordinator for the Media Communication department at Southern Wesleyan University. Before settling in academia, Knight started in radio, then moved to television, eventually producing the Good Morning Houston show on KTRK-TV for 12 years. Knight also formed his own business, Knight Line Production, where he created TV commercials and did other media projects for clients. Knight also did stringer work for ABC, HBO, NBC, and Paramount Pictures.

Lara Lengel began her research on Arab Islamic identity and intercultural communication as a Fulbright Research Scholar in Tunisia (1993–1994). Her refereed research appears as lead articles in *Text and Performance Quarterly, Journal of Communication Inquiry,* and *Convergence: The International Journal of Research into New Media Technologies,* and *International Journal of Health Communication,* and in numerous others including *Studies in Symbolic Interaction, Gender & History, Journal of International and Intercultural Communication, Feminist Media Studies,* and *International Journal of Women's Studies.* She and colleagues have been awarded nearly $500,000 in grants

xiv *Contributors*

from Fulbright-Hayes, U.S. Department of State Middle East Partnership Program, and U.S. Department of State Bureau of Educational and Cultural Affairs to develop international university and professional partnerships in the Middle East and North Africa. She has directed and codirected study abroad programs in China, Italy, and Morocco.

Kevin Marinelli is Visiting Assistant Professor of Rhetoric at Davidson College. His scholarship engages the intersection of critical theory and materiality within a rhetorical framework. His work has appeared in *Rhetoric Society Quarterly*, *Argumentation and Advocacy* and *Memory Studies*. His latest publication, "Placing Second: Navigating Transferential Space at the *Silent Gesture* Statue of Tommie Smith and John Carlos," addresses the affective dimension of transferential space in public memory. His essay, "Revisiting Edwin Black: Exhortation as a Prelude to Emotional-Material Rhetoric," addresses the neurobiological implications for the rhetorical style of exhortation. Marinelli is currently writing on the tension between the perceived threats of emotion fatigue and emotional manipulation in public mourning.

Samuel Mateus, PhD, is Professor of Rhetoric and Communication at Madeira University and researcher on visual rhetoric. He has examined the nature of pathos and its role on contemporary advertising at Labcom. IFL and ICNOVA. He is author of the Portuguese e-book Introduction to Rhetoric in the 21th Century (Labcom Books, 2018) and co-editor of From Multitude to Crowds: Collective Action and the Media (Peter Lang, 2015).

Michael Mayne received his Ph.D. in English from the University of Florida and currently teaches at Denison University. His research focuses on twentieth-century American literature and culture. His essay, "Agnes Smedley's *Daughter of Earth* and Representations of the Social," is included in the forthcoming collection, *Representations of Poverty in American Popular Culture.*

George F. (Guy) McHendry, Jr. is an Assistant Professor in the Department of Communication Studies at Creighton University. McHendry received his PhD from the University of Utah in 2013. His research examines rhetorical enactments of security in airport security checkpoints. In particular, McHendry is interested in examining the affective dimensions of travelers and Transportation Security Administration officers.

Lucy J. Miller is a Lecturer in the Department of Communication at Texas A&M University. Her work appears in *Spectator* and *Participations: Journal of Audience and Reception Studies*. She is also coeditor with Amanda R. Martinez of *Gender in a Transitional Era: Changes and Challenges* (Lexington Books, 2015).

Julie D. Nelson is an Assistant Professor at North Carolina Central University, where she teaches courses in rhetoric and composition. Her research interests include rhetorical theory, affect and emotion studies, and archival work. She has published work in *Enculturation, Radical Pedagogy,* and *Composition Forum.*

Adam Smidi is a Graduate Teaching Associate and PhD student in the School of Media and Communication at Bowling Green State University. His research focuses on how mosque organizations can better foster organizational identification with their diverse stakeholders. His study, "Freedom for Whom? The Contested Terrain of Religious Freedom for Muslims in the United States," co-authored with Lara Lengel, is published in The Rhetoric of Religious Freedom in the U.S. His co-authored work is published in the journal *India Quarterly* and has received a 2017 Top Paper Award by the Spiritual Communication Division of the National Communication Association.

Jeffrey St. Onge is an Assistant Professor of Communication and Media Studies at Ohio Northern University. His research focuses on rhetoric and media, with a particular interest in how rhetorical criticism can be used to shape political culture toward more productive ends. His work has appeared in *Rhetoric and Public Affairs, Rhetoric Society Quarterly,* and *Rhetoric Review,* among other venues.

Paul Stenner has held a Chair in Social Psychology at The Open University in the United Kingdom since September 2011. Prior to that, he was professor of psychosocial studies in the School of Applied Social Science at the University of Brighton. He has also held lectureships and senior lectureships in Psychology at University College London, The University of Bath, and The University of East London. He has held, or currently holds, honorary positions at the Department of Social and Biological Communication at the Slovak Academy of Sciences, the University of Brighton, the University of Bath, and University College London, and he has recently taught courses at the Universitat Autònoma de Barcelona, Spain, the University of Copenhagen, Denmark, and the Benemérita Universidad Autónoma de Puebla, Mexico. He has published and edited more than 100 articles and books on a wide range of topics, many of which focused on affect theory.

David Stubblefield is an Assistant Professor of English at Southern Wesleyan University, where is he is also Senior Publishing Editor for the Carolina Institute of Faith and Culture. He is ABD in the University of South Carolina's Composition and Program Rhetoric, where he is finishing a dissertation entitled *A Deconstructed Humanism: Internal Difference and the Affirmation of Privileged Terms.* David also holds an MA in Philosophy from the University of South Carolina. He specializes in Rhetorical Theory, the History of Composition, and Continental Philosophy.

Editors

Carlton Clark is a Lecturer in the English Department at the University of Wisconsin—La Crosse, where he teaches writing and American Literature. He earned his PhD in Rhetoric from Texas Woman's University. He has published work in *Erfurt Electronic Studies in English, Kairos: A Journal for Teachers of Writing in Webbed Environments, Teaching English in the Two-Year College, Technological Forecasting and Social Change, Kybernetes: The International Journal of Cybernetics, Systems and Management Sciences*, and *Research Paradigms and Contemporary Perspectives on Human-Technology Interaction*. His primary research interest is the social systems theory of Niklas Luhmann. He blogs on social systems theory at socialsystemstheory.com.

Lei Zhang is an Assistant Professor of English and Journalism at the University of Wisconsin—La Crosse, where she teaches rhetoric, journalism, and new media studies. She also serves as the faculty advisor for the student newspaper, *The Racquet*. She received her master's in Journalism from the University of North Texas and PhD in Rhetoric from Texas Woman's University. Her research interests include intercultural rhetorics, new media studies, and discourse analysis. She has published work in *Rhetoric Review* and *Kybernetes: The International Journal of Cybernetics, Systems and Management Sciences,* among other venues.

Introduction

Heartfelt Reasoning, or Why Facts and Good Reasons Are Not Enough

Carlton Clark and Lei Zhang

Following two surprising political events that occurred in 2016, the victory of the "Leave" campaign in the Brexit vote and the U.S. election of Donald Trump, we felt an increased urgency to understand how persuasion actually happens in contemporary, information-overloaded contexts. In putting together this collection of essays, we wanted to advance the understanding of persuasion—for two and a half millennia the province of rhetoric—across a wide variety of disciplines. We believe the issues discussed in this collection are urgent and deserve to reach a wide audience. Thus, the essays are written in a style intended to appeal to the well-educated generalist rather than to specialists alone. We have attempted to remove or translate academic jargon into language understandable across disciplines. But in addressing a wide audience, we have had to walk a fine line, seeking to produce neither an oversimplified, "affect and persuasion made easy" text nor an overly technical, jargony, narrowly focused book.

Affect or emotion, which we treat in this introductory essay as synonymous,[1] may serve as a disciplinary node where a wide range of research fields can meet. Thus, this collection ambitiously aims to establish communication between fields such as rhetorical studies, cultural studies, mass media and communication studies, sociology, psychology, philosophy, neuroscience, cognitive science, political science, gender studies, and various design disciplines (architecture, fashion design, urban design, etc.). Design is particularly important as these disciplines concern style and function and human beings respond emotionally to style.

Emotional appeals have become an increasingly important element of persuasion in almost every aspect of our lives. For example, in the 2016 U.S. presidential election, emotions such as fear, anger, and even hate played an enormous role in voter persuasion. When it comes to U.S. national elections, the conventional wisdom has long been that economic issues carry the most weight—recall the slogan adopted by Bill Clinton's 1992 presidential campaign, "It's the economy, stupid."[2] However, in the fall of 2016, with the U.S. unemployment rate at a seven-year low, the economy was not the top concern.

Donald Trump won the white working-class vote by roughly a 2 to 1 margin; however, it wasn't fear for their jobs that motivated Trump voters.

2 Carlton Clark and Lei Zhang

According to The Public Religion Research Institute and *The Atlantic Monthly*, it was white working-class Americans' fear of cultural change, not economic distress, that put Trump in the White House. As Cox, Lienesch, and Jones put it, "White working-class voters who say they often feel like a stranger in their own land and who believe the U.S. needs protecting against foreign influence were 3.5 times more likely to favor Trump than those who did not share these concerns."[3] Trump's message of exclusion of immigrants and restoring America to its former greatness resonated with voters who fear they are rapidly becoming a minority demographic in twenty-first-century America. On the other hand, Hillary Clinton lost the election, at least in part, due lack of voter trust,[4] a powerful emotion in politics. Deep-seated sexism and misogyny also clearly played a major role, along with the fact that Clinton was successfully portrayed "the status quo candidate" in a time of change.[5]

Political campaigners know very well that campaigns cannot be fought with facts alone, especially in this digital age when campaign grounds have increasingly been moved to social media, online news, and blog sites. Cambridge Analytica, the firm that played an important role in the Brexit campaign and Trump's successful presidential bid, understands the role of emotions in propaganda campaigns exceptionally well.[6] Mark Turnbull, Cambridge Analytica's managing director, acknowledged the firm's focus on manipulating voters' emotions in a candid private conversation recorded by British Chanel 4's undercover journalists:

> The two fundamental human drivers when it comes to taking information onboard effectively are hopes and fears and many of those are unspoken and even unconscious. You didn't know that was a fear until you saw something that just evoked that reaction from you. And our job is to get, is to drop the bucket further down the well than anybody else, to understand what are those really deep-seated underlying fears, concerns. It's no good fighting an election campaign on the facts because actually it's all about emotion. The big mistake political parties make is that they attempt to win the argument rather than locate the emotional center of the issue, the concern, and speaking directly to that.[7]

There is nothing shocking in this revelation. Effective propaganda has always manipulated people's emotions, regardless of what age we live in. Online information wars among political candidates simply mean faster message delivery and more digital tools to understand what those underlying fears and hope are, allowing campaigns to better tailor their messages and microtarget crucial voters.

We might like to believe that human beings usually employ their reasoning capacity to find the truth or reach understanding. But in a much-discussed 2011 article, Hugo Mercier and Dan Sperber argued that the primary function of reasoning is argumentative. When engaged in a debate or discussion, we typically reason in order to find arguments to support a predetermined conclusion, not to discover the truth.[8] Thus, argument tends to reinforce polarization of views rather than mutual understanding or the advancement of knowledge. But the news is not all bad. Mercier and Sperber write that "contrary to common bleak assessments of human reasoning abilities, people are quite capable of reasoning in an unbiased manner, at least when they are evaluating arguments rather than producing them, and when they are after the truth rather than trying to win a debate."[9] However, it's hard to separate evaluation and production because when evaluating arguments we produce more arguments.

As indicated by Mercier and Sperber's study, among others, it has become clear that facts and reason alone are not the answer to our problems. Where decision-making is concerned, access to reliable information does not always produce rational, sound decisions. Thus, the Information Deficit Model (IDM), which holds that lack of information is responsible for lack of understanding (of science in particular), has been declared dead.[10] Today, thanks to information technology, we have more facts, more reasons, and more arguments at our fingertips than ever before. And tomorrow we will have even more facts and reasons and arguments than today. There are nearly 200 million active websites, meaning sites with a unique hostname that users are actually visiting, on the World Wide Web. According to Internet Live Stats, Google processes over 40,000 search queries on average per second.[11] We have information, but without some degree of emotional appeal, reasonable arguments supported by facts do not persuade or move us. For example, an August 2016 poll by NBC News found that 72% of registered Republican voters, despite all the evidence to the contrary, still doubted President Obama's citizenship.[12] As long as an affective bias exits, we might not even *notice* an opposing argument; or if we do notice the argument, we won't care enough to attend to it. As Silvan Tomkins put it, "A world experienced without any affect would be a pallid, meaningless world. We would know that things happened, but we could not care whether or not they did."[13]

When analyzing our decision-making and openness to persuasion, we must realize that the human brain isn't really just one organ. Neuroscience identifies four regions of the brain that evolved at different times. The most primitive region, sometimes called the "reptilian" brain, is responsible for vital functions such as heartbeat and respiration. Above the reptilian brain lies the midbrain, which contains key areas involved in regulating sleep, appetite, motivation, and attention. Surrounding the midbrain is the limbic system, which is critically involved in relationships and emotion. The outermost and most recent brain region to evolve is the cortex, which allows language, abstract thought, and planning. It is also critical to understand that "these brain regions work in concert, so it is impossible to separate 'rational thought' from emotion. Even the most sophisticated decisions and analyses require positive and negative emotion; otherwise, it is impossible to determine which choice or idea is 'better' and which isn't. Valuing anything—even an idea—as 'good' or 'bad' requires feeling."[14]

Clearly, then, emotion is not simply a weakness or evolutionary vestige like the appendix, tailbone, or wisdom teeth—far from it. For instance, when it comes to moral reasoning—that is, making decisions on how a person ought to behave—it is now generally accepted that both rational and emotional processes come into play. According to the dual-process model, "a moral judgment is the outcome of a rapid, affect-laden process and a slower, deliberative process. If these outputs conflict, decision time is increased in order to resolve the conflict."[15] Consider parity products. For instance, when making a decision between several brands of shampoo that have very similar ingredients and sell for about the same price, the typical shopper may make a choice based, not solely on brand recognition, but on design features, such as the color or shape of the bottle, features that evoke a subtle emotional response. The concept of "sexy packaging" is based on this premise. For instance, in reference to packaging of perfumes and colognes, Gabriella Zuckerman, president of Gabriella Z Ltd., a beauty-products marketing and development firm, stated, "In a saturated market like fragrances, packaging is critical."[16] As one award-winning package designer said, when it comes to men purchasing a brand of cologne, "Hopefully he likes the fragrance and wants to wear it, but the initial purchase is because they like the bottle."[17]

Of course, this is not really news. Professional organizations have been established to capitalize on this affective bias. For example, the Design & Emotion Society, based in The Netherlands, was established in 1999 as "an international network of researchers, designers and companies sharing an interest in experience driven design. The network is used to exchange insights, research, tools and methods that support the involvement of emotional experience in product design."[18] Novel, interesting design or style gets our attention.[19] As Richard Lanham argued in *The Economics of Attention*, we are not living in an information economy but rather an attention economy. Economics is the science of managing scarcity, but there is no scarcity of information; we are drowning in it. The scarce resource is human attention, and we all end up competing for one another's attention. As Lanham argues, in the attention economy, style moves to the foreground and "substance" recedes to the background. When the substance is pretty much the same, the packaging of the shampoo or cologne takes primacy over the substance inside the bottle.

Furthermore, if we do not incorporate emotional responses, making a trivial decision might take much longer and cause more stress.[20] With respect to decision-making, one area of research compares "neurotypical individuals" with individuals meeting the criteria for autism spectrum disorder (ASD) or alexithymia, a condition characterized by difficulties identifying and describing one's own emotions. In the hypothetical case of choosing a shampoo, a person on the autism spectrum might experience significant stress, especially if she feels pressured to make the decision quickly. One study found that decision-making in ASD was associated with anxiety, exhaustion, problems engaging in the process, and a tendency to avoid decision-making.[21] Both ASD and alexithymia, also known as "emotional blindness," have been associated with atypical decision-making[22] as well as atypical moral reasoning.[23] Alexithymia and ASD are often co-occurring, as alexithymia characterizes under 10% of the typical population but approximately 50% of the ASD population, and co-occurring alexithymia, rather than ASD alone, may account for the observed atypical moral reasoning.[24] It appears that emotional signals are not perceived, and thus, not integrated into decision-making in persons with alexithymia.[25] Consequently, a person with alexithymia tends to make utilitarian rather than empathy-based decisions.[26] Other studies have supported the theory that neurotypical persons base their judgments of the moral acceptability of behavior on their emotional response to that behavior, while people on the autism spectrum show more logical consistency and rely on their own established rules to judge moral acceptability.[27]

Temple Grandin, the well-known professor of animal behavior and writer and speaker on autism, described her situation this way: "Nonautistic people seem to have a whole upper layer of verbal thinking that is merged with their emotions. By contrast, unless I panic, I use logic to make all decisions; my thinking can be done independently of emotion. In fact, I seem to lack a higher consciousness composed of abstract verbal thoughts that are merged with emotion."[28] For Grandin, the absence of abstract thoughts when making decisions is usually not a problem. She thinks in pictures and can make rapid choices between various visual scenarios. In life-and-death situations, this mode of thinking has distinct advantages. On the other hand, a trip to the grocery store may present significant problems.

Even for Grandin, however, thinking alone, even in pictures, is not enough to make a meaningful life. Grandin emphasizes that she does have emotions, but those emotions, being intense and fleeting, are more like those of a child than an adult. As she puts it, "My emotions are simpler than those of most people. I don't know what complex emotion in a human relationship is. I only understand simple emotions, such as fear, anger, happiness, and sadness. I cry during sad movies, and sometimes I cry when I see something that really moves me. But complex emotional relationships are beyond my comprehension."[29] Given that Grandin can describe her emotions, she appears to be autistic but not alexithymic. If Grandin were alexithymic, she probably wouldn't have devoted her career to the humane treatment of livestock animals. Although Grandin clearly demonstrates empathy, deliberative or rule-based decision-making has been associated with increased perceived permissibility of accidentally harming others.[30] In other words, if harm accidentally results from well-intended actions,

6 Carlton Clark and Lei Zhang

the alexithymic individual is less likely than the neurotypical person to be emotionally troubled.

As Paul Stenner writes, "Alexithymia means, literally, the inability to assign words to emotions. Alexithymia describes a series of psycho-behavioural characteristics that are expressed in the etymology of the word itself: from the Greek *a-* (lack), *lexis-* (word) and *thymos-* (mood, feeling or emotion), alexithymia means literally without words for emotions."[31] The discussion of *thymos* brings us back to classical rhetoric.

We can draw a connection here with the Greek rhetorical concept of the enthymeme, which is often misrepresented as a truncated syllogism—that is, a syllogism where the audience fills in an unstated premise. In the *Rhetoric*, Aristotle, speaking of previous writers on rhetoric, states, "Now, the framers of the current treatises on rhetoric have constructed but a small portion of that art. The modes of persuasion are the only true constituents of the art: everything else is merely accessory. These writers, however, say nothing about enthymemes, which are the substance of rhetorical persuasion, but deal mainly with non-essentials."[32] Aristotle also calls the enthymeme "the most effective of the modes of persuasion."[33] Clearly, the enthymeme is a big deal; therefore, it would not make sense for it to be nothing more than an incomplete syllogism, which could be "fixed" by inserting the unstated premise. The common misrepresentation of the enthymeme as an informal logic or quasi-logic[34] has served to subordinate the ethical and affective appeals to the logical appeal, and it ultimately leads to a very restricted view of argumentation. This is a view that, Jeffrey Walker argues, "leaves little room for the affective dimensions of argumentation, or for argumentational procedures that cannot be resolved into straightforwardly 'syllogistic' ... representations."[35] Enthymeme derives from *thymos*, "meaning 'heart' or 'mind' or 'spirit' as the seat of emotion, thought, wish, desire, intentionality, or will. In one's *thymos* one considers things, draws inferences, becomes impassioned, forms desires, has intentions, and makes plans."[36] As a form of heartfelt reasoning, then, the enthymeme negates the reason/emotion dichotomy. The ancient Greek arts of rhetoric, drama, and poetry were all forms of argumentation; they addressed arguments to an audience in the form of heartfelt reasoning. The goal was to stir the thoughts and feelings of an audience. This is where affect fits into rhetorical argumentation. Thus, contemporary psychology and neuroscience, along with the affective turn more generally, appear to be turning (not necessarily turning back, but just turning) to ancient Greek poetics and rhetoric.

Overview of the Chapters

The book proceeds in four parts. Part I offers an overview of affect theory and the "affective turn." Part II considers affect within the contexts of rhetorical theory and cultural studies. Part III considers the role of affect and affective appeals in the mass media, and Part IV focuses more narrowly on how affective appeals were deployed in the 2016 U.S. presidential election.

More specially, in Part I, the contributors present an overview of the "affective turn," questioning some of the now taken-for-granted positions. In Chapter 1, Kevin Marinelli argues that the burgeoning study of affect offers a potential node of interdisciplinary collaboration; yet, its heterogeneity can also undermine a coherent framework of analysis. Marinelli aims to facilitate an interdisciplinary, collaborative approach to research on affect by tracing its respective discussions across the disciplines. To this end, Marinelli provides an introduction to affect theory by surveying its three dominant paradigms: classical rhetoric, cultural studies, and neuroscience. Paul Stenner, in Chapter 2, draws on three decades of work as a social psychologist to outline three key sources of the affective turn, each of which presents a different concept of affect (affect as autonomous virtual intensity, as drive amplification, and as unconscious psychic energy). Stenner also comments on the widespread view that affect and emotion are two very different things. Stenner is not in principle opposed to making an affect/emotion distinction. His concern is with *the way* this distinction has been drawn by influential advocates of the affective turn. Although the affective turn has often been represented as a turn away from the discursive turn—an umbrella term covering the linguistic turn, rhetorical turn, social construction, semiotics, and various interpretations of postmodernism and poststructuralism—Stenner argues that the turn to affect is not a rejection but rather an extension or deepening of the discursive turn. In Chapter 3, David Stubblefield also observes that the contemporary affective turn has been framed as a reaction against the discursive turn. From the perspective of the affective turn, the discursive turn privileged symbolic representations, and thus, had little to say about the role of matter, bodies, and the affects that circulate between them. While Stubblefield sees much that is new in the contemporary turn to affect, he argues that affective experience has always played a central role in Western thought. To support this claim, he discusses two earlier positions on affect: the moral interpretation and the romantic interpretation of affect.

The contributors to Part II demonstrate that a rhetoric that relies solely on logic, evidence, and facts usually fails to persuade. In Chapter 4, Samuel Mateus shows how the mid-twentieth-century establishment of argumentation as an academic field conspicuously omitted any serious discussion of the emotions. He argues that, in contrast to classical treatises on rhetoric, major modern texts such as Toulmin's *The Uses of Argument* (1958) and Perelman and Olbrechts-Tyteca's *The New Rhetoric* (1958, original French edition) limited the scope of rhetoric by paying little attention to affective appeals. In Chapter 5, Michael Mayne analyzes white nationalism as a rhetoric of nostalgia. He argues that nostalgias are intrinsically reactionary, not because they always define a conservative social order, though

8   *Carlton Clark and Lei Zhang*

they usually do, but because they always insist that an ideal order once existed, and our uncritical longing for an idealized past prevents a critical analysis of the present and restricts possibilities for progressive social transformations. Extending the examination of ideology, in Chapter 6, Phil Bratta questions the separation affect and ideology, arguing that ideology and affect often work in a symbiotic way. Bratta argues that many ideologies are saturated with affect and many affective experiences are ideological. Using Donald Trump's defense of Confederate statues as a case study, Bratta argues that Trump's rhetoric draws on an ideology (a system of ideas, concepts, or theories) and manipulates a culturally situated affect—fear. Although much of Trump's rhetoric rests on logical fallacies—and fallacious arguments are ubiquitous in contemporary society—we should give greater attention to how an argument breaks through the fallacy to convince an audience. Merely documenting reasoning fallacies does not get us very far in confronting pressing public issues.

In Chapter 7, Julie D. Nelson takes a close look at the affective rhetoric surrounding North Carolina's House Bill 2, better known as the Bathroom Bill. Through a survey of queer affect scholarship, Nelson identifies four functions of affect: attaching, accumulating, creating public spaces, and generating public sentiments. More than just personal feelings, affects circulate among people. Nelson examines how attaching negative affects like shame and fear to queer and transgender bodies shaped the public debate, contributed to the relative success of HB2, and turned the bathroom into a symbolic cultural, affective site. In the final chapter of Part II, Lara Lengel and Adam Smidi extend the analysis of the circulation of affect, arguing that the circulation of negative affects contributes to "post-truth" affective politics. Lengel and Smidi trace the rise in dis/misinformation about Muslims in the United States and argue that anti-Muslim rhetoric constitutes some of the most dangerous forms of post-truth affective politics. This chapter looks closely at how the mass media amplified and intensified the circulation of post-9/11 affects, particularly anxiety, anger, and fear.

The authors featured in Part III analyze affect as it circulates in the mass media, including television commercials, film, and public health and anti-terrorism campaigns. In Chapter 9, Lewis Knight and Chad Chisholm explore the role of affect in beer commercials. They argue that producers of select beer commercials construct narratives that produce affective responses in consumers by appealing to unconscious, internalized archetypes. In particular, Knight and Chisholm argue that American men who "came of age" before the turn of the millennium are targets for beer commercials that invoke Ulysses S. Grant and Robert E. Lee archetypes. Next, Jaimee Bodtke and George F. (Guy) McHendry, Jr. critique a public health campaign designed to raise awareness about sexually transmitted infections (STIs), arguing that the campaign utilized affective rhetorical appeals of disgust and abjection to promote feelings of shame and, thus, stigmatized and marginalized sufferers of STIs. Bodtke and McHendry also describe how they actively intervened in this public health campaign and ultimately persuaded the organization behind the campaign to make changes. In Chapter 11, Charlotte Kent critiques the New York Metropolitan Transit Authority's (MTA's) "If You See Something, Say Something" public awareness campaign, which fueled feelings of fear and paranoia as it recruited ordinary citizens into the war on terror. Kent goes on to discuss, as cases of "aesthetic politics," three works of art that appropriated the MTA's slogan. Kent argues that these artistic efforts questioned the rhetoric and affective limitations of the patriotism, vigilance, and caution promoted by the MTA campaign. Next, Charles (Chuck) F. Aust explores the perhaps counterintuitive fact that "tearjerker" movies often bring comfort and consolation to viewers. Aust argues that viewers of tearjerker movies experience, temporally contiguous to their crying, comforting feelings associated with their own memories, which are activated by pivotal emotion-laden events involving film characters with whom they have developed a parasocial relationship. Aust's chapter intersects nicely with Chapter 2, where Stenner discusses a study led by Hertha Sturm that found that young children described a particular short film as both sad and pleasurable. Brian Massumi discusses the Sturm study in his often-cited 1995 article, "The Autonomy of Affect,"[37] but Stenner finds a number of problems with Massumi's interpretation of Sturm's research.

Finally, in Part IV, the contributors analyze how strong affects/emotions were aroused and manipulated in the 2016 U.S. presidential election. Jeffrey St. Onge draws connections between affect theory, meme theory, and democracy as a way to explain the political rise of Donald Trump. St. Onge argues that memes functioned to spread anger/rage through digital media and, in so doing, created an ideal condition for Trump's populist candidacy. Next, in Chapter 14, Lucy J. Miller argues that Trump makes rhetorical appeals to fear and anger to drive his audience away from designated others and toward himself. While Trump's appeals to emotion are not new in politics, what is interesting is his disregard for credible supporting facts; therefore, fact-based argument alone is not effective in countering Trump's rhetoric. Miller goes on to present an example of a productive response to post-truth discourse: Emma Gonzalez's speech delivered on February 18, 2018 in the aftermath of the shooting at Marjory Stoneman Douglas High School, a speech that combined genuine emotion with credible supporting facts. Extending the discussion of the "post-truth era," in the next chapter, Kayla Keener considers how specific instances of fake news concerning the 2016 election and the Trump presidency have circulated through digital media and popular discourse, highlighting the ways that fake news is consumed, spread, and believed by individuals on *all* points of the ideological spectrum. Fake news is able to deceive news consumers across partisan lines by specifically targeting preexisting fears and beliefs, mimicking the aesthetics of mainstream news websites, and circulating through social media. In the final chapter, Jamie Capuzza analyzes how gender politics permeated the 2016 election from beginning to end. Sexist and misogynist discourses are both grounded in and have the potential to evoke strong affective responses. Thus, Capuzza demonstrates the usefulness of affect theory in advancing an understanding of meta-sexist discourse, or how we talk about sexism and misogyny. In 2016, the discourse on sexism and misogyny produced affective polarization, as both the Clinton and the Trump campaigns used misogyny and alleged misogyny, as framed by Trump, to motivate their bases and reinforce feelings of interconnectedness among their followers.

To sum up, this book illustrates how the study of affect intersects in different disciplinary fields. We hope the essays lead to more interdisciplinary conversations about the important functions of affect in rhetorical persuasion. The centuries-long attempt to separate reason from affect, along with the associated siloing of academic fields, has held back our understanding of persuasion and limited our ability to negotiate an increasingly complex, information-saturated global society. We hope to contribute to productive change.

Notes

1 Paul Stenner, in Chapter 2, argues, *contra* arguments made by Brian Massumi and others, that emotion and affect are not actually two very different things.
2 This statement was a later variation of a statement by James Carville, "The economy, stupid."
3 Daniel Cox, Rachel Lienesch, and Robert P. Jones, "Beyond Economics: Fears of Cultural Displacement Pushed the White Working Class to Trump | PRRI/The Atlantic Report," *PRRI*, May 5, 2017. Available www.prri. org/research/white-working-class-attitudes-economy-trade-immigration-election-donald-trump/.
4 "Why Hillary Clinton Lost the Election: The Economy, Trust and a Weak Message," *The Guardian*, November 9, 2016. Available www.theguardian. com/us-news/2016/nov/09/hillary-clinton-election-president-loss.
5 Dana Milbank, "Commentary: Hillary Clinton Should Make Elizabeth Warren Her Running Mate," *The Chicago Tribune*, March 5, 2016. Available www.chicagotribune.com/news/opinion/commentary/ct-hillary-clinton-elizabeth-warren-running-mate-perspec-0307-20160306-story.html.
6 Hannes Grassegger and Mikael Krogerus, "The Data That Turned the World Upside Down," *Motherboard*, January 28, 2017. Available https://motherboard. vice.com/en_us/article/mg9vvn/how-our-likes-helped-trump-win.
7 Nancy LeTourneau, "Why Was Cambridge Analytica so Interested in Tapping into Our Fears?" *Washington Monthly*, March 21, 2018. Available https:// washingtonmonthly.com/2018/03/21/why-was-cambridge-analytica-so-interested-in-tapping-into-our-fears/.
8 Hugo Mercier and Dan Sperber, "Why Do Humans Reason? Arguments for an Argumentative Theory," *Behavioral and Brain Sciences* 34, no. 2 (2011): 57–74. doi:10.1017/S0140525X10000968.
9 Ibid., 72

10 Paul McDivitt, "The Information Deficit Model Is Dead. Now What? Evaluating New Strategies for Communicating Anthropogenic Climate Change in the Context of Contemporary American Politics, Economy, and Culture," Order No. 10124052, University of Colorado at Boulder, 2016.

11 Internet Live Stats. March 31, 2018. Available www.internetlivestats.com/total-number-of-websites/.

12 Josh Clinton and Carrie Roush, "Poll: Persistent Partisan Divide Over 'Birther' Question," *NBC News*, August 10, 2016. Available www.nbcnews.com/politics/2016-election/poll-persistent-partisan-divide-over-birther-question-n627446.

13 Silvan Tomkins, *Exploring Affect: The Selected Writing of Silvan S. Tomkins*, edited by E. Virginia Demos (Cambridge: Cambridge University Press, 1995), 88.

14 Maia Szalavitz and Bruce Perry, *Born for Love: Why Empathy Is Essential—And Endangered* (New York: HarperCollins, 2010), 18.

15 Denise Dellarosa Cummins and Robert C. Cummins, "Emotion and Deliberative Reasoning in Moral Judgment," *Frontiers in Psychology* 3 (2012): 328. doi.org/10.3389/fpsyg.2012.00328.

16 Ian Murphy, "Perfume Bottles Make a Fashion Statement," *Marketing News* 28, no. 25 (December 5, 1994): 6. Available https://libweb.uwlax.edu/login?url=https://search-proquest-com.libweb.uwlax.edu/docview/216403871?accountid=9435.

17 Ibid., 6.

18 The Design and Emotion Society. Accessed March 28, 2018. Available www.designandemotion.org.

19 Petronio A. Bendito, "Aspects of Visual Attraction: Attention-Getting Model for Art and Design," *Journal of Visual Literacy* 25, no. 1 (Spring 2005): 67–76.

20 Lydia Luke, Isabel C.H. Clare, Howard Ring, Marcus Redley, and Peter Watson, "Decision-Making Difficulties Experienced by Adults with Autism Spectrum Conditions," *Autism* 16, no. 6 (2011): 612–621.

21 Ibid.

22 Punit Shah, Caroline Catmur, and Geoffrey Bird, "Emotional Decision-Making in Autism Spectrum Disorder: The Roles of Interoception and Alexithymia," *Molecular Autism* 7 (2016):43. doi:10.1186/s13229-016-0104-x.

23 Rebecca Brewer, A.A. Marsh, C. Catmur, EMCardinale, S. Stoycos, R. Cook, et al., "The Impact of Autism Spectrum Disorder and Alexithymia on Judgments of Moral Acceptability," *Journal of Abnormal Psychology* 124 (2015): 589–95.

24 Ibid.

25 Anil K. Seth, "Interoceptive Inference, Emotion, and the Embodied Self," *Trends in Cognitive Science* 17 (2013): 565–73.

26 Ibid.

27 Ibid.

28 Temple Grandin, "My Mind Is a Web Browser: How People with Autism Think," *Cerebrum* 2, no. 1 (Winter 2000): 14–22.

29 Temple Grandin, *Thinking in Pictures: My Life with Autism* (New York: Vintage Books, 2006), 91.

30 Indrajeet Patil and Giorgia Silani, "Reduced Empathic Concern Leads to Utilitarian Moral Judgments in Trait Alexithymia," *Frontiers in Psychology* 5 (2014): 501.

31 Paul Stenner, "Is Autopoietic Systems Theory Alexithymic? Luhmann and the Socio-Psychology of Emotions," *Soziale Systeme* 10 (2004): Heft 1, S. 159–185.

32 Aristotle, *Rhetoric*, I.1.3. Translated by W. Rhys Roberts. Internet Classic Archives. http://classics.mit.edu/Aristotle/rhetoric.1.i.html.
33 Ibid., I.1.11.
34 Chaim Perelman and Lucie Olbrechts-Tyteca, *The New Rhetoric*, 193.
35 Jeffrey Walker, *Rhetoric and Poetics in Antiquity* (Oxford: Oxford University Press, 2000), 170.
36 Ibid., 173.
37 Brian Massumi, "The Autonomy of Affect," *Cultural Critique* 31, no. 2 (1995): 83–109.

Bibliography

Brewer, Rebecca, Abigail A. Marsh, Caroline Catmur, Elise M. Cardinale, Sarah Stoycos, Richard Cook, and Geoffrey Bird. "The Impact of Autism Spectrum Disorder and Alexithymia on Judgments of Moral Acceptability." *Journal of Abnormal Psychology* 124, no. 3 (2015): 589–595.

Clinton, Josh, and Carrie Roush. "Poll: Persistent Partisan Divide Over 'Birther' Question." *NBC News*, Aug 10, 2016. www.nbcnews.com/politics/2016-election/poll-persistent-partisan-divide-over-birther-question-n627446

Cox, Daniel, Rachel Lienesch, and Robert P. Jones. "Beyond Economics: Fears of Cultural Displacement Pushed the White Working Class to Trump, PRRI/The Atlantic Report." *PRRI*. www.prri.org/research/white-working-class-attitudes-economy-trade-immigration-election-donald-trump/

Cummins, Denise Dellarosa, and Robert C. Cummins. "Emotion and Deliberative Reasoning in Moral Judgment." *Frontiers in Psychology* 3 (2012): 328. doi.org/10.3389/fpsyg.2012.00328

Grassegger, Hannes, and Mikael Krogerus. "The Data That Turned the World Upside Down." *Motherboard* (Jan 28 2017). https://motherboard.vice.com/en_us/article/mg9vvn/how-our-likes-helped-trump-win

Internet Live Stats. (March 31, 2018). www.internetlivestats.com/total-number-of-websites/

LeTourneau, Nancy. "Why Was Cambridge Analytica So Interested in Tapping into Our Fears?" *Washington Monthly*, March 21, 2018. https://washingtonmonthly.com/2018/03/21/why-was-cambridge-analytica-so-interested-in-tapping-into-our-fears/

Luke, Lydia, Isabel C.H. Clare, Howard Ring, Marcus Redley, and Peter Watson. "Decision-Making Difficulties Experienced by Adults with Autism Spectrum Conditions." *Autism* 16, no. 6 (2011): 612–621.

Massumi, Brian. "The Autonomy of Affect." *Cultural Critique* 31, no. 2 (1995): 83–109.

McDivitt, Paul. "The Information Deficit Model is Dead. Now what? Evaluating New Strategies for Communicating Anthropogenic Climate Change in the Context of Contemporary American Politics, Economy, and Culture." Order No. 10124052, University of Colorado at Boulder, 2016. https://libweb.uwlax.edu/login?url=https://search-proquest-com.libweb.uwlax.edu/docview/1807432622?accountid=9435

Mercier, Hugo, and Dan Sperber. "Why Do Humans Reason? Arguments for an Argumentative Theory." *Behavioral and Brain Sciences* 34, no. 2 (2011): 57–74. doi:10.1017/S0140525X10000968.

Milbank, Dana. "Commentary: Hillary Clinton Should Make Elizabeth Warren Her Running Mate." *The Chicago Tribune* (March 5, 2016). www.chicagotribune.com/news/opinion/commentary/ct-hillary-clinton-elizabeth-warren-running-mate-perspec-0307-20160306-story.html

Murphy, Ian. "Perfume Bottles Make a Fashion Statement." *Marketing News* 28, no. 25 (December 5, 1994): 6. https://libweb.uwlax.edu/login?url=https://search-proquest-com.libweb.uwlax.edu/docview/216403871?accountid=9435

Patil, Indrajeet, and Giorgia Silani. "Reduced Empathic Concern Leads to Utilitarian Moral Judgments in Trait Alexithymia." *Frontiers in Psychology* 5 (2014): 501.

Perelman, Chaim, and Lucy Olbrechts-Tyteca. *The New Rhetoric: A Treatise on Argumentation*. Notre Dame, IN: University of Notre Dame Press, 1969.

Petronio A. Bendito. "Aspects of Visual Attraction: Attention-Getting Model for Art and Design." *Journal of Visual Literacy* 25, no. 1 (Spring 2005): 67–76.

Seth, Anil K. "Interoceptive Inference, Emotion, and the Embodied Self." *Trends in Cognitive Sciences* 17, no. 11 (2013): 565–573.

Shah, Punit, Caroline Catmur, and Geoffrey Bird. "Emotional Decision-Making in Autism Spectrum Disorder: The Roles of Interoception and Alexithymia." *Molecular Autism* 7, no. 1 (2016): 43.

Stenner, Paul. "Is Autopoietic Systems Theory Alexithymic? Luhmann and the Socio-Psychology of Emotions." *Soziale Systeme* 10 (2004): Heft 1, S. 159–185.

Szalavitz, Maia, and Bruce Perry. *Born for Love: Why Empathy Is Essential—and Endangered*. New York: HarperCollins, 2010.

Temple, Grandin. "My Mind is a Web Browser: How People with Autism Think." *Cerebrum*, 2 no. 1 (Winter 2000): 14–22.

Temple, Grandin. *Thinking in Pictures: My Life with Autism*. New York: Vintage Books, 2006.

The Design, and Emotion Society. Accessed March 28, 2018. www.designandemotion.org

Tomkins, Silvan. *Exploring Affect: The Selected Writing of Silvan S. Tomkins*. Edited by E. Virginia Demos. Cambridge: Cambridge University Press, 1995.

Tomkins, Silvan S. *Affect Imagery Consciousness: Volume I: The Positive Affects*. New York: Springer, 1962.

Walker, Jeffrey. *Rhetoric and Poetics in Antiquity*. Oxford: Oxford University Press, 2000.

"Why Hillary Clinton Lost the Election: The Economy, Trust and a Weak Message." *The Guardian* (November 9, 2016). www.theguardian.com/us-news/2016/nov/09/hillary-clinton-election-president-loss

Part I

Theorizing Affect and/or Emotion

1 Three Affect Paradigms

The Historical Landscape of Emotional Inquiry

Kevin Marinelli

Perhaps no concept of human inquiry currently generates more excitement than that of affect. From rhetoric to cultural studies to affective neuroscience, a growing number of scholars investigate the ineffable energy of human activity identified as affect. The trend presents both opportunities and challenges. On one hand, the burgeoning study of affect offers a potential node of interdisciplinary collaboration. On the other hand, its heterogeneity can also undermine a coherent framework of analysis. Various scholarly communities apply the term in different contexts with different inflections. Scholars consequently wind up talking past one another despite their common interests and collaborative potential. Our challenge, then, is to facilitate interdisciplinary dialogue while also preserving the richness of our respective traditions. We certainly do not want to become dogmatic in our vocabulary or homogenize our perspectives for the sake of clarity, but we should at least remain cognizant of how different academic circles define our common terminology. Only then will we begin to craft a multidimensional theory of affect utilizing the numerous insights at our disposal.

This chapter provides an introduction to affect theory by surveying its three dominant paradigms: classical rhetoric (affect as pathos); cultural studies (affect as extra-discursive energy); and neuroscience (affect as pre-cognitive emotion). The topology does not connote a rigid structure of affect scholarship so much as highlight dominant themes of discussion. Its purpose is to illuminate the range of seminal projects defining affect studies while focusing on their common roots and points of departure. By engaging the evolution of affect studies in this way, we may begin to transform multidisciplinary interest into interdisciplinary conversation. The chapter moves spatially and chronologically across the disciplines from classical antiquity to present day. First, we engage Aristotle's concept of pathos in classical rhetoric. Second, we trace the evolution of affect in cultural studies from the rationalist philosophy of Benedict de Spinoza through the post-structural insights of Gilles Deleuze and Felix Guattari. Third, we trace the development of affect studies in the life sciences from the evolutionary biology of Charles Darwin through the affective neuroscience of Paul Ekman and others. Finally, we touch upon notable intersections of affect scholarship whose multimodal perspectives offer unique insights into the human condition. First, a word on the challenge set before us.

The concept of affect, much like the phenomenon it identifies, remains notoriously difficult to manage. Scholars generally describe affect as the ineffable dimension of human activity. Some use it to describe a facet of human emotion, while others situate it in discourse and culture. In either case, affect generally refers to human activity operating outside the parameters of traditionally perceived "reason." Beyond that, there exists little consensus on the topic. We find as many definitions of affect as there are people studying it.[1] In that way, the concept functions more as a theoretical placeholder than a clearly defined phenomenon. Affect appears to us much like dark matter appears to theoretical physicists: overwhelming evidence suggests it exists, but no one agrees on what exactly "it" is. Biologists, for example, find evidence of affect in the human flashes of rage or fear that sometimes exceed our conscious judgment of a situation. Cultural theorists find evidence in discursive formations whose rhetorical life often exceeds the intentionality of its participants. This chapter attempts to situate these seemingly disparate perspectives in an ongoing conversation beginning in classical antiquity with the emergence of rhetorical studies.

Affect in Classical Rhetoric

Modern theories of affect evolve from classical insights concerning human motivation in public affairs.[2] Emotion becomes an important topic of discussion with the proliferation of public oratory in the fifth century BCE. Scholars quickly recognize the capacity of orators to stir and manipulate emotional states in their audiences for personal gain. The philosophy of Plato, for example, articulates a critical response to what he perceives as the "non-rational" dimension of rhetoric.[3] To clarify his position, Plato assigns three components to the soul: reason, emotion, and desire (we will return to the concept of desire in the next section).[4] The topology marks a perceived dichotomy between emotion and reason that persists today.[5] Still, perhaps in light of his disdain for it, Plato offers considerably minimal insight on the phenomenon of emotion itself. We locate some of the earliest sophisticated treatment on emotion in the work of his successor, Aristotle.[6]

Aristotle engages emotion most extensively in Book II of the *Rhetoric*. Emotion is defined as desire accompanied by a particular form of pleasure or pain facilitated by situational premises.[7] Specifically, Aristotle engages the rhetorical production of emotion, which he identifies as pathos. According to Aristotle, "The emotions [pathê] are those things through which, by undergoing change, people come to differ in their judgments and which are accompanied by pain and pleasure, for example, anger, pity, fear, and other such things and their opposites."[8] We may likewise define pathos as a rhetorically generated emotion aimed to induce audience judgment. The emphasis on judgment is essential for Aristotle to rescue rhetoric from the caricature of emotional manipulation circulating in Plato's Academy at the time.[9] By connecting emotion to human reason in the form of pathos, Aristotle effectively legitimizes the practice of rhetoric in general and the study of emotion in particular. In other words, because pathos is rooted in reason, it is not necessarily bad. Thus, for the first time, emotional rhetoric becomes aligned with reasoned deliberation.

Aristotle's reasonable treatment of emotion offers a wealth of psychological insight. Specifically, it reveals an emotional logic philosophers had previously ignored. In turn, thinkers could now consider emotion in the context of rational decision-making. In the same gesture, however, Aristotle effectively narrows the scope of emotional rhetoric by situating it squarely in logical premises.[10] The nonrational generation of emotion, by contrast, located in rhetorical devices such as physical delivery, receive no vindication in the *Rhetoric*.[11] Likewise, scholarly interest in emotion becomes relatively confined to conscious judgment and beliefs, while emotional activity exceeding perceived reason remains marginalized.[12] Thus, even as emotion earns a place within the rhetorical canon, it nevertheless remains subservient to the more dignified form of rational deliberation.[13] For centuries to follow, rhetoricians interested in emotion focus primarily on pathos while minimizing the potential affectivity of extra-discursive emotional appeals.[14] Accordingly, phenomena such as physicality and tonality (identified today as modes of affect) are effectively excluded from the purview of rhetorical criticism.[15]

Aristotle expands his insights on emotion in the *Nicomachean Ethics*. Here, emotion functions not merely as a conduit of public judgment but also, and more importantly, as an ancillary of human virtue. Like his predecessor, Aristotle situates emotion within a topology of the soul. For Aristotle, however, the soul comprises feelings, capacities, and states. The framework, in turn, provides a more nuanced perspective on the interaction between reason and emotion.[16] The two need not necessarily oppose one another as Plato had argued. Instead, emotion can serve as a valuable aid in the pursuit of reason. Aristotle defines the three categories as follows. First, a feeling refers to "whatever implies pleasure or pain."[17] Second, a capacity is "what we have when we are said to be capable of these feelings."[18] Finally, a state refers to our quality of being when experiencing such feelings.[19] To feel good about doing good things implies a positive state, whereas feeling bad about doing good things implies a negative state. Likewise, virtue is a state of being connected to a feeling or emotion.[20]

In the construction of human virtue, Aristotle argues, individuals must cultivate the appropriate emotional disposition toward acting appropriately. Put simply, one must strive to feel good about doing good. In this way, emotion becomes a central facet of ethical life. Additionally, one must cultivate an emotional disposition autonomously, free from the manipulation

20 Kevin Marinelli

of others. Virtue can be cultivated, e.g., nurtured in children by parents and teachers, but it cannot be manipulated, e.g., rhetorically generated by orators or emotional events.[21] The rhetorical generation of pity, for example, marks a negative, and likewise, unintentional emotion.[22] Accordingly, to help someone out of pity fails to constitute human action because it hinges on an involuntary reflex rather than reasoned deliberation.[23] Because it fails to constitute human action, it fails to constitute ethical behavior, since only humans are capable of such behavior. In this way, Aristotle's treatment of emotion in the *Ethics* and the *Rhetoric* operate similarly. Each model values emotion only insofar as it coordinates with reason. Aristotle transforms Plato's binary between reason and emotion into a binary between reasoned and unreasoned emotion. In doing so, Aristotle articulates but refrains from engaging the dimension of emotional activity identified today as affect.

The Aristotelian conception of emotion informs a considerable portion of emotion studies in philosophy and the social sciences still today. Even as more and more scholars emphasize the importance of emotion in public life, reason remains paramount. Moral philosopher Martha Nussbaum, arguably the leading advocate of Aristotelian ethics, aims to demonstrate the cognitive mediation of human emotion, i.e., emotions as judgments, in her political philosophy.[24] While Nussbaum does amend features of Aristotle's philosophy in light of contemporary scientific insights, she nevertheless privileges a theory of emotional cognition over the concept of affect to which we turn next.

Affect in Cultural Studies

The contemporary study of affect complements the Aristotelian emphasis on reasoned deliberation by examining the ineffable side of emotional life. The scholarship typically falls within either cultural studies or affective neuroscience. In cultural studies, scholars draw on a myriad of theorists, including David Hume, William James, Henri Bergson, Sigmund Freud, and Jacques Lacan. Its primary foundation centers on the work of seventeenth-century philosopher, Benedict de Spinoza.[25] In this section, I ground the critical-cultural approach to affect in the work of Spinoza and his twentieth-century admirers, Gilles Deleuze and Felix Guattari.

We find the centerpiece of Spinoza's work on affect in his magnum opus, the *Ethics*. The work provides some of the most profound insights into human motivation since Aristotle. Aristotle provides a major influence on Spinozan philosophy, and their perspectives share significant parallels.[26] Both consider the ethical utility of bodily affection. Spinoza, for example, communicates the ethical centrality of affect by devoting the third and central part of his treatise to the concept. Both aim to collapse dominant binaries between reason and emotion. Both privilege reason, but nevertheless surpass their contemporaries concerning their insights on the bodily mediation of human activity. Both argue only positive emotions accompany reason. Additionally, Spinoza's definition of affect as the potential to increase or diminish one's "power of acting" echoes Aristotle's concept concerning the "capacity" of the soul to feel appropriately.[27] Still, Spinoza also distinguishes himself from Aristotle by delving further into the psyche of human motivation. In doing so, Spinoza effectively redefines common terms such as *affect* and *desire* into philosophical concepts penetrating the primal abyss of the human condition. These concepts are worth close attention as they continue to spark spirited academic discussion today.

According to Spinoza, the essence of humanity is located in desire. All human beings strive to preserve their being.[28] When preservation is related to the body, we call it appetite.[29] When we consciously direct our appetite to the mind, we call it desire.[30] Desire takes the form of affections or feelings.[31] Thus, although we first become conscious of our appetites on the surface of our bodies, those feelings actually correspond to more primal forces, which Spinoza labels affects. The three primary affects are pleasure, pain, and desire.[32] Spinoza explains, "By affect I understand affections of the body by which the body's power of acting is increased or diminished."[33] The "power of acting," however, is not as simple as it seems. Spinoza defines action as non-passionate affects, or acts of the mind, as opposed to acts resulting from outside forces (similar again to Aristotle). In other words, action always corresponds with reason, and, by extension, Nature/God.[34] Passions, by contrast, refer to affects resulting from an external cause, and therefore, diminish one's power to act (reasonably).[35] Only non-passionate affects, because they relate to the mind, can increase one's power to act.[36] Put simply, humans act in accordance with reason and Nature/God only when motivated by affects of the mind.

Thus far, Spinoza appears to reinforce the perennial reason-emotion dichotomy articulated by Plato, and softened, but nevertheless advanced, in the work of Aristotle. Spinoza clearly privileges the will of the mind over the passions of external forces, and he clearly maintains a transcendental notion of reason. It is important to note, however, that Spinoza identifies the mind operating in tandem with the human body. The distinction between mind and body, then, is merely a conceptual one.[37] Likewise, Spinoza asserts, ideas that fail to recognize the existence of the body are inherently flawed.[38] Genuine action therefore recognizes the contingency of reason upon the human body.[39] Spinoza states, "An affect therefore is an imagination, insofar as [the affect] indicates the constitution of the body."[40] Some contemporary thinkers, including neuropsychologist Antonio Damasio, interpret that passage to suggest Spinoza shared the growing contemporary view that mind is simply a construction of the human body.[41] In any case, Spinoza certainly intimates that viewpoint by emphasizing the inextricability of the two.

22   *Kevin Marinelli*

The philosophy of Spinoza offers a number of prescient insights into the human condition. First, Spinoza clears the space to conceptualize what contemporary thinkers label "embodied cognition," claiming the human mind is in fact a construction of the body informed by a host of material constraints.[42] Second, Spinoza distinguishes between affect and affection to demonstrate the underlying forces of human emotions. To that effect, Spinoza defines affection as the body's consciousness of a thing, namely, an affect or a passion. Thus, it becomes the ethical responsibility of the human subject to investigate one's affections to understand their causes. Ultimately, Spinoza challenges readers to pursue a radically conscious appetite in the form of desire. Although desire can never be fully satisfied, it nevertheless brings one closer to Truth/Nature/God through the pursuit of understanding.[43] Third, and connected to that challenge, Spinoza reverses traditional assumptions about human motivation. According to Spinoza, "[W]e neither strive for, nor will, neither want nor desire anything because we judge it to be good; on the contrary, we judge something to be good because we strive for it, will it, want it, and desire it."[44] In other words, affect does not follow from a conceptual judgment as Aristotle had suggested. Instead, judgment follows affect to produce a mental state. The profound reversal of traditional logic will play an influential role in shaping nineteenth- and twentieth-century human inquiry, specifically, for Nietzsche, and, later, in the field of psychoanalysis.[45]

Psychoanalysis remains especially indebted to the Spinozan concepts of affect and desire. Following Freud, Lacan identifies desire as the insatiable driving force of the human psyche.[46] Unlike Spinoza, however, Lacan does not privilege embodied reason. In fact, he moves in almost the opposite direction. According to Lacan, there exists an irreconcilable chasm between human subjectivity and material embodiment, which produces the affective dimension of lived experience.[47] The chasm constrains the representational limits of speech and often manifests in human anxiety (one of the few affects Freud or Lacan engage in depth).[48] Lacan's treatment of affect and desire presents a twofold legacy. On one hand, Lacan bequeaths a more theoretically sophisticated framework of desire concerning the construction of language. On the other hand, his minimal engagement with affect aims to diminish Spinoza's reflections on embodied cognition.[49] Lacan's failure to more fully engage the discursive life of affect gradually inspires a profound backlash to psychoanalysis in the post-structural work of Deleuze and Guattari.[50]

Deleuze and Guattari provide their most succinct examination of affect in their essay, "Percept, Affect, and Concept," which explores the circulation of affect in works of art.[51] Whereas Lacan conceptualizes the impossibility of fixed meaning from the perspective of a "lack," or inability to fully articulate one's subject position, Deleuze and Guattari engage the phenomenon from the perspective of discursive "excess." In other words, communication always produces more than what the author intends to

Three Affect Paradigms 23

say. Communication also affects the receiver of the message in ways that exceed conscious interpretation. This is what Deleuze and Guattari call affect. The authors define affect, perhaps counterintuitively, as the "non-human becomings of man." By nonhuman, the authors refer to the ways in which communication exceeds the parameters of reason. All communication includes traces of nonhuman phenomena, which Deleuze and Guattari encourage their readers to explore; thus the phrase, nonhuman becoming. The process of becoming marks a central theme in their work. They celebrate becoming as a disintegration of stable opinions, concepts, and identities.[52] In the process of becoming nonhuman, they argue, individuals reclaim the fluidity and multiplicity of lived experience.[53] To borrow from Lawrence Grossberg, studying affect allows us "to see multiplicities instead of simple difference."[54]

Still, two key differences between Spinoza and Deleuze/Guattari emerge concerning agency and reason. First, Deleuze and Guattari assign affect much greater autonomy than does Spinoza. Whereas Spinoza arguably focuses primarily on the relationship between affect and the body, Deleuze and Guattari focus on the cultural circulation of affect in the realms of art and politics. The human body becomes implicated in the circulation of affect, but it does not encapsulate it. Affect neither begins nor ends with the individual.[55] To that effect, Sara Ahmed defines emotion (synonymous with affect) as an effect of contact between bodies, which, in turn, shapes the surfaces of those bodies.[56] It does not, however, begin within the body. Spatially, one could say affect roams the outer terrain of discourse.[57] We frequently come into contact with it, yet we remain unable to capture or even signify it. Thus, while Deleuzian philosophy marks a rejuvenated interest in human sensation on one hand, it further destabilizes human agency on the other.

Second, Deleuze and Guattari effectively release affect from the Spinozan clutches of reason. The authors ultimately envision a world of "heterogeneous elements" guided by no foundational structure: reason, God, desire, etc.[58] For Spinoza, individuals must learn to understand their affects in order to transform them into clear, uninhibited ideas. This is what Spinoza calls human freedom.[59] For Deleuze and Guattari, individuals must aspire in the opposite direction. The purpose of becoming nonhuman is to celebrate affect, to destabilize apparently singular concepts and consider the multitude of potentialities life offers. The authors identify the art of nonhuman becoming as affect.

Deleuze and Guattari do not argue affect is necessarily good, nor do they privilege affect over reason. The very distinction between affect and reason, they would argue, marks a false dichotomy. Instead, the authors merely attempt to demonstrate the discursive dimension of affect in everyday life—the unintelligible discourse shaping reality. To accept concepts at face value, then, is to ignore the "discursive regimes" structuring social norms.[60] To that extent, the historical analyses of Michel Foucault

24   *Kevin Marinelli*

provide a useful complement to Deleuzian philosophy by grounding affect in concrete material practices.[61] Foucault, of whom Deleuze and Guattari were mutual admirers, spent his career exploring various forms of discourse exceeding the traditional parameters of speech. Instead, he explored how material relationships, such as the spatial structures of prisons, produced discursive effects, such as panopticism—where individuals internalize modes of surveillance so that actual surveillance is no longer necessary.[62] Foucault identifies the coordination of such practices as discursive regimes.[63] Locating discursive regimes does not guarantee their collapse, according to Foucault, but it is a necessary step in the process of human emancipation. The endeavor merely aims to identify the discursive context shaping reality at any given moment, what Foucault calls a discursive formation.

Today, cultural critics employ a combination of Spinozan, Freudian, Lacanian, and Deleuzian perspectives on affect. Following Spinoza, Brian Massumi highlights the visceral embodiment of political discourse.[64] Scholars such as Lawrence Grossberg and Nigel Thrift, by contrast, move away from the body to extend the Deleuzian project of locating the "regimes of signification" governing popular culture.[65] To that effect, Grossberg defines emotion as an "articulation of affect and ideology."[66] Lauren Berlant primarily approaches affect from a Lacanian perspective, incorporating themes such as fantasy and objects of desire into her cultural critique.[67] Despite their points of departure, virtually all critical-cultural examinations of affect share a common appreciation for the power of discourse to structure cultural norms beyond the limits of representation and perceived reason.

Affect in the Life Sciences

In the life sciences, scholars examine the production of emotion from a biological perspective instead of a discursive one. One of its most vibrant subdisciplines is affective neuroscience, which studies the relationship between emotion and the central nervous system. Breakthroughs in affective neuroscience allow us to correlate emotions with neural activity in specific areas of the brain. Further, the research demonstrates that while some of our emotions correlate with neural activity in the neocortex (the most recently evolved and uniquely human outer shell of the brain, where language is activated), other especially powerful emotions correlate with neural activity in subcortical regions of the brain shared by many animals.[68] The discovery leads many scientists to distinguish between human cognitive emotions on one hand and primal "affects" on the other. It also compels many to consider the emotional experiences of animals in a more humane light.[69] In this light, emotion is commonly defined as the bodily experience of a mental state in relation to a particular object, whereas affects refer to "states of feeling or action readiness that do not bear on some particular object."[70] This section traces the scholarly conversation surrounding affect and emotion in the life sciences from the nineteenth century to present day.

The trajectory of affective neuroscience dates back to the pioneering work of Charles Darwin in *The Expression of Emotions in Man and Animals*. As the title suggests, Darwin believed he had observed a series of universally shared emotional expressions across the human species and several of its animal relatives. Darwin argues emotional activity must therefore produce, directly and indirectly, bodily responses that eventually become connected to specific emotions, whether necessary or unnecessary for survival, by function of habit.[71] The observation allows Darwin to connect emotions to biological processes including activity in the central nervous system, which will become central to the development of affective neuroscience in the twentieth century. Additionally, Darwin's attention to biological processes as a form of human communication will later inform contemporary theories of material rhetoric.[72] Nevertheless, Darwin's description of emotion as the sensational experience of a mental state remains relatively conventional.[73] This definition will inspire a series of critiques that will, in turn, facilitate theories of affect down the road.[74]

Within a couple decades, scholars begin to challenge key Darwinian assumptions. Most notably, philosopher and physician William James, along with physician Carl Lange, respectively, invert Darwin's description of emotional states to argue that physiological conditions in fact produce mental states. For Darwin, again, emotion marks the sensory experience of a mental state accompanied by bodily expressions. For James and Lange, however, emotion marks the sensory experience of a physiological transformation, accompanied by a mental state. In other words, our hearts do not pump quickly because we are afraid; instead, we become afraid when we notice our hearts pumping quickly. The emotional state still marks a biologically determined relationship between sensory experience and bodily expression, but the sequence is inverted. The explanation eventually becomes known as the James-Lange theory of emotion.

The James-Lange theory facilitates the study of affect by conceptualizing emotion beyond the prototypical emotional episode. Prototypical emotional episodes refer to emotions mediated by conscious cognitive judgments concerning an object.[75] Again, Darwin recognized that bodily expressions often manifest unconsciously, but he did not consider the possibility that emotions could do the same. Today, scholars generally agree on a hybrid of both theories, arguing that emotional states can be induced by mental states, physiological changes, or a combination of both. Lisa Feldman Barrett and Karen Lindquist go so far as to offer a theory of emotional embodiment in which mind and body operate in fluid cooperation, thereby making it impossible to assign a determining factor.[76] In any case, the James-Lange theory allowed scientists to consider biological and psychological functions of emotion outside the realm of prototypical emotional episodes.

The contemporary study of affect begins with the work of psychologist Silvan Tomkins. Tomkins was among the first to identify a set of core emotions, which he labeled affects.[77] Tomkins' student, Paul Ekman, later substantiates his mentor's insights by conducting a landmark experiment on emotional recognition.[78] The study also supports Darwin's early intuitions concerning the universal expression of certain emotions and, by extension, the biological evolution of emotion itself. Ekman, however, takes the hypothesis a step further to consider how certain emotions are biologically distinct from other emotions, not simply in terms of their affection but additionally through a whole range of physiological activity.[79] Ekman labels these affects "basic emotions."

Today a number of core/basic emotion topologies exist.[80] Despite general disagreement on what precisely constitutes a core emotion—Ekman later went on to proclaim, "All emotions are basic"—the significance of such work concerns the scientific evidence that human (and many nonhuman) animals appear biologically hardwired for particular emotional responses transcending cultural norms or conscious emotional assessments.[81] Jaak Panksepp and Lucy Biven, for example, argue that because the affects correspond to neural activity in the subcortical brain (the primitive area of the brain shared by primates), we can rightly assume our nonhuman relatives share these same emotions, and therefore, deserve more humane treatment.[82] Whatever position one assumes in the unfolding debate over affect, one cannot ignore the tremendous insights into emotional activity that affective neuroscience continues to provide.

Whither Affect Studies?

Today, the scholarly landscape of affect encompasses a wide range of disciplinary perspectives. A growing number of social scientists now incorporate neuroscientific insights into the examination of emotion in politics and society.[83] While rationalist perspectives still dominate the scene of social science in many respects, the traditional dichotomy between reason and emotion appears to be steadily eroding. Unfortunately, however, there remains a disconnect between studies of affect in the life sciences and those in cultural studies, respectively. In cultural studies, scholars increasingly turn to Deleuzian philosophy while minimizing the biological labor of affect and the emotional events it facilitates. In neuroscience, biologists and psychologists continue to explore affect as a bodily phenomenon while typically minimizing its discursive-cultural constraints.[84] In each case, scholars often subscribe to one paradigm without considering alternative perspectives. For these reasons, the study of affect as a form of embodied-discursive cognition remains underdeveloped. Ironically, such division undercuts precisely what makes affect so intellectually provocative. The phenomenon of affect reminds us, above all, that human processes do not take place in a vacuum—psychological, cultural, or biological. Affect, like rhetoric, is a process informed by biological and discursive phenomena simultaneously. Its scholarly investigation likewise demands more than multidisciplinary perspectives. It needs genuine interdisciplinary consideration.

To illustrate the disciplinary constraints of affect studies, I turn to an interview with Lawrence Grossberg featured in the *Affect Theory Reader*. Here Grossberg takes issue with Brian Massumi's 2005 study concerning the affects evoked by color-coded terror alerts.[85] Grossberg argues the study privileges bodily affects without fully considering the discursive regimes engendering those affects in the first place.[86] The merits of Grossberg's criticism notwithstanding, he nevertheless appears to express a general reservation toward discussing bodily affects whatsoever. Students of cultural studies are likewise disciplined to uphold the theoretical boundary between discourse and biology preventing interdisciplinary collaboration. Still, Grossberg's reservation is partially warranted. The moment we begin to locate discursive phenomena in the body, scientific inquiry has a way of appropriating and monopolizing the conversation. Historically, scientific inquiry has helped reduce a range of complex discursive phenomena to seemingly fixed, isolatable objects—precisely what Deleuze and Guattari rail against. Oppositely, however, many life scientists criticize cultural studies for its absence of scientifically measureable assumptions—it's all discourse, in other words. There must be room for discussion across these perspectives.

Fortunately, an increasing number of scholars incorporate a combination of perspectives to facilitate what we may call a paradigm of embodied-discursive-cognition.[87] Anna Gibbs, for example, offers a beautiful intervention concerning the mutual interest of science and the humanities in relation to affect.[88] Similarly, rhetorical critics, Celeste Condit and Debra Hawhee, remain at the forefront of emotional-material rhetoric.[89] The emerging paradigm situates the biological constraints of cognition on equal footing with the discursive constraints of public culture to produce a more holistic (yet not totalizing) understanding of affect in everyday life. The capacity of rhetoric and communication studies to drive this conversation should come as no surprise. As this chapter has illustrated, communication scholars initiated discussions of affect as early as classical Antiquity. By appreciating the evolution and trajectories of this conversation, they may continue to offer significant insight still today, identifying new biological and discursive capacities for human transformation.

Notes

1 See, for an example of the variety of perspectives circulating across critical-cultural studies, Melissa Gregg and Gregory J. Seigworth, eds., *The Affect Theory Reader* (Durham, NC: Duke University Press, 2010); for philosophy, see Peter Goldie, ed., *The Oxford Handbook of Philosophy of Emotion* (New York: Oxford University Press, 2010); for neuroscience, see Paul Ekman and

28 *Kevin Marinelli*

Richard J. Davidson, *The Nature of Emotion: Fundamental Questions* (New York: Oxford University Press, 1994). Although these bodies of scholarship inform one another to some extent, they largely remain isolated discussions.

2 Historically, and still today in the vernacular, the terms *affect* and *emotion* often appear synonymously. A formal distinction does not begin to emerge until the seventeenth century, as the next section of this chapter illustrates. See Daniel Gross, *The Secret History of Emotions: From Aristotle's Rhetoric to Modern Brain Science* (Chicago, IL: University of Chicago Press, 2007).

3 See, for example, Plato, *Gorgias*, trans. Robin Waterfield (New York: Oxford University Press, 1998).

4 Plato, *Republic*, trans. G.M.A. Grube (Indianapolis, IN: Hackett Classics, 1992), 95, 434d.

5 Although the reason-emotion binary is typically attributed to Plato, it is generally imprudent to attribute cultural frameworks to a single author. More accurately, Plato's articulation of the reason-emotion binary was so effective it carries implications to this day.

6 George Kennedy, in Aristotle, *On Rhetoric, A Theory of Civic Discourse*, trans. George Kennedy (New York: Oxford University Press, 1991), 122.

7 See, for example, Aristotle's definition of anger, *On Rhetoric*, 124, 1378a.

8 Aristotle, *On Rhetoric*, 121, 1378a.

9 W.W. Fortenbaugh, *Aristotle on Emotion* (New York: Harper and Row, 1975), 17.

10 Edwin Black, *Rhetorical Criticism: A Study in Method* (Madison, WI: University of Wisconsin Press, 1965) 132–147.

11 Aristotle, *On Rhetoric*, 121, 1378a.

12 See, for example, Aristotle, *On Rhetoric*, 218–219, 1404a.

13 Not all scholars entirely agree with this interpretation. See, for example, Susan Jarrett, *Rereading the Sophists: Classical Rhetoric Refigured* (Carbondale, IL: Southern Illinois University Press), 8.

14 Edwin Black, *Rhetorical Criticism: A Study in Method* (Madison: University of Wisconsin Press, 1978).

15 Ibid.

16 Aristotle, *Nicomachean Ethics*, in *Selections*, trans. and eds. Terence Irwin and Gail Fine (Indianapolis, IN: Hackett, 1995), 347–449, 1105b, 371.

17 Ibid.

18 Ibid.

19 Ibid.

20 Ibid.

21 Ibid., 1155a, 417.

22 Ibid.

23 Ibid., 1110a, 379.

24 See, for example, Martha Nussbaum, *Upheavals of Thought: The Intelligence of Emotions* (New York: Cambridge University Press, 2003).

25 Spinoza grew up under the Hebrew name, Baruch, but assumed the name Benedict when excommunicated from the Jewish community.

26 See Heidi M. Ravven, "Notes on Spinoza's Critique of Aristotle's *Ethics*: From Teleology to Process Theory," *Philosophy and Theology* IV (Fall 1989): 3–32.

27 Benedict de Spinoza, *The Ethics and Other Works*, trans. and ed. Edwin Curley (Princeton, NJ: Princeton University Press, 1994), 154.

28 de Spinoza, *The Ethics and Other Works*, 160.

29 Ibid.

30 Ibid.

31 Ibid.

Three Affect Paradigms   29

32 Ibid., 189.
33 Ibid., 154.
34 Ibid., 239.
35 Ibid., 158, 234.
36 Ibid., 186.
37 Ibid., 205.
38 Ibid.
39 Ibid.
40 Ibid.
41 See, for example, Antonio Damasio, *Looking for Spinoza: Joy, Sorrow and the Feeling Brain* (New York: Harvest, 2003), 12.
42 de Spinoza, *The Ethics and Other Works*, 123.
43 Ibid., 250.
44 Ibid., 160.
45 See, for example, Friedrich Nietzsche, *The Genealogy of Morality*, trans. Maudemarie Clark and Alan Swenson (Indianapolis, IN: Hackett, 1998); See also Sigmund Freud, *The Interpretation of Dreams*, trans. Joyce Crick (New York: Oxford University Press, 1999).
46 See Sigmund Freud, *Group Psychology and the Analysis of the Ego* (New York: Empire Books), 13. Jacques Lacan, *Écrits*, trans. Bruce Fink (New York: W. W. Norton and Company, 2006), 35–39.
47 Lacan, *Écrits*, 92.
48 See Roberto Harari, *Lacan's Seminar on "Anxiety": An Introduction* (New York: Other Press, 2001).
49 The degree to which Lacan engages affect remains debated. See, for example, Colette Soler, *Lacanian Affects: The Function of Affect within Lacan's Works* (New York: Routledge, 2016).
50 Their most elaborate critique of psychoanalysis is located in their seminal work, *A Thousand Plateaus: Capitalism and* Schizophrenia, trans. Brian Massumi (New York: Continuum, 2002).
51 Gilles Deleuze and Felix Guattari, *What is Philosophy?* trans. Hugh Tomlinson and Graham Burchell (New York: Columbia University Press, 1994).
52 Ibid., 167.
53 Ibid.
54 Lawrence Grossberg, *Cultural Studies in the Future Tense* (Durham, NC: Duke University Press, 2010), 16.
55 Ibid., 178.
56 Sara Ahmed, *The Cultural Politics of Emotion* (New York: Routledge, 2004), 10.
57 A number of critical geographers build on the spatial metaphors of Deleuze and Guattari to reconsider the production of social space in contemporary society. See, for example, Edward Buendia, Robert Helfenbein, and Nancy Ares, eds., *Deterritorializing/Reterritorializing: Critical Geography of Educational Reform* (Rotterdam, Netherlands: Sense Publishers, 2017). See also Arun Salanha, *Space after Deleuze* (New York: Bloomsbury, 2016).
58 Deleuze and Guattari, *What is Philosophy?* 99.
59 de Spinoza, *The Ethics and Other Works*, 248.
60 see Michel Foucault, *Discipline and Punish*, trans. Alan Sheridan (New York: Vintage, 1995).
61 Ibid.
62 Ibid., 216.
63 Michel Foucault, *Discourse/Power: Selected Interviews and Other Writings 1972–1977* (New York: Pantheon Books, 1980), 113.
64 Brian Massumi, *Politics of Affect* (Malden, MA: Polity, 2015), vii.

30   *Kevin Marinelli*

65 See Grossberg, "Affect's Future," in Gregg and Seigworth, 315. See also Nigel Thrift, *Non-Representational Theory: Space, Politics, Affect* (New York: Routledge, 2007).
66 Grossberg, "Affect's Future," 316.
67 See Lauren Berlant, *Cruel Optimism* (Durham, NC: Duke University Press, 2011).
68 Jaak Panksepp and Lucy Biven. *The Archaeology of Mind: The Neuroevolutionary Origins of Human Emotions* (New York: W. W. Norton and Company, 2004), 10.
69 Panksepp and Biven, *The Archaeology of Mind*, 11.
70 Nico H. Frijda, "Minimal Cognitive Prerequisites for Emotion," in Paul Ekman and Richard J. Davidson, eds., *The Nature of Emotion: Fundamental Questions* (New York: Oxford University Press, 1994), 199.
71 See Charles Darwin, *The Expression of Emotions in Man and Animal* (CreateSpace Independent Publishing Platform), 1.
72 See, for example, George Kennedy, "A Hoot in the Dark: The Evolution of Generic Rhetoric," *Philosophy and Rhetoric* 25, no. 1 (1992): 1–21.
73 Darwin, *The Expression of Emotions in Man and Animal*, 1.
74 Ibid.
75 James A. Russell and Lisa Feldman Barrett, "Core Affect, Prototypical Emotional Episodes, and Other Things Called *Emotion:* Dissecting the Elephant," *Journal of Personality and Social Psychology* 76, no. 5 (1999): 806.
76 Lisa Feldman Barrett and Karen Lindquist, "The Embodiment of Emotion," in *Embodied Grounding: Social, Cognitive, Affective and Neuroscientific Approaches* (New York: Cambridge University Press, 2008).
77 Silvan Tomkins, "Evolution and Affect," in *Affect, Imagery Consciousness, Volumes I and II* (New York: Springer Publishing Company, 2008), 83–94.
78 Ekman's survey was similar to, but more scientifically reliable than, Darwin's initial survey in that it used a control group. Its participants of Papua New Guinea were isolated from exposure to outside cultural norms concerning the expression of emotions. Without such information available to them, one could reasonably conclude their answers were based on biology, not culture.
79 Paul Ekman, "An Argument for Basic Emotion," *Cognition and Emotion* 6, no. 3/4 (1992): 169–200, 170.
80 See the list compiled by Andrew Ortony and Terence J. Turner, "What's Basic About Basic Emotions," *Psychological Review* 97, no. 3 (1990): 315–331.
81 Paul Ekman, "All Emotions Are Basic," in Paul Ekman and Richard Davidson, eds., *The Nature of Emotion* (New York: Oxford University Press, 1994), 15–19, 15.
82 By contrast, culturally contingent emotions, e.g., shame, correspond to a combination of neural activity in the subcortical regions of the brain along with the neocortex. Jaak Panksepp and Lucy Biven, *The Archaeology of Mind: Neuroevolutionary Origins of Human Emotion* (New York: W. W. Norton and Company, 2012).
83 See for example, Jon Elster, *Alchemies of the Mind: Rationality and the Emotions* (New York: Cambridge University Press, 1999); see also George Marcus, *The Sentimental Citizen* (University Park, PA: Pennsylvania State University Press, 2002); see also Monica Greco and Paul Stenner, *Emotions: A Social Science Reader* (New York: Routledge, 2009).
84 See, for example, Lisa Feldman Barrett, *How Emotions Are Made* (New York: Macmillan, 2017); see also Jaak Panksepp, *Affective Neuroscience: The Foundations of Human and Animal Emotions* (New York: Oxford University Press, 2004); see also Paul Ekman and Richard J. Davidson, eds., *The Nature of Emotion: Fundamental Questions* (New York: Oxford University Press, 1994).

85 Lawrence Grossberg, "Affect's Future," 316.
86 Ibid. To read Massumi's critique, see Brian Massumi, "Fear (The Spectrum Said)," *Positions* 13. no. 1 (2005).
87 See, for example, Jean Decety and Thalia Wheatley, *The Moral Brain: A Multidisciplinary Perspective* (Cambridge, MA: MIT Press, 2015).
88 Anna Gibbs, "After Affect: Sympathy, Synchrony, and Mimetic Communication," in Gregg and Seigworth.
89 Celeste Condit, "Pathos in Criticism: Edwin Black's Communism-as-Cancer Metaphor," *Quarterly Journal of Speech* 99, no. 1 (January 2013): 1–26; See also Debra Hawhee, *Moving Bodies: Kenneth Burke at the Edges of Language* (Columbia: University of South Carolina Press, 2009).

Bibliography

Ahmed, Sara. *The Cultural Politics of Emotion*. New York: Routledge, 2004.

Aristotle. *"Nicomachean Ethics."* In *Selections*. Translated by Terence Irwin and Gail Fine, 347–449. Indianapolis, IN: Hackett, 1995.

Aristotle. *On Rhetoric, A Theory of Civic Discourse*. Translated by George Kennedy. New York: Oxford University Press, 1991.

Barrett, Lisa Feldman. *How Emotions Are Made*. New York: Macmillan, 2017.

Barrett, Lisa Feldman, and Karen Lindquist. "The Embodiment of Emotion." In *Embodied Grounding: Social, Cognitive, Affective and Neuroscientific Approaches*, 237–262. Edited by Gún R. Semin and Eliot R. Smith. New York: Cambridge University Press, 2008.

Condit, Celeste. "Pathos in Criticism: Edwin Black's Communism-as-Cancer Metaphor." *Quarterly Journal of Speech* 99, no. 1 (January 2013): 1–26.

Black, Edwin. *Rhetorical Criticism: A Study in Method*. Madison: University of Wisconsin Press, 1965.

Buendia, Edward, Robert Helfenbein, and Nancy Ares. *Deterritorializing/Reterritorializing: Critical Geography of Educational Reform*. Rotterdam, Netherlands: Sense Publishers, 2017.

Damasio, Antonio. *Looking for Spinoza: Joy, Sorrow and the Feeling Brain*. New York: Harvest, 2003.

Darwin, Charles. *The Expression of Emotions in Man and Animal*. CreateSpace Independent Publishing Platform, 1872.

Decety, Jean, and Thalia Wheatley. *The Moral Brain: A Multidisciplinary Perspective*. Cambridge, MA: MIT Press, 2015.

Deleuze, Gilles, and Felix Guattari. *A Thousand Plateaus: Capitalism and Schizophrenia*. Translated by Brian Massumi. New York: Continuum, 2002.

———. *What is Philosophy?* Translated by Hugh Tomlinson and Graham Burchell. New York: Columbia University Press, 1994.

Elster, Jon. *Alchemies of the Mind: Rationality and the Emotions*. New York: Cambridge University Press, 1999.

Ekman, Paul. "All Emotions Are Basic." In *The Nature of Emotion*, edited by Paul Ekman and Richard Davidson, 15–19. New York: Oxford University Press, 1994.

———. "An Argument for Basic Emotion." *Cognition and Emotion* 6, no. 3/4 (1992): 169–200.

Ekman, Paul, and Richard J. Davidson. *The Nature of Emotion: Fundamental Questions*. New York: Oxford University Press, 1994.

32   *Kevin Marinelli*

Fortenbaugh, W.W. *Aristotle on Emotion*. New York: Harper and Row, 1975.

Foucault, Michel. *Discipline and Punish*. Translated by Alan Sheridan. New York: Vintage, 1995.

———. *Discourse/Power: Selected Interviews and Other Writings, 1972–1977*. New York: Pantheon Books, 1980.

Freud, Sigmund. *Group Psychology and the Analysis of the Ego*. Translated by James Strackey. New York: Empire Books, 1920.

———. *The Interpretation of Dreams*. Translated by Joyce Crick. New York: Oxford University Press, 1999.

Frijda, Nico H. "Minimal Cognitive Prerequisites for Emotion." In *The Nature of Emotion: Fundamental Questions*, edited by Paul Ekman and Richard J. Davidson, 59–67. New York: Oxford University Press, 1994.

Gibbs, Anna. "After Affect: Sympathy, Synchrony, and Mimetic Communication." In *The Affect Theory Reader*, edited by Melissa Gregg and Gregory J. Seigworth, 186–205. Durham, NC: Duke University Press, 2010.

Goldie, Peter. *The Oxford Handbook of Philosophy of Emotion*. New York: Oxford University Press, 2010.

Greco, Monica, and Paul Stenner. *Emotions: A Social Science Reader*. New York: Routledge, 2009.

Gregg, Melissa, and Gregory J. Seigworth. *The Affect Theory Reader*. Durham, NC: Duke University Press, 2010.

Gross, Daniel. *The Secret History of Emotions: From Aristotle's Rhetoric to Modern Brain Science*. Chicago, IL: University of Chicago Press, 2007.

Grossberg, Lawrence. "Affect's Future: Rediscovering the Virtual in the Actual." In *The Affect Theory Reader*, edited by Melissa Gregg and Gregory J. Seigworth, 309–338. Durham, NC: Duke University Press, 2010.

———. *Cultural Studies in the Future Tense*. Durham, NC: Duke University Press, 2010.

Harari, Roberto. *Lacan's Seminar on "Anxiety": An Introduction*. New York: Other Press, 2001.

Hawhee, Debra. *Moving Bodies: Kenneth Burke at the Edges of Language*. Columbia: University of South Carolina Press, 2009.

Jarrett, Susan. *Rereading the Sophists: Classical Rhetoric Refigured*. Carbondale: Southern Illinois University Press, 1991.

Kennedy, George. "A Hoot in the Dark: The Evolution of Generic Rhetoric." *Philosophy and Rhetoric* 25, no. 1 (1992): 1–21.

Lacan, Jacques. *Écrits*. Translated by Bruce Fink. New York: W. W. Norton and Company, 2006.

Marcus, George. *The Sentimental Citizen*. University Park: Pennsylvania State University Press, 2002.

Massumi, Brian. *Politics of Affect*. Malden, MA: Polity, 2015.

———. "Fear (The Spectrum Said)." *Positions*, 13, no. 1 (2005): 31–48.

Nietzsche, Friedrich. *The Genealogy of Morality*. Translated by Maudemarie Clark and Alan Swenson. Indianapolis, IN: Hackett, 1998.

Nussbaum, Martha. *Upheavals of Thought: The Intelligence of Emotions*. New York: Cambridge University Press, 2003.

Ortony, Andrew, and Terence J. Turner. "What's Basic about Basic Emotions?" *Psychological Review* 97, no. 3 (1990): 315–331.

Panksepp, Jaak. *Affective Neuroscience: The Foundations of Human and Animal Emotions*. New York: Oxford University Press, 2004.

Panksepp, Jaak, and Lucy Biven. *The Archaeology of Mind: The Neuroevolutionary Origins of Human Emotions*. New York: W. W. Norton and Company, 2004.

Plato. *Gorgias*. Translated by Robin Waterfield. New York: Oxford University Press, 1998.

———. *Republic*. Translated by G.M.A. Grube. Indianapolis, IN: Hackett Classics, 1992.

Ravven, Heidi M. "Notes on Spinoza's Critique of Aristotle's *Ethics*: From Teleology to Process Theory." *Philosophy and Theology* IV (Fall 1989): 3–32.

Russell, James A., and Lisa Feldman Barrett. "Core Affect, Prototypical Emotional Episodes, and Other Things Called Emotion: Dissecting the Elephant." *Journal of Personality and Social Psychology* 76, no. 5 (1999): 805–819.

Salanha, Arun. *Space after Deleuze*. New York: Bloomsbury, 2016.

Soler, Colette. *Lacanian Affects: The Function of Affect within Lacan's Works*. New York: Routledge, 2016.

de Spinoza, Benedict. "The Ethics." In *The Ethics and Other Works*. Translated by Edwin Curley. Princeton, NJ: Princeton University Press, 1994.

Thrift, Nigel. *Non-Representational Theory: Space, Politics, Affect*. New York: Routledge, 2007.

Tomkins, Silvan. "Evolution and Affect." In *Affect, Imagery Consciousness, Volumes I and II*, 83–94. New York: Springer Publishing Company, 2008.

2 Bridging the Affect/ Emotion Divide

A Critical Overview of the Affective Turn

Paul Stenner

Introduction

A veritable torrent of academic activity has recently identified itself as being part of a turn to affect. However, the concept of affect at play in this work is neither singular nor clear. This confusion is acknowledged by key figures within the affective turn. Seigworth and Gregg, for example, state that "first encounters with theories of affect might feel like a momentary (sometimes more permanent) methodological and conceptual free fall."[1] The main section of this chapter will provide an overview of three key sources of the affective turn, each of which presents a different concept of affect (affect as autonomous virtual intensity, as drive amplification, and as unconscious psychic energy). Through a critique of Massumi's affect/ emotion distinction, I will then question perhaps the one thing that scholars of the affective turn appear to agree about: that affect and emotion are two very different things.

In questioning this distinction, my intention is neither to deny the organic substructure of affective experience nor the importance of feelings that are felt only as vague "atmospheres," nor the value of a distinction between the virtual and the actual (explained below). Nor do I question the existence of brain structures affording a rapid and unconscious thalamo-amygdala pathway for processing the emotional relevance of sense data around 10 msec faster than would be required by the neocortical-amygdala pathway.[2] This finding fleshes out earlier findings that question whether high-level cognition is a necessary condition for all emotional response.[3] Each of these matters is certainly worth attending to, and I am not in principle against the use of the words "affect" and "emotion" to mark some of these distinctions. My concern is rather with the way this distinction *has* been drawn by influential advocates of the affective turn. This has led to an unfortunate tendency to polarize affect and emotion and to arbitrarily assign emotion to conditions that are conscious, personal, and tied to clear socially available meanings.[4] Emotions like jealousy, as I will show in the first section below, are never clearly personal. It is also highly likely that they always involve unconscious phases and typically implicate electro-dermal activity and other autonomic responses. In the view I offer, the

Bridging the Affect/Emotion Divide   35

affective turn should be considered, not as a rejection, but as a deepening of the discursive turn that, as I will show in the second section below, preceded it. In raising this theoretical problem, my aim is not to accelerate the sense of conceptual free fall, but to clarify some of the confusion within affect studies. I will begin by drawing upon my own experience as a social psychologist with a research interest in the emotions that began nearly 30 years ago.

A Summary of My Own Approach to the Emotion of Jealousy

First, it is necessary for me say something about emotion, which has been a vast, complex, and multifaceted topic within psychology for over a century.[5] To set the scene, a bit of background is required. In 1992, I completed a PhD in the Departments of Psychology and Sociology at the University of Reading, UK. In addition to surveying the scientific literature on emotion and/or affect, my PhD work used a range of methods to examine how ordinary people experience and make sense of jealousy. This work can be considered as an early contribution to critical discursive psychology and my aim was to provide empirical support for a non-dogmatic social constructionist approach to the emotions. Now, in one sense, it is important to understand that my work, like that of several others, was a protest against the dominant tradition of experimental psychology within social psychology and psychology more broadly. At the risk of oversimplifying (and there are many exceptions), the core of this tradition effectively ignored the societal and interpersonal context and treated psychological processes as universally shared properties of the individual mind/brain. These processes and properties were assumed ultimately to be reducible to brain activity and the job of the psychologist was to tease them apart in carefully designed experiments. Again, with some notable exceptions, emotions were approached—if approached at all—as objectively demonstrable entities or behaviors to be observed from the outside, and rarely, for example, as felt experiences (indeed much work built upon the behaviorist tradition of explicitly rejecting the very concept of "felt experience"). The aim, to put it crudely, was to replace the incurably subjective accounts of lay people with a scientifically objective understanding of emotions. The basic idea was that a better understanding of the psychological facts would enhance our capacity to control conduct. A typical example of this style of thinking presents jealousy (in this case, an understanding of male sexual jealousy informed by a rather crude sociobiological assumption of reproductive "fitness") as an innate urge to dominate female partners in order to enhance a man's confidence that he is the father of her children.

My own research made three related contributions. First, it showed that jealousy is much more complicated and better understood as a multiplicity of often very different experiences, each shaped by cultural contexts and

36 *Paul Stenner*

symbolic resources. I was interested in occasions of jealous experience as they unfold, event by event, in concrete interpersonal settings as parts of real historical and cultural contexts. It quickly became clear that there was enormous variety, not just with respect to scenes that get called "jealousy" but also with respect to how those scenes are understood from different perspectives, and subsequently, acted upon. Since the aim of mainstream psychology was to find the universal natural mechanism "behind" ordinary talk and experience, this variety in ways of "constructing" jealousy was almost completely ignored in the existing literature, and so I used a technique called Q methodology to empirically demonstrate what I described as a "manifold" of multiple situated understandings. For short, this contribution could be called "jealousy as manifold."[6]

Second, it was abundantly clear to me that the ways in which people talk about and make sense of jealousy are an integral part of actual occasions of experience, and can profoundly shape *what is made of* those experiences as they unfold through time. To the extent that scientific theories of jealousy enter into those ways of talking, they too become a *part of* jealous experiences. My research indicated some of the ways in which scientific accounts of jealousy get incorporated, sometimes critically, as part of lay accounts, and thus, function within the psychosocial power dynamics of communication. The account of jealousy as innate response to infidelity threat, for instance, was both used and challenged as part of legal arguments in cases of partner abuse. From my perspective, this kind of psychological knowledge did not offer an objective "view from nowhere," but was part of the subject matter social psychologists like myself wanted to study. I adopted a critical stance with respect to the knowledge claims of psychological science, and observed what I called the "social life" of that knowledge, as it was used as a cultural resource. This second contribution assumes a rather different ontology of the person than that presupposed by the mainstream experimental approach. The latter ultimately assumes the person to be a fixed and finite psychobiological mechanism governed by discoverable laws. I took the view, by contrast, that the human being is a social creature with an interest in its own being, and that the answers we propose to questions concerning our own being contribute to what we in fact become. For short, this second contribution could be called "jealousy as (in part at least) reflexively self-created process."

Third, my research clarified why emotions like jealousy are poorly understood as individual-level phenomena. An experience of jealousy always involves *relationships,* and indeed, always implies at least three parties: the one who is jealous (that a valued relation might be interrupted), the valued party in that relation, and a third figure (the rival) who threatens to interrupt the bond between the first two. To focus on the individual alone is to miss at least two-thirds of the action, including the ways in which jealousy is negotiated and attributed within those relationships in scenes of communication. But also, not all triadic configurations involving rivals with subjects and objects of desire are experiences of jealousy. To give just one example, if a person desires an object belonging to a "rival" but can claim no rights to that object, their experience is better described as envy. Iago is envious in relation to Othello, and so, he manipulates events so that Othello is jealous (feeling that his rightful relation to Desdemona is being intruded upon by Cassio). It is this specific triadic configuration involving the actual or potential loss or transgression of a valued relation that makes a given experience a suitable candidate for being called "jealousy." As Proust put it, what is needed for jealousy is that "our predilection should become exclusive," or to use an expression from Simone De Beauvoir, the interruption of "an intimacy that used to belong only to me."[7] For short, this third contribution could be called "jealousy as relational configuration."

This third "relational" contribution helps explain the first "manifold" contribution about diversity of experience. Jealousy is not some inherent feature or quality that can be abstracted from that configuration; it is the *feeling of that configuration*. For this reason, many diverse events and qualities of experience can happily be called "jealousy," so long as this basic pattern obtains. The quality of the actual experience may therefore vary enormously, since the jealous subject can be *angry* like Shakespeare's Othello,[8] *fearful* like Proust's Swann,[9] or *destroyed* like de Beauvoir's Monique[10] (or *erotic* like Kundera's Terez, *dramatic* like Nabokov's Humbert, "*jerked around*" like Saunders' Jeff, and so on).

The Affective Turn and the Discursive Turn

What does this summary of my work on jealousy have to do with affect as it is discussed within the affective turn? Many today would say that jealousy has nothing to do with affect, since jealousy is an emotion while affect, by definition, implies "vital forces beyond emotion."[11] No less an authority than Brian Massumi himself insists that one of his "clearest lessons … is that emotion and affect … follow different logics and pertain to different orders."[12] Furthermore, my discussion of jealousy is not just concerned with feelings but deals with how people think and talk about jealousy. Affect, again by contrast, can never be put into words or thought about because, according to these authors, it is precisely that which *escapes* consciousness and discursive communication. Massumi states that affect has nothing to do with consciousness or discourse. Referring to the autonomic nervous system (which automatically governs processes like heart rate, respiration, and skin conductance), he insists on the "irreducibly bodily and autonomic nature of affect."[13]

Furthermore, these "affective turn" writers often present themselves as being *against* a form of social science that analyses how discursive practices "construct" versions of reality. Patricia Clough, for example, presents her work and that of her colleagues as being all about "toppling … semiotic

38 *Paul Stenner*

chains of signification and identity and linguistic-based structures of meaning making" from their "privileged position."[14] The affective turn, for Clough, Massumi, Seigworth, Gregg, and numerous other influential North American scholars, is precisely a turn *against* what is sometimes called the "discursive turn" (i.e., the turn toward social constructionism) that preceded it. From this perspective, my approach (for part of my research, I did indeed analyze discourse from transcribed interviews) is precisely what the affective turn is against, and my subject matter (the emotion of jealousy) is precisely what must not be mistaken for the true gold of affect.

The affective turn, as is becoming more apparent, is not just a fascination with an apparently new subject matter ("affect"), but is part of a much broader mutation in knowledge and knowledge practices. It is "a new understanding of human being and a new politics of the living"[15] or even "the overarching project of rethinking the human in the wake of a sustained critique of Western rationality."[16] When the intellectual stakes are as grand as this, it is easy for little details to get passed over. It is easy for the affective turn to take the form of something closer to a cult movement or the movement of an artistic *avant-garde*. And it is easy for the term "affect" to serve as the buzzword or keystone for such a movement. But it must be said that in this respect, the term affect functions a little like the term "discourse" did, or does, among advocates of the discursive turn. Movements like social constructionism, postmodernism, post-structuralism, and deconstruction also presented themselves as part of a "rethinking of the human in the wake of a sustained critique of Western rationality." The term "discourse" also carried, or carries, the excitement of a thrilling new breakthrough in thought, and functions as its symbol for the new collective that rallies around it. This symbolic and collective function can make the meaning of words like "discourse" and "affect" appear very vague and wooly indeed, as if something important might be lost were too much clarity to intrude. And it also enhances the tendency to simplify and parody the work of those who function as the "other" to the new truth of the *avant-garde*. But these dangers are especially evident with the term "affect," since whatever affect is, it is "in essence beyond ordinary experience."[17] The affective turn, we might say, stands up for those unnamed and unnamable possibilities that must forever remain virtual. Affect is not ... *yet*. Not *quite*.

I have suggested that my own interest in jealousy during the late 1980s and early 1990s expressed a more widespread interest in exploring emotions and psychological phenomena more generally as complex, relational, processual, and multiple in nature, and as bound to changing cultural and historical circumstances. Around that time, this sort of critical reflection on psychology coalesced, for better or for worse, under the label of "social constructionism."[18]

Having completed my PhD and having secured a full-time post in London as a university lecturer, I was in a good position to keep a close eye on, and contribute to, what would become the "affective turn," as it began in the mid-1990s. During that time, I created and taught (first at the University of East London and then at University College, London) a final year undergraduate course entitled "Affect in affective climate," and I was particularly interested in the fact that scholars from many disciplines (here, the core disciplines were philosophy, cultural studies, sociology, and queer theory) were becoming newly interested in the emotions. In the following section, I wish to distinguish just three of the important tributaries that contributed toward influencing the affective turn, each of which operates with a rather different concept of affect. For the sake of simplicity I will concentrate on three publications that appeared in 1995.

1995, or Three Key Influences on the Affective Turn

Affect as Autonomous Virtual Intensity: Brian Massumi

The first publication I will discuss is Massumi's highly creative but somewhat chaotic article entitled "The Autonomy of Affect."[19] Massumi is a philosopher with an interest in cultural studies. He drew heavily and partially upon Deleuze's readings of Bergson and Spinoza to critique the limitations of discursive approaches and to champion affect for what he called its autonomy from discourse. As he put it in a later publication, his project was an effort to "part company with the linguistic model at the basis of the most widespread concepts of coding."[20] By the autonomy of affect Massumi really means its openness, and hence, its potential for novelty and disruption, but he also plays with autonomy as a political concept and, as we shall see, as a concept pertaining to the autonomic nervous system.

Using one of Bergson's favorite distinctions, Massumi defines affect as something virtual as distinct from something actual. This distinction is quite abstract, but in essence very simple: the virtual is an undifferentiated potential whose openness is necessarily closed down as soon as it is actualized as some concrete occurrence or entity. Although it quickly becomes highly complex, to give a simplified example, as you enter the cinema you might see any number of the films that are on offer: but when it comes to it, you must choose one and forsake the others (and even if you opt to drop into several films for five minutes only, or to sit outside instead, it is *that* which you actualize, and not your other options). The actual is thus always a limitation or reduction or subtraction with respect to the buzzing possibilities of the virtual which, as it were, hover around any given actual. Massumi extends this distinction to the dimension of feeling. He defines "emotion" as something "actual," and thus, as necessarily something that is more limited and concrete than "affect," defined as virtual. By reason of its virtuality, affect, as Massumi puts it, "escapes confinement."[21] On this basis, Massumi insists that affect and emotion belong to distinct registers that must not be confused, the former being an open, autonomous, and

40   *Paul Stenner*

virtual "intensity" that escapes the confinements of structured, conscious meaning (which he calls "quality") that, for him, characterizes emotion (these terms will be clarified below).

Massumi thus equates affect with intensity, and contrasts it with what he calls quality, which he identifies with emotion. In a densely complex and controversial argument, "quality" and "intensity" are presented as two distinct systems that operate in parallel. Taking the example of an image of a snowman, "quality" is identified with a "signifying order" that indexes the experience of the image to conventionally accepted and shared meanings (e.g., "this is a snowman"). The "intensity" of the image, on the other hand, is identified by Massumi with the strength and duration of its effects (and in particular, the effects the image has upon the electrodermal activity of a person's skin). For Massumi, intensity and quality are always copresent in any given situation, but follow different logics and come in different mixtures, the latter perpetually capturing the former, but never quite succeeding, since intensity always escapes its fate of being fixed by qualities.

Emotion (as quality) is thus defined by Massumi in relation to the capture and taming of affect (as intensity), and is associated with the higher order processes of meaning-making, consciousness, and communication that are often grasped with concepts of discourse (and semiosis more generally). Affect, in turn, is defined as an unstructured, unassimilable remainder, associated with the virtual potentialities of the autonomic nervous system, and with an asubjective and pre-personal connective logic that operates outside of consciousness and beyond the normativities of social order. Affect, in short, escapes articulation in discourse. In this way, Massumi is able to observe that approaches that take discourse as their keynote tend be concerned only with "quality" at the expense of "intensity," and yet, of the two, intensity is arguably the vital factor and the unacknowledged source of novelty. Massumi's work is thus understandable as a prolonged critique of what he sees as an endemic neglect of intensity/affect, and a plea for its decisive relevance for any understanding of the emergence of *novelty* in evolving systems of all kinds.

To make proper sense of this argument, it is necessary to dissect it in some detail and to relate it to some of the psychological theories that he borrows and adapts. Massumi's 1995 article begins with a fascinating but highly selective, and at times, misguided interpretation of a series of quite conventional social psychological experiments. The experiments were led by the German psychologist Hertha Sturm to investigate how psychological reactions to film can be modified by voice-overs with different characteristics. Sturm became interested in a short film shown on German TV that had excited some attention from parents because some of their children had reported being disturbed by the film. Sturm wanted to know what it was about the film that made it so disturbing to these children. The film shows a snowman melting on the roof garden of the man who built it.

Bridging the Affect/Emotion Divide 41

The man watches and then takes it to the mountain where it can stay intact longer, and bids it farewell. The experiment involved modifying certain aspects of the film. It involved showing this film to children under three conditions: the original film (which involved no dialogue), a "factual" condition (in which a voice-over was added, giving factual statements about the action), and an "emotional" condition (in which the voice-over articulated and expressed the emotional feel of the action).

In each condition, the children who watched were asked to (1) rate the film on a "pleasant-unpleasant" scale and (2) on a "happy-sad" scale, and they were also tested (3) on their memory of the film while (4) a number of physiological measures were taken (heart rate, breathing, and electrodermal activity). The basic idea, then, was to manipulate the independent variables (the three conditions in which the film was presented) and to examine the effects this has on the dependent variables (1, 2, 3, & 4). On average, memory was best for the emotional version and worst for the factual version, and pleasantness was highest for the original wordless version and lowest for the factual version. Massumi claims to find this "a bit muddling," and unravels an elaborate theory to explain his muddle. However, it seems to me that there is reason to question this sense of muddle, and hence, the need to explain it. First, it seems obvious that a film designed to be impactful without words would be enjoyed more in exactly that form (i.e., that the original format would be judged more pleasant). It seems equally obvious that superimposing a dull factual narrative would both spoil it for the children and, for this very reason, make it less memorable (explaining why the "factual" format was found least pleasant and least memorable). Also, it seems perfectly logical that adding the "emotional" narrative would enhance memory on a test that requires the child to recall using language (since they have been given some workable language for this as part of the film in this condition), and might not spoil the film quite as much as the factual voiceover (thus explaining why the "emotional" format might be more pleasant than the factual, but less pleasant than the original format, while being more memorable than both).

Nevertheless, Massumi describes these results as if they were highly counterintuitive. He then identifies a further "surprise": generally speaking, those scenes in the film that were rated most pleasant on the pleasant/unpleasant scale were also rated most sad on the "happy/sad" scale. It is in order to explain this finding—and also some physiological findings noted below—that Massumi elaborates his complex network of theoretical distinctions starting with content/effect and moving onto quality/intensity, mutating into "redundancy of signification"/"redundancy of resonance" and culminating in the "emotion/affect" distinction that, for many, would come to define the field of affect studies. Again, however, it seems quite obvious that when people (children and adults alike) view a sad film, the bits that are likely to be most enjoyed (and hence, rated as more "pleasant") are precisely the sad bits, just as the best bits of a horror movie are the scenes that are scary. If we are disappointed by tear-jerkers that fail to jerk tears and by horror movies that fail to scare, then there is plenty of scope for describing a film enjoyable for its sadness as simultaneously sad and pleasant. This finding is only "strange" if it is assumed that the children cannot enjoy the sadness they feel when watching a film. Indeed, it is this assumption that seems strange to me, and not the idea that the participants might have used the "pleasantness" scale to indicate their enjoyment. If we don't make this assumption, there is no problem left for Massumi's complex chain of conjectures to explain.

Nevertheless, Massumi goes on to "explain" this alleged "crossing of semantic wires"[22] (pleasantness = sadness) by making use of another perfectly understandable result that he finds confusing: namely, that heart rate and breathing depth were highest in the factual condition, while electrodermal activity (skin-conductance) was highest in the original version. He presents this, rather dramatically, in terms of the children being "physiologically split: factuality made their heart beat faster and deepened their breathing, but it made their skin resistance fall. The original nonverbal version elicited the greatest response from their skin. Galvanic skin response measures *autonomic* reaction."[23] Of course, all three are in fact measures of autonomic reaction, and all three are measures of intensity (since intensity is effectively the strength or concentration of a process, a faster heart rate is more intense than a slower one, for example).

Again, this notion of participants being "physiologically split" is a highly problematic inference. In fact, many years of studying the relationships between these measures of autonomic nervous system activity have shown remarkably variable correlations between measures of heart rate, breathing rate, skin-conductance, and so on. In a classic article, Taylor and Epstein warned against assuming homogeneity.[24] To give just one example, they reported high correlations (+.65) between heart rate and skin conductance among experienced parachutists undertaking a jump, but correlations closer to zero (and sometimes negative) for novices. The notion of being "physiologically split," in short, presupposes a general coherence or homogeneity between these physiological measures that ought not to have been assumed. Indeed, these sorts of findings led most psychologists to abandon the concept of a measure of general arousal.[25] Abandoning general arousal called into question the simple distinction between a nonspecific arousal component of motivation (typically called intensity) and an evaluational component which specifies motivational direction and content. It was this oversimplified distinction, for example, that had animated Schachter & Singer's famous two-factor theory of emotions with its crude double act of the undifferentiated energy of autonomic physiological arousal and the informational business of cognition. For these authors, "emotion" is always a combination of the two factors of intensity provided by undifferentiated autonomic arousal, and cognition that qualifies and differentiates that arousal, taking psychosocial variables

Bridging the Affect/Emotion Divide 43

into consideration. Their famous experiments tried, largely unsuccessfully, to show that the same intensity of arousal (produced by injecting participants with adrenalin), could be an ingredient in either anger or joy emotional experiences depending upon the manner in which the cognitive system qualified that artificially induced intensity with a meaning and direction. Tomkins wryly notes that the Schachter and Singer experiments became classics because they satisfied two conditions: they need to be believed and they are not read.[26]

Through his surprise at the lack of correlation between heart rate and electrodermal activity, Massumi perpetuates this now long outdated assumption of a homogenous arousal system supplying intensity. Furthermore, on the basis of his surprise, he proceeds to finesse the situation by speculating that intensity "is embodied in purely autonomic reactions most directly manifested in the skin—at the surface of the body" whilst "[d]epth reactions belong more to the form/content (qualification) level, even though they also involve autonomic functions such as heartbeat and breathing."[27] As well as being unsubstantiated, this distinction clearly compromises the integrity of Massumi's "intensity/quality" distinction and his troublesome identification of affect with autonomic arousal. Based on the idea that of the three autonomic nervous system (ANS) measures used, electrodermal activity is perhaps the least accessible to conscious control, he is arbitrarily limiting the meaning of "intensity" to electrodermal activity. This gives him the illusion of having identified a pure form of intensity that is uncontaminated by "quality." He wants us to believe that the original version of the film had a pure and direct influence on the children's skin conductance, while the factual version impacted heart rate and breathing indirectly via the mediation of conscious meaning (this is not to deny the findings, nor indeed that the skin may have a special motivational significance for feelings and may have been a better indicator of enjoyment in Sturm's study). He further wants us to believe that this direct relationship between image and skin involves a paradoxical logic for which, miraculously, sadness can be pleasant, because no semantic or semiotic "ordering" (no "content" or "quality") can be at play. I hope my criticism has made clear that:

a   there is no need for an elaborate explanation for why sadness can be pleasant;
b   there is no reason to be surprised at the lack of correlation between heart rate, breathing, and skin conductance;
c   electrodermal activity is not a pure form of autonomic intensity;
d   there is no basis for identifying affect with this purified notion of intensity;
e   emotion should not be identified, as did Schachter and Singer, with qualified general arousal, especially given the problematic nature of the latter concept.

44 *Paul Stenner*

Nevertheless, having extracted his idiosyncratic concept of affect, Massumi goes on to give it a distinctively political relevance, arguing that it "holds a key to rethinking postmodern power after ideology." He famously discussed Ronald Reagan's political appeal in terms of his transmission of affective potentials that were circulated by the mass media and then actualized as qualified contents by those at the receiving end. In this way, Massumi argues—or rather asserts—that Reagan was able to "produce ideological [i.e. discursive] effects by non-ideological [i.e. affective] means."[28] Reagan's mesmeric voice, for instance, can be thought of as transmitting affective potentials that many TV viewers actualized as an emotion of confidence. The suggestion is that Reagan's political appeal was less about the content of his policies and the meaning of his statements, and more about the affective intensity and atmosphere he was able to generate within a mediatized system. Now, it is certainly true that persuasive communication draws upon far more than rational argumentation to create its effects, and that figures like Reagan exploited this as much as they were able. It is also true that contemporary social systems of control rely heavily upon the subtle manipulation and modulation of feelings using open-ended, free-floating, networked, and ultra-rapid modes of technology. Where old forms of discipline barked discursively organized orders to a massified and pacified cohort, contemporary control is more about the continual stimulation and modulation of feelings and desires. But none of this justifies or clarifies the idea that Reagan's appeal was about intensity/affect as distinct from quality/emotion.

Even on its own terms, Massumi's account is thoroughly contradictory. He happily moves from announcing his clearest lesson, "that emotion and affect … follow different logics and pertain to different orders"[29] to, just a few pages later, asserting that "What is being termed affect in this essay is precisely this two-sidedness, the simultaneous participation of the virtual in the actual and the actual in the virtual, as one arises from and returns to the other."[30] If affect belongs to a virtual order that is fundamentally different to the actual order of emotion, then surely it cannot, without evident inconsistency, also fundamentally belong to both of these orders, linking them in a two-sided way.

Affect as Biological Equipment for Drive Amplification: Sedgwick and Frank's Appreciation of Silvan Tomkins

The second publication from 1995 was an article called "Shame in the cybernetic fold," written by the famous queer theorist Eve Sedgwick and her collaborator, Adam Frank. This article shares with Massumi's (1) a critical attitude toward the social constructionism of the discursive turn, and (2) the feature of critiquing discursive approaches by way of an engagement with experimental social psychology. It begins with a scathing attack on the assumptions of critical discursive theory. The three most

Bridging the Affect/Emotion Divide 45

significant of these assumptions are, first, that theories grounded in biology are necessarily conservative; second, that human language provides the best model for understanding representation; and third, that dualisms of all kinds must be endlessly deconstructed.[31]

To challenge these assumptions, Sedgwick and Frank championed the theory of affect proposed by the U.S. psychologist Silvan Tomkins. During the time I was working on my PhD thesis, Tomkins' work was little known and very rarely discussed. I had encountered it as a precursor to the work on universal facial expressions of emotion undertaken by Paul Ekman. In part at least, Tomkins' lack of impact within psychology was attributable to the fact that his work was unusually "philosophical" in nature, although he engaged deeply with the existing biological and psychological literature. Indeed, he had studied philosophy at Harvard in the 1930s (A.N. Whitehead was one of his philosophical influences). Tomkins' main contribution was his four-volume work *Affect Imagery Consciousness*, which was published between 1962 and 1991. He argued consistently and at length for the existence of a small number of basic biologically hardwired affects. Each of these affects varied in intensity, and so Tomkins included a low-intensity version (e.g., fear) and a high-intensity version (e.g., terror). The complete set includes distress/anguish, shame/humiliation, fear/terror, anger/rage, interest/excitement, enjoyment/joy, surprise/startle, disgust, and dissmell.

Tomkins theorized what he called "the affect system" as effectively an amplifier of drive signals. The drive system, for Tomkins, is the motivational system—shared in common with many animals—that ensures our organic sustainability. Put simply, we seek water thanks to the drive signal we call "thirst," we eat thanks to a hunger drive and we reproduce thanks to a sex drive. Tomkins reasoned that an affect system had evolved to supplement the drive system, because the drive system alone had proved insufficiently motivating. Like drives, affects function by using organic processes to generate "signals" which, when experienced by the organism, motivate it to action. But whereas drive signals tend to specify the when, where, and the how of the required action, affect signals motivate in a more general and diffuse manner. Hunger, for instance, is always about food and about getting it into one's belly via the mouth, but anger can be "about" many things, and the actions taken to assuage it can be several in nature. The sex drive inclines one toward a concern with sex, but thanks to the affect of interest, a creature can be curious and seek out all kinds of possibilities. The affect system, thus, introduces a much richer and more varied realm of potential values into the life of an organism.

For Tomkins, each affect is hypothesized to be triggered by an innate activating mechanism and to find its primary instantiation in the face. Indeed, although each affect has multiple physical aspects (characteristic body-postures, particular patterns of ANS activity, specific vocalizations, etc.), Tomkins' main criterion for the existence of an affect is the

46 *Paul Stenner*

demonstrable existence of a unique facial expression (the smile of joy, the snarl of anger, the blush of shame, and so forth). Furthermore, the motivating affect signal that is experienced is quite literally *the feeling of* the face (along with the other relevant organic processes). It is these feelings that qualify the world we encounter with the felt tinge of value (a situation becomes exciting or scary or shameful, etc.). For Tomkins, the world can take on these values only thanks to affects which, in his theory, are triggered by patterns of neural stimuli with different densities of neural firing (the so-called innate activating system). This means that it is not "the external world" that triggers affects, but differential patterns of neural firing (which may or may not be related to events in the "outside" world). In short, if neural stimulation is on the increase, this triggers startle (if the increase is sharp and sudden) or fear (if it is less sudden) or interest (if it is gradual). Distress follows from a sharp increase in neural stimulation that is sustained in time, and anger when the stimulation is more intense. Joy is triggered by the sudden reduction of stimulation. For example, if a sudden noise produces a sharp increase in density of neural firing in the hearer, then all else being equal, this would trigger surprise. But it would trigger distress if that high density continued, followed by anger if the volume were to increase, followed by joy if it were to stop. This theory (and it remains a theory) permits any given affect to be triggered by any event, so long as that event produces the requisite alteration in density of neural firing.

So, in short, Tomkins' theory gives us: (1) evidence for the existence of nine distinguishable affects; (2) a theory of an innate trigger for each proposed affect; and (3) a theoretical account of the motivational function of that affect system. Sedgwick and Frank, correctly in my view, saw this theory as a challenge to the prevalent dogma among social theorists that biology is necessarily essentialist and determining (since in Tomkins' account, the innate system supplies the basis for value of any kind, and does not assume mechanistic determinism) and that discourse is the primary mode of representation (since affects provide meaning in a sense that can be prior to language). For me, it was remarkable to observe how rapidly Tomkins' work moved, in a matter of a couple of years, from relative obscurity to being "flavor of the month" among many cultural theorists and social scientists.

Affect as Largely Unconscious Psychic Energy: Elliot and Frosh's Psychosocialized Freud

The third publication from 1995 was a volume edited by Elliott and Frosh entitled *Psychoanalysis in Context*.[32] This text formed part of a resurgence of interest in, and revaluation of, psychoanalytic theory and its application to sociological questions that is now at the core of "psychosocial studies." Actually, I am using this book as a symbol for the awakening of interest in

Bridging the Affect/Emotion Divide 47

affect within psychoanalytical psychosocial studies. Dating from Freud's work, there has been much theorization of affect, wherein affect refers to the adventures of unconscious energy as it is "stored up" in the ego, "invested" in objects, and so forth. Only limited aspects of this dynamic process are consciously available to ordinary people (e.g., as experiences of "anxiety," "fear," "anger," "jealousy," etc.). It is worth noting that Tomkins engaged in a sustained critique of Freud's tendency to reduce the affects to modifications of basic drives (especially the sex drive), and indeed, the old idea of drive energy (to which ideas become attached) still animates much psychoanalytic thought.

André Green, who is the main psychoanalytic authority on affect, points out that in France the adjective "affectif" and the verb "affecter" are part of everyday vocabulary, while in the United Kingdom, the term "emotion" is typically preferred for talking about roughly the same thing, and "affective" has a more neutral ring. Freud himself used a mixture of terms including Affekt, Gefühl, and Empfindung (each of which has been translated into English and French in multiple ways, including feeling, sentiment, emotion, affect, affection, and sensation).[33] Since, as a science and a clinical practice, psychoanalysis concerns the dynamic influence of what is not conscious (or at least, of feelings—often disturbing—that motivate us, and yet, cannot easily be put into words), then the ordinary terminology and lay theories are necessarily considered partial and distorted. What we consciously think of as our emotions (if we use that word) is revealed by the psychoanalyst to be something rather different, and so another term is arguably needed. In psychoanalytic therapy, for example, what the client may think of at one moment as love or hatred toward the analyst is viewed by the analyst as something very different, with a different nature and origin (the so-called "transference"). Freud's engagement with transference is important also because it extended the frame of the intelligible field of study of affectivity from the individual to the relationship between two people (the transference concerns the feelings a patient develops for their analyst). It is obvious that the transference cannot be understood by considering an individual alone. Others, like Bion extended the intelligible field still further, considering the affectivity of group dynamics.[34]

It is also important to note that there is a great deal of variability both within the work of individual psychoanalytic thinkers and between different thinkers. For Green, for example, the entire tradition of Lacanian psychoanalysis is basically Freud without the affect.[35] Since psychoanalysis is a clinical practice as well as a science, psychoanalysts are not purely concerned with an objective description and conceptualization of affect but also with its experience and management or navigation. It is evidently easier to talk about what is said about affect than about affect itself. For psychoanalysts, affect challenges thought, and the question of the relationship between affect and discourse (or "representation") becomes directly salient. Affect, from a psychoanalytic perspective, is intelligible and

48   *Paul Stenner*

communicable only insofar as it is associated with a certain representation mediated by words, and typically the process of therapy is conceived as a way of rendering something like pure affect "graspable" and "digestible" by thought.[36]

Whilst *Psychoanalysis in context* was not specifically about emotion or affect, it began with a critical recognition that Freud's practice functioned to colonize "otherness" and to "make it amenable to the demands of rationality,"[37] and it reflects critically upon this "imperialism" in ways that mirror Massumi and Sedgwick and Frank. The book expresses the new "psychosocial" interest in the affective and unconscious basis of creativity and social life that would become a key theme within the affective turn. Furthermore, the ambivalent relation the psychosocial tradition has to the discursive turn is summed up in Ian Craib's description of social constructionism as a mass manic psychosis.[38]

The Affective Turn and the Separation of Affect and Emotion

The earliest use of the phrase "affective turn" that I have come across was by Anu Koivunen in 2001. She used it as the title of her preface to the published proceedings of a feminist conference to mark a renewed interest in "affects, emotions and embodied experiences" in many disciplines.[39] Note that Koivunen does not use the word "affective" to contrast with emotion, but includes "affects, emotions and embodied experiences" in the same broad category of the "affective." Koivunen thus used "affective turn" to refer to a broad-based increase of interest among social scientists in emotional themes. We might just as well call it an "emotional turn." Much of the work included, in fact, adopts a broadly social constructionist or post-structuralist theoretical framework and, in this sense, is part of the discursive turn. In other words, it rebels against the idea that emotion is a basic biological force contrasted with reason and proper to the natural sciences.[40]

To avoid confusion, I suggest that we reserve the phrase "affective turn" for the later development that I have been tracing above and that was indeed predicated upon a sharp distinction between affect and emotion. The phrase made its first appearance in the title of a book in 2007, thanks to Patricia Clough and Jean Halley.[41] Where Koivunun used affect as a generic term, Clough and Halley use it in a sense that is both more limited and more ambitious. For Clough, affect designates the quite specific avant-garde intellectual movement—mostly located within the humanities—that turns against the postmodern, deconstructionist, or discursive turn usually associated with social constructionism by turning to a concept of affect that is sharply distinguished from emotion. In this sense, it builds upon the criticisms of "discourse" that appeared in the three tributaries discussed above.

Bridging the Affect/Emotion Divide   49

Affect, in this sense, is not only strictly separated from discursive practices but is defined as being in principle inaccessible to discursive articulation. It is an autonomous and pre-personal force or capacity that precedes, or perhaps exceeds, consciousness. The starting point for this affective turn, as we have seen, is the idea that the discursive turn led to a monopoly of concern with discursive processes and to the neglect of a vast and vital territory of affective dynamics and forces. If for advocates of the discursive turn, discourse symbolized a principle of progressive freedom from naturalistic essentialism, then for advocates of the affective turn discourse symbolized, on the contrary, a certain entrapment within a spider's web of meaning better grasped as discursive imperialism. The key, from this perspective, is to articulate an ontology capable of recognizing "the virtual," and granting it a reality, even if that reality is, by definition, not actual: "one of the surest things that can be said of affect and its theorization is that they will exceed, always exceed the context of their emergence, as the excess of ongoing process."[42] Again, it is this sense of the "virtual" that always exceeds the "actual" that informs the firm affect/ emotion distinction: "affect is ... vital forces insisting beyond emotion"[43] or "affect is ... synonymous with *force*," or "affect can be understood then as a gradient of bodily capacity."[44] In this respect, it is Massumi's work that has exerted the greatest influence on the affective turn, where affect stands for the "virtual as cresting in a liminal realm of emergence" that is "not directly accessible to experience."[45] I have already presented a criticism of the way in which Massumi crafts a concept of affect as pure intensity. I will now criticize the way in which he justifies this distinction by recourse to the philosophy of Spinoza.

Massumi describes Spinoza as being "a formidable philosophical precursor on many of these points: on the difference in nature between affect and emotion; on the irreducibly bodily and autonomic nature of affect ..."[46] It seems to me, however, that Spinoza does not distinguish between affect and emotion and does not argue for the irreducibly autonomic nature of the former. Here, I will address just the first point.[47] Spinoza wrote in Latin and used the term *affectus* (as well as the variants *afficio* and *affectio*), and to my knowledge, he never used the word emotion, which was barely used until the early nineteenth century (though in many English translations of his work, *affectus* is often translated as "emotion"). For Spinoza, the affections of a body are the modifications that occur in the course of an encounter with another body. Spinoza discusses the affects at great length in his most famous book, the *Ethics*.[48] When Spinoza deals with concrete examples of affects, far from marking a difference in nature from emotion, he discusses what we would now call emotions. That is to say, he discusses experiences that we would call anger, fear, joy, jealousy, envy and so forth. The important thing is his *approach* to these emotions, which always emphasizes modifications wrought by encounters. Anger, for Spinoza, is thus a particular kind of modification that occurs in particular types of encounters.

50 *Paul Stenner*

It is important, however, to understand that Spinoza does not limit his understanding of affects to human emotions. On the contrary, as a philosopher, Spinoza is looking for a much broader generality. Here, we find a real basis for a distinction between affect (as applicable ontologically) and emotion (the specifically anthropological manifestation of affects), albeit one Spinoza does not make using those terms. For him, *all* entities are to be understood in relation to the affects they are capable of in their encounters with other entities. His philosophy is thoroughly relational in that anything that exists does so as a function of its relations, and hence, of the affects it is capable of going through. All finite entities in nature are affected/modified by other entities in nature. This is also the relational basis for a process philosophy because it starts with, and foregrounds, the idea that affect is a reciprocal process of affecting and being affected. When it comes to human beings, those affects often take the form of emotions (but not exclusively, since feelings of hunger, sensations of touch, etc., are not emotions in the modern sense).

Importantly, the distinction I have just described is not the one Massumi draws, but rather the difference between a concept applied in a maximally general and ontological way (we might even use the scary word "metaphysical"), and a concept applied in a specific, and, in this case, specifically *anthropological,* way (pertaining to human beings). Since the bodies of both are modified in the process of their encounters, the ontological concept of *affectus* applies equally to snails and to people, but this does not mean that the experiences of snails and people are the same. A snail is not capable of being affected and of affecting others in the manner that we call "envy" and, perhaps, in some respects, we humans are not capable of being affected in the manner of a snail. We sometimes give the name "emotions" to these specific human affects (i.e., to affects at the specifically anthropological level), and we might need another name for the specifics of the snail's affections. From Spinoza's perspective, both specific sets could quite properly be called—using the more general category—affects: "The things we have shown so far are completely general and do not pertain more to man than to other individuals, all of which, though in different degrees, are nevertheless animate."[49]

Something similar can be said about the affect/emotion distinction as it pertains to the second and third streams of influence described above. Tomkins himself did not draw the distinction between affect and emotion that is now routinely assumed among scholars of the affective turn. Like Spinoza, when Tomkins discusses the affects that make up the affect system, he refers to what ordinary people would call emotions: the experiences we call anger, fear, shame, disgust, joy, and so forth. In his published work, Tomkins uses the word "emotion" very rarely, and the reason that he prefers the word "affect" is that he wanted a more scientific sounding word that would allow him and his readers to step back from routine and common-sense assumptions about emotions (although some interpreters of his work use the word "emotions" to denote complex blends of experience involving scripts). In short, what ordinary so-called "lay folk" call their "emotions," the scientist—with the benefit of their objective research—recognizes as proper to an innate system of affects. A very similar use of the term "affect" is made by Panskepp in the research program he calls "affective neuroscience."[50] Likewise, within the psychoanalytical tradition, Green takes the position that affect should be a metapsychological term and not a descriptive term with a specific referent. The word "affect" should thus be reserved for use as a categorical term that groups together "all the nuances that German (Empfinding, Gefühl) or French (émotion, sentiment, passion etc.) bring to this category."[51]

Conclusion

If my analysis is correct, then the affective turn—so long as it is based on something like Massumi's affect/emotion distinction—turns on flimsy ground indeed. In questioning the separation of affect and emotion within the literature of the affective turn, my intention is not to insist that there is no value in, for example, a distinction between the virtual and the actual, or in attending to affective experiences that are vaguely felt or felt only as "atmospheres," or in exploring unconscious forces, or impulses that are shared with other animals. On the contrary, these things are certainly worth attending to. My concern, rather, has been with an unfortunate tendency to polarize affect and emotion and to arbitrarily assign emotion to conditions which are conscious, personal, and tied to clear socially available meanings. Emotions are never clearly personal and it is likely that they always involve unconscious phases and typically implicate electrodermal activity and other autonomic responses. In my view, the affective turn should be considered, not as a rejection, but as a deepening of the discursive turn and as a continuation of the important project of a new understanding of human being in the wake of a sustained critique of Western rationality. That project must necessarily involve a sustained engagement with the affective dimensions of experience, conduct, and communication, and it must, in my view, transgress the usual boundaries between the natural sciences, the social sciences, and the humanities.

Notes

1 Greg Seigworth and Melissa Gregg, "An Inventory of Shimmers," in Melissa Gregg and Gregory J. Seigworth, eds., *The Affect Theory Reader* (Durham, NC: Duke University Press, 2010), 44.
2 Jo LeDoux, *The Emotional Brain* (New York: Simon & Schuster, 1996).
3 In psychology this was called the debate over "affective primacy". Zajonc, for example, demonstrated that subjects can "prefer" stimuli they have not consciously perceived. Zajonc R, "Feeling and Thinking: Preferences Need No Inferences," *American Psychologist* 35 (1980): 151–175.

4 Part of the confusion is that the same words have been used to mark different, and sometimes opposite distinctions. Within Damasio's neuroscience, for instance, emotion designates an innate bioregulatory device and he reserves the word "feeling" for the conscious experience of these biological processes, whilst "the word "affect" ... should be used only to designate the entire topic of emotion and feeling". Antonio Damasio, "A Second Chance for Emotion," in R.D. Lane and L. Nadel, eds., *Cognitive Neuroscience of Emotion* (Oxford: Oxford University Press, 2000), 12–23, 16.

5 For an overview, see Paul Stenner, "Emotion: Being Moved Beyond the Mainstream," in Ian Parker, ed., *Handbook of Critical Psychology* (London: Routledge, 2015), 43–51.

6 Paul Stenner and Rex Stainton Rogers, "Jealousy as a Manifold of Divergent Understandings: A Q Methodological Investigation," *The European Journal of Social Psychology* 28 (1998) 71–94.

7 Simone de Beauvoir, *The Woman Destroyed*, 122–123.

8 Damn her, lewd minx! O, damn her!
Come, go with me apart; I will withdraw,
To furnish me with some swift means of death
For the fair devil.

9 "It is not even necessary for that person to have attracted us, up till then, more than or even as much as others. All that was needed was that our predilection should become exclusive. And that condition is fulfilled when – in this moment of deprivation – the quest for the pleasures we enjoyed in his or her company is suddenly replaced by an anxious, torturing need, whose object is the person alone, an absurd, irrational need which the laws of this world make it impossible to satisfy and difficult to assuage—the insensate agonizing need to possess exclusively." Proust, Marcel, *In Search of Lost Time*, 277.

10 "Another woman was stroking his cheek, as soft as this silk, as warm and gentle as this pull-over—that I cannot bear ... Between them there is an intimacy that used to belong only to me ... My heart is being sawn in two with a very fine-toothed saw." Simone De Beauvoir, *The Woman Destroyed*, 122–123.

11 Seigworth and Gregg, "An Inventory," 1.

12 Brian Massumi, "The Autonomy of Affect," *Cultural Critique* 31, no. 2 (1995): 83–109, 88.

13 Ibid., 89.

14 Patricia Clough, "The Affective Turn: Political Economy, Biomedia and Bodies," in Gregg and Seigworth, 223.

15 Couze Venn, "Individuation, Relationality, Affect: Rethinking the Human in Relation to the Living," *Body and Society* 16, no. 1 (2010): 129–161, 159.

16 Anna Gibbs, "After Affect: Sympathy, Synchrony, and Mimetic Communication," in Gregg & Seigworth, 188.

17 Steven Dexter Brown and Ian Tucker, "Eff the Ineffable: Affect, Somatic Management, and Mental Health Service Users," in Gregg and Seigworth.

18 Peter Berger and Thomas Luckmann had famously called their treatise on the sociology of knowledge *The Social Construction of Reality* (Harmondsworth: Penguin, 1966). This title caught on and in 1979 Jeff Coulter applied a variant of this sociology in an important book called *The Social Construction of Mind* (London: Palgrave, 1979). To my knowledge, the first psychology book bearing the phrase was Ken Gergen and Keith Davis *The Social Construction of the Person* (London: Springer Verlag, 1985), swiftly followed by Rom Harré's edited volume *The Social Construction of Emotions* (London: Routledge, 1987). Celia Kitzinger, who completed her PhD at Reading shortly before my own published that work under the title *The Social Construction of Lesbianism* (London: Sage, 1987). My own PhD was an effort to lend some empirical

substance to what was then a predominantly theoretical concern with the issues recently opened up by the thesis of the social construction of emotions.

19 Brian Massumi, "The Autonomy of Affect," 1995, 83–109.

20 Brian Massumi, *Parables for the Virtual: Movement, Affect, Sensation* (Durham, NC: Duke University Press, 2002), 4.

21 Massumi, "The Autonomy of Affect," 1995, 228.

22 Ibid., 85.

23 Ibid., 84.

24 Stuart P. Taylor and Seymour Epstein, "The Measurement of Autonomic Arousal: Some Basic Issues Illustrated by the Covariation of Heart Rate and Skin Conductance," *Psychosomatic Medicine* 29, no. 5 (1967): 514–525.

25 G. Robert J. Hockey, Michael G.H. Coles and Anthony W.K Gaillard, *Energetics and Human Information Processing* (Dordrecht, Netherlands: Martinus Nijhoff Publishers, 1986).

26 Silvan S. Tomkins, "The Quest for Primary Motives: Biography and Autobiography of an Idea," *Journal of Personality and Social Psychology* 41, no. 2 (1981): 306–329.

27 Massumi (1995). "The Autonomy of Affect." 85

28 Massumi, 102.

29 Massumi, 88.

30 Massumi, 96.

31 Eve Kosovsky Sedgwick and Adam Frank, "Shame in the Cybernetic Fold: Reading Silvan Tomkins," *Critical Inquiry* 21, no. 2 (1995): 496–505.

32 Anthony Elliott and Stephen Frosh, eds., *Psychoanalysis in Context: Paths between Theory and Modern Culture* (London: Routledge, 1995).

33 André Green, "The Conception of Affect," *International Journal of Psychoanalysis* 58, no. 2 (1977): 129–156.

34 Wilfred R. Bion, *Experiences in Groups and Other Papers* (London: Tavistock, 1961), 14.

35 André Green, *The Fabric of Affect in the Psychoanalytic Discourse* (London: Routledge, 1999), xv.

36 See Matte Blanco, *Thinking, Feeling and Being* (London: Routledge, 1988).

37 Elliot and Frosh, *Psychoanalysis in Context*, 2.

38 Ian Craib, "Social Constructionism as a Social Psychosis," *Sociology* 31, no. 1 (1997): 1–15. Craib suggests that social constructionists suffer from a delusion (that the world is constructed) which functions to defend them from a confrontation with their powerlessness to explain that world. They imagine they are lucid and rational, but all the while their thinking is shaped and determined by the affect.

39 Anu Koivunen, "The Affective Turn?" *Preface to the Proceedings of the Conference Affective Encounters: Rethinking Embodiment in Feminist Media Studies,* 2001.

40 It is not coincidental that feminism was a significant influence since feminists were amongst the first to point out the masculinist bias at play in the old Platonic, Augustinian, Cartesian and Kantian dogma whereby reason must assert itself as (transcendent) "master" over the (natural) passions and sentiments.

41 Patricia Clough and Jean Halley, eds., *The Affective Turn: Theorizing the Social* (London: Duke University Press, 2007).

42 Seigworth and Gregg, "An Inventory," 5.

43 Op cit., 1.

44 Op cit., 2.

45 Massumi, "The Autonomy of Affect," 1995, 92.

46 Ibid., 88–89.

47 The second claim made by Massumi is equally false, since Spinoza nowhere argues for the "irreducibly bodily and autonomic nature of affect". In the first

54 *Paul Stenner*

place, as Massumi is well aware, Spinoza is most famous for what is called his thought/extension parallelism. This means that he resolutely refuses to separate mind/thought from body/extension and instead bases his entire philosophy upon the argument that these are not two separate substances, but one substance which can be made to show up to an observer under two different attributes. There is no "irreducibly bodily" event for Spinoza, since each and every event can be considered under at least the two attributes "thought" and "extension". For a more detailed account, see Paul Stenner, *Liminality and Experience: A Transdisciplinary Approach to the Psychosocial* (London: Palgrave, 2018).

48 Baruch Spinoza, *Ethics: Including the Improvement of the Understanding*, trans. R.H.M. Elwes (New York: Prometheus books, 1677/1989).

49 Spinoza, 89 (13th proposition of Part 2).

50 Jaak Panksepp, *Affective Neuroscience: The Foundations of Human and Animal Emotions* (Oxford, Oxford University Press, 1998).

51 Green, *The Fabric of Affect in the Psychoanalytic Discourse*, ü8.

Bibliography

Berger, Peter, and Luckmann, Thomas. *The Social Construction of Reality.* Harmondsworth: Penguin, 1966.

Bion, Wilfred R. *Experiences in Groups and Other Papers.* London: Tavistock, 1961.

Blanco, Matte. *Thinking, Feeling and Being.* London: Routledge, 1988.

Brown, Steven Dexter, and Tucker, Ian. "Eff the Ineffable: Affect, Somatic Management, and Mental Health Service Users." In *The Affect Theory Reader*, edited by Melissa Gregg and Gregory J. Seigworth, 229–249. Durham, NC: Duke University Press, 2010.

Clough, Patricia, and Halley, Jean. *The Affective Turn: Theorizing the Social.* London: Duke University Press, 2007.

Clough, Patricia. "The Affective Turn: Political Economy, Biomedia and Bodies." In *The Affect Theory Reader*, edited by Melissa Gregg and Gregory J. Seigworth, 206–228. Durham, NC: Duke University Press, 2010.

Coulter, Jeff. *The Social Construction of Mind.* London: Palgrave, 1979.

Craib, Ian. "Social Constructionism as a Social Psychosis." *Sociology* 31, no. 1 (1997): 1–15.

Damasio, Antonio. "A Second Chance for Emotion." In *Cognitive Neuroscience of Emotion*, edited by R.D. Lane and L. Nadel, 12–23. Oxford: Oxford University Press, 2000.

De Beauvoir, Simone. *The Woman Destroyed.* New York: Harper Perennial Modern Classics, 1967.

Elliott, Anthony, and Frosh, Stephen. *Psychoanalysis in Context: Paths between Theory and Modern Culture.* London: Routledge, 1995.

Gergen, Ken, and Davis, Keith. *The Social Construction of the Person.* London: Springer Verlag, 1985.

Gibbs, Anna. "After Affect: Sympathy, Synchrony, and Mimetic Communication." In *The Affect Theory Reader*, edited by Melissa Gregg and Gregory J. Seigworth, 186–205. Durham, NC: Duke University Press, 2010.

Green, André. "The Conception of Affect." *International Journal of Psychoanalysis* 58, no. 2 (1977): 129–156.

Green, André. *The Fabric of Affect in the Psychoanalytic Discourse*. London: Routledge, 1999.

Harré, Rom. *The Social Construction of Emotions*. London: Routledge, 1987.

Hockey, G. Robert J., Michael G.H. Coles, and Anthony W.K. Gaillard. *Energetics and Human Information Processing*. Dordrecht, Netherlands: Martinus Nijhoff Publishers, 1986.

Kitzinger, Celia. *The Social Construction of Lesbianism*. London: Sage, 1987.

Koivunen, Anu. "The Affective Turn?" *Preface to the Proceedings of the Conference Affective Encounters: Rethinking Embodiment in Feminist Media Studies*, 2001.

Kosovsky Sedgwick, Eve, and Frank, Adam. "Shame in the Cybernetic Fold: Reading Silvan Tomkins." *Critical Inquiry* 21, no. 2 (1995): 496–505.

LeDoux, Jo. *The Emotional Brain*. New York: Simon & Schuster, 1996.

Massumi, Brian. "The Autonomy of Affect." *Cultural Critique* 31, no. 2 (1995): 83–109.

Massumi, Brian. *Parables for the Virtual: Movement, Affect, Sensation*. Durham, NC: Duke University Press, 2002.

Panksepp, Jaak. *Affective Neuroscience: The Foundations of Human and Animal Emotions*. Oxford: Oxford University Press, 1998.

Proust, Marcel. *In Search of Lost Time, Volume 1, Swann's Way*. Translated by C.K. Scott Moncrieff and Terrence Kilmartin. London: Vintage Books, 2005.

Seigworth, Greg, and Gregg, Melissa. "An Inventory of Shimmers." In *The Affect Theory Reader*, edited by Melissa Gregg and Gregory J. Seigworth, 1–28. Durham, NC: Duke University Press, 2010.

Spinoza, Baruch. *Ethics: Including the Improvement of the Understanding*. Translated by R.H.M. Elwes. New York: Prometheus books, 1989.

Stenner, Paul, and Stainton Rogers, Rex. "Jealousy as a Manifold of Divergent Understandings: A Q Methodological Investigation." *The European Journal of Social Psychology* 28 (1998): 71–94.

Stenner, Paul. "Emotion: Being Moved Beyond the Mainstream." In *Handbook of Critical Psychology*, edited by Ian Parker, 43–51. London: Routledge, 2015.

Stenner, Paul. *Liminality and Experience: A Transdisciplinary Approach to the Psychosocial*. London: Palgrave, 2018.

Taylor, Stuart P, and Epstein, Seymour. "The Measurement of Autonomic Arousal: Some Basic Issues Illustrated by the Covariation of Heart Rate and Skin Conductance." *Psychosomatic Medicine* 29, no. 5 (1967): 514–525.

Tomkins, Silvan S. "The Quest for Primary Motives: Biography and Autobiography of an Idea." *Journal of Personality and Social Psychology* 41, no. 2 (1981): 306–329.

Venn, Couze. "Individuation, Relationality, Affect: Rethinking the Human in Relation to the Living." *Body and Society* 16, no. 1 (2010): 129–161.

Zajonc, R. "Feeling and Thinking: Preferences Need No Inferences." *American Psychologist* 35 (1980): 151–175.

3 We Have Never Been Rational

A Genealogy of the Affective Turn

David Stubblefield

One of the more significant developments in the humanities over the last few decades has been an increasing interest in the notion of affect, so much so that some have spoken and written about "the affective turn" in the humanities, a turn that challenges traditional ways of thinking about rationality, bodies, and the forces that drive human behavior. While this turn consists of a loose set of largely heterogeneous theories from a variety of disciplines, it can be understood as challenging a long-standing assumption within the Western tradition that explicit symbolic processes such as conscious thoughts, beliefs, and feelings are the primary agencies that drive human behavior.

More particularly, the contemporary turn to affect is motivated by the perceived limits of a variety of theoretical movement in the 1980s and 1990s, which it reads as the most recent instance of this tendency to privilege the role of symbolic action. That is, much of the affective turn is motivated by the belief that the linguistic turn, social construction, semiotics, and various interpretations of postmodernism and poststructuralism, all privilege symbolic representations and, in doing so, have little to say about the role of matter, bodies, and the material affects that circulate among them.[1]

One critic of this belief in the primacy of the symbolic, Donovan O. Schaefer, speaks of what he calls "the linguistic fallacy," which assumes that the only reason bodies act is "because a particular textual regime has told them to."[2] According to Schaefer, affect theory exposes this fallacy and intervenes in the name of the myriad of nonlinguistic forces that make bodies act. Thus, he asserts that "affect theory—examining the mobile materiality of the body—thematizes the way that world prompts us to move before language."[3] Therefore, contrary to the tendency to focus on the symbolic, Schaefer and other theorists of the affective turn draw our attention to the "materiality" of affective and bodily experience, or the way that affect acts on, directs, orients, or conditions thinking (cognition) and feeling (perception) before these processes begin. Building on this line of thinking the moral psychologist, Johnathan Haidt, has argued that contrary to the traditional understanding of moral reasoning where our reasoning processes determine our affective experience, affect is "the horse" that leads the way and reason is the "rider" that follows.

While this central provocation—that conscious symbolic activity is not the only thing that motivates action—can be grasped fairly easily, the task of defining affect and understanding how it works has proven to be much more difficult. Indeed, reducing such a concept to a rigid definition may not be possible or desirable; however, a historical approach that locates the concept of affect within the Western intellectual tradition can provide a much needed sense of how the term has been used in the past and how the current use of the term both extends and differentiates itself from this history. To this end, I will provide a genealogy of the concept of affect by discussing two of its most historically significant interpretations: what I will call the moral interpretation and the Romantic interpretation. In both cases, affective experience will be seen to play a central role in human life and its possibilities.

The Centrality of Symbolic Behavior in the Western Tradition

According to Aristotle, humans may be distinguished from other animals by their possession of *logos*, a term most often translated as rationality, but also bearing connotations of language and law. While other animals are capable of sensation and appetite, Aristotle claims, only man possesses *logos*. This possession, then, delineates humanity from the surrounding world, marking it as different in *kind* from other forms of existence, and drawing clear boundaries between *logos* and its nonrational other.

In the twentieth century, the defining feature of humankind often becomes "symbolic activity," a broader term encompassing any use of communicative means to represent one's experience. This behavior can include painting, music, and overtly linguistic behaviors, such as writing and speaking. Thus, Ernst Cassirer in his 1944, *An Essay on Man,* argues that "instead of defining man as an *animal rationale*, we should define him as an animal *symbolicum*"[4] For Cassirer, this drive to produce symbols, whether these symbols are mathematical, mythical, linguistic, or artistic, is synonymous with the human spirit and its desire to transcend sensible experience by endowing it with form. Likewise, in 1963, Kenneth Burke's "Definition of Man" famously categorizes man as "the symbol-using (symbol-making, symbol-misusing) animal, inventor of the negative (or moralized by the negative), separated from his natural condition by instruments of his own making, goaded by the spirit of hierarchy (or moved by the sense of order), and rotten with perfection."[5] Thus, like Cassirer's understanding of "Man," Burke's definition, while somewhat more ambivalent about the results of symbolic action, focuses on the way that symbols allow man to separate from nature and seek a higher sense of morality, order, and truth.

While Aristotle's definition intimately weds man's existence to *logos*, we can think of theorists such as Cassirer and Burke as working within

58   *David Stubblefield*

and expanding an Aristotelian paradigm, which privileges humanity's capacity to transcend his natural experience by standing outside of its empirical experience and representing that experience for the purpose of understanding it. By attaching normative significance to this capacity, the nonsymbolic, preconscious aspects of human life become nonessential, or when indulged at the expense of the "higher," "rational" symbolic aspects, even destructive. Unlike other forms of life, humans are not simply at the mercy of their affective experiences. They categorize, know, and transmit their experience through symbols, and then make generalizations and predictions about the future.

Moreover, the capacity for symbolic action is what allows humanity to create civilized forms of collective existence. As Cicero explains, the ability to speak and, therefore, to persuade each other is "our greatest advantage over brute creation" and such an art is a "power ... strong enough ... to gather scattered humanity into one place, or lead it out of its brutish existence in the wilderness up to our present condition of civilization."[6] Thus, symbolic behavior, perhaps the most readily recognized form of which is language, saves the collective life of humankind from regressing to savage forms of existence by subordinating violence and conflict into verbal or symbolic disputations and disagreements.

The Moral Interpretation of Affect

This wedding of the symbolic to man's proper nature and to the possibility of civilized existence lays the foundation for understanding what I will call the moral interpretation of affect. Because human nature is rational, one becomes more fully human to the degree that one exercises this rationality and subjects one's affective experience to a symbolic order. In other words, this interpretation insists that our affective experience ought to be subservient to, reinforce, or be sublimated into a particular symbolic order, whether this order be cultural, natural, or divine. Hence, it posits a moral hierarchy whereby symbolic representations *ought* to be primary and affective experience *ought* to be supplementary, and in doing so, it likewise posits that reversing this order undermines, imprisons, or perverts both human nature and human civilization.[7]

Mapping this tradition, Teresa Brennan notes that "the earliest Western records of the transmission of affect ... make them demons or deadly sins."[8] She adds that the seven deadly sins—pride, sloth, envy, lust, anger, gluttony, and avarice—are "affects rather than actions."[9] She also maps these sins onto what she sees as the unofficial list of "psychological sins" of the twentieth century: narcissism (pride), inertia (sloth), envy (envy), objectification (lust), aggression (anger), greed (gluttony), and obsessionality (avarice).[10] For Brennan, these "sins" or affects are states of affliction that undermine human agency by enacting physiological transformations in bodies that orient them toward certain self-destructive ways of thinking, feeling, and behaving[11] As such, these affects are essentially *opposed* to the kind of existence that would be in line with one's true nature.

In order to understand how this happens, one must understand the subjective passivity that is associated with affective experience. According to Brennan, "to be the object of affects is to be in passive relation to them."[12] Such passivity undermines the ideals of freedom, autonomy, and rationality, which have been valued by traditional forms of Western morality, making affect, in Brennan's word's, "opposed to the integrity of the organism's expression"[13] and leading us to understand affects as "invaders that work against our true nature." Moreover, affects so overwhelm the subject that they render her *inert,* forcing her to repetitively act out *fixed* patterns of thought and behavior. The envious, gluttonous, or narcissistic person repeats the same affective relations again and again. Thus, subjective passivity makes humanity vulnerable to a persuasive force that overpowers the subject's conscious will. As Saint Paul says, "I do not understand what I do. For what I want to do I do not do, but what I hate I do …. Now if I do what I do not want to do, it is no longer I who do it, but it is sin living in me that does it."[14] In other words, the "sinful," affective self undermines the conscious, rational self. Being open to this sort of affective possession leaves sinners in a constant battle to subjugate or expel affectivity and to act in accordance with the true integrity of his being.[15]

In order to draw out this position on affect, it will be helpful to consider how Augustine describes the difference between sexuality in a postlapsarian and a prelapsarian humanity:

> In Paradise, if culpable disobedience had not been punished with another disobedience, marriage would not have known this resistance, this opposition, this struggle between the libido and will. On the contrary, our private parts, like all the other parts of the body, would have been at the service of the will. That which was created for this end would have sown the field of generation, as the hand sows the earth. … Man would have sown his seed and woman would have received it in her genitals, only when necessary and to the degree necessary, as a result of the will's command, and not due to the excitation of the libido.[16]

In other words, in Paradise, humanity's will was ordered by God and, therefore, commanded his body according to divine law, using its organs for the right purpose, at the right time, and in the right fashion. However, after the Fall, the libido, as part of humanity's flesh becomes disconnected from this order, and, therefore, vulnerable to affective excitations from external sources that are not in alignment with the divine knowledge.

In fact, this rationalist moral theology suggests that it would be better for humans if affects did not exist at all. Giorgio Agamben describes what procreation would be like in Augustine's Paradise: "with the signal of the

60   *David Stubblefield*

will, the genitals would have been aroused, just as easily as we might raise a hand, and the husband would impregnate his wife without the burning stimulation of libido."[17] In this picture, man would not need affective excitations to accomplish this act and would simply deposit his seed without the whole play of bodies, subjection, and desire. As Augustine states, "It would have been possible for man to transmit his seed to his wife without harming her physical integrity."[18] Thus, in an ideal world, affect would not exist and the fact that it does is an unfortunate part of man's fallen condition.

However, despite this disparaging view of affect, this line of rationalist Christian theology[19] comes to insist that fallen man actually *needs* affect to supplement his imperfect nature and imperfect reason. After the Fall, the wholesale expulsion of affect is not an option, and the best humanity can do is to subject the affective excitations to a higher, divine order. Hence, the Church eventually comes to recognize that appeals to our intellect do not always persuade our natures, and some affective experiences, like sacred music and art, are a necessary evil, needed to reinforce Christian discourse.

We can see this failure of rationality to persuade in our everyday lives. For example, if we were purely rational beings, then once a cigarette smoker heard the following rational argument—"If you want to live, then you will stop smoking. You want to live. Therefore, you should stop smoking"—then this person would stop immediately. That is, once the argument was understood, then a purely logical nature would execute the argument in the same way that a computer does. However, it can hardly be disputed that many smokers hear this argument and continue to smoke, leading us to the inevitable conclusion that our nature is not purely rational and, thus, forcing us to confront the limits of rationality as a means of persuasion. The question, then, becomes how do we actually persuade this not-fully-rational-nature—which ideally would be as rational as possible, but which nonetheless remains bound to and often seems to require "non-rational" and affective forms of persuasion? How do we understand a nature in which the affective experiences of embarrassment, pride, the fear of losing love, or the desire to please a newfound mate who disproves of smoking, and not an argument in the form of *modus ponens*[20], often proves to be a more effective means of persuading someone of the need to stop smoking? Persuading someone to adopt rational conclusions, it seems, often requires affect even if affective experience is not necessarily rational.

Thus, this moral interpretation of affect ends up valuing affect, but doing so carefully and cautiously inside of a moral hierarchy that subordinates it to an order of symbolic meanings. Despite its calls to renounce affective experience, ultimately, it understands affect as a kind of *pharmakon*, both a poison and a cure. On the one hand, affective experiences render the subject passive and undermine its agency, and are, therefore, very likely to be expelled as a kind of poison; on the other hand, these experiences come back into the moral fold as a cure for a fallen nature that is seldom compelled to desire the right things by rational arguments. In the end, rationalist theology appears as a particular way of modulating affect, much more than a way of eliminating it.

The Romantic Interpretation of Affect: Curing Affective Alienation through Art

One place we might expect to find a less ambiguous affirmation of affective experience would be art. Art would seem to openly affirm affective experience. For example, one can think of the Romantic glorification of the sublime experience of things like thunderstorms, or the sensation of beauty involved in experiencing the grandeur of nature. In fact, if Cicero celebrated the accomplishments of modern civilization as a means of sublimating a largely affective and potentially violent existence into language, then Romantic conceptions of art have often sought to recover something of this "lost" affective experience. According to this interpretation of affect, civilization represses affect, and thereby, alienates human life from an important part of its nature or even severs its connection with nature itself.

This Romantic approach to affect is perhaps best encapsulated by the German notion of *Schein*, a term that was critical to the German aesthetic tradition. While the term is etymologically related to the English word "shine," the term is often translated as "sensuous appearance" or "beautiful appearance." Hegel famously defined the beautiful as "*das sinnliche Scheinen der Idee*"—the sensuous appearance or "shining" of the idea. Thus, *schein* suggests an intellectual intuition of objects that is affective in nature, and which, therefore, overcomes the dichotomy of affect and cognition brought about by the fall into the alienation of modern, technological civilization.

For Romantics, this alienation of human nature caused by modern civilization is evident in forms of technical labor, which reflects this bifurcation and incompleteness. In the words of Schiller,

> the enjoyment is separated from labor, the means from the end, exertion from recompense. Eternally fettered to a single little fragment of the whole, man fashions himself only as fragment; ever hearing only the monotonous whirl of the wheel which he turns, he never develops the harmony of his being, and instead of shaping the humanity that lies in his nature, he becomes the mere imprint of his occupation, his science.[21]

As with the moral interpretation of affect, humans are still bifurcated. But this time, it is not affective experience cutting us off from rationality,

62   David Stubblefield

instead it is rationality (science, technology) repressing or distorting our natural affective experience, as human nature finds itself "ever hearing only the monotonous whirl of a wheel" at the expense of the "harmony of his being." The Romantic interpretation of affect seeks to overcome the modern bifurcation of sensibility and reason by recovering the "lost" affective dimension of human life. The privileged site for doing this is art—and the discipline that has most rigorously theorized the nature of art is aesthetics, or "the science of sensation."

We can see this Romantic approach to affect in the aesthetic theory of Herbert Marcuse, particularly in his work *Eros and Civilization*, where "the aesthetic dimension" possesses the potential to restore our erotic and "sensuous drives and instincts which have been pushed underground by civilization." Marcuse characterizes the aesthetic dimension as an affirmation of affective experience, where affective experience is understood as a special kind of cognition: "The basic experience of this dimension is sensuous rather than conceptual; the aesthetic perception is essentially intuition, not notion. The nature of sensuousness is 'receptivity,' cognition through being *affected* by given objects. It is by virtue of its intrinsic relation to sensuousness that the aesthetic function assumes its central position."[22] Thus, for Marcuse's aesthetics, affective experience is not opposed to cognition, nor is it reluctantly brought in as an aid to understanding. Instead, it offers the potential for a special kind of cognition, which he calls aesthetic perception,

For Marcuse, aesthetic perception is possible because of the imagination's power to remember archetypal figures that precede the entry into the repressive order/regime of civilization and that are buried in the human psyche. One archetype Marcuse discusses is the figure of Orpheus, the poet whose song recalls an original harmony between humanity and nature. We can see this harmony in the description of Orpheus' song in Rilke's *Sonnets to Orpheus*:

> Almost a maid, she came forth shimmering
> From the highest happiness of song and lyre,
> And shining clearly through her veils of spring
> She made herself a bed within my ear
> And slept in me. All things were in her sleep:
> The trees I marveled at, the enchanting spell
> Of the farthest distances, the meadows deep,
> Within her slept the world. You singing god, o how
> How did you perfect her so she did not long
> To be awake? She rose and slept.
> Where is her death?[23]

By containing all things, Orpheus' song recalls an original harmony with nature, a harmony receptive to all things including death.

We Have Never Been Rational 63

Orpheus' song, partly because of its receptivity and non-opposition to death, liberates objects from being perceived solely in terms of social utility or humanity's self-interest to preserve its own existence, allowing us to be affected by them, to experience their own intrinsic nature, and to think differently about their possibilities. Marcuse explains, "Trees and animals respond to Orpheus's language .... The Orphic Eros awakens and liberates potentials that are real in things animate and inanimate, in organic and inorganic nature—real but in the un-erotic reality suppressed. These potentialities circumscribe the *telos* inherent in them as: 'just to be what they are,' 'being there,' existing."[24]

This concept of "disinterested," affective cogitation is difficult to grasp; therefore, an example might be helpful. While modern man, according to this Romantic interpretation of affect, may see a field of grass as a site for a future strip mall, aesthetic perception is the moment where we are affected by the grass, the trees, and the flowers themselves. This experience involves not only a sensual perception of these objects but also the cognitive grasping of grass as grass, the trees as trees, and the flowers as flowers. These two tasks (one affective, the other cognitive), for Marcuse, cannot be separated.

In a sense, art recalls a primordial experience of these objects that took place prior to man's entry into civilization and the resulting bifurcation of his senses and intellect. There was a time, we can assume, when humans did not look at trees as lumber to build cabins, or grass and flowers as something to be cleared so roads could be built. Art, for Marcuse, captures something of the original perception of these objects. Hence, during moments of aesthetic perception, our capacity to be affected by objects is, at the same time, our capacity to cognize these objects in themselves and their intrinsic possibilities outside of their utility for human civilization. Thus, affect and cognition are combined in a unitary act of aesthetic perception where form and matter achieve beautiful appearance, or *Schein*.

For many aesthetic theorists working in the Romantic tradition, affective cogitation takes on a critical function. By affording a disinterested, nonutilitarian experience of objects, art undermines the "false" forms of rationality in which they are currently embedded: "Only in the 'illusory world' [of art] do things appear as what they are and what they can be. By virtue of this truth (which art alone can express in sensuous representation) the world is inverted—it is the given reality, the ordinary world which now appears as untrue, as false, as deceptive reality."[25] Thus, aesthetic perceptions, by bringing us into the truth of what things are and what they can be, dialectically negates the existing ways of thinking that have defined these objects. Moreover, failing to critique the existing rationality amounts to succumbing to it. As Theodore Adorno claims, "*Schein* is dialectical as a reflection of truth; to reject all *Schein* is to become its victim all the more fully."[26] And to the degree that aesthetic perception involves a utopian form of thinking, its function will perhaps forever remain critical and negative.

64 *David Stubblefield*

For Marcuse, art cannot become part of the existing order of society without losing its critical function and exists primarily as a critique of this society aimed at creating "a new sensibility," or a new way of thinking and feeling. Thus, he insists that every authentic work of art would be "subversive of understanding and perception, an indictment of the established reality principle, the appearance of the image of liberation."[27] Art, then, provides an affective cogitation of objects, which reworks our capacity of thinking and feeling.

Conclusion

While the contemporary affective turn has stressed the novelty of the affective experience, since the beginning of the Western tradition, affective experience has been a critical part of human experience, particularly in moral theology and art. Much of the perceived novelty of the affective turn likely lies in its contrast to the linguistic turn and various forms of semiotics and textualism that flourished in the 1980s and 1990s. Claiming that the affective turn has exaggerated its novelty certainly does not mean that affect is somehow unimportant. If anything, it means the exact opposite: affect and its modulation into various forms of art and theology have always played an absolutely critical role in Western thought. In fact, if rationality means separating ourselves from or eliminating affective experience, then we have never been rational.

Notes

1 Patricia T. Clough, *The Affective Turn: Theorizing the Social.* Edited by Melissa Gregg and Gregory J. Seigworth (Durham, NC: Duke University Press, 2007).
2 Donovan O. Schaefer, *Religious Affects: Animality, Evolution, and Power* (Durham, NC: Duke University Press, 2015).
3 Ibid.
4 Ernst Cassirer, *An Essay of Man* (New Haven, CT: Yale University Press), 26.
5 Kenneth Burke, *Language as Symbolic Action* (Berkeley and Los Angeles: University of California Press), 16.
6 Marcus Tullius Cicero, H. Rackham, and E. W. Sutton, *De Oratore* (Cambridge, MA: Harvard University Press, 1988), xx.
7 The use of the term *ought* is often understood as necessarily asserting a moral claim.
8 Teresa Brennan, *The Transmission of Affect* (Ithaca, NY: Cornell University Press, 2004), 97.
9 Ibid., 98–99.
10 Ibid., 99.
11 See Brennan 1, 5, and 6. Brennan differentiates affect from feeling saying that difference between the two terms is "the difference between what I feel with and what I feel." Later on, she defines feelings as "sensations that have found a match in words."
12 Ibid., 101.

13 Ibid., 99.

14 Romans 7:15–17.

15 Far from being somehow unique to Christian thought, this tension between affect and signification has extended into nearly every facet of life. Dolar explains that "the birth of opera was accompanied by the dilemma of *prima la musica, e poi le parole* ("first the music, then the words"), or the other way around, the dramatic tension between the word and the voice was put into its cradle," adding that "the entire history of opera from Montiverdi to Strauss can be written through the spyglass of this dilemma" Mladen Dolar, *A Voice and Nothing More.* Cambridge, MA: MIT Press, 2006, 30.

16 Quoted in Giorgio Agamben, *Nudities* (Stanford, CA: Stanford University Press, 2011), 69.

17 Agamben, 69.

18 Quoted in Agamben, 69.

19 It would be completely misleading to attribute this moral interpretation of affect to Christianity as such, although this sometimes happens. Brennan, for one, argues that faith, hope and love are perhaps the best example of an affirmative interpretation of affective experience. To the degree that these virtues are central to the Christian experience, Christianity would arguably represent one of the best examples of interpreting affective experience in a favorable light.

20 The rule of logic stating that if a conditional statement ("if p then q") is accepted, and the antecedent (p) holds, then the consequent (q) may be inferred.

21 Friedrich Schiller, "Letters on Aesthetic Education," 22 quoted in Marcuse, *Eros and Civilization,* 186.

22 Ibid., 176.

23 quoted in Marcuse, 162.

24 Ibid., 165.

25 Herbert Marcuse, *The Aesthetic Dimension: Toward a Critique of Marxist Aesthetics* (Boston, MA: Beacon Press, 1978), 54.

26 Sven Lutticken. "Shine and Shein" *e-flux Journal* 61 January 2015. Accessed February 8, 2018, p. 6. www.e-flux.com/journal/61/61008/shine-and-schein/.

27 Marcuse, *Aesthetic Dimension,* x–xi.

Bibliography

Agamben, Giorgio, et al. *Nudities.* Stanford, CA: Stanford University Press, 2011.

Brennan, Teresa. *The Transmission of Affect.* Ithaca, NY: Cornell University Press, 2004.

Burke, Kenneth. *Language as Symbolic Action: Essays on Life, Literature, and Method.* Berkeley and Los Angeles: University of California Press, 1966.

Cassirer, Ernst. *An Essay on Man: An Introduction to a Philosophy of Human Culture.* New Haven, CT: Yale University Press, 1972. Print.

Cicero, Marcus T., et al. *De Oratore.* Cambridge, MA: Harvard University Press, 1988.

Clough, Patricia T. *The Affective Turn: Theorizing the Social* ed. Mellisa Gregg and Gregory J. Seigworth. Durham, NC: Duke University Press, 2007.

Dolar, Mladen. *A Voice and Nothing More.* Cambridge, MA: MIT Press, 2006.

Gregg, Melissa, and Gregory J. Seigworth. *The Affect Theory Reader.* Durham NC, Duke University Press, 2011.

Hardt, Michael. "Affective Labor." *Boundary* 26, no. 2 (1999): 89–100.

66   David Stubblefield

Marcuse, Herbert. *Eros and Civilization: A Philosophical Inquiry into Freud.* Boston, MA: Beacon Press, 1966. Print.

Marcuse, Herbert. *The Aesthetic Dimension: Toward a Critique of Marxist Aesthetics.* Boston, MA: Beacon Press, 1978.

Massumi, Brian. *Parables for the Virtual: Movement, Affect, Sensation.* Durham, NC: Duke University Press, 2007.

Massumi, Brian. *The Politics of Affect.* Cambridge: Polity Press, 2015.

Schaefer, Donovan O. *Religious Affects: Animality, Evolution, and Power.* Durham, NC: Duke University Press, 2015.

Part II

Affect in Rhetorical and Cultural Theory

4 Affective Rhetoric
What It Is and Why It Matters

Samuel Mateus

Introduction

Theorists and practitioners of rhetoric have long known that emotions play a key part in persuasion. Aristotle discusses emotions in terms of understanding and influencing the audience's frame of mind. Aristotle's *Rhetoric* states, "Now the proofs furnished by the speech are of three kinds. The first depends upon the moral character of the speaker, the second upon putting the hearer into a certain frame of mind, the third upon the speech itself, in so far as it proves or seems to prove."[1] He realizes that in order to persuade, it is not sufficient to use reasonable speech (*logos*) or to appeal to the speaker's own character (*ethos*); it is also necessary to put audiences into the appropriate emotional state. Aristotle not only recognizes the significance of emotions in rhetoric, but also explains the importance of understanding how and under which circumstances they can be best elicited.

In 55 BCE, Marcus Tullius Cicero, emphasizing what Aristotle's *Rhetoric* had already established, admonishes the speakers of his day not to neglect the power of specific emotions. In *De Oratore*, Cicero posits that the manipulation of feelings could, indeed, sway opinion to the orator's side while implying that those who master the arousal of emotions and frame the argument in emotional terms are among the most effective practitioners of rhetorical persuasion: "Thus, as everyone knows, the virtue of oratory is most effectively displayed in arousing anger, disgust, or indignation of an audience, or in turning them from such excitement of feeling to mercy and pity; and here no one but a man who has made himself thoroughly familiar with the characters of men (...) will ever be able to produce by his words the effect which he desires."[2] And Quintilian, in Book VI of his *Institutio Oratoria*, presents emotional appeals as a main rhetorical strategy to sway the judges in court. In Chapter 1, he deals with the use of emotions in the peroration, or closing argument, while in Chapter 2 he gives advice in the specific use of emotions in a trial.[3]

Even if emotions and *pathos* are a major part of Aristotle, Cicero, and Quintilian's teachings on rhetoric, the twentieth-century professionalization of the field of argumentation as an academic discipline had

70   *Samuel Mateus*

the consequence of marginalizing affective appeals. Beginning in the mid-twentieth century, effective deployment of emotional appeals lost its value because argumentation theory tended to consider emotions impediments to rational argumentation.[4] Consequently, modern reformulation of the art of rhetoric marginalized appeals to an audience's emotions. For example, Stephen Toulmin's model of argument[5], which is widely taught in the schools, focuses on probabilistic logic and does not consider the impact of feelings, affects, or emotions.[6] As Schroeder writes, "Toulmin's approach also fails to account for affective and stylistic appeals of persuasion, which are essential. Students who are presented with the Toulmin model are not being taught how to appeal to an audience's emotions, to which Aristotle devotes a significant portion of his *On Rhetoric*."[7] We should note that while the Toulmin model of argument is included in rhetoric textbooks, Toulmin is not a rhetorician but a philosopher. Another influential mid-twentieth-century text, *The New Rhetoric* of Perelman & Olbrechts-Tyteca, while giving great impetus to the modern "rediscovery of rhetoric," has little to say on the role of emotions in argumentative or persuasive discourse.[8] *The New Rhetoric*, as well as Perelman's *The Realm of Rhetoric,* emphasizes practical, probabilistic reasoning.[9]

Breaking with the modern rewriting of the art of rhetoric, this chapter discusses the central role of emotions in rhetorical persuasion. It contends we need to bring rhetoric and eloquence to the forefront of contemporary communicative studies, and demonstrates how the appeal to emotions is crucial to most of today's persuasive communication. A full appraisal of its significance should pay attention, for instance, to the emotional role of images, symbols, and pictorial metaphors[10] in media communication such as advertising, films, or digital environments. Media are ubiquitous and they constitute rhetorical-communicative devices that highlight the exercise of emotions with persuasive intent. Although in psychiatry and psychology "emotion" and "affect" are conceptually distinct notions,[11] for the purposes of this chapter, I treat them as interchangeable terms. I follow the Merriam-Webster Dictionary's definition of affect as "the conscious subjective aspect of an emotion considered apart from bodily changes; also: a set of observable manifestations of a subjectively experienced emotion."[12] In simple terms, affect refers to the experience of feeling or emotion arising in specific situations.

Today's mass media communication seems to enact specific forms of emotional-based persuasion. Many messages appear to rely, not on logic, but on emotional appeals. In such cases, as in luxury-items advertising, persuasion is not based exclusively on argumentation but also rooted in an affective structure of persuasion. "Pure," logical argumentation will seldom be enough to win acceptance or "close the sale." Audiences need also to *desire* what the rhetor claims. In other words, they need to *identify* with the rhetor.[13] Affective rhetoric, then, is a different kind of rhetoric of identification. It is a type of rhetorical process that is precisely developed by the coincidence of the audience's aspirations and speaker's motivations. As Kenneth Burke remarks, "A is not identical with his colleague, B. But insofar as their interests are joined, A is identified with B. Or he may identify himself with B even when their interests are not joined, if he assumes that they are, or is persuaded to believe so."[14] Some contemporary messages persuade precisely by triggering the mechanisms of desire and identification. And they do so using emotional—not logical or ethical—rhetorical appeals. In order to illustrate this kind of rhetoric, I highlight three domains—Media Communication, Argumentation, and Politics—where emotional persuasion has potentially major implications. Ultimately, I hope to demonstrate what affective rhetoric is and why it matters.

Affective Rhetoric: Definition

Burke defines rhetoric as "the use of language as a symbolic means of inducing cooperation in beings that by nature respond to symbols."[15] With a slight change, I define affective rhetoric as the use of affective means of persuasion to induce cooperation in beings that, by nature, respond not just to symbols but to the emotions they trigger. The subtle difference is that affective rhetoric encompasses both symbolic and emotional means by which people construct reality and establish cooperation and identification. Discourses and practices shape the way we see the world. Symbols, of course, are crucial to that endeavor, but so are affects. As social beings, we communicate by feeling the symbols. Indeed, we share common feelings through which we establish our collective identity (e.g., emotions triggered by the national anthem).

In speaking of "affective rhetoric," I am not just referencing appeals to emotions as extensively studied by argumentation theory[16] but, instead, I am claiming that an affective energy circulates among signs, images, sounds and communities.[17] This circulation of signs, gestures, images, and speeches throughout society can be used not just to promote solidarity and unity but also to create commonality and cohesion. The repetition, insistence, and reutilization of symbols elicit emotional responses that grow more intense by their recurrence. In other words, since emotions have the power to shape our ways of life, they constitute a material rhetoric. This concept "urges historians and theorists of rhetoric to address the body as well as the mind—to consider in addition to modes of argument lines of affect and swells of passion, and in addition to enthymemes and topics, heat and impression."[18] In sum, emotions have affective power that can lead to collective politics, social alliances, or even help to foster national identities.[19]

Affects may be rhetorically deployed, and rhetoric is inseparable from the social construction of meaning. Affective rhetoric is, therefore, an implicit dimension of all rhetorical activity.[20] It is interesting that George Kennedy links rhetoric not just to a kind of energy but also to a mental or emotional energy: "Rhetoric, in the most general sense, may thus be identified with the energy inherent in an utterance (or an artistic representation): the mental or emotional energy that impels the speaker to expression, the energy level coded in the message, and the energy received by the recipient who then uses mental energy in decoding and perhaps acting on the message. Rhetorical labor takes place."[21] In other words, rhetoric is imbued with emotional energy.

Therefore, affective rhetoric could be described as the emotional side of rhetoric, and rhetoricians may study how affects (including passions, moods, feelings, or sentiments) are socially and culturally deployed to persuade. It concerns the ways in which affects intervene, shape, and influence persuasion. The study of affective rhetoric is about explaining how social mobilization of affects leads to rhetorical persuasion. With this understanding, researchers may analyze different situations, from interpersonal communication, media communication or advertisement, to emotional argumentation[22] and political speech. Note that "affective rhetoric" does not address specific emotions. Rather, it refers to the mobilization of affects as a function of the emotional framing of persuasive appeals. Rhetoric becomes affective when it is based not only in the verbal side of human communication but strategically integrates appeals to emotion, which may be communicated nonverbally, to achieve persuasion. Affective rhetoric can, therefore, refer to nonverbal forms of communication. In fact, emotions themselves may assume a communicative function.[23] In sum, the way we experience the world beyond a rigid, verbal symbolic framing is at the heart of the exploration of affects and emotional persuasion.

Now, let's take the example of one of the latest TAG Heuer advertisements in its *"Don't Crack Under Pressure"* campaign (Figure 4.1). This is a good example of working with persuasive images at an affective level. Starting with its slogan, the advertisement uses emotional processes of persuasion to trigger immediate associations with the thrill of Formula 1 motor racing. But it is not just that. The word *"Congratulations"* forges a link between the success of the racecar driver with the (expected success of) the consumer. Notice that this ad does not deal with complex arguments, nor does it rationally emphasize any advantages or merits of this luxury watch brand. Indeed, there are few words. This ad does not persuade through verbal deliberation or argumentative reasoning. Instead, it relies totally on the emotional structure of affective rhetoric to connect with the audience, making a bold association between the winning, competitive spirit, and the triumphant qualities of Max Verstappen with the potential buyer of the watches. Here, we may observe how it convinces others to buy products, not by rational, *logos*-based argumentation, but by activating deep emotional mechanisms (*pathos*) like the desire to be successful, strong, or distinct. This is a thoroughly emotional kind of persuasion.

Moreover, the ad "promises" not a physical, tangible, or material thing, but a particular emotional experience associated with owning a

Affective Rhetoric 73

Figure 4.1 Verstappen's Congratulations advertisement.
Credits: © TAG Heuer - used with permission.

material object: a TAG Heuer watch. The ad, in other words, is selling an emotional experience. The rhetorical message is not about the watch, but about you (the consumer) and how this special watch can make you feel stronger and better, instilling a sense that you will not *"Crack Under Pressure."* Thus, the appeal works through emotional identification. The ad alludes to the experience of not giving in. It is based on affects that are rhetorically intended to transfer the quality of never giving up, from the watch to the wearer. Consumers are persuaded and drawn to the brand, in great part, because TAG Heuer's rhetorical message makes them *feel something special* about the object it sells and *appeals to their desire* to assume those qualities.

Ultimately, this example reflects a general tendency of affective rhetoric in advertising: to encourage the perception of augmenting self-esteem by the purchase of a product. In this kind of persuasive intent, the product is represented as offering a way to meet personal, psychological, and social needs of approval, appreciation, or economic affirmation. In acquiring a watch, individuals are offered an opportunity to emotionally recreate themselves and their relationships to the world.

Affective rhetoric takes up where logic and evidence leave off. Logical argumentation and empirical evidence are of primary importance. Nonetheless, there are cases where logic, words, and critical reasoning are inconclusive. In those cases, affects can be especially useful and help compensate for the inadequacy of formal knowledge.[24] Love, anger, guilt, compassion, fear, and pride are culturally infused with value, pointing to what is worth doing or preserving. They guide our ways of thinking and acting upon the world. Persuasion based on emotions can, thus, influence our thinking and doing by determining how we feel. In the TAG Heuer watch ad, consumers are persuaded by an emotion of winning and being resilient. It is a case of inducing rhetorical identification by the use of emotionally laden symbols.

Affective Rhetoric—Why It Matters

Affects or emotions perform primal functions in social interaction. For example, *emotional states are adaptive mechanisms* allowing us to deal with both internal and external events on which our success or survival depend.[25] Additionally, *emotions are key players in guiding actions*. When you feel confident, you tend to engage with other persons more and be more convincing when explaining a subject. Also, affects can be crucial in motivating action[26] by automatically or unconsciously classifying *stimuli* as good or bad. They may, therefore, function as somatic markers: when a positive marker is associated with the outcome, we are drawn to it.[27] Without emotions, decisions lack meaning; therefore, choices are more difficult to make.

Finally, *emotions can function as signaling mechanisms*[28] *or communication systems*[29] where individuals assess the type of situation from the emotional expressions of other individuals. If a group of people are all laughing and smiling, the social situation is (probably) not a menacing one. So, the extent or type of affective response (e.g., fear evoked by "quit smoking" ads) helps a person focus on the new, important information, and select those aspects more pertinent for understanding the situation. Depending upon

Affective Rhetoric 75

how people feel about an object, they may focus on different aspects of information.[30]

Rhetoricians accept the fact individuals are diverse and undertake distinct goals. In order to pursue their objectives in harmony with others, people must take into account their differences and negotiate ways to accommodate them in order for individuals to get the results they want. Emotional states or affects are central tools to negotiate these differences. The rhetorical role of affects constitutes, therefore, an important resource to negotiate and deal with people's diverse goals. Since emotions can be universally shared, they form an effective basis for understanding.

We point to three domains where affects are of utmost importance to rhetoric: *Media Communication, Argumentation and Politics*.[31] First, discourses containing affective content are pervasive in social life[32] including media communication. As cultural ways of feeling, emotions entail ideas about what is appropriate to feel as well as when, where, and how to feel something.[33] Because mass media communication is central in the dissemination of messages, one should not disregard how media-communicated emotions inspire certain ways of thinking, acting, and feeling. Affective rhetoric is, then, important to describe the cultural productions of meaning in society and the use, in mass media communication such as advertising, of specific affective ways to persuade.

Second, since a large part of rhetoric is argumentative, affective rhetoric is important because it may lead us to conclude that not only are appeals to emotion ubiquitous but they also have a legitimate and central place in argumentation.[34] Even if they can be used fallaciously, affects and emotions do not entail weak argumentation, nor do they necessarily subvert critical discussion. Most practical argumentation is based on presumptive reasoning: claims based on them are not decisive or absolute. Yet, emotions can steer the resolution of conflicting opinions.[35] We must study the use of emotions since persuasion is ubiquitous and conclusions are frequently drawn based on the discursive construction of emotional positions.[36] As a matter of fact, we may mobilize affects for argumentative purposes. In this case, argumentative conclusions would be derived from affective positioning and negotiation.[37] To conclude, affective rhetoric is important at the argumentative level for two main reasons: besides being a recurrent theme in everyday rhetoric and argumentation (ex: *ad hominem, ad misercordiam, ad baculum* arguments), affective rhetoric points to the fact that argumentation is often emotionally shaped.

Third, we should pay careful attention to affective rhetoric because it plays a central part on political communication. Given that we inhabit an affective world, the ways we use words and images to describe governments and policies have a great influence on how we think and act politically. From a political standpoint, affective rhetoric is crucial for determining how information is processed, how mood is used by politicians

76 *Samuel Mateus*

to generate identification, or how political figures will be remembered in the future.[38] Hence, researches have concluded that both successful and unsuccessful presidential candidates use emotional language and charismatic communication in order to influence voters.[39] Affective displays are inescapable in today's politics, and they have been shown to influence voters more than the candidate's party affiliations or ideology.[40] Moreover, leaders perceived as faking or adulterating emotions are seen as less genuine and trustworthy.[41] Many successful politicians never hesitate to show appreciation and love for the spouses, for instance, and their public affective displays may be a contributing factor to their popularity. To consider affective rhetoric in politics is, then, to examine the conditions through which we perceive politicians and how we are influenced (and persuaded) by their various emotional displays.

Mass media communication, argumentation, and politics are, thus, three of the many fields where affects play a crucial role. Rhetoricians would, thus, be tasked with scrutinizing the use of emotions and elucidating how affects are indeed decisive factors in the persuasive appeal of many contemporary media, as well as non-media messages.

Conclusion

Rhetoric may be considered an inventive attitude toward language and the world.[42] Emotions are just another way in which humans construct meaning. Affective rhetoric is an inventive attitude based on the way the rhetor makes the audience *feel a message*. There may not be a single, absolute, or imperative argumentative, or rational expression of a thesis. Messages may be communicated not by reason and logic alone but also by the creative and social expression of organized feelings. One can simply ask: would rhetoric without any emotional resonance still be rhetoric?[43]

This chapter briefly schematized what can be understood by affective rhetoric and three domains where affects are at the core of persuasion. I hope to have demonstrated that a rhetorical understanding of affects is indispensable to negotiating the politics of everyday life. Affects transform our conception of what it means to be intelligent, just, or desirable; they have a major effect on what it takes to be a good citizen, friend, or romantic partner. Consequently, affective rhetoric is key to questioning how we are persuaded, not merely by facts but also by the way facts are felt. It is also crucial to recognize how affective messages are built, particularly when the mass media are central agents in setting cultural trends. These trends may well have an emotional dimension and may shape the ways we precisely feel (or should feel) in a given situation. Indeed, gaining a thorough understanding how affect-based persuasion works is a central challenge of current rhetorical scholarship.

Notes

1 Aristotle, *The Art of Rhetoric* (London: Harper Press, 2012), 1356 a.
2 Marcus Tullius Cicero, *De Oratore* (London: Forgotten Books, 2012), 22.
3 Marcus Fabius Quintilian, *The Institutio Oratoria*, trans. H. E. Butler (Cambridge, MA: Harvard, 1953).
4 Claire Polo, Christian Plantin, Kristine Lund and Gerald Niccolai, "Quand construire une position émotionnelle, c'est choisir une conclusion argumentative: le cas d'un café-débat sur l'eau potable au Mexique," *Semen – Revue de sémio-linguistique des textes et discours* 1, no. 35 (2013): 8.
5 Stephen Toulmin, *The Uses of Argument* (Cambridge: Cambridge University Press, 1958).
6 *The Uses of Argument* contains no index entry for the words "emotion" or "*pathos.*"
7 Christopher Schroeder, "Knowledge and Power, Logic and Rhetoric, and Other Reflections in the Toulminian Mirror: A Critical Consideration of Stephen Toulmin's Contributions to Composition," *JAC* 17, no. 1 (1997): 102.
8 Chaïm Perelman and Lucie Olbrechts-Tyteca, *Traité de l'argumentation: la nouvelle rhétorique* (Paris: Presses Universitaires de France, 1958).
9 Chaïm Perelman, *The Realm of Rhetoric* (Notre Dame, IN: University of Notre Dame Press, 1982): viii.
10 Charles Forceville, *Pictorial Metaphor in Advertising* (London and New York: Routledge, 1996).
11 Batson, C. D., Shaw, L. L., & Oleson, K. C, "Differentiating Affect, Mood, and Emotion: Toward Functionally based Conceptual Distinctions," in *Review of Personality and Social Psychology*, edited by M. S. Clark, vol. 13 (1992), 294–326.
12 "Affect." *Merriam-Webster.com*. Merriam-Webster, n.d. Web. 10 Feb. 2018.
13 Kenneth Burke, *A Rhetoric of Motives* (Berkeley and Los Angeles: University of California Press, 1969).
14 Ibid., 20.
15 Ibid., 46.
16 Sahbi Benlamine, Maher Chaouachi, Villata Serena, *et al.* "Emotions in Argumentation: An Empirical Evaluation," *International Joint Conference on Artificial Intelligence, IJCAI* (2015): 156–163.
17 James Zappen, "Affective Rhetoric in China's Internet Culture," *Present Tense* 6, no. 1 (2016): 1.
18 Debra Hawhee and Cory Holding. "Case Studies in Material Rhetoric: Joseph Priestley and Gilbert Austin," *Rhetorica: A Journal of the History of Rhetoric* 28, no. 3 (2010): 265.
19 Sara Ahmed, *Cultural Politics of Emotion* (London: Routledge, 2004), 62.
20 James Zappen, "Affective Rhetoric in China's Internet Culture," *Present Tense* 6, no. 1 (2016): 6.
21 George A. Kennedy, *Comparative Rhetoric: An Historical and Cross-Cultural Introduction* (New York: Oxford University Press, 1998).
22 Michael A. Gilbert, "What Is an Emotional Argument? Or Why Do Argument Theorists Quarrel with Their Mates?" *ISSA Conference*. June (1994).
23 Anne Bartsch and Susanne Hübner, "Towards a Theory of Emotional Communication," *CLCWeb: Comparative Literature and Culture* 7, no. 4 (2005): 1–8.
24 James Averill, "The Rhetoric of Emotions, with a Note on What Makes Great Literature Great," *Empirical Studies of the Arts* 19, no. 1 (2001):14.
25 Dolores Cañamero and Walter Van de Velde, "Socially Emotional: Using Emotions to Ground Social Interaction," *Proceedings from AAAI Fall Symposium* (1997): 12.

78 Samuel Mateus

26 Peters, E., Lipkus, I. and Diefenbach, M. A. "The Functions of Affect in Health Communications and in the Construction of Health Preferences," *Journal of Communication* 56 (2006): 142.
27 Damásio, António. *Descartes; Error: Emotion, Reason, and the Human Brain* (New York: Putnam, 1994).
28 Cañamero and Van de Velde, "Socially Emotional," 12.
29 Anne Bartsch and Susanne Hübner,"Towards a Theory of Emotional Communication," *CLCWeb: Comparative Literature and Culture* 7, no. 4 (2005): 2.
30 Peters, E., Lipkus, I. and Diefenbach, M. A. "The Functions of Affect in Health Communications and in the Construction of Health Preferences," *Journal of Communication* 56 (2006): 147.
31 The division in three areas does not mean there are no other relevant domains on the role of emotions in rhetoric. This distribution mainly reflects the great interest that studying the consequences of emotions in society, argumentation and politics has arisen in recent years in a number of different works.
32 Frank Furedi, *The Culture of Fear; Risk Taking and the Morality of Low Expectations* (London: Cassel, 1997).
33 Donileen R Loseke, "Examining Emotion as Discourse: Emotion Codes and Presidential Speeches Justifying War," *Sociological Quarterly* 50 (2009): 498.
34 Douglas Walton, *The Place of Emotion in Argument* (Pennsylvania: Pennsylvania State University Press, 1992), 1.
35 Ibid.
36 Christian Plantin, *Les Bonnes Raisons des Émotions – Principes et méthode pour l'étude du discours émotionné* (Berne: Peter Lang, 2011).
37 Polo, *Semen – Revue de sémio-linguistique des textes et discours*, 9.
38 Stephen Utych, "Negative Affective Language in Politics," *American Politics Research* 46, no. 1 (2017): 77–102.
39 Willis, S., Sweida, G. L., Glassburn, S., Sherman, C. L., and Bligh, M. C. "Charismatic and Affective Rhetoric in a Presidential Campaign." In *Communication and Language Analysis in the Public Sphere*, edited by R. P. Hart, 120–137 (London: IGI Global, 2013).
40 Erik Bucy, "Emotional and Evaluative Consequences of Inappropriate Leader Displays," *Communication Research* 27, no. 2 (2000): 194–226.
41 Lars Glaso and Stale Einarsen, "Emotion Regulation in Leader – Follower Relationships," *European Journal of Work and Organizational Psychology* 17, no. 4 (2008): 482–500.
42 Daniel Gross, *The Secret History of Emotion – from Aristotle's Rhetoric to Modern Brain Science* (Chicago, IL and London: The University of Chicago Press, 2006), 15.
43 Plantin, *Les Bonnes Raisons des Émotions*, 47.

Bibliography

Ahmed, Sara. *Cultural Politics of Emotion*. London: Routledge, 2004.
Aristotle. *The Art of Rhetoric*. London: Harper Press, 2012.
Averill, James. "The Rhetoric of Emotions, with a Note on What Makes Great Literature Great." *Empirical Studies of the Arts* 19, no. 1 (2001): 5–26.
Bartsch, Anne, and Susanne Hübner. "Towards a Theory of Emotional Communication." *CLCWeb: Comparative Literature and Culture* 7, no. 4 (2005): 1–8.
Batson, C. D., Shaw, L. L., and Oleson, K. C. "Differentiating Affect, Mood, and Emotion: Toward Functionally based Conceptual Distinctions." In *Review of Personality and Social Psychology*, edited by M. S. Clark, Thousand Oaks, CA: Sage Publications, Inc. vol. 13, 294–326, 1992.

Benlamine, Sahbi, Maher Chaouachi, and Serena Villata, et al. "Emotions in Argumentation: An Empirical Evaluation." *Proceedings of the Twenty-Fourth International, International Joint Conference on Artificial Intelligence, IJCAI* Buenos Aires, Argentina. (2015): 156–163.

Bucy, Erik. "Emotional and Evaluative Consequences of Inappropriate Leader Displays." *Communication Research* 27, no. 2 (2000): 194–226. doi:10.1177/00 9365000027002004

Burke, Kenneth. *A Rhetoric of Motives.* Berkeley and Los Angeles: University of California Press, 1969.

Cañamero, Dolores, and Walter Van de Velde. "Socially Emotional: Using Emotions to Ground Social Interaction." *Proceedings from AAAI Fall Symposium* (1997): 10–15.

Cicero, Marcus Tullius. *De Oratore.* London: Forgotten Books, 2012.

Damásio, António. *Descartes' Error: Emotion, Reason, and the Human Brain.* New York: Putnam, 1994.

Forceville, Charles. *Pictorial Metaphor in Advertising.* London and New York: Routledge, 1996.

Furedi, Frank. *The Culture of Fear; Risk Taking and the Morality of Low Expectations.* London: Cassel, 1997.

Gilbert, Michael. A. "What Is an Emotional Argument? Or Why Do Argument Theorists Quarrel with Their Mates?" *ISSA Conference.* June, 1994.

Glaso, Lars, and Stale Einarsen. "Emotion Regulation in Leader – Follower Relationships." *European Journal of Work and Organizational Psychology* 17, no. 4 (2008): 482–500. doi:10.1080/13594320801994960

Gross, Daniel. *The Secret History of Emotion – from Aristotle's Rhetoric to Modern Brain Science.* Chicago, IL and London: The University of Chicago Press, 2006.

Hamblin, Charles. *Fallacies.* Methuen, 1970.

Hawhee, Debra, and Cory Holding. "Case Studies in Material Rhetoric: Joseph Priestley and Gilbert Austin." *Rhetorica: A Journal of the History of Rhetoric* 28, no. 3 (2010), 261–289. doi:10.1525/rh.2010.28.3.261

Kennedy, George. A. *Comparative Rhetoric: An Historical and Cross-Cultural Introduction.* New York: Oxford University Press, 1998.

Loseke, Donileen R. "Examining Emotion as Discourse: Emotion Codes and Presidential Speeches Justifying War." *Sociological Quarterly* 50 (2009): 497–524. doi:10.1111/j.1533-8525.2009.01150.x

Perelman, Chaïm. *The Realm of Rhetoric.* Notre Dame, IN: University of Notre Dame Press, 1982.

Perelman, Chaïm and Lucie Olbrechts-Tyteca. *Traité de l'argumentation: la nouvelle rhétorique.* Paris: Presses Universitaires de France, 1958.

Peters, E., Lipkus, I., and Diefenbach, M. A. "The Functions of Affect in Health Communications and in the Construction of Health Preferences." *Journal of Communication* 56 (2006): 140–162. doi:10.1111/j.1460-2466.2006.00287.x

Plantin, Christian. *Les Bonnes Raisons des Émotions – Principes et méthode pour l'étude du discours émotionné.* Berne: Peter Lang, 2011.

Polo, Claire, Christian Plantin, Kristine Lund, and Gerald Niccolai. "Quand construire une position émotionnelle, c'est choisir une conclusion argumentative: le cas d'un café-débat sur l'eau potable au Mexique". *Semen - Revue de sémio-linguistique des textes et discours* 1, no. 35 (2013): 41–64.

Quintilian, Marcus Fabius. *The Institutio Oratoria.* Cambridge, MA: Harvard, 1953.

Schroeder, Christopher. "Knowledge and Power, Logic and Rhetoric, and Other Reflections in the Toulminian Mirror: A Critical Consideration of Stephen Toulmin's Contributions to Composition." *JAC* 17, no. 1 (1997): 95–107.

Toulmin, Stephen. *The Uses of Argument*. Cambridge: Cambridge University Press, 1958.

Utych, Stephen. "Negative Affective Language in Politics." *American Politics Research* 46, no. 1 (2017): 77–102.

Walton, Douglas. *The Place of Emotion in Argument*. Pennsylvania: Pennsylvania State University Press, 1992.

Willis, S., Sweida, G. L., Glassburn, S., Sherman, C. L., and Bligh, M. C. "Charismatic and Affective Rhetoric in a Presidential Campaign." In *Communication and Language Analysis in the Public Sphere*, edited by R. P. Hart, 120–137. London: IGI Global, 2013.

Zappen, James. "Affective Rhetoric in China's Internet Culture." *Present Tense* 6, no. 1, (2016): 1–8.

5 White Nationalism and the Rhetoric of Nostalgia

Michael Mayne

On June 17, 2015, Dylan Roof killed nine African Americans after participating in a Wednesday night Bible study at one of America's oldest churches in Charleston, South Carolina. In his last blog post, Roof identifies as a white nationalist and explains the role organizations like the Council of Conservative Citizens (CofCC), which evolved from the White Citizens Councils of the Civil Rights era, played in his indoctrination.[1] After the massacre, Roof's fondness for Confederate iconography initiated momentum in dismantling Confederate memorials, which then invigorated resistance by white nationalist groups like the CofCC. This resistance became national news two years later when a white supremacist killed an anti-racist activist and injured 19 others during the Unite the Right protest in Charlottesville, North Carolina. Unite the Right was a white nationalist spectacle organized around the preservation of a General Robert E. Lee statue in the city's Emancipation Park. The two-day event was five times larger than any other rally hosted by white supremacists in the past ten years, and it was promoted through an extensive network of white nationalist websites and social media platforms.[2]

The prominence of white nationalism has risen in American society, necessitating our investigation and comprehension of its rhetorical tactics.[3] White nationalists are white supremacists who understand "race" as a knowable fact and understand "nation" as the social structure of a racial group. They seek the restoration of white supremacy in their communities because they believe alien and inferior races are replacing their culture. Actions such as the defense of white supremacist memorials are not just about historical commemoration according to the CofCC; they are "about defending the images of White history, White heroes, and White America" and affirming the "spirits of our ancestors within us."[4] While this sentiment has proliferated in disparate communities and resonated across relatively diverse demographics, it consistently articulates an affective rhetoric of loss and longing. White nationalism posits the object of loss and longing as a prelapsarian homeland, the poetics of an authentic white collective that manifests in affective experiences like Confederate nostalgia and rhetorics like Unite the Right's motto: "You Will Not Replace Us." Their mantra was popularized through Unite the Right's Twitter

82   *Michael Mayne*

account[5] and repeated at the rally,[6] but it originally became viral after Identity Evropa chanted it in protest during a live-streamed anti-Trump art performance in early 2017.[7] This white nationalist group later clarified what was being replaced with a banner in support for another Confederate memorial in Florida: "You Will Not Replace Us: Our Past, Our Culture, Our People."[8] Donald Trump, who frequently promotes white nationalists,[9] echoed this rhetoric on Twitter less than a week after the fatal rally: "Sad to see the history and culture of our great country being ripped apart with the removal of our beautiful statues and monuments. ... [They] will be greatly missed and never able to be comparably replaced!"[10]

The logic of white nationalism, I argue, can best be understood with a focus on its affective character and a comparison between this character and the affective mode of nostalgia. I emphasize the social significance of affect and suggest nostalgia often persuades individuals to invest in reactionary versions of society like patriarchy and white supremacy by romanticizing the past. Affect, Caroline Williams argues, "is an inherently political concept" that represents "a dynamic process of production and circulation of forces and powers that create and mobilize political subjectivity."[11] In other words, affect can coordinate emotions collectively and help shape the ways individuals participate in society. Because of this function, the concept of affect helps us comprehend how political subjectivity is created and mobilized in social discourse. According to Brian Massumi, affect itself is neither reactionary nor progressive; it is "the ongoing force of the social taking evolving form."[12] While this force mobilizes the social agency of individuals, affect can also limit the capacity of our agency when it, as Susan Ruddick warns, is "constituted passively."[13] Nostalgia's uniquely uncritical narratives trigger a passive emotional investment that encourages individuals to understand a fantastic past as an ideal future. In my example of this mode, white nationalism's nostalgic yarns situate white supremacy as a prefigurative utopia that corrals and pacifies the agency of individuals by severely disciplining their vision of possible versions of social organization.

The history of the word "nostalgia" begins in 1688 as a neologism in a medical student's dissertation. Johannes Hofer combined the Greek terms for a return home (*nostos*) and the pain (*algia*) of longing to diagnose a mysterious ailment found among people living abroad.[14] According to Hofer, the victim "wanders around sadly, scorns foreign manners, seized by a distaste of strange conversations ... makes a show of delight of the fatherland [and experiences] weakness, anxiety, palpitation of the heart, frequent sighs, stupidity of the mind."[15] While the experience of longing itself is unmediated desire, Janice Doane and Devon Hodges assert that nostalgia "is not just a sentiment but also a rhetorical practice."[16] And this practice of nostalgia, Michael Dwyer emphasizes, is a "fundamentally *productive* affective engagement."[17] Many recent theories of nostalgia attempt to rehabilitate the term by suggesting a progressive potential. Svetlana

White Nationalism and the Rhetoric of Nostalgia   83

Boym's representative example of these perspectives classifies good and bad versions: "restorative" nostalgia essentializes the past and manifests itself in reactionary nationalisms, while "reflective" nostalgia emphasizes a critical reading of history and a longing for "new flexibility, not the reestablishment of stasis."[18] While the concept of nostalgia may indeed have progressive potential as a critical heuristic device, the rhetoric of nostalgia—idealized myths of the past that haunt the present—is always reactionary because its uncritical longing for and celebration of home always argues for a previous version of society.

Nostalgia does not just select and esteem moments of promise embedded in the past. Nostalgia's longing and celebration posit a singular and essentialist conception of the past, which prevents an understanding of history itself. Instead of comprehending history as a process that reveals our ability to transform the present, people slip into the "clutches of the transcendent traps of nostalgia," as Erin Manning observes, where "memory is trapped in an air-tight cell of linear narrative."[19] Most importantly, in rhetorics of nostalgia, according to Lynne Huffer, "an immutable lost past functions as a blueprint for the future, cutting off any possibility for uncertainty, difference, or fundamental change."[20] When individuals invest in conjured fantasies scripted by old social forms, this investment guides people away from challenges to traditional social dogmas like white supremacy by directly or indirectly affirming them. "[I]n all its manifestations," Susan Bennett insists, "nostalgia is, in its praxis, conservative."[21] Praxis, or the combination of theory and practice, instigates social transformations. Nostalgias are intrinsically reactionary, not because they always define a conservative social order, though they usually do, but because they always insist that an ideal order once existed, and our longing for this halcyon moment's return limits the possibilities of progressive social transformations. White nationalism is a prototypical version of this dynamic.

White nationalists variously identify as identitarians, racialists, race realists, white advocates, white separatists, citizenists, and civic nationalists. Two things distinguish them from other white supremacists like neo-Nazis, skinheads, and racist militia, criminal, and prison groups: white nationalists usually disavow the label "white supremacist" and they have a relatively specific agenda. Geert Wilders, a Dutch white nationalist, succinctly describes their perspective:

> Ordinary people are well aware that they are witnessing a population replacement phenomenon. Ordinary people feel attached to the civilization which their ancestors created. They do not want it to be replaced by a multicultural society where the values of the immigrants are considered as good as their own. It is not xenophobia or islamophobia to consider our Western culture as superior to other cultures – it is plain common sense.[22]

84   *Michael Mayne*

White nationalists esteem their version of white European cultural history and consider the immigration of nonwhites, the decline of white birth rates, and changing cultural norms as obvious and ominous threats. Steve King, an American white nationalist and Iowa Congressman who used to display a Confederate flag on his desk, concurs with Wilders: "It's simple logic ... we're not replacing ourselves.... [T]he majority of the people who established the foundation of Western civilization were white" and "the United States is moving towards becoming a white minority."[23] Motivated by these dreams of a state premised on ethnic essentialism, the white nationalist agenda includes a moratorium on immigration from nonwhite and/or Muslim countries, the expulsion of undocumented nonwhite immigrants, the repeal of the 1960s immigration reforms that removed national origins quotas, the repeal of Civil Rights laws, the end of affirmative action programs, the end of "political correctness," and the "abolition of all multiculturalist curricula, 'sensitivity training,' and similar experiments in brainwashing."[24]

White nationalists employ a heavy dose of common sense—the logic of contrived consensus—to establish the validity of their imaginary community.[25] Common sense affirms immediate impressions through the omission of history. For example, think of the rhetorical question "How many women have written great symphonies?" used to validate a natural difference of creative competence between genders by erasing the historical context of patriarchy in these cultural productions. Rhetorically, this move involves elements of *doxa* (self-evident truths) processed through the inductive reasoning of *topoi* formulas. *Topoi* are generic and popular prompts that utilize common sense as the argument's premise.[26] For example, an argument that advocates free food for children might employ the *topos*, "children are innocent." *Topoi* often form the lynchpin of affective rhetorical strategies because they posit an unmediated truth that triggers an uncritical appreciation of the argument's logic. No one wants a truth violated, everyone wants a truth maintained, and *topoi* help affirm subjective positions as truths. Therefore, as Ruth Wodak and Salomi Boukala point out, *topoi* "are widely adopted in prejudiced and discriminatory discourses," discourses that would collapse with the comprehension of history.[27]

The rhetoric of white nationalism and the rhetoric of nostalgia share three specific elements of *doxa*: authenticity, home, and restoration. Charted through the common sense of *topoi* formulas, this rhetoric suggests that authenticity is an essential character, home is sacred, and restoration is desirable. Rather than function as discrete themes, these rhetorical motifs overlap and work together. In the nostalgic rhetoric of white nationalism, whiteness is the authenticity of home in need of restoration. The affective content of these elements manifests itself in the terror of whiteness eclipsed, mourning the loss of home, and longing for its return.

Nostalgias are premised on the proposition that an ideal social order once existed and that our contemporary social order has regressed. In this rhetorical mode, according to Doane and Hodges, "the referent plays a crucial role: it acts as an authentic origin or center from which to disparage the degenerate present."[28] In white nationalist discourse, the referent of a white homeland acts as an authentic origin from which the present has degenerated into a cosmopolitan amalgamation. The concept of authenticity argues that identities are expressive of intrinsic qualities rather than discursive performances. Authenticity functions as a truth, a measure of singular, natural, and immutable essence, opposed to the fallacies of the transient, the circumstantial, the relational. White nationalists emphasize the authenticity of race, recognized through their impressions of history and contemporary life. "I'm not a racist," insists David Duke, perhaps America's most famous racist.[29] "I'm a race realist, and that simply means to recognize and understand the fact that there are racial differences and that these differences have an impact on society, education, crime, and many other aspects of life."[30] What this concept means in terms of whiteness rarely varies, and the white nationalist collective, Nationalist Front, provides a standard definition: "White is defined as those who are overwhelmingly the descendants of indigenous Europeans. Jews and other groups who have light skin but are not Europeans are separate ethnicities and thus should have their own homes."[31] Once they establish the salience of race's authentic essence, white nationalists can build a rhetorical strategy that emphasizes an emotional investment in its maintenance because anything that violates or diminishes whiteness becomes a threat to commonsense, scientific truth, and natural order.

Home—a metaphorical referent that provides the cornerstone for many traditions' cultural tropes—functions as the centerpiece of authenticity for white nationalism.[32] Nostalgic and white nationalist rhetoric exploit the emotional attachment many people have to the concept of home, popularly figured as a composite of love, safety, and security. According to Richard Spencer, founder of AltRight.com and president of the white nationalist National Policy Institute (sponsored by William Regnery, Jr.), "a homeland for all white people," America's "essential, historic people," is the movement's "grand goal."[33] The future posits an existential crisis for white nationalists, who see their homeland being "demographically conquered" by nonwhites and transformed into a foreign country.[34] Peter Brimlow, founder and editor of VDare.com, a white nationalist website named after the first known white child born in the Americas, was a senior editor at *Forbes* when he wrote one of the movement's seminal statements for the *National Review*. The "ideal of an American nation-state is in eclipse," he warns, because the country "has lost control of its borders."[35] He describes an Immigration and Naturalization Service waiting room as the "tenth Circle of Hell," which he compares to a New York subway, where "you find yourself in an underworld that is almost entirely colored."[36] In this scary portrait of home defiled, white

86 *Michael Mayne*

nationalists encourage an affective investment in their agenda to restore white supremacy. The *topos* of home's sacredness here becomes a truth to cherish and defend.

In late 2017, American white nationalists reposted a manifesto signed by ten European conservative public intellectuals who share their concern of a homeland under siege.[37] "A Europe We Can Believe In" nicely distills the logic of white nationalism's nostalgic *topoi* formulas of authenticity, home, and restoration in an affective mode: "Europe belongs to us, and we belong to Europe. These lands are our *home*; we have no other.... Ordinary landscapes and events are charged with special meaning—for us, but not for others.... This is the real Europe, our precious and irreplaceable civilization."[38] Europe is being lost to waves of immigration, the authors warn, and they echo white nationalists' most famous motto—"We must secure the existence of our people and a future for white children"[39]— with a program to "renew," "recover," and "restore" a "true" Europe "to hand on to our children."[40] Faced with anxiety about a present filled with strangers inside the gate, the past becomes the object of desire for a stable referent of purity and security, a desire Adolf Hitler defines as nostalgic: "a longing to return to the never-forgotten ancestral home."[41]

Called "white genocide" by white nationalists, this narrative of white civilization in crisis has entered mainstream political discourse with important rightwing politicians in Europe and the United States using the affective rhetoric of nationalism as a salve for frightful demographic predictions.[42] The process remains consistent: shade the present with existential dread and resentment and then herald a new morning of greatness, again. Donald Trump, for example, puts it this way: "The fundamental question of our time is whether the West has the will to survive."[43] The solution is the reclamation of the past as the blueprint for the future: "We are the fastest and the greatest community.... We write symphonies. We pursue innovation. We celebrate our ancient heroes [and] embrace our timeless traditions and customs."[44] Trump ticks off the primary tenets of white nationalism: white culture's uniqueness, superiority, innate sense of communal solidarity, and its threatened survival. The affective rhetorical touchstones of white nationalism's nostalgic mode are also here: fear of the present, recalling a beautiful moment of achievement, the desire for restoration, and a blueprint for the future featuring the coordinated traditions of an authentic national collective.

White nationalism and nostalgia are not reactionary because they affectively support singular forms of solidarity or fantasies about the past. They are reactionary because they reify social orthodoxies. The United States' social order has always been premised on de facto and de jure white supremacy,[45] but this does not mean it always will be. If, as Eric Hobsbawm advocates, we recognize that "human society is a successful structure because it is capable of change," we then also recognize that a genuine utopian version of the future recognizes that what follows the present remains undetermined.[46] However, nostalgia confuses the past with the possible. With its sepulchral dreams of a lost Eden that fetishize a former social order, nostalgia defers a critical analysis of history, which prevents a critical analysis of the present, and these critical faculties are the only tools we have to build a new future.

Notes

1 Dylan Roof, "rtf88," June 17, 2015, https://assets.documentcloud.org/documents/2108059/lastrhodesian-manifesto.pdf.
2 Anti-Defamation League, "Have Hate, Will Travel: The Demographics of Unite the Right," October 8, 2017, www.adl.org/blog/have-hate-will-travel-the-demographics-of-unite-the-right. See Jessie Daniels' *White Supremacy Online and the New Attack on Civil Rights* for a thorough review of the history, form, and content of white nationalism's internet presence (Lanham: Rowman & Littlefield, 2009).
3 Leonard Zesking lucidly charts this history of this prominence in *Blood and Politics: The History of the White Nationalist Movement from the Margins to the Mainstream* (New York: Farrar, Straus and Giroux, 2009). In their 2017 study of police data from 40 American cities, the California State University at San Bernardino Center for the Study of Hate and Extremism notes a "dramatic rise of white nationalism and reactive bigotry" ("Final U.S. Status Report: Hate Crime Analysis & Forecast for 2016–2017 [September 2017]: 21). Quincy Troup noted this spike in the backlash to President Barak Obama's election. "I believe," he said in the fall of 2011, "we have entered the state of full-blown white nationalism" ("My Take," *Black Renaissance Noire*, 11, no. 1 [Spring 2011]: 4–5.) A survey conducted by the University of Virginia Center for Politics after the Unite the Right rally affirms explicit or complicit support of significant white nationalist tenets among American whites: only 19% *agreed* that "Confederate monuments should be removed from all public spaces" and only 31% *disagreed* with the statement "America must protect and preserve its White European heritage."(Reuters/Ipsos/University of Virginia Center for Politics, "Condensed_FINAL_Tables_Aug21_to_Sep5_UVA_Race_prot," September 11, 2017).
4 Vanguard America, "On Charlottesville Rally: Why We Fight," July 10, 2017, CofCC, http://conservative-headlines.org/on-charlottesville-rally-why-we-fight/. This was posted on the CofCC website by Vanguard America, a white nationalist group that the Charlottesville killer posed with during the Unite the Right event.
5 Jason Kessler, Unite the Right @UniteTheRightVA, http://twitter.com/unitetherightva?lang=en, accessed November 21, 2017.
6 Naternot, "You Will Not Replace Us," Youtube video, 1:00, August 16, 2017, www.youtube.com/watch?v=ZSeDvZaz4nU.
7 Anti-Defamation League, "White Supremacists Adopt New Slogan: 'You Will Not Replace Us," June 9, 2017, www.adl.org/blog/white-supremacists-adopt-new-slogan-you-will-not-replace-us.
8 Identity Evropa, Twitter post, May 27, 2017, 5:08 p.m., https://twitter.com/IdentityEvropa.
9 Trump has retweeted white nationalists at least 12 times in the past two years, including six tweets from Jason Bergkamp (Oct. 7, Oct. 13, Nov. 3, Nov. 6, Nov. 7, 2015, and Apr. 19, 2016), two from @whitegenocideTM (Jan. 22 and Feb. 20, 2016); one from @EustaceFash (Feb. 23, 2016); and three from Jayda Fransen (Nov. 29, 2017) (Donald Trump, Twitter posts,

88 *Michael Mayne*

https://twitter.com/realDonaldTrump). According to one study, about 30% of Trump's retweets are from accounts that follow white nationalists (Nicholas Confessore, "For Whites Sensing Decline, Donald Trump Unleashes Words of Resistance," *New York Times*, July 13, 2016, www.nytimes.com/2016/07/14/us/politics/donald-trump-white-identity.html).

10 Donald Trump, Twitter posts, August 17, 2017, 8:07 a.m. and 8:21 a.m., https://twitter.com/realDonaldTrump.

11 Caroline Williams, "Affective Processes without a Subject: Rethinking the Relation between Subjectivity and Affect with Spinoza," *Subjectivity* 3, no. 3 (2010): 246–247.

12 Ibid.

13 Susan Ruddick, "The Politics of Affect Spinoza in the Work of Negri and Deleuze," *Theory, Culture, & Society*, 27, no. 4 (2010): 29.

14 Svetlana Boym, *The Future of Nostalgia* (New York: Basic Books, 2001), 3.

15 Quoted in Alexander V. Zinchenko, "Nostalgia: Dialogue Between Memory and Knowing," *Russian Social Science Review*, 53, no. 1 (January–February 2012): 70.

16 Janice Doane and Devon Hodges, *Nostalgia and Sexual Difference: The Resistance to Contemporary Feminism* (New York: Methuen, 1987): 3.

17 Michael D. Dwyer, *Back to the Fifties: Nostalgia, Hollywood Film, and Popular Music of the Seventies and Eighties* (Oxford: Oxford University Press, 2015): 22.

18 Boym, 49–50.

19 Erin Manning, *Always More Than One: Individuation's Dance* (Durham, NC: Duke University Press, 2013), 57.

20 Lynne Huffer. *Maternal Pasts, Feminist Futures: Nostalgia, Ethics, and the Question of Difference* (Stanford, CA: Stanford University Press, 1998), 19.

21 Susan Bennett, Quoted in Alastair Bonnett, *Left in the Past: Radicalism and the Politics of Nostalgia*, (New York: Continuum, 2010): 2.

22 Geert Wilders, "The Failure of Multiculturalism and How to Turn the Tide," March 25, 2011, www.geertwilders.nl/index.php/in-english-mainmenu-98/in-the-press-mainmenu-101/77-in-the-press/1740-speech-geert-wilders-in-rome-25th-of-march-2011Bottom of Form.

23 Steve King, Interview with Jan Mickelson, March 13, 2017, *WHO Newsradio 1040*, http://media.ccomrcdn.com/media/station_content/1165/2017/03/mp3/default/part_1_-_jan_mickelson_with_re_0_1489429024.mp3.

24 Samuel T. Francis, "The Return of the Repressed," National Policy Institute, September 10, 2006, www.npiamerica.org/research/category/the-return-of-the-repressed.

25 In his landmark argument, Benedict Anderson suggests that nations are socially constructed "imagined communities" rather than representations of intrinsic ethnic or cultural characteristics. See *Imagined Communities: Reflections of the Origin and Spread of Nationalism*, Revised edition, London: Verso, 2006.

26 See Ruth Wodak and Salomi Boukala, "European Identities and the Revival of Nationalism in the European Union: A Discourse Historical Approach," *Journal of Language and Politics*, 14, no. 1, (2015): 94.

27 Ibid.

28 Doane and Hodges, 8.

29 David Duke, Interview with Russ Nieli in Carol M. Swain and Russ Nieli, *Contemporary Voices of White Nationalism in America* (New York: Cambridge University Press, 2003): 180.

30 Ibid.

31 Nationalist Front, "Fourteen Points," 2017, www.nfunity.org/14-points/.

White Nationalism and the Rhetoric of Nostalgia 89

32 See Paul Chilton and Mikhail Ilyin, "Metaphor in Political Discourse: The Case of the "Common European House," *Discourse & Society*, 4, no. 1 (1993): 8.

33 Al Letson and Richard Spencer, "A Frank Conversation with a White Nationalist," November 10, 2016, *NPR*, www.revealnews.org/episodes/a-frank-conversation-with-a-white-nationalist/.

34 Lawrence Murray, "Mapping the Rising Tide," August 9, 2016, https://atlantic centurion.wordpress.com/2016/08/09/mapping-the-rising-tide/.

35 Peter Brimelow, "Time to Rethink Immigration?" *National Review* (22 June 1992): 34 & 30.

36 Ibid., 30. Nonwhite immigrants are not the only ones to blame: Brimlow claims that "a significant part of the black community has succumbed to social pathology" and alerts us to "the emergence of a strange anti-nation inside the U.S. – the so-called 'Hispanics'" (Ibid., 40 & 45).

37 See VDare.com, October 14, 2017, www.vdare.com/letters/a-reader-alerts-us-to-the-paris-statement-a-europe-we-can-believe-in; The American Notice, November 18, 2017, http://allrightforum.blogspot.com/2017/11/a-europe-we-can-believe-in.html; and Forza Nuova U.S.A., December 29, 2017, www.usa.forzanuova.info/2017/12/29/philosophers-warn-europe-protect-borders-restore-marriage-if-you-want-to-survive/.

38 The True Europe, "The Paris Statement: A Europe We Can Believe In," https://thetrueeurope.eu/a-europe-we-can-believe-in/, accessed October 21, 2017.

39 Ant-Defamation League, "14 Words," www.adl.org/education/references/hate-symbols/14-words, accessed October 21, 2017.

40 Ibid.

41 Adolf Hitler, *Mein Kampf*, Translated by Ralph Manheim (Boston, MA: Houghton Mifflin Company, 1943): 13.

42 In Europe, I am thinking of prominent political parties like Austria's Freedom Party, France's National Front, Alternative for Germany, Greece's Golden Dawn, Holland's Party for Freedom, Movement for a Better Hungary (Jobbik), Northern Ireland's Democratic Unionist Party, and Poland's Law and Justice Party. In the United States, I am thinking of figures like Pat Buchanan, Steve King, Kris Kobach, Carl Paladino, Jeff Sessions, and Tom Tancredo.

43 Donald Trump, "Remarks by President Trump to the People of Poland," July 6, 2017, www.whitehouse.gov/briefings-statements/remarks-president-trump-people-poland/.

44 Ibid.

45 See Barbara Jeanne Field's "Slavery, Race and Ideology in the United States of America" for a discussion about the origins of what we now call white nationalism (*New Left Review*, 1, no. 181 [May–June, 1990]: 95–118). In his *White Nationalism, Black Interests: Conservative Public Policy and the Black Community*, Ronald W. Walters outlines white nationalism as a structural imperative of American domestic policy (Detroit: Wayne State University Press, 2003). Y. N. Kly calls this imperative America's "anti-social contract" (*The Anti-Social Contract*, Atlanta: Clarity, 1989).

46 Eric Hobsbawm, *On the Edge of the New Century: In Conversation with Antonio Polito*, Translated by Allan Cameron (New York: The New Press, 2000), 6. Hobsbawm also suggests that one important element in reactionary versions of history consistently posits a kind of homeland, or "the need for the 'permanent' and the 'fundamental' which takes on a great psychological importance not only for individuals, but also for communities, particularly in the latter half of the twentieth century, an era of change and constant insecurity. Even

90 *Michael Mayne*

in areas where it is not possible to live in isolation, such as the United States where wave after wave of new arrivals come to settle, we can see the emergence of a need to have priority, to be able to say, 'We are here, this is our land, the others came later, and we are the ones who have always been here.' It is a kind of secular version of eternity" (Ibid., 28).

Bibliography

Anderson, Benedict. *Imagined Communities: Reflections of the Origin and Spread of Nationalism.* Revised edition. London: Verso, 2006.

Ant-Defamation League. "14 Words." www.adl.org/education/references/hate-symbols/14-words (Accessed October 21, 2017).

———. "Have Hate, Will Travel: The Demographics of Unite the Right." October 8, 2017. www.adl.org/blog/have-hate-will-travel-the-demographics-of-unite-the-right (Accessed September 10, 2017).

———. "White Supremacists Adopt New Slogan: 'You Will Not Replace Us.'" June 9, 2017. www.adl.org/blog/white-supremacists-adopt-new-slogan-you-will-not-replace-us (Accessed September 13, 2017).

Bonnett, Alastair. *Left in the Past: Radicalism and the Politics of Nostalgia.* New York: Continuum, 2010.

Boym, Svetlana. *The Future of Nostalgia.* New York: Basic Books, 2001.

Brimelow, Peter. "Time to Rethink Immigration?" *National Review* 44, no. 12 (June 22, 1992): 30–46.

California State University at San Bernardino Center for the Study of Hate and Extremism. "Final U.S. Status Report: Hate Crime Analysis & Forecast for 2016–2017." September 2017.

Chilton, Paul, and Mikhail Ilyin. "Metaphor in Political Discourse: The Case of the "Common European House." *Discourse & Society* 4, no. 1 (1993): 7–31.

Confessore, Nicholas. "For Whites Sensing Decline, Donald Trump Unleashes Words of Resistance." July 13, 2016. *New York Times*, www.nytimes.com/2016/07/14/us/politics/donald-trump-white-identity.html) (Accessed August 31, 2017).

Daniels, Jessie. *White Supremacy Online and the New Attack on Civil Rights.* Lanham, MD: Rowman & Littlefield, 2009.

Doane, Janice, and Devon Hodges. *Nostalgia and Sexual Difference: The Resistance to Contemporary Feminism.* New York: Methuen, 1987.

Dwyer, Michael D. *Back to the Fifties: Nostalgia, Hollywood Film, and Popular Music of the Seventies and Eighties.* Oxford: Oxford University Press, 2015.

Field, Barbara Jeanne. "Slavery, Race and Ideology in the United States of America." *New Left Review* 1, no. 181 (May–June, 1990): 95–118.

Francis, Samuel T. "The Return of the Repressed." *National Policy Institute.* September 10, 2006. www.npiamerica.org/research/category/the-return-of-the-repressed (Accessed September 11, 2017).

Hitler, Adolf. *Mein Kampf,* Translated by Ralph Manheim. Boston, MA: Houghton Mifflin Company, 1943.

Hobsbawm, Eric. *On the Edge of the New Century: In Conversation with Antonio Polito.* Translated by Allan Cameron. New York: The New Press, 2000.

Huffer, Lynne. *Maternal Pasts, Feminist Futures: Nostalgia, Ethics, and the Question of Difference.* Stanford, CA: Stanford University Press, 1998.

Identity Evropa. Twitter post. May 27, 2017, 5:08 p.m. https://twitter.com/IdentityEvropa.

Kessler, Jason. Twitter post. August 12, 2017, 6:24 p.m. http://twitter.com/unitetherightva?lang=en.

King, Steve. Interview with Jan Mickelson. March 13, 2017. *WHO Newsradio 1040*, http://media.ccomrcdn.com/media/station_content/1165/2017/03/mp3/default/part_1_-_jan_mickelson_with_re_0_1489429024.mp3 (Accessed September 11, 2017).

Kly, Y. N. *The Anti-Social Contract*. Atlanta, GA: Clarity, 1989.Letson, Al, and Richard Spencer. "A Frank Conversation with a White Nationalist." November 10, 2016, *NPR*, www.revealnews.org/episodes/a-frank-conversation-with-a-white-nationalist/ (Accessed September 12, 2017).

Manning, Erin. *Always More Than One: Individuation's Dance*. Durham, NC: Duke University Press, 2013.

Murray, Lawrence. "Mapping the Rising Tide." August 9, 2016. https://atlanticcenturion.wordpress.com/2016/08/09/mapping-the-rising-tide/ (Accessed September 11, 2017).

Naternot. "You Will Not Replace Us." Youtube video, 1:00. www.youtube.com/watch?v=ZSeDvZaz4nU (August 16, 2017).

Nationalist Front. "Fourteen Points." www.nfunity.org/14-points/ (Accessed September 11, 2017).

Roof, Dylan. "rtf88." June 17, 2015. https://assets.documentcloud.org/documents/2108059/lastrhodesian-manifesto.pdf (Accessed September 3, 2017).

Ruddick, Susan. "The Politics of Affect Spinoza in the Work of Negri and Deleuze." *Theory, Culture, & Society* 27, no. 4 (2010): 21–45.

Swain, Carol M., and Russ Nieli. *Contemporary Voices of White Nationalism in America*. New York: Cambridge University Press, 2003.

The True Europe. "The Paris Statement: A Europe We Can Believe In." https://thetrueeurope.eu/a-europe-we-can-believe-in/ (Accessed October 21, 2017).

Troup, Quincy. "My Take." *Black Renaissance Noire* 11, no. 1 (Spring 2011): 4–5.

Trump, Donald. "Remarks by President Trump to the People of Poland." July 6, 2017. www.whitehouse.gov/briefings-statements/remarks-president-trump-people-poland/ (Accessed October 4, 2017).

———. Twitter post. August 17, 2017, 8:07 a.m. https://twitter.com/realDonaldTrump.

———. Twitter post. August 17, 2017, 8:21 a.m. https://twitter.com/realDonaldTrump.

University of Virginia Center for Politics. "Condensed_FINAL_Tables_Aug21_to_Sep5_UVA_Race_prot." Reuters/Ipsos/University of Virginia Center for Politics (Accessed September 11, 2017).

Vanguard America. "On Charlottesville Rally: Why We Fight." July 10, 2017. http://conservative-headlines.org/on-charlottesville-rally-why-we-fight/ (Accessed September 10, 2017).

Walters, Ronald W. *White Nationalism, Black Interests: Conservative Public Policy and the Black Community*. Detroit, MI: Wayne State University Press, 2003.

Wilders, Geert. "The Failure of Multiculturalism and How to Turn the Tide." March 25, 2011. www.geertwilders.nl/index.php/in-english-mainmenu-98/in-the-press-mainmenu-101/77-in-the-press/1740-speech-geert-wilders-in-rome-25th-of-march-2011Bottom of Form (Accessed September 12, 2017).

Williams, Caroline. "Affective Processes without a Subject: Rethinking the Relation between Subjectivity and Affect with Spinoza." *Subjectivity* 3, no. 3 (2010): 246–262.

Wodak, Ruth, and Salomi Boukala. "European Identities and the Revival of Nationalism in the European Union: A Discourse Historical Approach." *Journal of Language and Politics* 14, no. 1, (2015): 87–109.

Zesking, Leonard. *Blood and Politics: The History of the White Nationalist Movement from the Margins to the Mainstream.* New York: Farrar, Straus and Giroux, 2009.

Zinchenko, Alexander V. "Nostalgia: Dialogue between Memory and Knowing." *Russian Social Science Review* 53, no. 1 (January–February 2012): 68–81.

6 They Believe Their Belief

Rhetorically Engaging Culture through Affect, Ideology, and *Doxa*

Phil Bratta

Introduction

Three days after the August 2017 "Unite the Right" rally, which included white supremacists and nationalists carrying torches and chanting "Blood and soil!," "You will not replace us!," and "Jews will not replace us!" to protest the removal of the Robert E. Lee statue in Charlottesville, Virginia, President Donald Trump responded to the weekend's events about the removal of Confederate statues in the United States: "George Washington was a slave owner ... So will George Washington now lose his status? Are we going to take down statues to George Washington? How about Thomas Jefferson?"[1] One fallacy of Trump's argument is faulty analogy because Washington and Jefferson, unlike Lee, did not take up arms against the United States. Another fallacy is that Trump's reasoning is embedded in a classic slippery slope argument, which suggests that the acceptance of one action will certainly lead to a number of other events that are undesirable. With no evidence of statements or plans by others to remove the statues of George Washington or Thomas Jefferson, Trump presents a false dilemma in which an "either/or" situation is on our hands and a simple "yes" or "no" decision must be made. Embedded within this line of argument is a particular ideology (a system of ideas, concepts, or theories), but also an affect—one that many might label as fear—that is situated culturally.

Not all affect theorists, however, think of affect as a cultural phenomenon, and many scholars suggest a partition between affect and ideology.[2] According to one view, affect emerges before cognition and is a kind of pre-cultural, pre-subjective experience, i.e., an event that operates outside of or prior to cultural influence.[3] Although individuals are subject to the symbols, symbolic practices, and ideological meanings—primarily through language—of a culture, individuals also have experiences that cannot be reduced to any cultural logic or even a conscious registering.[4] In other words, the structure and uses of language only capture the symbolic, while affect, as an indescribable phenomenon, according to this view, operates in different ways and logics than language and reason.[5] That is, affect—à la Brian Massumi and Steven Shaviro—is a primary and nonconscious experience[6] that is not necessarily filtered through cultural elements, such as language. This approach to studying affect is primarily responding to scholarship on cultural theory that emphasizes language, symbolicity, and subjectivity, and it offers the concept of affect as acultural, nonrepresentational phenomena that work at a physiological level.[7] This means, for example, that regardless of one's language (e.g., English, French, German, etc.) or subjectivity (white, Black, heterosexual, homosexual, man, woman, transgender, and so forth), one will likely experience affect in the same way.

In contrast, critical and cultural theorists usually study how ideology is communicated and circulated by culture. Ideology is a system that communicates and establishes a set of ideas about people, bodies, history, and practices. Ideology disseminates from institutions, such as school, church, mass media, and others, and notably through the discourses of those institutions. While discourse is typically associated with simply the presence of written and/or spoken communication, discourse also involves rules for what is permitted and forbidden in writing and speaking, often based on the historical context.[8] Classical rhetoricians spoke of these rules as decorum. In other words, discourses always have a set of formal and informal rules and practices. Moreover, these rules and practices point toward the dynamics of social power and ideology. The weakness, however, is that critical analysis, with its primary focus on ideological critique, often ignores or downplays[9] the affective dimension of human experience, focusing overwhelmingly on "content and structures of signification."[10]

My claim is that ideology and affect often work in a symbiotic way. Of course, there are ideologies with seemingly little affect undergirding them. For example, on the surface, the idea that "justice is blind" presents a cultural meaning about equality and objectivity. This ideology suggests that laws apply universally or that laws are factual and natural with no human influence (and hence, no affect). Likewise, there are affects that do operate in a kind of acultural way. For instance, consider that when we watch a horror movie and a monster or ghost appears suddenly to frighten other characters, we may feel jolted out of our seat or feel as if the hair on our arms and neck stands up. However, most ideologies are saturated with affect and many affective experiences are ideological. Identifying the connection between affect and ideology can often best be located in various arguments, hence making rhetoric—in its common definition of the study and use of persuasion—a promising object of analysis for studying both affect and ideology.

Many scholars who do not have dominant cultural subjectivities (white, male, and/or heterosexual) have shown how affect connects to culture through language. For example, Frantz Fanon proposed the idea of "affective erethism," an internalized colonial process and phenomenon in which Black women (but also Black men) are made to feel inferior and aspire "to gain admittance to the white world,"[11] and which is created by various kinds of information in cultural media, such as books, movies, newspapers, and advertisements.[12] Claudia Garcia-Rojas also shows how "White affect studies, [which] draws from Western-European theories to establish a sociopolitical structure of affects ... positions White affects as universal, concrete, and true."[13] She offers productive insights into understanding how "lesbian and queer women of color" use language to "examine and expose systems of power and oppression," as they "theoriz[e] a language of self" outside White affect studies scholarship and discourse.[14] As these scholars illuminate, affect and any affective experiences are not culturally homogenous. Culture, language, race, gender, class, sexuality, nationality, and dis/ability structure and influence how affects are understood, engaged, and experienced. I want to contribute to these scholars' arguments by encouraging a much-needed attention to the ways in which scholars of color, lesbian, gay, bisexual, transgender, and queer (LGBTQ) scholars, and women have continually illuminated the connection between culture and affect, as well as positioning affects as particular and not universal. As I show below, Sara Ahmed is influential to my larger argument as she provides rich ideas in thinking about culture and affect.

In the rest of this chapter, I first discuss in more detail affect and culture, underscoring the need to put scholarship on affect and culture in continuing conversation with each other. This leads me to argue that if we are to understand one of the things that rhetoric does, we need to engage with a new term: *affective cultures*. Affective cultures are shared values, practices, discourses, systems, and institutions that respond to cultural narratives loaded with ideology and affect. A cultural narrative gives "structured form in which stories advance explanations for the ways of the world"[15] for a collection of individuals who identify similarly, as well as differently with others. A cultural narrative presents seemingly coherent, sequenced ideas and events that inform a collection of individuals about its place in the world. For instance, the American Dream is a cultural narrative: anyone can achieve success, prosperity, and upward mobility through hard work and determination, regardless of one's race, ethnicity, gender, sex, and dis/ability. Many Americans, as well as foreigners and immigrants, believe this cultural narrative to be true. These Americans, foreigners, and immigrants constitute an affective culture, which means the individuals become activated, charged, and mobilized through a distinct rhetorical concept: *doxa*, or common belief. Affective cultures *believe* in cultural narratives. Affective cultures are extremely diverse and wide-ranging in size, as for example, college sports culture or military culture or the LGBTQ community or American culture writ large. The individuals in each of these cultures (and others) participate in particular rituals, use language in certain ways, emphasize specific ideas to create shared values, and build or are built by institutions, such as family, school, government, church, organization, and others. After presenting an overview of affective cultures, as well as *doxa*, I conclude this chapter by returning to Trump's argument to show how Trump appeals to an affective culture to gain support from his base.

96   *Phil Bratta*

Affect and Culture

One way— though not the only way—of describing affect is by tracing the concept from Baruch Spinoza to Henri Bergson, through Gilles Deleuze and Felix Guattari, and on to Brian Massumi, Melissa Gregg and Gregory J. Seigworth, Patricia Clough, Sara Ahmed, and others. In this chapter, I draw from these scholars' work to argue that affect has three qualities. First, affect can be understood as a body's capacity to affect and be affected.[16] In other words, affect is a particular potential—an openness for the body to have a felt experience, and it changes and moves in relation to a body's proximity to other bodies (human, nonhuman animal, social, things, and so forth). Bodies, as Deleuze and Guattari contend, are "nothing but affects and local movements, differential speeds."[17] A body, or as they name *haecceity*, "consist[s] entirely of relations of movement and rest between molecules or particles, capacities to affect and be affected."[18] Second, affect is often described as a social phenomenon, meaning that affect is not an internalized state of experience—a common understanding of emotion. Emotions, for some theorists, are internalized states of the individual and often understood as stemming from irrationality in the mind. On the other hand, affect, it is commonly argued, is not personal feelings. As Clough notes, affect is "irreducible to the individual, the personal, or the psychological."[19] That is, affect cannot simply be understood by studying one person, or one person's subjective experience, or one person's psychological state. Finally, affect has been described as the intensities in the in-betweeness of bodies.[20] Intensities are forces that cause bodies to relate to themselves *and* other bodies in an experience. Take, for example, the intensities involved in the following scenario: a thoroughbred horse, plow horse, and plow—all of which are types of bodies—are on a field. When the horses move about the field, they do so at different speeds and intensities. The plow horse's exertion and experience is more closely related to the plow than the thoroughbred, consequently developing a commonality with the plow technology and movement.[21] We might say that the plow horse's embodied experience is an affective one.

Similar to the term "affect," "culture" carries many definitions across a number of disciplines. More than 300 definitions exist.[22] For the purposes of this chapter, I use the word "culture" as specifically related to humans, although many scholars in a variety of disciplines are studying and showing that nonhuman animals also have behaviors and communicative practices that could constitute a culture. Nevertheless, culture, as Robin Boylorn and Mark P. Orbe argue, is a term that has been defined in various ways over time and detailed with various qualities.[23] For instance, Raymond Williams designates culture as "a whole way of life,"[24] which includes shared artifacts, beliefs, institutions, practices, and rituals. Chris Weedon, Andrew Tolson, and Frank Mort, however, note that "language is seen as important in Williams's definition of culture,"[25] and many other scholars have noted that humans' ability to use language in complex ways to make symbolic meanings is a key feature of culture. Suffice it to say, a culture and individuals within that culture continually construct, deliver, and consume symbolic meanings. For instance, American culture produces an ideology of masculinity in various ways, such as in advertisements. In many cologne magazine ads, you find a man with no shirt, muscular arms and torso, and a woman enthralled with him. Of course, the company's goal is to sell the product; but the company is part of a culture that constructs and delivers messages about what it means to be and act a man (attraction of women/heterosexuality, strength for dominance, and others). Through the visual appearance of the man (i.e., his built body, posture, desirable looks) and the woman (i.e., captivated and seduced), viewers consume the image and its symbolic meanings, developing a sense of masculinity, manhood, and relations between men and women.

The cologne advertisement and many other cultural productions use rhetoric to communicate ideologies and symbolic meanings. Rhetoric is cultural and aids in creating meaning (what it means to be a man, a woman, white, Black, Christian, Muslim, rich, poor, etc.). But rhetoric also operationalizes affect, creating situations where, as Jennifer Edbauer notes, "meaning and feeling always shadow the other in rhetoric without reducing to the other."[26] Edbauer argues that because we are bodies, we experience an entanglement of meaning and feeling when we use rhetoric. That is, rhetoric allows us to create ideas that signify and are felt through the body. Edbauer concludes with a call for rhetoricians and compositionists to address the tension between representation (cultural meanings) and nonrepresentational practices, as well as examine culture beyond *simply* signification, or ideology. The concept of affective cultures takes up Edbauer's call by specifically honing in on the affective dimensions of subjects in a culture, particularly in terms of how ideology and affect build up within a culture over time and orient subjects within and across cultures to each other. Affective cultures are forged, distributed, and sustained by the work of rhetoric, whether in writing, speech, image, sound, performance, and so forth.

Affective Cultures

Affective cultures feel the intensities (forces that cause bodies to relate to themselves *and* other bodies) of ideologies (ideas, concepts, or theories that provide cultural meaning), particularly in the rhetorical operations of an argument. The idea of affective cultures builds from Sara Ahmed, who connects affect to culture. Ahmed proposes that the "cultural politics of emotion" direct our attention to how "emotions work by working through signs and on bodies to materialise the surfaces and boundaries that are lived as worlds."[27] "Emotions," for Ahmed, "are not 'in' either the individual or the social, but produce the very surfaces and boundaries that allow the individual and the social to be delineated as if they are objects."[28] She notes the subtle difference between emotion and affect in which the latter involves objects that "become sticky."[29] However, this notion of stickiness differs from common understandings of merely one object sticking to another, as, for instance, with a piece of tape sticking to paper. Instead, Ahmed remarks, "Rather than using stickiness to describe an object's surface, we can think of stickiness as an effect of surfacing, *as an effect of the histories of contact between bodies, objects, and signs.*"[30] In other words, affect creates and is created by situations that make us become attached to objects and/or people. Objects—whether a material object or an immaterial object, such as language—resonate with our bodies, shaping and orienting them to other bodies and society. For instance, the statues Trump references are material objects. His argument is also an object—connected to, but also distinct from his body and subject position. Both the statues and argument involve rhetoric for the general public, and they shape and charge affective cultures.

As an affect-loaded object and its signifying messages enter into public space, affective cultures feel the effect of the object and signification. In feeling the effect, affective cultures come to better understand where they align in society. Take, for example, the cologne advertisement mentioned above. The affective culture of heterosexual men might engage with the object (the image) and signification (masculinity) to learn their place in society: men are valued as men for their muscular physique and ability to attract women. Coming to understand one's "place" in society is also a cultural narrative. That is, the effects of an object and signification, as well as the stickiness and response to the effects, also create cultural narratives, which, Ahmed also points out, is an important part of the circulation of emotions. These narratives, then, produce "others" by inclusion and exclusion of certain populations based on social identities (race, gender, sexuality, class, nationality, creed, and so forth). Similarly, affective cultures operate within cultural narratives. In addition to emotions shaping cultural narratives, rhetoric runs through various parts of cultural narratives.

Similar to Ahmed's argument on the cultural politics of emotion where cultures invest belief into narratives, affect works from a rhetorical concept: *doxa*, or common belief. Affective cultures respond to and are undergirded by *doxa*. Plato regarded *doxa* as distinctly different from reason and as a tool used by the sophists, teachers of rhetoric in ancient Greece, to manipulate audiences. *Doxa*, according to Plato, is the opposite of and inferior to *episteme*,[31] which typically has been translated as knowledge, understanding, or science. John Muckelbauer remarks, "Plato championed *episteme*—true knowledge of essences—in contrast to *doxa*—fallible beliefs about appearances."[32] It makes sense that Plato would oppose the sophists and devalue *doxa* because of his own belief in Truth and ideal forms. By juxtaposing *episteme* and *doxa*, Plato could argue that if scholars and teachers taught and strived for knowledge, individuals might not be negatively influenced by the masses—one of the effects of *doxa*—as well as resistant to

They Believe Their Belief 99

rhetoric. For Plato, rhetoric merely works on an audience's opinions (*doxa*), and rhetoric is simply flattery with no basis or investment in knowledge, Truth, or certainty.[33] Of course, rhetoric (and knowledge, Truth/truth, and certainty) is more complex than Plato's assertion. As a foundation for the way that affective cultures engage in the world, *doxa* is more important than ever to understand how rhetoric works upon audiences. We live in a world where beliefs carry the weight of experiences, perceptions, and realities. Beliefs often trump facts and sound reasoning. Indeed we may be in an age where *doxa* has triumphed over *episteme*.[34] For affective cultures, beliefs are ideological and affective, moving the individuals of an affective culture to reinforce (typically those who are already in power and in dominant positions) or challenge/change (typically those who are in marginalized or oppressed positions) their social position and our collective social life.

In returning to Trump's slippery slope argument, we can see how Trump caters to beliefs by evoking affect (i.e., fear) and ideology (a system of ideas, concepts, or theories) in the cultural narrative of his argument. Of course, Trump's argument impacts different affective cultures differently: it might incite one affective culture (conservative American protesters), undermine another affective culture (counter-protestors and anti-racist activists), and deny justice and acknowledgement for yet another affective culture (African Americans/Black people). But Trump's argument attempts to resonate most powerfully with the affective culture of white America. Part of the cultural narrative is a belief in a nationalistic principle: an unwavering honor and respect for the history of the United States. This principle, as well as the belief in this principle, finds its way into the cultural narrative embraced by Trump: while the racist history of the United States and Confederate general Lee and racist policies of Washington and Jefferson are present— both in the representation of the statues and Trump's remark that "George Washington was a slave owner"—they are also dismissed as irrelevant to our contemporary moment. That was just the way people thought back then. Slave owners didn't mean any harm. We can't judge them by our modern standards. The fallacy in Trump's argument relies upon this cultural narrative, but his argument also elicits a sense of fear. Fear is an affect, and it undergirds the narrative as a *felt truth*, a *felt fact*: white Americans are losing their history and stronghold on the politics and culture of the United States, thus potentially making whites a minority with no more power.

Accompanying the fear created in the narrative is an ideological belief that Trump hopes to tap into in order to move the affective culture of white America. That belief is the notion that white American history is righteous and, consequently, white Americans are innocent and superior to nonwhites and citizens of other countries. Their superiority and history, however, are being erased, hence the fear. In this view, the ideology that the United States is a great nation built by hardworking white Americans is at risk of crumbling as it continues to both acknowledge the nation's violent, exploitative, and oppressive history ("George Washington was a slave owner") and conceal that history (in this instance, the past is the past and has no effect upon the present). Moments later in Trump's speech, Trump notes this of U.S. history: "[Thomas Jefferson] was a major slave-owner. Now, are we going to take down his statue? So you know what? It's fine. You're changing history. You're changing culture. And you had people, and I'm not talking about the neo-Nazis and the white nationalists, because they should be condemned totally. But you had many people in that group other than neo-Nazis and white nationalists."[35] As an affective culture, white Americans who resist the removal of the Confederate statues would fear the potential dissolution of U.S. history. Trump also suggests a pure, well-meaning, and innocent quality to many who were protesting, even drawing on the rule of law to support his remark: "you had a lot of people in that group that were there to innocently protest and very legally protest."[36] By shifting attention to the "innocence" of individuals protesting the statue removal, Trump attempts to represent them as more important than the white nationalists and supremacists who expressed racism and hatred, suggesting there were only a few bad people. Such a suggestion shifts the identity of the group to victims of a number of culprits and threats: the "liberal" media, hostile liberals/progressives (counter-protesters), the rise and success of African American/Black people (e.g., with the last eight years of having Barack Obama as President), the decline of white dominance and power, and the perceived marginalization of white people.

By being victims of these perpetrators and threats, white Americans who align with Trump's argument can understand a more coherent and cohesive cultural narrative. Undergirding that narrative is a belief that Trump taps into: these white Americans, and by extension U.S. history, are righteous, egalitarian, and not racist; those slave owners may have been racist, but the nation has moved forward into a kind of post-racist society; furthermore, the greatness of the forefathers outweighs the violent exploitation and oppression of African Americans/black people, and we must preserve, through such statues and monuments, the rich history of the United States. The belief in this narrative allows the affective culture to feel a nationalism, even when that nationalism is a peculiar combination of The Confederate States of America and The United States of America, and a rationale for not removing the statues. Additionally, as the belief goes, Trump opens the opportunity for white Americans to now claim that not only does prejudice and discrimination happen to white people, but racism (i.e., a reverse racism) emerges whenever white history—a particular white history understood as an account of a pure, great, and innocent civilized White nation—is removed, attacked, or eradicated.

Trump attempts to create rhetorical power through a combination of fear and belief in a cultural narrative. White Americans who fear the Other and already hold the belief that they are losing their culture could not care less whether or not Trump's argument is sound or valid. While at times rhetoric works to persuade an audience through a number of devices and sound arguments, rhetoric often mobilizes affect and ideology to tap into the beliefs of an affective culture. This helps explain why there is such difficulty in persuading individuals of an affective culture to change their ideas. Affective cultures—and those individuals of affective cultures—*believe* their beliefs, regardless of an argument's (lack of) evidence. That is, many arguments are effective because they appeal to already-held beliefs of an affective culture.

Conclusion

Similar to Ahmed's ideas about the cultural politics of emotion, affective cultures engage in the world by their encounters with affect-forming cultural objects, whether that object is a material object, such as the Robert E. Lee statue, or a politician's argument, such as Trump's. Many of these objects are presented in cultural narratives (including the cultural narrative as an object in and of itself). Through a slippery slope argument, Trump reinforces an already existing cultural narrative about the United States and white Americans in order to impact a specific affective culture. That is, the cultural narrative delivers an ideology that is affective, which Trump hopes will tap into the beliefs of the affective culture. Such slippery slope arguments, as well as a variety of other kinds of arguments (deductive, inductive, abductive) and types of reasoning (sound, valid, or fallacious), will typically engage and move affective cultures through already-held beliefs.

When we conduct rhetorical analyses or create arguments, we must be attentive to the ways that ideology, affect, and *doxa*/belief operate jointly. When doing analyses, we need to keep in mind that the validity and/or soundness of an argument may be irrelevant because of what affective culture the argument attempts to reach. Fallacious arguments are ubiquitous, and we should definitely point them out. In studying them, however, we should give greater attention to why and how fallacious arguments are rhetorically effective on an audience. In doing so, the idea of affective cultures as they are grounded in ideology, affect, and *doxa*/belief provides an opening into understanding the power of rhetoric, often referred to as rhetorical consequentiality. In other words, we could better understand why many arguments are effective by attending to how *doxa*/belief functions for impact. Additionally, when we use rhetoric to make arguments, we need to not only be sure that we identify the beliefs of an affective culture, but bring to light the ethical or unethical qualities of those beliefs. Doing so, in some instances, may reveal unjust and inhumane qualities of those beliefs. This means being attentive to history, cultural identity, and embodied experiences with language. In doing so, the study and use of rhetoric can continue an activist agenda for the betterment of society through ethical engagements with language.

Notes

1 Lisa Marie Segarra, "Read the Transcript of President Trump's 'Blame on Both Sides' Comments on Charlottesville," *Time*, last modified August 15, 2017. http://time.com/4902144/donald-trump-charlottesville-blame-both-sides-kkk-nazi/
2 Brian Massumi, *Parables for the Virtual: Movement, Affect, Sensation* (Durham, NC: Duke University Press, 2002), 3; Christoffer Kølvraa, "Affect, Provocation, and Far Right Rhetoric," in Britta Timm Knudsen and Carsten Stage, eds., *Affective Methodologies: Developing Cultural Research Strategies for the Study of Affect* (New York, NY: Palgrave Macmillan, 2015), 183.
3 Ibid.
4 Lisa Blackman, "Researching Affect and Embodied Hauntologies: Exploring an Analytics of Experimentation," in Britta Timm Knudsen and Carsten Stage, eds., *Affective Methodologies: Developing Cultural Research Strategies for the Study of Affect* (New York, NY: Palgrave Macmillan, 2015), 33.
5 Brian Massumi, *Parables for the Virtual: Movement, Affect, Sensation* (Durham, NC: Duke University Press, 2002), 25–27.
6 Steven Shaviro, *Post-Cinematic Affect* (Winchester, UK and Washington, USA: 0-Books, 2009), 3.
7 Terese Brennan, *The Transmission of Affect* (Ithaca, NY: Cornell University Press, 2004).
8 Michel Foucault, *The Archaeology of Knowledge*, trans. A.M. Sheridan Smith (New York, NY: Pantheon Books, 1972), 38.
9 Daniel Chandler, *Semiotics: The Basics*, 2nd ed. (London and New York, NY: Routledge, 2007). 216 (original emphasis).
10 Britta Timm Knudsen and Carsten Stage, "Introduction: Affective methodologies," in Britta Timm Knudsen and Carsten Stage, eds., *Affective Methodologies: Developing Cultural Research Strategies for the Study of Affect* (New York, NY: Palgrave Macmillan, 2015), 2.
11 Frantz Fanon, *Black Skin, White Masks*, trans. Richard Philcox (New York, NY: Grove Press, 2008), 41.
12 Ibid., 130–131.
13 Claudia Garcia-Rojas, "(Un)Disciplined Futures: Women of Color Feminism as a Disruptive to White Affect Studies," *Journal of Lesbian Studies* 21, no. 3 (2017): 254–255.
14 Ibid., 255–258.
15 Chris Barker, *Cultural Studies: Theory and Practice*, 4th ed. (London: Sage Publications, 2012), 35.
16 Baruch Spinoza, *The Ethics. The Collected Works of Spinoza, volume 1*, ed. and trans. Edwin Curley (Princeton, NJ: Princeton University Press, 1985).
17 Gilles Deleuze and Felix Guattari, *A Thousand Plateaus: Capitalism and Schizophrenia*, trans. Brian Massumi (1980; repr. Minneapolis, MN: University of Minnesota Press, 1980), 260.
18 Ibid., 261.
19 Patricia Ticineto Clough, "Introduction," in Patricia Ticineto Clough and Jean Halley, eds., *The Affective Turn: Theorizing the Social* (Durham, NC and London: Duke University Press, 2007), 3.
20 Melissa Gregg and Gregory J. Seigworth, "An inventory of shimmers," in Melissa Gregg and Gregory J. Seigworth, eds., *The Affect Theory Reader* (Durham, NC and London: Duke University Press, 2010), 1.
21 I give my gratitude to Jenny Rice for providing this example at the 2017 Rhetoric Society of America Institute.

22 John R. Baldwin, Sandra L. Faulkner, Michael L. Hecht, and Sheryl L. Lindsley, eds., *Redefining Culture: Perspectives Across the Disciplines* (Mahwah, NJ: Lawrence Erlbaum Associates, 2006).

23 Robin Boylorn and Mark P. Orbe, "Introduction: Critical Autoethnography as Method of Choice," in Robin M. Boylorn and Mark P. Orbe, eds., *Critical Autoethnography: Intersecting Cultural Identities in Everyday Life* (London and New York, NY: Routledge, 2014), 15.

24 Raymond Williams, *Culture and Society* (Garden City, NY: Anchor Books, 1958), xvii.

25 Chris Weedon, Andrew Tolson, and Frank Mort, "Introduction to Language Studies at the Centre," in Stuart Hall, Dorothy Hobson, Andrew Lowe, and Paul Willis, eds., *Culture, Media, Language: Working Papers in Cultural Studies 1972–79* (London and New York, NY: Birmingham, UK: Academic Division of Unwin Hyman (Publishers) Ltd, 1980), 168.

26 Jennifer Edbauer, "(Meta)Physical Graffiti: "Getting Up" as Affective Writing Model," *JAC* 26, no. 1 (2005): 151 (original emphasis).

27 Sara Ahmed, *The Cultural Politics of Emotion* (New York, NY: Routledge, 2004), 191.

28 Ibid., 10.

29 Ibid., 11.

30 Ibid., 90 (original emphasis).

31 Plato, *Gorgias*, trans. Benjamin Jowett (Project Gutenberg, The Project Gutenberg EBook of Gorgias, 2008), n.p. www.gutenberg.org/ebooks/1672

32 John Muckelbauer, *The Future of Invention: Rhetoric, Postmodernism, and the Problem of Change* (Albany, NY: State University of New York Press, 2009), 151–152.

33 Plato, *Phaedrus*, trans. Benjamin Jowett (Project Gutenberg, The Project Gutenberg EBook of Phaedrus, 2008), n.p. www.gutenberg.org/ebooks/1636

34 Scott Sundvall, "The First 100 Days of an Electrate President: Post-Truth, Alternative Facts, and Fake News in the Third Sophistic," *Textshop Experiments* 3, (Summer 2017): n.p. http://textshopexperiments.org/textshop03/first-100-days-of-an-electrate-president

35 Lisa Marie Segarra, "Read the Transcript of President Trump's 'Blame on Both Sides' Comments on Charlottesville," *Time*, last modified August 15, 2017. http://time.com/4902144/donald-trump-charlottesville-blame-both-sides-kkk-nazi/

36 Ibid.

Bibliography

Ahmed, Sara. *The Cultural Politics of Emotion*. New York, NY: Routledge, 2004.

Baldwin, John R., Sandra L. Faulkner, Michael L. Hecht, and Sheryl L. Lindsley, eds. *Redefining Culture: Perspectives across the Disciplines*. Mahwah, NJ: Lawrence Erlbaum Associates, 2006.

Barker, Chris. *Cultural Studies: Theory and Practice*, 4th ed. London: Sage Publications, 2012.

Blackman, Lisa. "Researching Affect and Embodied Hauntologies: Exploring an Analytics of Experimentation." In *Affective Methodologies: Developing Cultural Research Strategies for the Study of Affect*, edited by Britta Timm Knudsen and Carsten Stage, 25–44. New York, NY: Palgrave Macmillan, 2015.

Boylorn, Robin M., and Mark P. Orbe. "Introduction: Critical Autoethnography as Method of Choice." In *Critical Autoethnography: Intersecting Cultural Identities in Everyday Life*, edited by Robin M. Boylorn and Mark P. Orbe, 13–26. London and New York, NY: Routledge, 2014.

Brennan, Terese. *The Transmission of Affect*. Ithaca, NY: Cornell University Press, 2004.

Chandler, Daniel. *Semiotics: The Basics*. 2nd ed. London and New York, NY: Routledge, 2007.

Clough, Patricia Ticineto. "Introduction." In *The Affective Turn: Theorizing the Social*, edited by Patricia Ticineto Clough with Jean Halley, 1–33. Durham, NC and London: Duke University Press, 2007.

Deleuze, Gilles, and Felix Guattari. *A Thousand Plateaus: Capitalism and Schizophrenia*. Translated by Brian Massumi. Minneapolis, MN: University of Minnesota Press, 1987.

Edbauer, Jennifer. "(Meta)Physical Graffiti: "Getting Up" as Affective Writing Model." *JAC* 26, no. 1 (2005): 131–159.

Fanon, Frantz. *Black Skin, White Masks*. Translated by Richard Philcox. New York, NY: Grove Press, 2008.

Foucault, Michel. *The Archaeology of Knowledge*. Translated by A. M. Sheridan Smith. New York, NY: Pantheon Books, 1972.

Garcia-Rojas, Claudia. "(Un)Disciplined Futures: Women of Color Feminism as a Disruptive to White Affect Studies." *Journal of Lesbian Studies* 21, no. 3 (2017): 254–271.

Gregg, Melissa, and Gregory J. Seigworth. "An Inventory of Shimmers." In *The Affect Theory Reader*, edited by Melissa Gregg and Gregory J. Seigworth, 1–25. Durham, NC and London: Duke University Press, 2010.

Knudsen, Britta Timm, and Carsten Stage. "Introduction: Affective methodologies." In *Affective Methodologies: Developing Cultural Research Strategies for the Study of Affect*, edited by Britta Timm Knudsen and Carsten Stage, 1–22. New York, NY: Palgrave Macmillan, 2015.

Kølvraa, Christoffer. "Affect, Provocation, and Far Right Rhetoric." In *Affective Methodologies: Developing Cultural Research Strategies for the Study of Affect*, edited by Britta Timm Knudsen and Carsten Stage, 183–200. New York, NY: Palgrave Macmillan, 2015.

Massumi, Brian. *Parables for the Virtual: Movement, Affect, Sensation*. Durham, NC: Duke University Press, 2002.

Muckelbauer, John. *The Future of Invention: Rhetoric, Postmodernism, and the Problem of Change*. Albany, NY: State University of New York Press, 2009.

Plato. *Gorgias*. Translated by Benjamin Jowett. Project Gutenberg, The Project Gutenberg EBooks, 2008. www.gutenberg.org/ebooks/1672.

Plato. *Phaedrus*. Translated by Benjamin Jowett. Project Gutenberg, The Project Gutenberg EBook of Phaedrus, 2008. www.gutenberg.org/ebooks/1636.

Segarra, Lisa Marie. "Read the Transcript of President Trump's 'Blame on Both Sides' Comments on Charlottesville." *Time*, last modified August 15, 2017. http://time.com/4902144/donald-trump-charlottesville-blame-both-sides-kkk-nazi/.

Shaviro, Steven. *Post-Cinematic Affect*. Winchester, UK and Washington, USA: 0-Books, 2009.

Spinoza, Baruch. *The Ethics. The Collected Works of Spinoza, Volume 1*. Edited and Translated by Edwin Curley. Princeton, NJ: Princeton University Press, 1985.

Sundvall, Scott. "The First 100 Days of an Electrate President: Post-Truth, Alternative Facts, and Fake News in the Third Sophistic." *Textshop Experiments* 3, (Summer 2017): n.p. http://textshopexperiments.org/textshop03/first-100-days-of-an-electrate-president.

Weedon, Chris, Andrew Tolson, and Frank Mort. "Introduction to Language Studies at the Centre." *Culture, Media, Language: Working Papers in Cultural Studies 1972–79*, edited by Stuart Hall, Dorothy Hobson, Andrew Lowe, and Paul Willis, 167–176. Birmingham, UK: Academic Division of Unwin Hyman (Publishers) Ltd, 1980.

Williams, Raymond. *Culture and Society.* Garden City, NY: Anchor Books, 1958.

7 Governing Bodies

The Affects and Rhetorics of North Carolina's House Bill 2

Julie D. Nelson

When North Carolina House Bill 2 (HB2) was signed into law by Governor Pat McCrory in March 2016, many considered it to be the most anti-LGBTQ legislation in the United States at the time. Popularly called the "Bathroom Bill," HB2 responded to a Charlotte, NC City Council ordinance that prohibited public facilities from discriminating against people based on sexual orientation or gender identity. To undermine the ordinance, HB2 denied cities and municipalities the power to pass similar protections for LGBTQ people. Responses to the bill quickly engulfed news and social media, and supporters and critics alike zeroed in on the provision that transgender people were required to use public bathrooms according to the sex on their birth certificates.[1] The bathroom became the battleground—touted either as a culturally constructed space reinforcing antiquated notions of gender identity or as a necessarily regulated space, for the safety of women and children. Americans remain sharply divided over transgender issues and the existence of transgender identity,[2] and like most social issue debates, public exchanges are often heated. In the United States, LGBTQ people are the most likely minority group to be targets of hate crimes,[3] and the rhetorics of and responses to HB2 reveal some of the public sentiments that contribute to this disturbing trend.

Media coverage, no doubt, influenced the public reception of HB2, yet impassioned feelings circulating among citizens also propelled and sustained LGBTQ-phobic reactions to the bill. Using affect theory to analyze the public response to HB2 reveals how particular ideas and messages "caught on" in ways that inspired significant cultural shifts. Viral media trends that amass collective feelings shape pubic sentiments, as we have seen in countless occasions in the last decade.[4] This chapter illustrates how attaching negative affects like shame and fear to queer and transgender bodies contributed to the relative success of HB2. After a brief overview of the bill and its partial repeal, I survey select affect theories from queer scholarship to consider how affects shape queer identities and cultural responses to transgender and gender nonconforming people. Finally, I analyze a few examples of HB2 rhetorics to show how affects accumulated and shaped the debate, especially as the bathroom became a symbolic cultural, affective site.

HB2 Background

The impact of North Carolina's HB2 has been far reaching, despite its partial repeal in March 2017. Following McCrory's signing of the law, many companies and people—ranging from Lionsgate and PayPal to Ringo Starr and Bruce Springsteen—publicly boycotted the state, calling HB2 a civil rights violation. In May 2016, the U.S. Department of Justice sued McCrory, stating the bill violated the Civil Rights Act, Title IX, and the Violence Against Women Act. The Associated Press estimated a loss of nearly $4 billion in state revenue over 12 years because of the massive boycott.[5] As the economic impact of the bill became clearer, many North Carolina residents protested, leading to McCrory narrowly losing his reelection bid in 2016. However, because of widespread Republican control in the state, it was only after the NCAA threatened to move another year of tournaments from North Carolina and gave a 48-hour deadline that HB2 was partially repealed. To appease the NCAA, the bathroom provision was removed, but the bill still prohibited local governments from passing nondiscrimination protections for LGBTQ people; many critics called it a "fake repeal" or "HB2.0." The relative success of the bill—its year-long existence and its remaining mostly in tact—has encouraged sixteen states to pursue similar bills, though no other has been passed into law at the time of writing.

Queer Theory

Emerging in the last decades of the twentieth century, queer theory extends feminist critiques of patriarchal, essentialist notions of gender and sexuality. Rather than accepting "gender" and "sexuality" as natural and innate human characteristics, queer theorists consider how these concepts are culturally constructed and socially controlled. Throughout history, many Western scholars categorized the world in binaries or dichotomies (e.g., male-female, white-black, West-East, logic-emotion, hetero-homo, normal-deviant, etc.). In recent decades, however, cultural and queer theorists have argued that this organization of the world is reductive and inherently biased, since one side is always privileged and considered ideal, i.e., male, white, West, logic, hetero, and normal. Queer theorists argue that sexual/gender binaries fail to capture the complexities of human identity, e.g., people who are pansexual, transgender, asexual, intersex, etc. In addition to using "queer"[6] to stand in for identities outside of traditional sexual/gender binaries, some scholars and activists self-identify as "queer" to reject reductive labeling.

Queer theories work to deconstruct heteronormativity (the belief that male-female relationships are natural or right) and the assumption that "male" and "female" are static identities determined at birth. Thus, queer theorists scrutinize cultural practices that reinforce heteronormativity, restrictive identity politics, and LGBTQ-phobic beliefs. These exclusionary practices are learned and enforced through language but also on the level

108 *Julie D. Nelson*

of the body. Our bodies have physiological reactions that respond to our interactions and environments, for example, the warmth of happiness, the tensing of fear, or the cringe of disgust. For those who identify as or appear queer, exclusion and acceptance can be felt and understood in their bodies. Affect theories focus on how bodily feelings and intensities shape our understandings of the world and our interactions in it. Thus, for queer theorists, affect scholarship is useful in probing the feelings, emotions, and desires that make up and marginalize queer identities. For analyzing HB2, queer affect theory is useful not just because queer people were the targets of the legislation but also because it provides a theoretical framework to better conceptualize and probe the experience of queer people in our culture.

Queer Affects

Queer theorists have identified several functions of affect as it relates to queer identities, experiences, and discourses in American culture. These functions—that affects attach, accumulate, create public spaces, and generate public sentiments—are essential for understanding how affects travel and contribute to significant cultural shifts. This section gives a select overview of affect theory as it has been used to advance queer scholarship. Many scholars in the humanities and social sciences have developed affect theories from philosophers like Brian Massumi who strictly defines affect as operating outside of conscious awareness. However, queer theorists tend to rely on psychologist Silvan Tomkins' affect theory, developing a more fluid definition of affect that is often used interchangeably with concepts like feeling, emotion, or mood. Eve Kosofsky Sedgwick was largely responsible for integrating Tomkins' affect theory into queer scholarship, asserting that affects have a kind of freedom: "affects can be, and are, attached to things, people, ideas, sensations, relations, activities, institutions, and any number of other things, including other affects."[7] While some affects—understood broadly to be feelings, responses, or emotions—have cultural histories, they may emerge in surprising ways. For example, negative affects are often attached to painful experiences, but positive affects can also attach to painful experiences. Sedgwick identifies attachment as one of the primary functions of affects, which is important for understanding how particular ideas and bodies carry histories of affective associations with them.

Many queer theorists have written about shame as a common affect attached to queer identity. Shame is directly related to one's identity as it fits—or more likely does not fit—within a particular place and time. When educational, legal, religious, cultural, and media institutions continually reinforce what is "normal," they attach negative affects to nonconforming identities. As Sedgwick describes, "shame is both peculiarly contagious and peculiarly individuating."[8] Shame is unique in marking groups of people as "deviant" and in directing negativity inward, toward oneself. According to Elspeth Probyn, shame shapes how bodies interact and how we understand the social. Also following Tomkins, Probyn suggests shame occurs when interest and joy are taken from someone: "At that moment the sheer disappointment of loss translates into shame that attacks your sense of self: the entrails of who you thought you were are suddenly displayed for all to judge."[9] Attaching shame to queer bodies influences social interaction and how people understand their place in the world. This attachment process can be obvious or subtle, e.g., a stranger scowls in a public bathroom, a social media post uses an antigay slur, the news media covers an LGBTQ hate crime, a physician assumes a patient is cisgender,[10] or a barista uses the wrong pronoun. All of these interactions attach negative affects to one's identity, and they accumulate to shape one's life. Megan Watkins asserts that continued experiences with particular affects can create dispositions that encourage people to act and react in certain ways.[11] Repeated experience with negative affects will begin to shape how one feels, sees oneself, and what s/he believes is possible. Watkins points our attention to a second function of affect: its ability to accumulate, shaping one's sense of self and being in the world.

While many queer affect theories focus on the development of individual queer identity, they also describe how public spaces are similarly created and regulated by affects. Lauren Berlant asserts that public spaces are affective, where cultural divisions and practices work to include some people and keep others out.[12] These divisions and practices are often subtle. For example, even though African Americans are no longer required to use separate water fountains and bathrooms in the U.S., racial segregation is still enforced through contemporary economic, educational, and real estate practices that work to keep African Americans out of affluent white neighborhoods and public spaces. Sara Ahmed argues that "bodies are gendered, sexualized, and raced" by how they are extended into or are restricted within space.[13] Bodies that are welcomed in public spaces are "extended" because they can move freely, without suspicion or challenge to their identities. Ahmed describes, "For bodies that are not extended by the skin of the social, bodily movement is not so easy. Such bodies are stopped, where the stopping is an action that creates its own impress. Who are you? Why are you here? What are you doing?"[14] Questioning people's belonging is a practice that excludes minority groups, implicitly bolstering some identities and not others in public spaces. Through this process, gender nonconforming or queer people are "made socially present as deviant."[15] A third function of affect is its extension and limitation of people's social capacities, through attaching affects to people based on their appearance and perceived identities.

Repeated public affects constitute collective/cultural feelings, similar to what Berlant describes as an "affective public sphere"; in other words, prevalent and routinely expressed feelings and emotions influence public space by connecting some people and not others. In addition to shame inwardly shaping a queer person, fear of queer people is a defining affect in LGBTQ-phobic public sentiments. Ahmed describes "compulsory

110 *Julie D. Nelson*

heterosexuality"[16] as an underlying cultural principle that positions queerness as a threat to the legitimacy of heterosexual life and reproduction.[17] From the Bible to biology textbooks, heterosexuality is purported to be the natural or intended way of being in our culture. The threat of queerness, according to Ahmed, "works to enable some bodies to inhabit and move in public space through restricting the mobility of other bodies to spaces that are enclosed or contained."[18] Compulsory heterosexuality affords cisgendered people the privilege of judging and restricting queer bodies' movement in public spaces, e.g., through explicit legislation like HB2 or in everyday interactions that make queer people feel unwelcome. Many of our contemporary affective public spheres are sustained through digital discourses and networks; thus, it is necessary to scrutinize digital communities as much as geographic ones. The fourth function and cumulative manifestation of affect is generating public sentiments that inform how we understand and interact with other people.

While this brief overview is far from comprehensive in explicating how affects shape public sentiments toward social issues or legislation, it begins to identify some of the main roles affect played in circulating HB2 rhetorics. The many functions of affect (only some of which were detailed here) often work simultaneously; thus, the following section will point to isolated moments when affects played a significant role in the response to HB2. Because affect, by any of its definitions, resists capture and reduction, affective analysis can only ever be approximate, especially done in retrospect. Yet looking for the affects that fueled pro-HB2 rhetorics is necessary for considering its cultural resonance and how we might censure LGBTQ-phobic movements.

Affective Analysis

HB2 is especially rich for analysis, given that it was enforced largely on an affective—and not legal—level. The text of the bill failed to include guidelines that named specific crimes related to the legislation or correlating punishments. Because of this, several of North Carolina's largest police departments admitted they were taking no steps to enforce the bill, citing lack of guidelines and resources to assign officers to patrol bathrooms.[19] Thus, for the year that the bathroom provision of HB2 was in effect, it was largely symbolic—a cultural/collective judgment about the legitimacy and morality of queer bodies in public spaces. Still, the bill was effective in creating an affective public sphere, wherein citizens could feel emboldened to scrutinize bodies, looking for queer or "inappropriately" gendered people. Even if mostly symbolic, the bill implicitly mandated that people publicly dress and act according to traditional expectations for the sex written on their birth certificates.

Because our cultural understanding of the bathroom itself is affectively rooted in feelings of secrecy, vulnerability, and shame, HB2 rhetorics that focus on the bathroom successfully invoke our personal feelings and embarrassments attached to our own bodily functions. We are taught from an early age to keep biological processes like urinating, defecating, and menstruating concealed, upholding notions that they are dirty, foul, or unseemly processes. In the United States, where puritanical principles remain, the public bathroom is a place where privacy is believed to be necessary to maintain modesty and purity. Because our culture hides biological functions,[20] we attach shame to natural bodily processes, and bathrooms become the symbolic representation of our feelings toward our messy, smelly bodies. Thus, the affective history of the bathroom in our culture may intensify the fear some feel about a perceived "threat" entering that space. The "freedom of affects," as Sedgwick calls it, allows them to attach to our own bodily processes, perceptions of others, and public spaces.

The very exercise of publicly declaring one's identity through entering a public bathroom may inspire shame in those who appear to be or are gender nonconforming. Transgender activist Hunter Shafer, who was in high school during HB2, describes what it was like choosing which public bathroom to use early in her transition: "I felt like an outlaw every time I had to pee, as if this natural bodily function were some unforgivable act."[21] Words like "outlaw" and "unforgiveable" capture how negative affects accumulated to make Shafer feel deviant or shameful. Though she was never punished by the law, the affects of HB2 were powerful in shaping how she understood herself and interacted with the world. Shafer describes avoiding public bathrooms as much as possible, denying her biological needs to keep from deciding between "male" or "female." Repeated experiences with affects create dispositions, as Watkins suggests, that in turn extend and restrict one's opportunities.

In addition to attaching negative affects to queer-appearing bodies, pro-HB2 rhetorics relied on two central tropes: "privacy" and "security." Supporters implied that queer people are a threat to both, reviving long-standing LGBTQ-phobic beliefs that queer people are predators, mentally ill, or sexually deviant.[22] In a statement delivered in May 2016, defending the bill, McCrory presents "privacy" as a cherished American value that must be protected: "Our nation is dealing with a very new, complex, and emotional issue: how to balance the expectations of privacy and equality, in one of the most private areas of our lives: restrooms, locker rooms, or public shower facilities."[23] In emphasizing the "most private areas of our lives," McCrory taps into our shared vulnerability and shame about bodily functions, yet the irony remains that the bill lacks guidelines on how protecting privacy will be executed. As McCrory goes on, he attaches fear to an image that will become central to the pro-HB2 campaign: men invading women's bathrooms. Mentioning a similar bill in Houston, Texas, McCrory says, there were "major privacy concerns about males entering female facilitates or females entering male facilities."[24] While simply "entering" a facility does not sound threatening, the purposeful vagueness of "major concerns" allows audience members to imagine the possible transgressions. Despite offering no specific details about the Houston bill, McCrory incites fear of the unknown. Many HB2 supporters translated messages like this into scenarios in which men brazenly invade and assault women in public bathrooms.

Social media was central in spreading fear-inducing slogans and images—championing the "security" that HB2 endorsed. Organizations like Keep NC Safe and NC Values Coalition saturated their websites and social media feeds with slogans like "Men Do Not Belong in Women's Bathrooms, Showers, and Locker Rooms" or "Protect our Privacy: No Men in Women's Locker Rooms." One popular post included an image of a young girl looking into the mirror in a public bathroom with the slogan "Common Sense Bathroom Safety for Women and Children." The most successful pro-HB2 rhetorics ignored questions of gender identity entirely, and instead played into the fear of gender nonconforming people preying on innocent, defenseless women and children. Relying on the affective history attached to queer bodies, these rhetorics shape public sentiments about LGBTQ people. Shafer identifies the heteronormative forces at work in these arguments: "The most vulnerable victims of the law aren't even *all* trans men, women, or non-binary individuals, they're the people who don't directly fit into our idea of what a man or a woman looks like, whatever their identity may be."[25] Regulating people's gender identities, even if only affectively in side glances and social media posts, restricts the movements of queer and "queer-looking" people and condones questioning anyone who does not fit in. This creates public spaces in which some bodies are extended and other are not, as Ahmed describes. McCrory continues to extend the bodies of cis-gendered people by invoking a "common sense" argument in a 2016 campaign commercial: "other folks were actually pushing to make our schools allow boys to use girls' locker rooms and showers. Are we really talking about this? Does the desire to be politically correct outweigh our children's privacy and safety? Not on my watch."[26] Using "really" and "actually," McCrory attempts to cast his opponents' views as absurd and creates a false binary between children's safety and political correctness. The "common sense" argument illustrates how the very existence of queer people threatens heterosexual life, as Ahmed contends. Through viral sharing of pro-HB2 rhetorics, digital affective public spheres grew, propelling the movement and gaining the attention of mainstream media and the general public.

Despite the arguments from many supporters, HB2 is about much more than bathrooms. The bathroom is a symbolic, affective space that many pro-HB2 rhetorics exploit, yet closer analysis reveals how ingrained anti-LGBTQ sentiments are in our culture. Shafer asserts, "While the fight for the trans community's just use of restrooms is urgent and essential, the core issue is the deep-rooted transphobia that lies beneath this 'bathroom bill' controversy. Transphobia resides at the heart of HB2, a bill that appeals to a public still clinging to the gender binary and fearful depictions of those who reside outside of it."[27] The affects attached to HB2 systematically work to shame and promulgate fear toward queer people. As we work to undermine LGBTQ-phobic discourses and rhetorics, we must consider how feelings, emotions, and desires persuade us. Affect theory offers frameworks to recognize how affects accumulate, regulate public spaces, and shape cultural sentiments that define how we understand the world and relate to each other.

Notes

1 In North Carolina, transgender people must undergo sex-reassignment surgery before the state will reissue birth certificates with a change of sex.
2 Anna Brown, "Republicans, Democrats Have Starkly Different Views on Transgender Issues," *Pew Research Center*, November 8, 2017, www.pewresearch.org/fact-tank/2017/11/08/transgender-issues-divide-republicans-and-democrats.
3 Haeyoun Park and Iaryna Mykhyalshyn, "L.G.B.T. People Are More Likely to Be Targets of Hate Crimes Than Any Other Minority Group," *The New York Times,* June 16, 2016, www.nytimes.com/interactive/2016/06/16/us/hate-crimes-against-lgbt.html.
4 For example, viral media trends inciting protests of police brutality, purporting fake news to influence the election, or growing the collective voice of the #MeToo movement.
5 Emery P. Dalesio, "AP Exclusive: Price Tag of North Carolina's LGBT Law: $3.76B," *AP News*, March 27, 2017 https://apnews.com/fa4528580f3e-4a01bb68bcb272f1f0f8/ap-exclusive-bathroom-bill-cost-north-carolina-376b.
6 Hereafter, I use "queer" as an umbrella term to include all nonconforming gender identities and sexualities.
7 Eve Kosofsky Sedgwick, *Touching Feeling: Affect, Pedagogy, Performativity* (Durham, NC: Duke University Press, 2003) 19.
8 Ibid., 36.
9 Elspeth Probyn, *Blush: Faces of Shame* (Minneapolis: University of Minnesota Press, 2005) xii.
10 Cisgender refers to people whose gender identity aligns with their sex assigned at birth.
11 Megan Watkins, "Desiring Recognition, Accumulating Affect," in Melissa Gregg and Gregory J. Seigworth, eds., *The Affect Theory Reader* (Durham, NC: Duke University Press, 2010), 269–285.
12 Lauren Berlant, *The Female Complaint* (Durham, NC: Duke University Press, 2008).
13 Sara Ahmed, *Queer Phenomenology: Orientations, Objects, Others* (Durham, NC: Duke University Press, 2006), 5.
14 Ibid., 139.
15 Ibid., 21.
16 Ibid., 84. Coined by Adrienne Rich, "compulsory heterosexuality" refers to patriarchy's upholding of heterosexuality as natural and necessary.
17 Ibid., 91.
18 Sara Ahmed, *The Cultural Politics of Emotion* (New York: Routledge, 2012), 70.
19 Samantha Michaels, "We Asked Cops How They Plan to Enforce North Carolina's Bathroom Law," *Mother Jones*, April 7, 2016, www.motherjones.com/politics/2016/04/north-carolina-lgbt-bathrooms-hb2-enforcement/.
20 Think, for example, about missing or overly sanitized public discourses about masturbating, menstruating, childbirth, or bowel disorders.

114 *Julie D. Nelson*

21 Hunter Schafer, "Trans Activist Hunter Schafer on Why She's Fighting for Much More than Bathrooms," *Vice*, March 31, 2017, https://i-d.vice.com/en_us/article/43wwzq/trans-activist-hunter-schafer-on-why-shes-fighting-for-much-more-than-bathrooms.
22 Up until the 1970s in the U.S., homosexuality was listed as a mental disorder in the *DSM*.
23 Craig Jarvis, "McCrory Ad Focuses on 'Political Correctness,'" *The News & Observer*, September 7, 2016, www.newsobserver.com/news/politics-government/state-politics/article100347892.html.
24 Ibid.
25 Hunter Schafer, "Trans Activist."
26 Craig Jarvis, "McCrory Ad."
27 Hunter Schafer, "Trans Activist."

Bibliography

Ahmed, Sara. *The Cultural Politics of Emotion*. New York: Routledge, 2012.
———. *Queer Phenomenology: Orientations, Objects, Others*. Durham, NC: Duke University Press, 2006.
Berlant, Lauren. *The Female Complaint*. Durham, NC: Duke University Press, 2008.
Brown, Anna. "Republicans, Democrats Have Starkly Different Views on Transgender Issues." *Pew Research Center*, November 8, 2017. www.pewresearch.org/fact- tank/2017/11/08/transgender-issues-divide-republicans-and-democrats.
Dalesio, Emery P. "AP Exclusive: Price Tag of North Carolina's LGBT Law: $3.76B." *AP News*, March 27, 2017. https://apnews.com/fa4528580f3e4a01bb68bcb272f1f0f8/ap- exclusive-bathroom-bill-cost-north-carolina-376b.
Jarvis, Craig. "McCrory Ad Focuses on 'Political Correctness.'" *The News & Observer*, September 7, 2016. www.newsobserver.com/news/politics-government/state- politics/article100347892.html.
Michaels, Samantha. "We Asked Cops How They Plan to Enforce North Carolina's Bathroom Law." *Mother Jones*, April 7, 2016. www.motherjones.com/politics/2016/04/north- carolina-lgbt-bathrooms-hb2-enforcement/.
Park, Haeyoun, and Iaryna Mykhyalshyn. "L.G.B.T. People Are More Likely to Be Targets of Hate Crimes Than Any Other Minority Group." *The New York Times,* June 16, 2016. www.nytimes.com/interactive/2016/06/16/us/hate-crimes-against-lgbt.html.
Probyn, Elspeth. *Blush: Faces of Shame*. Minneapolis, MN: University of Minnesota Press, 2005.
Schafer, Hunter. "Trans Activist Hunter Schafer on Why She's Fighting for Much More than Bathrooms." *Vice*, March 31, 2017. https://i-d.vice.com/en_us/article/43wwzq/trans- activist-hunter-schafer-on-why-shes-fighting-for-much-more-than-bathrooms.
Sedgwick, Eve Kosofsky. *Touching Feeling: Affect, Pedagogy, Performativity*. Durham, NC: Duke University Press, 2003.
Watkins, Megan. "Desiring Recognition, Accumulating Affect." In *The Affect Theory Reader*, edited by Melissa Gregg and Gregory J. Seigworth, 269–285. Durham, NC: Duke University Press, 2010.

8 How Affect Overrides Fact

Anti-Muslim Politicized Rhetoric in the Post-Truth Era

Lara Lengel and Adam Smidi

Despite an "explosion of writing about affect,"[1] there is a surprising lack of research on affect and Muslims, and on the affective dimension of Islamophobia.[2] This is particularly remarkable given the vast increase of hate crimes and incidents of bias against Muslims in the United States, which, after increasing by 1,600% from 2000 to 2001, surged another 67% from 2014 to 2015, and has continued to rise since.[3]

In their study published in *Journal of Muslim Mental Health*, Mussarat Khan and Kathryn Ecklund argue, "Greater understanding of non-Muslims' affective response to Muslims might be useful information to guide efforts to reduce prejudice toward this group."[4] In response to the need for understanding, the lack of research on affect and Muslims, and the negative essentialism of Islam[5] in affective publics, this study analyzes the role of affect and emotion in rhetorical persuasion in the media concerning Islam, Islamophobia, Arab Americans, and Muslims both within and outside the United States.[6]

We aim to enhance the understanding of the intersections of affect and bias, and focus, specially, on affective resonance, the tendency for people to experience a similar affective response. Given that affective resonance is closely connected to the concept of models of affect circulation, a process of emotional transmission as a social process that, Teresa Bennett argues, "literally gets into the individual,"[7] we analyze, in particular, the impact of post-9/11 anxiety, anger, and fear on affective resonance, the degree to which the impact of the events of September 11, 2001 has continued to intensify and amplify the circulation of affect across communities.[8]

It is important to define and contextualize the phenomenon of affect as it relates to this study. As is evident throughout the various approaches addressed in this volume, there are many types of affect studies situated within three paradigms: first, the paradigm of classical rhetoric; second, cultural studies; and third, neuroscience.[9] Our study is informed by scholarship within the classical rhetoric paradigm, in particular, Plato's reason-emotion binary.[10] It is also informed by research emerging from neuroscientific and psychological approaches, such as the aforementioned study in the *Journal of Muslim Mental Health*.[11] We draw primarily on the

116　*Lara Lengel and Adam Smidi*

cultural studies paradigm, informed by key theorists,[12] critiques of this theoretical work,[13] and the few existing studies of affect and Islam.[14] In particular, Sara Ahmed's groundbreaking book, *The Cultural Politics of Emotion,* and her work on "affective economies" are useful as new methodological strategies for interpreting "the emotionality of texts" that lead to bias against, hatred for, and fear of Muslims as well as contentious topics, most notably international terrorism and the negative effect of immigration, for which Muslims are overwhelmingly blamed.[15]

The connection of affect to biases and anxieties concerning religion is substantial. In *Religious Affects: Animality, Evolution and Power,* Donovan Schaefer illustrates how the "affective turn" in religious studies helps to analyze "religious racialization" of Islamophobia that fuels a range of emotions, from apprehension to rage.[16] Religious conflict, Schaefer argues, is "a collision between embodied affective regimes, rather than a debate between rival worldviews."[17] Here we share two of the numerous examples of how persistent post-9/11 anti-Muslim rhetoric has been used for the past seven years to exacerbate this collision in affective regimes. The first example is Park51, an Islamic cultural center proposed to be built two blocks north of the site of the World Trade Center (WTC) ten years after the catastrophic events in lower Manhattan. Opponents of the center employed anti-Muslim rhetorical persuasion efforts, most notably the power of naming, to intensify the anger about and fear of Park51. Given its track record of anxiety-, fear- and anger-inducing "news,"[18] it is not surprising that Fox commentators first attached the misnomer "Ground Zero mosque" to Park51. Pamela Geller, whose organization, American Freedom Defense Initiative, is a designated hate group by multiple civil rights groups, one of which describes Geller as "the anti-Muslim movement's most visible and flamboyant figurehead,"[19] intensified emotions with her blogs about the "Monster Mosque" to be built in the "Shadow of World Trade Center Islamic Death and Destruction."[20] Analyzing the video blogging of this self-identified "human rights activist," Schaefer describes Geller as crackling "with energy, alive with hate and contempt ... Geller's project turns her very body into an affective vector."[21] The "affective vector," he argues, is inextricably linked with religious essentialism and the mediascapes that amplify the emotional debates about religion. Corporate, partisan media, thus, becomes a site for "production of affects—an economy of hate."[22]

A second example of the intensification of anti-Muslim bias and anxiety is the rhetorical persuasion centered around Sharia law. Around the same time as opposition to Park51, at least 100 anti-Sharia, or "anti-foreign law," bills or state constitutional amendments were introduced.[23] Based on our rhetorical analysis[24] of the bills and amendments, we found they disproportionally targeted Muslims and created a wave of Islamophobia and anti-Muslim fear and anger. The language of most of the anti-Sharia bills emerges from "American Laws for American Courts" sponsored by the American Public Policy Alliance[25] and written by attorney David Yerushalmi. What is particularly compelling to note is that Yerushalmi knew the effort would largely fail, legally. However, getting the bills and amendments passed was not the goal: "If this thing [anti-Sharia bill(s)] passed in every state without any friction, it would not have served its purpose," he said. "The purpose was heuristic–to get people asking this question, 'What is Sharia?'"[26] This question leads to fear of the unknown, confusion, anxiety, indignation, and further questions such as, "Can Sharia law override the U.S. Constitution?" and "Is Islam taking over America?" Answers to these questions are met with opportunities for dis/misinformation rather than occasions for rational debate or presentations of clarifying information such as the key principles of Sharia law—one being that Muslims follow established laws of the nation-states in which they live.[27] Strategic suppression of the fact that Sharia law will never take precedence over federal and state laws is an example of how limiting relevant information and deliberative dialogue about a concern can, in turn, limit the affective responses to it.

How Anti-Muslim Rhetoric Continues to Be Fueled by Affective Responses to 9/11

Most societies and cultural groups, Mai Al-Nakib argues, are "organized around a limited selection of tolerated affects."[28] Out of these tolerated affects, fear tops the list. From authors, to film directors, to psychologists, many concur that the most fundamental and primary affect is fear, and the strongest type of fear is fear of the unknown.[29] While it seems counterintuitive to consider fear as a tolerated affect, fear has been central to dominant mediated and political discourses concerning Islam and Muslims within and outside the United States and fear was unequivocally central to September 11, 2001.[30]

The catastrophic events on what is likely to be one of the most frightening days of our collective lives, caused tremendous affective response. Interestingly, many people, particularly those outside the United States, report that their initial reaction to the first televisual images of 9/11— the smoke billowing out of the WTC North Tower—was of watching a Hollywood horror or action/adventure film.[31] Like a horror film on a tape loop, 9/11 was seared in the world's mind through the incessant news footage of the devastation. Indeed, what Douglas Kellner has called "the most dramatic media spectacle in history,"[32] 9/11 solidified what is likely the most cohesive experience of affective resonance in contemporary history. The ceaseless mediation of 9/11 incited a cycle of emotions that commenced with a jolt of shock and disbelief, evolved to sorrow and grief, and persisted with two of the most sustainable affective responses— anger and fear.[33]

An "affective wave,"[34] an overwhelming collective experience of affective resonance, which began with the fear of the unknown the morning of September 11, quickly led to a rage-centered effort to "smoke out" America's enemies, including the 19 alleged terrorists whose names and faces were released by the Bush administration to the media and the public six days after the catastrophe. Given that the history of the term "affect" can be traced as far back as the seventeenth century, when it was aligned with "desire" or "passion" and opposed to "reason,"[35] it is not surprising that the anger and fear emerging on 9/11 could fuel the vast increase in hate crimes against Muslims in the United States (and elsewhere), the racial profiling, bias against, and stereotyping of persons of other faiths who "appeared" to be Muslims, and the support for government policy and securitization efforts that hurt most citizens to some extent, and Muslims in the United States to the most vicious extent. In their article, "Affective Politics after 9/11," Todd Hall and Andrew Ross note the events of 9/11 "generated an affective wave whose effects can be found in the reactions, choices, political opportunities, and strategies observable in their immediate aftermath, as well as more long-term shifts in the political environment."[36]

Consider, for a moment, that 9/11 never happened. What would the world be like today? Or consider, for example, if the catastrophe was caused by someone other than those individuals and the group identified in the official narrative and solidified in the images of that horrible day. Could the events of 9/11 be viewed afresh, without the media filters that subsequently shaped their interpretation and led to an intense emotion-laden rush to accuse, find blame, and retaliate? For illustration purposes, let's say the persons behind the attacks were a small, rogue element of the Guardia Svizzera Pontificia.[37] How would perceptions of 9/11 be different either within or outside the United States? How would U.S. citizens of Catholic faith be treated? Would there be retaliatory attacks on the Pope or others in Vatican City? Would the individuals and groups who have been demonized in the official narrative be perceived differently? Would the perpetrators of hate crimes and bias incidents target different individuals and groups?

"Historically," Debra Merskin argues, "a combination of (mis)information has worked to construct an enemy image in the popular imagination that has an important function in the maintenance of political power, or hegemony, through ideology."[38] Her work analyzing the construction of Arabs and Muslims as enemies also maintains that "a joining of politics and religion is useful in propagating hegemonic beliefs."[39] Given the widely accepted historical record confirming that numerous global conflicts were fought because of religion, is it possible that all Muslims have been held collectively responsible for 9/11? Further, could holding all Muslims responsible for 9/11 lead to fear and religious bigotry that can incite bias-based legislation and fuel hate crimes?

As these questions are pondered, consider Hall and Ross' suggestion that "affective dynamics shape beliefs, and motivations, but also political-strategic opportunities." These opportunities benefit from the play upon people's emotions which, in turn, "provoke politically advantageous emotional responses"[40] as well as "stimulate emergent collective solidarities"[41] such as the widespread Islamophobia emerging post-9/11.[42] The affective resonance of Islamophobia turned Muslims and Arab Americans "from invisible citizens to visible subjects,"[43] their visibility shaped by the limitations of the mediated discourses that began on 9/11 and have continued since.

Affect and Anti-Muslim Rhetoric in the Post-Truth Era

The waves of anti-Muslim affect since 9/11 have ebbed and flowed. There was a spike during debates about Park51, the push for anti-Sharia legislation, and after the November 13, 2015 murder of 130 persons in Paris for which ISIS took responsibility. One week after the Paris murders, then U.S. presidential candidate Donald Trump stated that there should be a complete ban on Muslims entering the U.S. and breathed new life into the erroneous "dancing Muslims" on 9/11, fanning the flames of anger and disgust that have made Islamophobia thrive since September 2001. Community leaders were quick to refute Trump's claim. For instance, Steven Fulop, Jersey City Mayor, asserted "Trump is plain wrong, and he is shamefully politicizing an emotionally charged issue." Fulop confirmed, "No one in Jersey City cheered on September 11th. We were actually among the first to provide responders to help in lower Manhattan."[44] He also said, "Trump needs to understand that Jersey City will not be part of his hate campaign. Clearly, Trump has memory issues or willfully distorts the truth."[45]

The willful distortion of truth has utility for many elite, who use affective rhetoric to shape perceptions that favor their position of power. In their influential analysis, *Manufacturing Consent*, Herman and Chomsky proposed a propaganda model that predicted that corporate-owned media would consistently produce news content that serves the interests of elitist regimes that control the world's power.[46] They argue that news passes through five filters before it reaches the intended audience. These filters determine what news is newsworthy, how they are covered, and how much coverage they receive. One filter that is particularly relevant to post-truth anti-Muslim rhetoric is that of the common enemy. When *Manufacturing Consent* was first published during the final days of the Cold War period, this filter manifested as anti-communism. In the more recent post-9/11 political climate, anti-communism was replaced by the so-called war on terror as a control mechanism,[47] with the subsequent affective impact of fear of Muslims. The fear mobilizes the dominant culture against the common enemy—the "terrorist"—while demonizing opponents of this rhetoric as unpatriotic or on the same side as the enemy.

Identifying the Manufacture of Affective Resonance: Guidelines for Questioning Post-Truth

Given the manufacture of fear of a common enemy and the polarizing manufacture of hate that fuels the Islamophobia industry, it is evident that media and political rhetoric since 9/11 has caused irrational fear and has led many Americans to equate the horrific acts of 9/11 with the Muslim population as a whole. In addition, 9/11 continues to be used to incite fear and anger as is the case with Trump's use of anti-Muslim rhetoric, particularly that which is based on falsehoods, in his speeches and interviews. Such rhetoric constrains and limits affective responses and privileges those who do not ask difficult questions about 9/11, the "war on terror," or anything critical of dominant politico-religious norms.

To critique how affect is used to incite and perpetuate bias, fear, and anger, we offer some guidelines for asking difficult questions. Engaging in active critical thinking in the post-truth era can start with revisiting confirmed "post-truths" (i.e., falsehoods). One can begin by analyzing the erroneous link of 9/11 to Saddam Hussein and the official lies about Hussein's weapons of mass destruction. In his critiques of Bush's "Axis of Evil" State of the Union address that highlighted a fabricated Al-Qaeda/Hussein nexus, and "endless insinuations about Iraq's weapons of mass destruction," Matthew Sparke assesses the success of this post-truth rhetoric: "[L]ong after the intelligence agencies had dismissed the stories of an Al Qaeda link, and even after the failure to find weapons of mass destruction after the war, nearly 70 percent of Americans still believe that Hussein had been personally involved in the 9/11 attacks."[48]

Revisiting proven fallacies through a rational, critical lens can facilitate questioning the affect-infused rhetoric vital to discursively construct the enemy "Other." Rational, critical thinking is also imperative to understand how basic or primary affects are used as foundational building blocks in the manufacture of an enemy. Primary affects such as fear and anger can incite people to act. The incessant mediated images of enemy faces—Mohammed Atta or Osama Bin Laden or Saddam Hussein—led people to act in a number of ways that supported the military-industrial complex,[49] most notably through enlisting in the U.S. military[50] to fight the enemy they unremittingly viewed on their television screens and covers of print media.

Questioning post-truth also requires a logical, political economy-centered analysis of why leaders lie, engage in fear-mongering, perpetuate the imagined enemy, and what they can gain from doing so.[51] The gains are often suppressed from public awareness, obscured through crony capitalism and corporate tax loopholes. The most glaring example is KBR. Between 2003 and 2013, the company was awarded $39.5 billion in contracts, many of which were "no-bid," for the Iraq war.[52] Until 2007, KBR was a subsidiary of Halliburton, which was also awarded government contracts in Iraq. Between 2000 and 2005, Halliburton made annual payments to its former chief executive, then U.S. Vice President Dick Cheney, who, when CEO of Halliburton, more than doubled the government contracts awarded to his company.[53] Given that the invasion of Iraq, according to Gearóid Ó Tuathail, was made possible by channeling "the public affect unleashed by 9/11,"[54] it is essential to ask questions about who has profited from 9/11 by interrogating who profited from the events, above all, the Iraq war, that politicians claimed were in direct response to 9/11. "The cultural politics of affect," Prys Gruffudd argues, "are indeed powerful forces in the manufacturing of consent for wars."[55]

Questioning post-truth also requires a holistic analysis that puts anger, anxiety, and fear into appropriate perspective. Consider, for instance, the affective politics of the color-coded terrorism Threat Level advisory scale. In his study on the Threat Level scale's capacity to incite affective resonance, Brian Massumi argues, "the affective reality of threat is contagious."[56] Since it was launched in March 2002 by the newly established Department of Homeland Security, the Threat Level scale has never been lowered to Green, which indicates a "low risk of terrorist attacks" or Blue ("general risk of terrorist attacks"). There is no level whatsoever for "no risk of terrorist attacks." Massumi notes, "Insecurity, the spectrum says, is the new normal."[57]

It is useful to put the terror Threat Level scale into perspective. According to reputable sources ranging from the National Safety Council, to the Centers for Disease Control and Prevention and the National Center for Health Statistics, to counter-terrorism analysts, to insurance, people are considerably more likely to be killed by drowning in their bathtub, or by their own furniture, than to be killed by a terrorist.[58] More distressingly, the lifetime risk of being killed in a car accident is 1 in 100. However, there is no affective resonance about the public health crisis of road safety. There is no Threat Level scale for every time we get into a car. Cars, bathtubs, and furniture have never been perceived as enemies, and while sharks could be perceived as "enemies,"[59] their risk is confined to the ocean. Massumi argues, "The alert system was introduced to calibrate the public's anxiety. In the aftermath of 9/11, the public's fearfulness had tended to swing out of control in response to dramatic, but maddeningly vague, government warnings of an impending follow-up attack. The alert system was designed to modulate that fear." Affective resonance, occurring across the "geographical and social differentials" of the United States, brought together a fearful citizenship that fell "into affective attunement."[60] Insecurity, "the new normal," became, as Massumi argues, that became, as Massumi argues, "not so much threatening as threat-generating: threat-o-genic."[61]

Finally, along with questioning the manufacture of threat, critical thinking entails questioning the notion of post-truth and, most crucially, questioning the notion of truth. In this "post-truth" era, it is imperative to ask whether there has ever been an era of truthful rhetoric. Given the close alignment of rhetoric and affect, does what resonates with an

122 *Lara Lengel and Adam Smidi*

audience supersede the pursuit of truth? Questioning post-truth requires more knowledge, for instance, more awareness about Islam, more understanding about political and media discourses about the Middle East and North Africa,[62] and more thoughtful efforts toward interfaith dialogue and community building.[63] Such knowledge can enhance critical thinking about how political rhetoric and corporate media discourses manufacture anti-Muslim sentiment, especially in the United States, and bolsters the affective resonance that materializes as manufactured, politically divisive misinformation, and as self-affirming "news" by deceptive partisan media outlets that have enabled subversion of reason and acceptance of affirmation over accuracy.

Notes

1 Lawrence Grossberg and Bryan G. Behrenshausen. "Cultural Studies and Deleuze-Guattari, Part 2: From Affect to Conjunctures," *Cultural Studies* 30, no. 6 (November 2016): 1001–1028.

2 Lorenz Trein, "Islamophobia Reconsidered: Approaching Emotions, Affects, and Historical Layers of Orientalism in the Study of Religion," *Method and Theory in the Study of Religion* (2017): 1–16, 4.

3 Federal Bureau of Investigation (FBI), "Hate Crime Statistics—2001," www.fbi.gov/about-us/cjis/ucr/hate-crime/2001/hatecrime01.pdf/view?searchterm=hate%20crime%202001; ProPublica, "Documenting Hate," February 2017, https://projects.propublica.org/graphics/hatecrimes/; Southern Poverty Law Center, "Post-Election Incidents Up to 1,372; New Collaboration with ProPublica," February 10, 2017, www.splcenter.org/hatewatch/2017/02/10/post-election-bias-incidents-1372-new-collaboration-propublica/. See, also, Ilir Disha, James C. Cavendish, and Ryan D. King. "Historical Events and Spaces of Hate: Hate Crimes against Arabs and Muslims in Post-9/11 America," *Social Problems* 58, no. 1 (2011): 21–46. In addition, between 2012 and 2015, there was a 253% increase in hate crimes targeting Muslims in Canada. See Amy Minsky, "Hate Crimes against Muslims in Canada Increase 253% Over Four Years. June 13, 2017, https://globalnews.ca/news/3523535/hate-crimes-canada-muslim/.

4 Mussarat Khan and Kathryn Ecklund, "Attitudes toward Muslim Americans Post-9/11," *Journal of Muslim Mental Health* 7, no. 1 (2012), para. 5. https://quod.lib.umich.edu/j/jmmh/10381607.0007.101/--attitudes-toward-muslim-americans-post-911?rgn=main;view=fulltext/.

5 Mehdi Semati, "Communication, Culture, and the Essentialized Islam," *Communication Studies* 62, no. 1 (2011): 113–126, 120.

6 Scholarly interest in Islam has "responded to the obsessions of the U.S. public sphere," Edwards argues, "where the religion is poorly understood and often defined in imprecise or fallacious ways, resulting in inaccurate references to and representations of both Islam and the 'Muslim' or 'Arab' worlds." For instance, "[w]hile not all Arabs are Muslim, and only about one-quarter of all Muslims are Arab, U.S. public discourse has often collapsed the religion and ethnicity through the logics of Orientalism". Brian T. Edwards, "Islam," in *Keywords for American Cultural Studies*, eds. Bruce Burgett and Glenn Hendler (New York: New York University Press, 2014), para 1. http://turing.library.northwestern.edu/login?qurl=http%3A%2F%2Fsearch.

How Affect Overrides Fact   123

credoreference.com%2Fcontent%2Fentry%2Fnyupacs%2Fislam%2F0/. See, also, Edward Said's tremendously influential work, *Orientalism* (London: Routledge and Keagan Paul, 1978).

7 Teresa Brennan, *The Transmission of Affect* (Ithaca, NY: Cornell University Press, 2004), 1. See, also, See Sarah Ahmed, *The Cultural Politics of Emotion*, 2nd ed. (Edinburgh: Edinburgh University Press, 2014).

8 Ana Pais, "Re-Affective the Stage: Affective Resonance as the Function of the Audience," *Humanities* 5, no. 79 (2016), 1–12, particularly pages 3 and 10.

9 See, for instance, Kevin Marinelli, "Three Paradigms of Affect," in this volume.

10 Plato, *Gorgias*, trans. Robin Waterfield (Oxford: Oxford University Press, 1998).

11 See Ivy Tso, Pearl H. Chiu, and Patricia J. Deldin, "Alterations in Affective Processing of Attack Images Following September 11, 2001," *Journal of Traumatic Stress* 24, no. 5 (2011): 538–545. See, also, work in the emerging field of neurotheology, for instance, Andrew Newberg, *Neurotheology: How Science Can Enlighten Us about Spirituality* (New York: Columbia University Press, 2018); Alireza Sayadmansour, "Neurotheology: The Relationship between Brain and Religion," *Iranian Journal of Neurology* 13, no. 1 (2014): 52–55.

12 Cultural studies scholars situate Benedictus (Baruch) de Spinoza (1632–1677), Gilles Deleuze (1925–1995), and Felix Guattari (1930–1992) as central to theorizing on affect. See Benedict de Spinoza, *The Ethics and Other Works*, ed. and trans. Edwin Curley (Princeton, NJ: Princeton University Press, 1994); *Complete Works/Spinoza*, trans. Samuel Shirley and others; ed. Michael L. Morgan (Cambridge/Indianapolis, IN: Hackett Publishing, 2002); Gilles Deleuze and Félix Guattari, *Mille Plateaux* (Paris: Minuit, 1980); tr. as *A Thousand Plateaus: Capitalism and Schizophrenia*, by Brian Massumi (Minneapolis: University of Minnesota Press, 1987); Gilles Deleuze, *Spinoza et le Problème de l'Expression* (Paris: Minuit, 1968); tr. as *Expressionism in Philosophy: Spinoza*, by Martin Joughin (New York: Zone Books, 1990); Gilles Deleuze, *Spinoza: Philosophie Pratique* (Paris: PUF, 1970/1981); tr. as *Spinoza: Practical Philosophy*, by Robert Hurley (San Francisco, CA: City Lights Books, 1988).

13 See, for example, Mai Al-Nakib, "Disjunctive Synthesis: Deleuze and Arab Feminism," *Signs: Journal of Women in Culture and Society* 38, no. 2 (2013): 459–482.

14 Catherine Lutz and Lila Abu-Lughod, *Language and the Politics of Emotion* (Cambridge: Cambridge University Press, 1990); Saba Mahmood, *Politics of Piety: The Islamic Revival and the Feminist Subject* (Princeton, NJ: Princeton University Press, 2005); Saba Mahmood, "Religious Reason and Secular Affect: An Incommensurable Divide?" in *Is Critique Secular? Blasphemy, Injury, and Free Speech*, eds. Talal Asad, Wendy Brown, Judith Butler, and Saba Mahmood (Berkeley: University of California Press, 2009), 64–100.

15 Sara Ahmed, *The Cultural Politics of Emotion*, 2nd ed. (Edinburgh: Edinburgh University Press, 2014), 13; Sara Ahmed, "Affective Economies," *Social Text* 79, 22, no. 2 (2004): 117–139.

16 Donovan Schaefer, *Religious Affects: Animality, Evolution and Power* (Durham, NC: Duke University Press, 2015), 128.

17 Schaefer, 134.

18 See Gregory J. Martin and Ali Yurukoglu, "Bias in Cable News: Persuasion and Polarization," *American Economic Review* 107, no. 9 (2017): 2565–2599; Tobin Smith, "FEAR and Unbalanced: Confessions of a 14-Year Fox News Hitman," *Medium*, May 26, 2017, https://medium.com/@tobinsmith_95851/how-roger-ailes-fox-news-scammed-americas-la-z-boy-cowboys-for-21-years-1996ee4a6b3e/.

19 Southern Poverty Law Center, "Pamela Geller," n.d., www.splcenter.org/fighting-hate/extremist-files/individual/pamela-geller.

20 Cited in Justin Elliot, "How the 'Ground Zero Mosque' Fear Mongering Began," *Salon*, August 16, 2010, www.salon.com/2010/08/16/ground_zero_mosque_origins/.

21 Ibid., 137.

22 Ibid., 138.

23 See, for instance, Yaser Ali, "Sharia and Citizenship—How Islamophobia Is Creating a Second-Class Citizenry in America," *California Law Review* 100, no. 4 (2012): 1027–1068; Sandya Bathija, "Sharia Charade: Politicians Fan Fear to Win Ballot Approval for Ban on Islamic Law," *Church & State* 63, no. 11 (2010): 253–254; Katherine Lemons and Joshua Chambers-Letson, "Rule of Law: Sharia Panic and the US Constitution in the House of Representatives," *Cultural Studies* 28, no. 5–6 (2014): 1048–1077.

24 Adam Smidi and Lara Lengel, "Freedom for Whom? The Contested Terrain of Religious Freedom for Muslims in the United States," in *The Rhetoric of Religious Freedom in the U.S.,* ed. Eric Miller (Lanham, MD: Lexington/Rowman & Littlefield, 2017), 85–99.

25 For more on the American Public Policy Alliance, non-profit organization established in 2009 to recruit lawyers who could serve as legislative sponsors for the anti-Sharia bills, see Carlo A. Pedrioli, "Constructing the Other: U.S. Muslims, Anti-Sharia Law, and the Constitutional Consequences of Volatile Intercultural Rhetoric," *Southern California Interdisciplinary Law Journal* 22 (2012): 65–108.

26 Cited in Smidi and Lengel, 88.

27 For analysis of similar legislation in Canada, see the article of legal scholar, Azeezah Kanji, "Anti-Sharia Hysteria Based on Unfounded Fears: Kanjii. *The Toronto Star*, March 9, 2017, www.thestar.com/opinion/commentary/2017/03/09/anti-sharia-hysteria-based-on-unfounded-fears-kanji.html.

28 Mai Al-Nakib, 466.

29 Nicolas Carleton, "Fear of the Unknown: One Fear to Rule Them All?" *Journal of Anxiety Disorders* 41, 5–21.

30 See, for example, Sara Ahmed, "The Politics of Fear in the Making of Worlds," *International Journal of Qualitative Studies in Education* 16, no. 3 (2003): 377–398; Evelyn Alsultany, *Arabs and Muslims in the Media: Race and Representations after 9/11* (New York: New York University Press, 2012); Evelyn Alsultany, "Arabs and Muslims in the Media after 9/11: Representational Strategies for a 'Postrace' Era," *American Quarterly* 65, no. 1 (2013): 161–169; Ames, Melissa, "Exploding Rhetorics of 9/11: An Approach for Studying the Role That Affect and Emotion Play in Constructing Historical Events," *Pedagogy: Critical Approaches to Teaching Literature, Language, Composition, And Culture* 17, no. 2, 177–202; Muniba Saleem, Sara Prot, Craig A. Anderson, and Anthony F. Lemieux, "Exposure to Muslims in Media and Support for Public Policies Harming Muslims," *Communication Research* 44, no. 6 (2017): 841–869; Cassandra Van Buren, "Critical Analysis of Racist Post-9/11 Web Animations," *Journal of Broadcasting & Electronic Media* 50 (2006): 537–554; Brigitte L. Nacos and Oscar Torres-Reyna, *Fueling Our Fears: Stereotyping, Media Coverage, and Public Opinion of Muslim Americans* (New York: Rowman & Littlefield, 2007); Lawrence Pintak, "Framing the Other: Worldview, Rhetoric and Media Dissonance since 9/11," in *Muslims and the News Media*, eds. Elizabeth Poole and John E. Richardson (London: I.B. Tauris, 2006), 188–198; Kimberly A. Powell, "Framing Islam: An Analysis of U.S. Media Coverage of Terrorism Since 9/11," *Communication Studies* 62 (2011): 90–112; Vit Šisler, "Digital Arabs: Representation in Video Games," *European Journal of Cultural Studies* 11 (2008):

203–220; Khalid Sultan, "Linking Islam with Terrorism: A Review of the Media Framing since 9/11," *Global Media Journal: Pakistan Edition* 9, no. 2 (Fall 2016): 1–10.

31 For more on the affective impact of horror, see Xavier Aldana Reyes, *Horror Film and Affect: Towards a Corporeal Model of Viewership* (London: Routledge, 2016).

32 Douglas Kellner, "9/11, Spectacle of Terror, and Media Manipulation: A Critique of Jihadist and Bush Media Politics," 2003, https://pages.gseis.ucla.edu/faculty/kellner/essays/911terrorspectaclemedia.pdf/.

33 Spinoza, Tompkins, and others, such as Rainer Mühlhoff, have identified "primary" or "basic" affects which include fear, anger, and sadness. Rainer Mühlhoff, "Affective Resonance and Social Interaction," *Phenomenology and the Cognitive Sciences* 14, no. 4 (2015): 1001–1019, 1015. For more on how governmental leaders "manipulate public affective responses to gain support for desired policies, such as mobilizing by 'fear mongering' or manipulating information," see Todd H. Hall and Andrew A.G. Ross, "Affective Politics after 9/11," *International Organization* 69 (Fall 2015): 847–879, 860. See, also, John J. Mearsheimer, *Why Leaders Lie: The Truth about Lying in International Politics* (Oxford: Oxford University Press, 2011).

34 Todd H. Hall and Andrew A. G. Ross, "Affective Politics after 9/11," *International Organization* 69 (Fall 2015): 847–879, 848.

35 *Oxford English Dictionary*, "Affect," https://en.oxforddictionaries.com/definition/affect/.

36 Hall and Ross, 848.

37 Guardia Svizzera Pontificia [Pontifical Swiss Guard] is the army of 135 soldiers, all Catholic Swiss citizens, responsible for the safety of the Pope and Vatican City. The Swiss Guard, founded January 22, 1506 by Pope Julius II, is the oldest continuously serving military unit in the world.

38 Debra Merskin, "The Construction of Arabs as Enemies: Post-September 11 Discourse of George W. Bush." *Mass Communication & Society* 7, no. 2 (2004): 157–175, 158.

39 Merskin, 161.

40 Hall and Ross, 848.

41 Ibid., 860.

42 See, for example, Randa Abdel-Fattah, "Taking Over: The Role of the Emotions in Islamophobia," Religions and Ethics Division, Australian Broadcasting Commission. August 24, 2016, www.abc.net.au/religion/articles/2016/08/24/4525791.htm/; Carmen Aguilera-Carnerero and Abdul Halik Azeez, "'Islamonausea, Not Islamophobia': The Many Faces of Cyber Hate Speech," *Journal of Arab & Muslim Media Research* 9, no. 1 (2016): 21–40; Becky L. Choma, Gordon Hodson and Kimberly Costello, "Intergroup Disgust Sensitivity as a Predictor of Islamophobia: The Modulating Effect of Fear," *Journal of Experimental Social Psychology* 48, no. 2 (2012): 499–506; Martha C. Nussbaum, *The New Religious Intolerance: Overcoming the Politics of Fear in an Anxious Age* (Cambridge, MA: Belknap Press of Harvard University Press, 2013); Hilary Pilkington, "'EDL Angels Stand Beside their Men…Not Behind Them': The Politics of Gender and Sexuality in an Anti-Islam(ist) Movement," *Gender & Education* 29, no. 2 (2017): 238–257; Bram Spruyt and Mark Elchardus, "Are Anti-Muslim Feelings More Widespread than Anti-Foreigner Feelings? Evidence from Two Split-Sample Experiments," *Ethnicities* 12, no. 6 (2012): 800–820.

43 Amaney Jamal and Nadine Naber, *Race and Arab Americans before and after 9/11: From Invisible Citizens to Visible Subjects* (Syracuse: Syracuse University Press, 2007).

44 Cited in Jill Colvin, "Trump Says He Saw People Celebrating 9/11 in New Jersey," *Real Clear Politics*, November 3, 2015, www.realclearpolitics.com/articles/2015/11/23/trump_says_he_saw_people_celebrating_911_in_new_jersey_128820.html/, para. 9.

45 Cited in Colvin, para. 12. See, also, Joanne Palmer, "They Didn't Dance: Jersey City's Mayor Steven Fulop Calls Out Donald Trump," *The Jewish Standard*, November 25, 2015, http://jewishstandard.timesofisrael.com/they-didnt-dance/.

46 Edward S. Herman and Noam Chomsky, *Manufacturing Consent: The Political Economy of the Mass Media* (New York: Pantheon Books, 1988).

47 Edward S. Herman and Noam Chomsky, *Manufacturing Consent: The Political Economy of the Mass Media*, 2nd ed. (New York: Pantheon Books, 2002).

48 Matthew Sparke, *In the Space of Theory: Postfoundational Geographies of the Nation-State*. (Minneapolis: University of Minnesota Press, 2005), 263.

49 An informal alliance of the military and related government departments with defense industries that is said to influence government policy.

50 Monica Davey, "Many Took Arms in Iraq with Images of September 11 Etched in Their Memories," *The New York Times*, April 6, 2003, section B7.

51 For more on how governmental leaders "manipulate public affective responses to gain support for desired policies, such as mobilizing by 'fear mongering' or manipulating information," see Todd H. Hall and Andrew A.G. Ross, "Affective Politics after 9/11," *International Organization* 69 (Fall 2015): 847–879, 860. See, also, John J. Mearsheimer, *Why Leaders Lie: The Truth about Lying in International Politics* (Oxford: Oxford University Press, 2011).

52 See Angelo Young, "And the Winner for the Most Iraq War Contracts Is … KBR, with $39.5 Billion in a Decade," *International Business Times*, March 19, 2013, www.ibtimes.com/winner-most-iraq-war-contracts-kbr-395-billion-decade-1135905/; Anna Fifield, "Contractors Reap $138bn from Iraq War," *Financial Times* (UK), March 18, 2013, www.ft.com/content/7f435f04-8c05-11e2-b001-00144feabdc0/.

53 See Jordi Palou-Loverdos and Leticia Armendáriz, *The Privatization of Warfare, Violence and Private Military & Security Companies: A Factual and Legal Approach to Human Rights Abuses by PMSC in Iraq* (Barcelona: Institute of Active Non-Violence, 2011); Robert Bryce and Julian Borger, "Cheney Is Still Paid by Pentagon Contractor," *The Guardian* (UK), March 12, 2013, www.theguardian.com/world/2003/mar/12/usa.iraq5/.

54 Gearóid Ó Tuathail, "Just Out Looking for a Fight: American Affect and the Invasion of Iraq," *Atipode* 35, no. 5 (2003): 856–870, 857.

55 Prys Gruffudd, "Nationalism," in *Introducing Human Geographies*, 3rd ed., eds. Paul Cloke, Philip Crang and Mark Goodwin (Abington: Routledge, 2005), 556–567, 563.

56 Brian Massumi, "Fear (The Spectrum Said)," *Positions* 13, no. 1 (2005): 31–48, 31.

57 Ibid.

58 Ronald Bailey, "How Scared of Terrorism Should You Be?" *Reason*, September 6, 2011, accessed March 12, 2018, http://reason.com/archives/2011/09/06/how-scared-of-terrorism-should/.

59 Phillip Bump, "Trump Seems to Think That Sharks Are Ocean Terrorists." *The Washington Post*, January 19, 2018, accessed March 1, 2018, www.washingtonpost.com/news/politics/wp/2018/01/19/trump-seems-to-think-that-sharks-are-ocean-terrorists/?utm_term=.6e0eae60bcdb/.

60 Massumi, 34.

How Affect Overrides Fact   127

61 Massumi, "Potential Politics and the Primacy of Preemption," *Theory and Event* 10, no. 2 (2007), doi:10.1353/tae.2007.0066. See, also, Marinelli, "Three Paradigms of Affect," in this volume.

62 See, for example, Victoria Newsom and Lara Lengel, "Framing Messages of Democracy through Social Media: Public Diplomacy 2.0, Gender, and the Middle East and North Africa," *Global Media Journal* 11, no. 21 (2012); Lara Lengel and Victoria Newsom, "Mutable Selves and Digital Reflexivities: Social Media for Social Change in the Middle East and North Africa," *Studies in Symbolic Interaction* 43 (2014): 85–119.

63 See Adam Smidi and Lara Lengel, "The Relevance of Interfaith Community-Building and *Khutab* [خطب] to Counter Islamophobia." Top Paper Award, Spirituality and Communication Division, 103rd Convention of the National Communication Association, Dallas, November 2017; Smidi and Lengel, "Freedom for Whom?"

Bibliography

Abdel-Fattah, Randa. "Taking Over: The Role of the Emotions in Islamophobia." Religions and Ethics Division, Australian Broadcasting Commission. August 24, 2016. www.abc.net.au/religion/articles/2016/08/24/4525791.htm (Accessed March 25, 2018).

Aguilera-Carnerero, Carmen, and Abdul Halik Azeez. "'Islamonausea, Not Islamophobia': The Many Faces of Cyber Hate Speech." *Journal of Arab & Muslim Media Research* 9, no. 1 (2016): 21–40.

Ahmed, Sara. *The Cultural Politics of Emotion*, 2nd ed. Edinburgh: Edinburgh University Press, 2014.

Ahmed, Sara. "Affective Economies." *Social Text* 79, 22, no. 2 (Summer 2004): 117–139.

Al-Nakib, Mai. "Disjunctive Synthesis: Deleuze and Arab Feminism." *Signs: Journal of Women in Culture and Society* 38, no. 2 (Winter 2013): 459–482.

Ali, Yaser. "Sharia and Citizenship—How Islamophobia Is Creating a Second-Class Citizenry in America." *California Law Review* 100, no. 4 (2012): 1027–1068.

Alsultany, Evelyn, *Arabs and Muslims in the Media: Race and Representations after 9/11.* New York: New York University Press, 2012.

Alsultany, Evelyn, "Arabs and Muslims in the Media after 9/11: Representational Strategies for a 'Postrace' Era," *American Quarterly* 65, no. 1 (2013): 161–169.

Ames, Melissa. "Exploding Rhetorics of 9/11: An Approach for Studying the Role That Affect and Emotion Play in Constructing Historical Events." *Pedagogy: Critical Approaches to Teaching Literature, Language, Composition, and Culture* 17, no. 2 (2017): 177–202.

Bailey, Ronald. "How Scared of Terrorism Should You Be?" *Reason*, September 6, 2011. http://reason.com/archives/2011/09/06/how-scared-of-terrorism-should/ (Accessed March 12, 2018).

Bump, Phillip. "Trump Seems to Think That Sharks Are Ocean Terrorists." *The Washington Post*, January 19, 2018. www.washingtonpost.com/news/politics/wp/2018/01/19/trump-seems-to-think-that-sharks-are-ocean-terrorists/?utm_term=.6e0eae60bcdb/ (Accessed March 1, 2018).

Bathija, Sandya. "Sharia Charade: Politicians Fan Fear to Win Ballot Approval for Ban on Islamic Law." *Church & State* 63, no. 11 (2010): 253–254.

Bryce, Robert, and Julian Borger. "Cheney Is Still Paid by Pentagon Contractor." *The Guardian* (UK), March 12, 2013. www.theguardian.com/world/2003/mar/12/usa.iraq5/ (Accessed December 17, 2018).

Choma, Becky L., Gordon Hodson, and Kimberly Costello. "Intergroup Disgust Sensitivity as a Predictor of Islamophobia: The Modulating Effect of Fear." *Journal of Experimental Social Psychology* 48, no. 2 (2012): 499–506.

Davey, Monica. "Many Took Arms in Iraq with Images of September 11 Etched in Their Memories." *The New York Times*, April 6, 2003, section B7.

de Spinoza, Benedict. *The Ethics and Other Works*. Edited and translated by Edwin Curley. Princeton, NJ: Princeton University Press, 1994.

———. *Complete Works/Spinoza*. Translated by Samuel Shirley and others; Edited by Michael L. Morgan. Cambridge/Indianapolis, IN: Hackett Publishing, 2002.

Deleuze, Gilles, and Félix Guattari. *Mille Plateaux*. Paris: Minuit, 1980; Translated by Brian Massumi, as *A Thousand Plateaus: Capitalism and Schizophrenia*. Minneapolis: University of Minnesota Press, 1987.

Deleuze, Gilles. *Spinoza et le Problème de l'Expression*. Paris: Minuit, 1968; Translated, by Martin Joughin, as *Expressionism in Philosophy: Spinoza*. New York: Zone Books, 1990.

———. *Spinoza: Philosophie Pratique*. Paris: PUF, 1970/1981. Translated by Robert Hurley, as *Spinoza: Practical Philosophy*. San Francisco, CA: City Lights Books, 1988.

Donohue, Brian. "Paterson Muslims Struggle to Overcome Stereotypes." *The Star-Ledger,* September 23, 2001. Republished November 20, 2015 and updated November 23, 2015. www.nj.com/news/index.ssf/2015/11/from_the_archives_paterson_muslims_struggle_to_ove.html (Accessed March 27, 2018).

Edwards, Brian T. "Islam." In *Keywords for American Cultural Studies*, edited by Bruce Burgett and Glenn Hendler (New York: New York University Press, 2014), para 1. http://turing.library.northwestern.edu/login?qurl=http%3A%2F%2F/ (Accessed December 15, 2017).

Grossberg, Lawrence, and Bryan G. Behrenshausen. "Cultural Studies and Deleuze-Guattari, Part 2: From Affect to Conjunctures." *Cultural Studies* 30, no. 6 (November 2016): 1001–1028.

Gruffudd, Prys. "Nationalism." In *Introducing Human Geographies*, 3rd ed., edited by Paul Cloke, Philip Crang, and Mark Goodwin, 556–567, Abington: Routledge, 2005.

Hall, Todd H., and Andrew A. G. Ross. "Affective Politics after 9/11." *International Organization* 69 (Fall 2015): 847–879.

Herman, Edward S., and Noam Chomsky. *Manufacturing Consent: The Political Economy of the Mass Media*. New York: Pantheon Books, 1988.

Herman, Edward S., and Noam Chomsky. *Manufacturing Consent: The Political Economy of the Mass Media*, 2nd ed. New York: Pantheon Books, 2002.

Jamal, Amaney, and Nadine Naber. *Race and Arab Americans before and after 9/11: From Invisible Citizens to Visible Subjects*. Syracuse, NY: Syracuse University Press, 2007.

Kellner, Douglas. "9/11, Spectacle of Terror, and Media Manipulation: A Critique of Jihadist and Bush Media Politics." 2003. https://pages.gseis.ucla.edu/faculty/kellner/essays/911terrorspectaclemedia.pdf/ (Accessed December 22, 2017).

Khan, Mussarat, and Kathryn Ecklund. "Attitudes toward Muslim Americans Post-9/11." *Journal of Muslim Mental Health* 7, no. 1 (2012). https://quod.lib.umich.edu/j/jmmh/10381607.0007.101/--attitudes-toward-muslim-americans-post-911?rgn=main;view=fulltext (Accessed March 28, 2018).

Lemons, Katherine, and Joshua Chambers-Letson. "Rule of Law: Sharia Panic and the US Constitution in the House of Representatives." *Cultural Studies* 28, no. 5–6 (2014): 1048–1077.

Lengel, Lara, and Victoria Newsom. "Mutable Selves and Digital Reflexivities: Social Media for Social Change in the Middle East and North Africa." *Studies in Symbolic Interaction* 43 (2014): 85–119.

Lutz, Catherine, and Lila Abu-Lughod. *Language and the Politics of Emotion.* Cambridge: Cambridge University Press, 1990.

Mahmood, Saba. *Politics of Piety: The Islamic Revival and the Feminist Subject.* Princeton, NJ: Princeton University Press, 2005.

Mahmood, Saba. "Religious Reason and Secular Affect: An Incommensurable Divide?" In *Is Critique Secular? Blasphemy, Injury, and Free Speech*, edited by Talal Asad, Wendy Brown, Judith Butler, and Saba Mahmood, 64–100. Berkeley: University of California Press, 2009.

Mansouri, M. Lobo, and A. Johns A. "Addressing the 'Muslim Question.'" *Journal of Muslim Minority Affairs* 35, no. 2 (2015): 165–170.

Marinelli, Kevin. "Three Paradigms of Affect." In *Emotion, Affect, and Rhetorical Persuasion in Mass Communication: Theories and Case Studies,* edited by Lei Zhang and Carlton Clark. New York: Routledge, 2018.

Massumi, Brian. "Fear (The Spectrum Said)." *Positions* 13, no. 1 (2005): 31–48.

Massumi, Brian. "Potential Politics and the Primacy of Preemption." *Theory and Event* 10, no. 2 (2007). doi:10.1353/tae.2007.0066.

Mearsheimer, John J. *Why Leaders Lie: The Truth about Lying in International Politics.* Oxford: Oxford University Press, 2011.

Mosher, Dave, and Skye Gould. "How Likely Are Foreign Terrorists to Kill Americans? The Odds May Surprise You." *Business Insider,* January 31, 2017. www.businessinsider.com/death-risk-statistics-terrorism-disease-accidents-2017-1/ (Accessed March 2, 2018).

Nacos, Brigitte L., and Oscar Torres-Reyna. *Fueling Our Fears: Stereotyping, Media Coverage, and Public Opinion of Muslim Americans.* New York: Rowman & Littlefield, 2007.

Newsom, Victoria, and Lara Lengel. "Framing Messages of Democracy through Social Media: Public Diplomacy 2.0, Gender, and the Middle East and North Africa." *Global Media Journal* 11, no. 21 (2012): 1–18.

Nussbaum, Martha C. *The New Religious Intolerance: Overcoming the Politics of Fear in an Anxious Age.* Cambridge, MA: Belknap Press of Harvard University Press, 2013.

Ó Tuathail, Gearóid. "Just Out Looking for a Fight: American Affect and the Invasion of Iraq." *Atipode* 35, no. 5 (2003): 856–870.

Palmer, Joanne. "They Didn't Dance: Jersey City's Mayor Steven Fulop Calls Out Donald Trump." *The Jewish Standard,* November 25, 2015. http://jewish-standard.timesofisrael.com/they-didnt-dance/ (Accessed December 17, 2017).

Pilkington, Hilary. "'EDL Angels Stand Beside their Men … Not Behind Them': The Politics of Gender and Sexuality in an Anti-Islam(ist) Movement." *Gender & Education* 29, no. 2 (2017): 238–257.

Palou-Loverdos, Jordi, and Leticia Armendáriz. *The Privatization of Warfare, Violence and Private Military & Security Companies: A Factual and Legal Approach to Human Rights Abuses by PMSC in Iraq.* Barcelona: Institute of Active Non-Violence, 2011.

Pintak, Lawrence. "Framing the Other: Worldview, Rhetoric and Media Dissonance since 9/11." In *Muslims and the News Media*, edited by Elizabeth Poole and John E. Richardson, 188–198. London: I.B. Tauris, 2006.

Plato, *Gorgias*. Translated by Robin Waterfield. Oxford: Oxford University Press, 1998.

Powell, K. A. "Framing Islam: An Analysis of U.S. Media Coverage of Terrorism since 9/11." *Communication Studies* 62 (2011): 90–112.

Said, Edward. *Orientalism.* London: Routledge & Kegan Paul, 1978.

Saleem, Muniba, Sara Prot, Craig A. Anderson, and Anthony F. Lemieux. "Exposure to Muslims in Media and Support for Public Policies Harming Muslims." *Communication Research* 44, no. 6 (2017): 841–869.

Schaefer, Donovan. *Religious Affects: Animality, Evolution and Power.* Durham, NC: Duke University Press, 2015.

Šisler, Vit. "Digital Arabs: Representation in Video Games." *European Journal of Cultural Studies* 11 (2008): 203–220.

Smidi, Adam, and Lara Lengel. "Freedom for Whom? The Contested Terrain of Religious Freedom for Muslims in the United States." In *The Rhetoric of Religious Freedom in the U.S.*, edited by Eric Miller, 85–99. Lanham, MD: Lexington/Rowman & Littlefield, 2017.

Smidi, Adam, and Lara Lengel. "The Relevance of Interfaith Community-Building and *Khutab* [خطب] to Counter Islamophobia." Top Paper of the Spirituality and Communication Division at the 103rd Convention of the National Communication Association, Dallas, November 2017.

Sparke, Matthew. *In the Space of Theory: Postfoundational Geographies of the Nation-State.* Minneapolis: University of Minnesota Press, 2005.

Spruyt, Bram, and Mark Elchardus. "Are Anti-Muslim Feelings More Widespread than Anti-Foreigner Feelings? Evidence from Two Split-Sample Experiments." *Ethnicities* 12, no. 6 (2012): 800–820.

Sultan, Khalid. "Linking Islam with Terrorism: A Review of the Media Framing since 9/11." *Global Media Journal: Pakistan Edition* 9, no. 2 (Fall 2016): 1–10.

Trein, Lorenz. "Islamophobia Reconsidered: Approaching Emotions, Affects, and Historical Layers of Orientalism in the Study of Religion." *Method and Theory in the Study of Religion* 29, no. 3 (2017): 1–16.

Van Buren, C. "Critical Analysis of Racist Post-9/11 Web Animations." *Journal of Broadcasting & Electronic Media* 50, no. 3 (2006): 537–554.

Part III
Affect in the Mass Media

9 "Lee's Filling—Tastes Grant!" The Affect of Civil War Archetypes in Beer Commercials

Lewis Knight and Chad Chisholm

American men who "came of age" before the turn of the millennium are targets for beer commercials that use Ulysses S. Grant and Robert E. Lee archetypes as their consumer psychographic constructs. Domestic beer companies heavily rely on the cultural footprint left behind by Grant and Lee when creating advertisements that are designed to link their products with masculine aspirations and old world virtues cherished and coveted by the targeted audience. These allusions to Grant and Lee in beer commercials are intended to produce unconscious affective experiences for the targeted audience in the hopes of guiding their choices as consumers.

Our case study examines three television commercials—Bud Light (Political) Party, Miller High Life, and Dos Equis' The Most Interesting Man—to illustrate the internalized archetypes as affective constructs for specific consumer groups. Grant represents working men (blue-collar archetypes) who hold strong convictions about the nature of community, citizenship, and family. Lee more represents sophisticated professionals (white-collar archetypes) who aspire to a more bourgeois lifestyle. Therefore, the targeted audience does not need to know the historical Grant or Lee in order to identify with the archetypal frames that these men represent.

In the 1980s, there was a renewed interest in the American Civil War that began to bridge over into our media and entertainment culture on a much larger scale than before. From the highly publicized Time-Life book series that began with the volume *Brother Against Brother: The War Begins* (1983)[1] to *North and South* (1985, 1986, and 1994),[2] which remains the seventh-highest rated television series of all time, to Ken Burns' critically acclaimed documentary series *The Civil War* (1990)[3] viewed by nearly 40 million people, and to this day, remains the most-watched documentary ever aired on PBS—the events and personalities from the Civil War began to leap from their historical epoch into contemporary culture, and there they have remained and dominated our subconscious perceptions ever since.

In the 1980s, the appearance of a Civil War-era figure sometimes only served to personify a sense of historical authenticity (if not moments of comic relief), such as the appearance of Abraham Lincoln in the movie

134   *Lewis Knight and Chad Chisholm*

Bill and Ted's Excellent Adventure (1989).[4] However, when it comes to beer commercials, such archetypal frames are far more crucial because Grant and Lee are often archetypes for American men who came of age before the millennium. While the references are not always overt, the Grant/Lee archetypical dynamic often tailors how advertisers pitch their beer products to the different parts of the American market. So how does this work?

In his essay "Grant and Lee: A Study in Contrasts," Bruce Catton conveys how the personal qualities of the two generals became models of ideal behavior for American men. Despite their different views on what constituted their "country," Catton argues that one of the characteristics that the generals shared was that each "saw his fate in terms of the nation's own destiny. As its horizons expanded, so did his. He had, in other words, an acute dollars-and-cents stake in the continued growth and development of his country."[5] These aspirational models for the strong and decisive American male reinforce the self-perception that beer consumers see in themselves.

The historical Ulysses S. Grant was born to much more humble and less-storied origins than his antagonist, Robert E. Lee. Furthermore, aside from being the self-assured and straightforward commander in wartime, Grant failed at almost all other professions he attempted.[6] However, as Catton argues, Grant came to represent a different class of men than his Confederate counterpart. Grant "was one of a body of men who owed reverence and obeisance to no one, who were self-reliant to a fault, who cared hardly anything for the past but who had a sharp eye for the future." According to Catton, their comportment was a result of their steadfast democratic beliefs:

> They stood for democracy, not from any reasoned conclusion about the proper ordering of human society, but simply because they had grown up in the middle of democracy and knew how it worked. Their society might have privileges, but they would be privileges each man had won for himself. Forms and patterns meant nothing. No man was born to anything, except perhaps to a chance to show how far he could rise. Life was competition.[7]

But when it comes to the unconscious appeals that are used in American beer commercials, why do Grant and Lee matter? The success (or sometimes failure) of these beer commercials often turns on the affect that these ads convey in their appeal to their male audiences and their individual social constructs. The lives of Grant and Lee took their place in the ongoing legendarium of American culture because of the values the two Civil War adversaries came to embody, and these commercials likewise draw on these traditions and cultural experiences in order to create similar unconscious emotional responses within their targeted audience in an effort to influence their choice of beer products.

Attitudes or behaviors that become part of ourselves through cultural and aspirational association are considered *internalized archetypes*, which many advertisements use as a persuasive device to shape consumer choice. Beer commercials best illustrate the affective relations between marketers and their consumer dynamic. For our case analysis, we define *affective appeal* as a rhetorical appeal to subconscious values and self-perceptions that have been internalized by the targeted audience. In order to develop these rhetorical triggers, advertisers use the study of psychographics to classify and categorize people according to their personal ambitions and attitudes as part of their marketing research.[8]

Before discussing how the choices of consumers and beer connoisseurs might be shaped by appealing to the Grant and Lee archetypes that exist in our popular culture, we must first establish how the aspirational nature of beer commercials depends on the deliberate use and adaptation of what Umberto Eco called *archetypal frames*. One example that illustrates how "frames" work in these advertisements is the Dos Equis character who is known as "The Most Interesting Man in the World."[9]

When featured in a commercial for Dos Equis, the pitch from the Interesting Man is familiar for many audiences: "I don't always drink beer, but when I do, I prefer Dos Equis. Stay thirsty, my friends." However, what audiences might miss is that the Interesting Man utters his short speech at the end of the advertisement, which comes after a lionizing monologue that proclaims his uniqueness from us. When French actor Augustin Legrand replaced Jonathan Goldsmith as the new Interesting Man, the pattern remained the same (even if the tempo was increased). In a recent Dos Equis commercial, the Interesting Man emerges from a space capsule at a wedding (where there happens to be an elephant), and the monologue proclaims that "he is the kind of man whose eye-contact technically counts as a first date" and "his passing remarks have been turned into screenplays," and so forth.[10]

The extoling adulation at the approach of the hero parallels and mimics the praise Grant received when he walked into a Washington ballroom as the declared savior of the Union, or that Lee received as the victor of Second Manassas and Chancellorsville during his visits to the Confederate capital in Richmond. Like the ancient heralds who walked before the conqueror in the triumphal procession, the Dos Equis narrator proclaims the glorious coming of a hero and draws on all of the appropriate forms and motifs that our culture has come to associate with the modern protagonist who, like Indiana Jones or James Bond, is the refined and accomplished man of the world. Similar to the historical Grant and Lee, the Interesting Man can keep his remarks brief because of the acclamation that goes before him: The Interesting Man speaks only toward the end of each advertisement because the power of his utterance hinges on the monologue that precedes it.

Dos Equis commercials are a pop cultural phenomenon because they contain what Eco, in his essay "*Casablanca*: Cult Movies and Intertextual

136 *Lewis Knight and Chad Chisholm*

Collage," calls *archetypical appeal*. Eco argues that in order for a movie to become a cult classic, it has to "provide a completely furnished world so that its fans can quote characters and episodes as if they were aspects of the fan's private sectarian world, a world about which one can make up quizzes and play trivia games so that the adepts of the sect recognize through each other a shared experience." The archetype of the Interesting Man is a "pre-established and frequently reappearing narrative situation" that Eco insists creates a "vague feeling of a déjà vu" that is important in creating a successful film (or, in this case, commercial) because "everybody yearns to see again" these things, which adds to the success of marketing the product.[11]

Eco identifies what he calls "frames" or situations that are easily identifiable for those who are consumers of film and media. The first type of frame, which Eco refers to as "common frames," are "stereotyped situations" with which the audience identifies—for the 1942 film *Casablanca*, the common frames include the jazz club, the cabaret singer, and the corrupt police officer. The second, "intertextual frames," which are stereotyped situations that the viewer recognizes through an established textual/cinematic history, is what happens when comedies and parodies quote lines out of context from movies such as *Braveheart* ("Freedom"), *Star Wars* ("I am your father"), or *Terminator* ("I'll be back"). Eco argues, "When you don't know how to deal with a story, you put stereotyped situations in it because you know that they … have already worked elsewhere."[12] While many commercials use "common" and "intertextual" frames, what elevates spots such as the Dos Equis' Interesting Man storyline into a cult classic is because it creates a character from a world so real for its consumer base that they are able to dissect the various commercials so that they can remember the quotable lines rather than the entire spot.[13] Indeed, this ability to create an original storyline that is integrated with familiar affective appeals is what makes Dos Equis' Interesting Man series more successful than other commercials that use a similar motif (such as the 2012 Bond-themed commercial by Heineken that used Daniel Craig cameos).

Domestic beer commercials in the United States are likewise full of "frames" and "archetypal appeals." These appeals, which trigger an aspirational affect, seemingly draw from the popular culture of the last 70 years. However, because our American popular culture often focuses on periods and personalities from American history, our past has also helped to shape our media-driven "frames," including the archetypes of Grant and Lee.

For the advertiser, the image and the product, when framed together successfully, begin to achieve a commercial symbiosis—that is, the product and its representative symbol achieve such a close association that they appear as one and the same. But who are these advertising frames intended to reach? Beyond the symbols of Lee and Grant that are based on documented evidence, both are emblematic of the broader warrior archetypes found in other cultures (such as Alexander the Great or Napoleon Bonaparte in European culture). The universality of these American archetypes go beyond these two historical figures: they affect a *hierarchy of influences* that transcends both the men and the time in which they lived. The hierarchy of influences is a psychographic theory that models the underlying forces or influences that guide individuals during their decision-making processes.[14] In other words, our social systems (such as our economically-driven media landscape) and institutions (such as our television programing or commodified information industries) have a subsuming influence over the decisions that we believe we make as individuals, including how we choose the beer we drink.[15]

The Grant and Lee archetypes appeal to this hierarchy of influences because many men aspire to be this warrior hero. As Catton says, in both Lee and Grant "there was an indomitable quality ... the born fighter's refusal to give up as long as he can still remain on his feet and lift his two fists," who nonetheless were able "to turn quickly from war to peace once the fighting was over."[16] Because American men prefer to see themselves in these aspirational figures, advertisers use heroic warrior archetypes such as Lee and Grant, which, in turn, serve as affective psychographics for a diverse number of current beer commercials such as the Bud Light (Political) Party advertisement that appeared during the 2016 Super Bowl and the Miller High Life ad that often appears as a brief web commercial.[17]

The choices of consumers, who might not have consciously used Grant and Lee as models, can also be shaped by appeals when beer commercials become popular culture phenomena. Bud Light and Miller High Life target similar income brackets, but use different affective rhetorical devices to appeal to their Grant and Lee parts of the market. For example, in some ways, The Most Interesting Man is a more modern and internationalized adaptation of the General Lee archetype. Much as the Dos Equis mascot represents the aspirations of their targeted audience to be paragons of refined masculinity, Catton points out that Lee likewise embodied the Lost Cause for those who fought for it:

> In the end, it almost seemed as if the Confederacy fought for Lee; as if he himself was the Confederacy ... the best thing that the way of life for which the Confederacy stood could ever have to offer. He had passed into legend before Appomattox. Thousands of tired, underfed, poorly clothed Confederate soldiers, long since past the simple enthusiasm of the early days of the struggle, somehow considered Lee the symbol of everything for which they had been willing to die. But they could not quite put this feeling into words. If the Lost Cause, sanctified by so much heroism and so many deaths, had a living justification, its justification was General Lee.[18]

Just as those ragged and defiant Confederate soldiers chose Lee to represent all of the principles and beliefs that, as Catton argues, they felt but "could not quite put this feeling into words," the brief "Miller High Life: Bottle

Hero" commercial performs a similar service for the aspirations of their male consumers. Widely used for online advertisements, with its charming music and simple "Welcome to the High Life" message, this beer spot appeals to a very Lee-like sense of premillennium nostalgia. The ad begins with its cabaret-sounding piano and brief yet genteel jingle—"If you've got the time, we've got the beer"—while illustrating a longneck bottle that seems chilled like champagne and yet gives off a candle-like aura.

The advertisement evokes feelings of old charm and southern comfort, but more than this, for the factory or construction worker with a middle-income lifestyle, it is their little step into sheer luxury. Much as some commercials depict a hot bubble bath as a leisurely pleasure when promoting cosmetic products,[19] the High Life commercial is likewise designed to affectively trigger psychographic self-affirmations of its intended audience.[20] More than this, as Catton conveys about Lee, the High Life commercial evokes a sense of leisure not for the privileged person, but of "a class of men with a strong sense of obligation to the community."[21] What Miller seems to say is, our beer is for the community-minded family man who gifts what he earns to others, and thus, a High Life beer at the end of the day is not merely his just dessert: it is his right for fulfilling his obligations to those who depend on him.[22]

However, if the brief and effective Miller High Life spot appeals to a Lee sense of nostalgia and idealism, the affective qualities of other American beer commercials seem to draw on different affective triggers. For example, Budweiser as the "king of beers" uses a different type of psychographic appeal in its Bud Light (Political) Party advertisement that appeared during the 2016 Super Bowl.[23] The Bud Light spot features comedians Seth Rogen and Amy Schumer traveling the country to make stump speeches for their Bud Light Party candidacy. The advertisement features many of the motifs of the 2016 presidential election—appeals to national identity, a sense of togetherness, bold proclamations and then backtracking, and so forth.

However, the genius of the Bud Light Party advertisement is that it relies not just on memes from the election, which would have risked tiring their audience, who by then were already becoming wary of political advertising. Instead, Budweiser makes use of intertextual frames such as bull riding, professional sports, cowboys, national monuments, inspiring music, and other stereotyped situations that their targeted audience would recognize. To return to Umberto Eco's theory, the question is what should the advertisers do when their motif is political but their audience is wary of politics? Once again, the answer is to "put stereotyped situations in it because you know that they ... have already worked elsewhere."[24] Aware of this, the Bud Light Party advertisers draw on a vast repertoire of popular culture that personifies the American double-ethos of endurance and confidence such as recognizable star power, appeals to patriotism, and political motifs such as "my fellow Americans."

For the Bud Light Party producers to do this, they inevitably had to appeal to a broad historical and cinematic history that touches on our American "deep sense of belonging to a national community," and this inevitably led them to draw on the General Grant archetype with themes of unity rather than division and a strong sense of national harmony.[25]

Indeed, these values of democracy, competition, achievement, and individualism are all compacted within the short Bud Light Party commercial. The spot begins with Schumer opening her speech with that familiar form of presidential address, and then, she and Rogen use some intertextual interplay from the script of the 1996 film *Independence Day* to talk about how beer can truly unite a divided nation.[26] The commercial races past a collage of familiar settings for an election year—hard hats and factories, basketball courts and rodeos, bars and farms, all of which culminates in a large rally with fireworks in front of the Lincoln Memorial. The enthroned Lincoln in the background—the president who said his trust in the victor of Vicksburg was "marrow deep"—is a direct affective reference to the Grant archetype.

The Bud Light Party commercial—with its political theme, double entendre, and use of celebrities—is tailor-made to address an audience that matches Catton's description of a General Grant: an audience that sees itself as "self-reliant to a fault" with "reverence and obeisance to no one." These motifs exist in the commercial to create a "preestablished and frequently reappearing narrative situation" that, Eco insists, creates a "vague feeling of a déjà vu."[27] All of this is designed so that the targeted audience—who has already projected into their politics their own "sharp eye for the future," as well as their intuitive sense of self-reliance and "obeisance to no one"—is prompted to make a choice that sounds like, "One Bud Light beer, please."[28] For beer marketers, such a connection between culture and product yields the desired result.

As noted above, despite their opposite views on what constituted their "country," Catton argues that both Grant and Lee saw their fates "in terms of the nation's own destiny." In history, as in legend, the two generals are most remembered both for their zeal for victory and their willingness to concede the end and move on regardless of who won or lost. These two characteristics seemed to have defined both Grant and Lee, and it is their legacy for generations of American men.

In the end, the reunified nation seems to have reciprocated this dedication because each American man was taught to revere and adapt these qualities as his own. Therefore, since both Grant and Lee were competitive, competition became a value for American men. Since both generals desired not just an end to the fighting, but a true spirit of resolve and brotherly assurance, our competitive American men were taught to value good sportsmanship even above victory itself, which has sublimated itself into our present sports culture.

The producers for these commercials appeal to these values in order to trigger an unconscious affect, and they also conversely change the way many of us think about beer. Because of the long-running framing within these commercials, these historical archetypes and beer products might have achieved an unconscious symbiosis for their targeted audience. When an American male who is enchanted by these affective appeals goes to order a beer, he might say, "I feel like a Miller High Life" or "I'll have a Bud Light," but his actual thinking might be more akin to, "I feel like a Robert E. Lee today" or "I'll have a General Grant tonight."

Notes

1 GloopTrekker, "Time Life Civil War Series Commercial," Filmed, 1991. YouTube video, 01:59. Posted May 31, 2010, www.youtube.com/watch?v=I7 wsmeomtzE.

2 Mark Bennett, "John Jakes' Journey to *New York Times* Bestseller List Included Boyhood Years in Terre Haute." *Tribune-Star*, August 11, 2007, www.tribstar. com/news/lifestyles/john-jakes-journey-to-new-york-times-bestseller-list-included/article_8a3877e1-8e78-593d-9de8-b878d396254a.html.

3 Patrick Kevin Day, "PBS to Air Remastered Version of Ken Berns '*The Civil War*,'" *The Los Angeles Times*, April 9, 2015, www.latimes.com/entertainment/tv/showtracker/la-et-st-pbs-to-air-remastered-version-of-ken-burns-the-civil-war-20150409-story.html.

4 While actor Robert V. Barron appears as the cinematic epitome of the lanky, long-faced, Abraham Lincoln, the character in the film does little to convey the personal or political qualities of the historical Lincoln. Director Stephen Herek mostly uses the Lincoln persona for historical affect and anachronistic humor.

5 Bruce Catton, "Grant and Lee: A Study in Contrasts," in *The Norton Reader*, eds. Linda Peterson, John Brereton, Joseph Bizup, Anne Fernald, Melissa Goldthwaite, and Charles Hood, 13th ed. (W.W. Norton and Company, December 2011), 168–173.

6 While there are numerous biographies on the careers of Ulysses S. Grant and Robert E. Lee, the authors found Shelby Foote's three-volume history *The Civil War: A Narrative* (New York: Random House, 1958, 1963, and 1974) very illustrative and detailed concerning the lives of the two men.

7 Catton, "Grant and Lee," 170.

8 Chris Anderson, *The Long Tail: Why the Future of Business is Selling Less of More* (New York: Hyperion e-books, 2008).

9 Michael Brüggemann, "Between Frame Setting and Frame Sending: How Journalists Contribute to News Frames," *Communication Theory* 24, no. 1 (2014): 61–82. doi.org/10.1111/comt.12027.

10 Dos Equis, "The Most Interesting Man in the World Addresses the Elephant in the Room," Filmed, May 2017. YouTube video, 00:32. Posted May 15, 2017, www.youtube.com/watch?v=FX4yPT4BJWk.

11 Umberto Eco, "Casablanca: Cult Movies and Intertextual Collage," in *Modern Criticism and Theory*, eds. David Lodge and Nigel Wood (Harlow: Pearson Education Limited, 2008), 462–465.

12 Ibid., 464.

13 Stephen Hartman, "Class Unconscious: From Dialectical Materialism to Relational Material," *Psychoanalysis, Culture & Society* 10 (2005): 121–137.

14 Pamela J. Shoemaker and Stephen D. Reese, *Mediating the Message in the 21st Century: A Media Sociology Perspective*, 2nd ed. (New York: Routledge 2014).

15 See the Adjusted Model for the Hierarchy of Influences (attached).

16 Catton, "Grant and Lee," 172.

17 *Psychographics* is the defining or profiling of individuals based on a complete analysis of their historical background and current psychosocial situation. Therefore, *affective psychographics* deals with how individuals respond intellectually and emotionally to specific stimuli.

18 Catton, "Grant and Lee," 170.

19 Carol Gilligan, *In a Different Voice: Psychological Theory and Women's Development* (Harvard University Press, 1982).

20 Miller High Life, "Miller High Life: Bottle Hero". Filmed, November 2016. YouTube video, 00:15. Posted November 23, 2016, www.youtube.com/watch?v=zbdHVrrKIcM.

21 Catton, "Grant and Lee," 169.

22 Arielle Emmett, "Whetting the Appetite for Storytelling," *American Journalism Review* (2007).

23 ABC News. "Super Bowl Ad: Amy Schumer, Seth Rogen Join Bud Light Party". Filmed, February 2016. YouTube video, 1:31. Posted February 3, 2016, www.youtube.com/watch?v=gcY4GRXMI2o.

24 Eco, "Casablanca," 462–465.

25 Catton, "Grant and Lee," 170.

26 The lines that Seth Rogen quotes are spoken by President Thomas Whitmore (played by Bill Pullman): "We will not go quietly into the night! We will not vanish without a fight! We're going to live on! We're going to survive! Today we celebrate our Independence Day!" *"Independence Day*: Quotes," IMDB, December 30, 2017, www.imdb.com/title/tt0116629/quotes/?tab=qt&ref_=tt_trv_qu.

27 Eco, "Casablanca," 462–465.

28 Daniel Luria, "Subjectivity and Dialectical Materialism," *Review of Radical Political Economics* (1974).

Bibliography

Anderson, Chris. *The Long Tail: Why the Future of Business Is Selling Less of More.* New York: Hyperion e-books, 2008.

Bennet, Mark. "John Jakes' Journey to New York Times Bestseller List Included Boyhood Years in Terre Haute." *Tribune-Star*, August 11, 2007. www.tribstar.com/news/lifestyles/john-jakes-journey-to-new-york-times-bestseller-list-included/article_8a3877e1-8e78-593d-9de8-b878d396254a.html.

Brüggemann, Michael. "Between Frame Setting and Frame Sending: How Journalists Contribute to News Frames." *Communication Theory* 24, no. 1 (2014): 61–82. doi.org/10.1111/comt.12027.

Catton, Bruce. "Grant and Lee: A Study in Contrasts." In *The Norton Reader*. 13th ed., edited by Linda Peterson, John Brereton, Joseph Bizup, Anne Fernald, Melissa Goldthwaite, and Charles Hood, 168–173. New York: W.W. Norton and Company, December 2011.

Day, Patrick Kevin. "PBS to Air Remastered Version of Ken Berns 'The Civil War.'" *The Los Angeles Times*, April 9, 2015. www.latimes.com/entertainment/tv/showtracker/la-et-st-pbs-to-air-remastered-version-of-ken-burns-the-civil-war-20150409-story.html.

Eco, Umberto. "Casablanca: Cult Movies and Intertextual Collage." In *Modern Criticism and Theory*, edited by David Lodge and Nigel Wood, 462–465. Harlow: Pearson Education Limited, 2008.

Emmett, Arielle. "Whetting the Appetite for Storytelling." *American Journalism Review* 29(6) (2007): 40–41.

Gilligan, Carol. *In a Different Voice: Psychological Theory and Women's Development.* Cambridge, MA: Harvard University Press, 1982.

Hartman, Stephen. "Class Unconscious: From Dialectical Materialism to Relational Material." *Psychoanalysis, Culture & Society* 10 (2005): 121–137.

Luria, Daniel. "Subjectivity and Dialectical Materialism." *Review of Radical Political Economics* 6(3) (1974): 61–68.

Shoemaker, Pamela J., and Stephen D. Reese. *Mediating the Message in the 21st Century: A Media Sociology Perspective.* 2nd ed. New York: Routledge, 2014.

10 Disgusting Rhetorics

"What's the Warts That Could Happen?"

Jaimee Bodtke and George F. (Guy) McHendry, Jr.

In the United States, more than 20 million sexually transmitted infections (STIs) are transferred each year. That means, at any given time, there are more than 110 million existing infections in the United States alone.[1] The Centers for Disease Control and Prevention (CDC) refers to these diseases as "an underestimated opponent in the public health battle" due to the major health and economic consequences STIs have on the United States.[2] This epidemic costs approximately $16 billion in health care costs and can lead to long-term health consequences such as infertility, pelvic inflammatory disease, ectopic pregnancy, and increased risk of HIV transmission.[3] According to the CDC, most new cases of STIs occur in young people for a variety of social and cultural reasons. Peer norms and lack of education influence these high rates, but barriers to testing and treatment remains the biggest indicator of the high STI rates. These barriers include inability to pay for testing or treatment, long wait times for testing, lack of transportation to testing facilities, and embarrassment attached to seeking STI services.[4] These barriers are set upon cultural norms where sex and sexual activity are seen as taboo topics while, at the same time, rape culture excuses men who use sexual violence to violate women's bodies. These cultural factors linger in the background of attempts to respond to STIs.

To curb this epidemic, various prevention efforts are in place in communities across the United States to manage and control the spread of STIs. The CDC called for a strengthening of public health infrastructure, an increase in health care access for underserved populations, and a modernization of surveillance techniques to move toward a better understanding of the burdens of sexually transmitted diseases in terms of physical health and other aspects of one's life.[5] Various education efforts, including but not limited to, billboard campaigns, social media promotions, and public service announcements exist to encourage utilization of this strengthened health infrastructure to improve knowledge of and access to services, as well as increase accuracy of surveillance techniques and efforts. Public health campaigns designed and distributed by community health agencies aim to foster conversation about STIs, encourage people to avoid unsafe sexual activity, and to promote testing and treatment for STIs.

144 *Jaimee Bodtke and George F. (Guy) McHendry, Jr.*

In this chapter, we critique one such campaign—a series of billboards placed around Omaha, Nebraska, designed to raise awareness about STIs. We focus on the Get Checked Omaha (GCO) campaign, which used striking visuals to draw attention to this issue. Using productive criticism (a method of rhetorical criticism that draws out ideological assumptions in a rhetorical artifact), we argue these billboards utilize affective rhetorical appeals of disgust and abjection, promoting feelings of shame, which reify social stigmas around STIs. The remainder of this chapter is divided into five sections: (1) We review public health campaign literature; (2) We describe the GCO campaign; (3) We discuss the ways affect, disgust, and abjection function as anchors for our use of productive criticism; (4) We analyze the campaign's affective rhetorical appeals; and (5) We discuss the social implications of our analysis for future public health campaigns and organizations.

Health Campaign Rhetoric

Numerous studies exist outlining strategies for effective persuasion in public health campaigns. We draw on research that examines how these strategies function and the social implications of these messages.

Strategies for Persuasion

Research examining public health campaigns offers various strategies for campaign design and implementation. Previous research suggests two key attributes for successful campaigns—crafting a message that connects to the audience personally[6] and an eye-catching design that drives viewership.[7] Theories of persuasion, for example, the activation model for information exposure that explains that persuasive messages are effective only when they stimulate enough (but not too much) arousal in the viewer, reinforce these findings.[8]

In the case of public health campaigns related to sexual behavior, advertisers need to reach high-sensation seekers.[9] High-sensation seekers enjoy new and intense experiences and enjoy the dangers associated with risky behavior, including unsafe sex.[10] High-sensation seekers, then, are the most in need of public health campaigns encouraging testing and treatment of STIs. Messages higher in sensation value often include visuals that are graphic in nature and appeal to emotions such as fear, shame, regret, and disgust.[11] Messages making use of shock tactics and including images that are distressing, threatening, and disturbing are common.[12] These graphic messages threaten viewers, hoping to generate fear of risky behaviors and encourage preventative measures.

Fear Appeals in Health & Persuasion

Theories surrounding fear appeals in health promotion campaigns indicate that fear appeals are successful in encouraging individuals to follow or avoid certain behaviors. Specifically, the Health Belief Model suggests that "cues make one feel threatened by the given hazard or disease and then these perceptions of threat should motivate protective behavior responses."[13] The Health Belief Model presents five factors that influence preventative behavior: perceived barriers to the recommended response, perceived benefits of the response, susceptibility to the hazard, severity of the hazard, and cues to action (i.e., billboard campaigns).[14] Persuasive efforts using this model show that preventative behavior is easy to adopt and that not adopting the behavior has severe consequences. Such appeals often revel in appeals to disgust to show the severity of the threat to one's identity as a clean and proper member of society. Conversely, such appeals suggest that those with an STI are unclean, improper, and socially unacceptable.

However, research also shows that public health campaigns that arouse fear are not necessarily effective in preventing or promoting particular behaviors. Shen suggests that public service announcements that arouse fear (through high sensation value and graphic imagery) are ineffective and often create undesired and/or unintended responses.[15] For audience members that are not high-sensation seekers, this intense messaging can cause offense.[16] Noar illustrates this danger clearly, noting it is difficult to "be persuasive without turning off or offending other audiences."[17] The complexities of audiences suggest public health officials and advertising agencies face a difficult rhetorical situation. For example, high-sensation messaging that uses fear appeals may not actually be effective for the target audience of high-sensation seekers. High-sensation seekers often attempt to reduce the affect of these appeals, responding with denial, defensiveness, avoidance, and counterarguments.[18] Arpan et al. suggest public health campaigns that use fear appeals are potentially least effective among individuals with the highest probability of engaging in risky behavior because of the defensiveness that may result in viewing the message.[19] These findings suggest that critics have ample reasons to approach fear appeals with skepticism.

Fear Appeals and Social Stigmas

As we have noted, extant research shows that the value of fear appeals in public health campaigns is contested. Often, the perceived effectiveness of fear appeals on changing or promoting health behaviors outweighs attention to negative social implications and/or dangers of these appeals. Engaging in such appeals also raises issues of power, marginalization, and stigmatization. Displaying negative emotional appeals to an entire community without understanding the consequences of discomfort, shame, guilt, humiliation, anxiety, etc., may be unethical and/or dangerous.[20] Such campaigns may define people with STIs as dishonorable, disgusting, and scary—it is through such rhetorics that social stigmas gain power and force. Or, as Du Pré notes, "One effect of social stigma is that people's

146 *Jaimee Bodtke and George F. (Guy) McHendry, Jr.*

individuality, even their humanity, is overshadowed by the discrediting characteristic."[21] This can even cause individuals to feel too ashamed to seek medical treatment.[22] Using rhetorical appeals of disgust may undermine public health campaigns. We use the GCO campaign as an exemplar of such appeals.

Get Checked Omaha

In Omaha, Nebraska (Douglas County), the rate of STIs is currently at an all-time high—30–50% higher than the national average.[23] Almost 5,000 cases of STIs were reported in Douglas County in 2015. This rate is particularly high for gonorrhea and chlamydia, which have been consistently higher than the national average since 1998.[24]

To combat the alarming rate of STIs, the Adolescent Health Project began in early 2015 with funding from the Women's Fund of Omaha. "The Adolescent Health Project seeks to create sustainable community-wide changes through a research-based, results focused, comprehensive approach that will: (1) increase the sexual knowledge and health of youth and, thereby, (2) decrease the number of youth engaging in risky sexual behavior and the rates of STDs and teen pregnancy."[25] To achieve these goals, the Adolescent Health Project focused on four primary initiatives: advocating for comprehensive sexual education, increasing access to contraception, enhancing capability of STD testing and treatment among area health providers, and launching a media campaign to increase awareness and promote STD testing.[26] GCO, an STI-focused media campaign, is one of the outcomes of this initiative.

GCO promotes the testing and treatment of STIs.[27] The campaign utilizes billboards, public transit posters, social media, and a variety of other forms of advertisement to achieve these goals. Initially, GCO placed three billboards at thirteen locations around high traffic areas of Douglas County. The billboards use a font that looks like infected skin to play on common idioms: "His and Herpes," "What's the Warts That Could Happen," and "Ignorance is Blisters" (Figure 10.1). The painful and disgusting skin is covered in hair, featuring oozing red blisters and warts, representing genital herpes or genital warts. According to Serve Marketing, the advertising agency that designed this campaign, the billboards are "cringe-worthy" and "unconventional" in an effort to increase conversation and promote STI treatment and testing.[28] Our analysis takes up the three billboards in Figure 10.1. We attend to the billboards' visual rhetoric, textual messages, affective rhetorics, and placement in the city of Omaha. Later in this chapter, we argue that these billboards generate forceful rhetorics that draw on affects of disgust and abjection to reinforce social stigmas around STIs. However, first we provide an overview of our critical approach to these billboards by connecting productive criticism and affect.[29]

Figure 10.1 © Serve Marketing. Used with permission.

Affective Rhetorical Criticism

We orient our reading of GCO's rhetorical appeals in the practice of productive criticism. In this section, we define productive criticism and discuss the key concepts we use to anchor our critique (affect, disgust, and abjection).

Productive Criticism

In this chapter, we draw from Ivie's work on productive criticism.[30] Productive criticism "intentionally produces a strategic interpretation, or structure of meaning, that privileges selective interests."[31] Productive criticism recognizes that rhetoric is ideological and tasks critics with making an artifact's politics visible, including how they mute or elide alternative worldviews. This approach obligates a rhetor/rhetorical critic with both analysis and political engagement in their areas of study: "Rather than dissipating scholarly energy in direct political action, productive critics can address the problematics of democratic culture thoughtfully and persuasively, enriching the social imaginary from which political actors may develop better strategies for bridging the human divide."[32] Later in the chapter, we discuss our efforts to share our research with GCO as an ideological intervention based in our critique. We employ productive criticism as a means of activating the concepts of affect, disgust, and the abject in rhetorical criticism.

Affect has emerged as a significant concept in rhetorical criticism and critical/cultural studies. We generate our conceptual basis for affect from the work of French philosopher Gilles Deleuze. Bonta and Protevi argue that Deleuze defines affect as, "the ('active') capacities of a body to act and the ('passive') capacities of a body to be affected or to be acted upon; in other words, what a body can do and what it can undergo."[33] This notion of affect, when bodies are acted upon, illustrates the ways GCO constructs certain bodies as disgusting. Affect is not merely emotion, but also marks a body's belonging to a world of encounters.[34] Affect, "sets the conditions for, and outlasts a particular human expression of emotion."[35] Affects are experiential rhetorics that use, reinforce, and create forceful embodied responses. Deleuze explains, "Something in the world forces us to think ... [to have] ... a fundamental *encounter* ... in a range of affective tones: wonder, love, hatred, suffering."[36] Encounters with affective rhetorics force our bodies into experiencing an experience.

Affective rhetorics are a powerful means by which *othered* bodies are shunned to the margins of society. Ahmed explains that affect allows, "the endless deferral of responsibility for injustice in the present."[37] For example, by emphasizing the negative affects around STIs, we focus on the individual person with the illness and ignore social factors that enable rampant spread of STIs. Rather than focusing on a culture that shames sexual activity, deficient education on *safe* sex, or lack of access to sexual and reproductive health care, individual bodies are targeted and held responsible for these affects. Affect is fundamentally about inclusion and exclusion: "Affect marks a body's *belonging* to a world of encounters."[38] Bodies that do not belong experience disgrace. Ahmed explains, "The subject, in turning away from another and back into itself, is consumed by a feeling of badness that cannot simply be given away or attributed to another."[39] Affects of abjection and disgust are a powerful way to push bodies to the margins.

Abject and Disgust

We are particularly interested in affective rhetorics of abjection and disgust. Bodies are not *naturally* disgusting; while they contain biological elements, our attitudes and judgment about bodies are socially constructed. Bodies are corporeal structures that gain meaning through their encounters in the world in particular historical moments. Cultural rhetorics situate *certain* bodies as desirable and expel *other* bodies as undesirable.[40] For example, different cultures define beauty in a myriad of ways. Examining the ideological work that defines disgust offers a way to understand the power relations used to sort bodies in a variety of cultural contexts.

Abjective rhetorics often function to call out those who produce disorder. The abject, Kristeva implores, "Is thus not lack of cleanliness or health that causes abjection but what disturbs identity, system, order. What does not respect borders, positions, rules."[41] Abjection is powerful because it arouses bodily danger. "Abjection acknowledges it [the body] to be in perpetual danger ... abjection itself is a composite of judgment and affect, of condemnation and yearning, of signs and drives."[42] Abjection affectively moves over the body, compelling collective revulsion to that which interrupts our belief in, and desire for, the purity of our anatomy.

Abjective and disgusting rhetorics marginalize pathologized bodies, casting them to the margins. Ahmed explains, "The body recoils from the object; it pulls away with an intense movement that registers in the pit of the stomach."[43] This intense movement away is the physical manifestation of disgust.[44] Pointedly, "to be disgusted is after all *to be affected by what one has rejected.*"[45] Disgusting bodies are those that should not be touched or encountered. Using appeals that draw on the abject or disgust create a social rupture, severing bodies (in our case, those with STIs) from belonging to the social order.

These appeals are particularly problematic in health campaigns. Wilcox explains, "The presence of the abject reminds us of the precariousness of bodies and subjectivity, and their indebtedness to one another in ways that collapse the distinction between self and body, nature and culture, order and disorder."[46] Affective rhetorics force certain bodies to be socially unacceptable. When the improper and unclean appears in public settings

150 *Jaimee Bodtke and George F. (Guy) McHendry, Jr.*

(e.g., GCO's billboards), viewers apprehend their bodily vulnerability, impelling them to turn away in disgust from the abject. Such campaigns aide in the marginalization of certain bodies and identities.[47] Moreover, associations between disgust and immoral/moral behavior degrade the dignity and humanity of those at the margins.[48] The force of these affects warrants our critical attention, especially when they take form in persuasive public health campaigns. In the next section, we proceed with our analysis via productive criticism, lending critical attention for the ways GCO invents ablest rhetorics via abject and disgust, marginalizing bodies as diseased others.

Get Checked Omaha's Affective Rhetorics

Our analysis unpacks three attributes which generate GCO's affective rhetorics. While there is overlap among these categories, we label them: (1) Design Form & Content, (2) Scale of Presentation, and (3) Abject Danger.

Design Form & Content

The message and type face of three billboards share common visual characteristics, generating affects of abjection and disgust. As discussed earlier, clean and unclean bodies are socially constructed through learned experiences and encounters with the world. The billboards read "His and Herpes," "What's the Warts that Could Happen?" and "Ignorance is Blisters." These phrases emphasize disgust as the bodily outcome of STIs. "Ignorance is blisters" plays on the common idiom, "Ignorance is bliss." The message is clear: if you do not get tested for STIs, you will not know if your body is grotesque.

Another billboard states, "What's the warts that could happen?" This, obviously, is a pun on the phrase "What's the worst that could happen?" The language emphasizes that the worst thing that could happen is contracting a disgusting STI. The infected body becomes the worst imaginable outcome of a sexual encounter. We vociferously question this rhetorical maneuver. As we mention in our introduction, the larger cultural context of sex-based violence where men too often victimize women and where access to reproductive health care is expensive and not always available suggests dire implications for framing STIs in this way. Further, the type face used by GCO intensifies the affective disgust of these slogans.

These slogans both tell and show disgust. Each letter of the slogan is formed to look like skin that is hairy, flaky, discolored, and covered with pus and sores (Figure 10.2). It is unclear where on the body the skin is from and the skin is free of gender markers, but it does contain a variety of hues. Displaying skin in this way decontextualizes it, disembodying the visible effects of STIs and robbing them of the context and lives of people who have STIs. Away from the private places where we usually attribute STIs—the genitals—they are placed openly in close proximity to the

Disgusting Rhetorics 151

Figure 10.2 © Serve Marketing. Used with permission.

public. These sores, blisters, and pus do not affect any specific body's genitals, but rather infect the public's body. This blotchy, diseased skin is captivating and repulsive. The body depicted in these letters has no particular identity other than the sores and pus that cover it—its identity is disgust.

Scale of Presentation

One of the authors of this chapter recalls the following scene:

> In a darkened lecture hall in an introductory biology class, the professor introduces a unit on health and disease. Three-hundred of us gazed upon the enormous projector screen, images of infected genitals replete with blood, pus, and open sores looked back at us. The professor bubbled with pleasure as our bodies audibly groaned. Our ablest-gaze denied these bodies' agency.

We do not use this anecdote to mock this professor, but to call attention to the normalization of displaying taboo bodies in pain as a means of teaching puritanical attitudes around sex. GCO's billboards show bodies with STIs on a grander scale, using the public's visual contact with warts, sores, and pus to generate affective rhetoric—exploiting disgust as a vehicle to show these bodies as abject.

The size of the billboards obligates our gaze—you cannot avoid seeing them. In compelling people to see the fleshy display, we are forced to make contact with STIs. "Disgust is clearly dependent upon contact: it involves a relationship of touch and proximity between the surfaces of bodies and objects."[49] The billboards become part of Omahans' daily commutes. At a stoplight at the intersection of Cuming Street and Saddle Creek Road, "His and Herpes" beckons a glance and forces contact with that which our bodies should not be. This proximity and contact, Ahmed suggests, is the signature of affects of disgust. The fleshy letters, too clever slogans, and enormous display drive disgust in a way that moves bodies with STIs involuntarily to the margins.

Abject Danger

Last, the othering of these bodies intensifies, making our obligated contact with them dangerous—completing the abjections of bodies with STIs. In taking a critical eye to danger here, we do not mean that STIs do not pose health risks to individuals or communities; instead we are critical of using disgust and abjection as an affective frame to *other* people with STIs. These affects reinforce cultural notions by which bodies with STIs are abject. The campaign affectively enables abjection by emphasizing the lurking danger of the public's ignorance: ignorance that your body may, in fact, be disgusting and that your bliss may be blisters. The unavoidable visibility and composition of the adverts violates normative "borders, positions, rules"—essential tenets of abjection.[50] As Kristeva argues, "Abjection acknowledges it to be in perpetual danger ... abjection itself is a composite of judgment and affect, of condemnation and yearning, of signs and drives."[51] STIs become a public threat, but one owned by the individual rather than society. They become a threat, an abject danger. In the face of this danger, the public is obliged to condemn those with STIs, pushing those with abject bodies to the margins. Bodies with STIs are undesirable. The need to expel the danger of STIs gains urgency because the threat lies at the heart of a basic social interaction: the functions and pleasures of sex. "What's the Warts That Could Happen?" is a declarative recognition that desire is linked to danger, a danger that must be repressed and marginalized. GCO utilizes affects of abjection and disgust to shame our desires, creating a grotesque display of bodies with STIs as a signal and warning that your body and your sexual desires need to "Get Checked."

Implications and Conclusions

The goal of our analysis is to explain the social consequences of placing these campaigns in the community. We argue that the fear appeals used by GCO, when viewed in their ideological context, marginalize people with STIs and warrant our critical analysis. This conclusion is drawn based on our analysis that suggests that in viewing this campaign, one's identity as "clean," "healthy," and "normal" is compromised and that this process marginalizes people who contract STIs. People with STIs are stigmatized because their infection overshadows their individuality and humanity.[52] These depictions are not natural, but cultural. Berger argues, "You painted a naked woman because you enjoyed looking at her, you put a mirror in her hand and you called the painting Vanity, thus morally condemning the woman whose nakedness you had depicted for your own pleasure."[53] GCO painted people with STIs as fleshy pus-filled sores, condemning them to scorn and abjection.

Productive criticism suggests that rhetorical criticism should be tied to advocacy and social intervention—we take that obligation seriously. After conducting our analysis, we discussed these findings with GCO, the organization responsible for this particular public health campaign. Over 90 minutes at their office, we participated in an open discussion about ways to advance their rhetorical appeals without affects of disgust and abjection. Representatives from the organization were receptive, and many shared our concerns about the negative social consequences these billboards fostered. Since the release of this campaign, GCO has created a new campaign, this time using friendly cartoon characters to represent different STIs. They hope this new campaign, among others, will encourage members of the community to get tested for STIs by providing more education and making STIs seem approachable instead of disgusting. This turn is an important consequence of our research. Based on our analysis, we argue that when designing public health campaigns, especially those that are focused on taboo or stigmatized issues, health promoters should take care not to target a particular subgroup of people. We argue that using disgust as a fear appeal is unethical because of the societal cost and implications it has for particular groups of individuals. Creating shame and stigma around a particular topic is unnecessary and counterproductive to the goal of many public health campaigns. By reflecting on these negative features, however, we see the potential power of rhetoric in public health campaigns to foster more positive feelings about taboo topics in an audience, promote awareness and acceptance of specific groups of people, and increase levels of comfort of communication about particular topics and participation in positive health behaviors.

Notes

1 CDC, "2015 STD Surveillance Report," Centers for Disease Control and Prevention. Last Modified October 2016. Accessed December 3, 2017, www.cdc.gov/std/stats15/std-surveillance-2015-print.pdf.
2 Ibid., v.
3 Ibid.; K. Owusu-Edusei, Jr et al., "The Estimated Direct Medical Cost of Selected Sexually Transmitted Infections in the United States, 2008," *Sexually Transmitted Diseases* 40, no. 3 (March 2013).
4 CDC, "2015 STD Surveillance," Centers for Disease Control and Prevention.
5 Ibid.
6 Seth M. Noar et al., "Assessing the Relationship between Perceived Message Sensation Value and Perceived Message Effectiveness: Analysis of PSAs from an Effective Campaign," *Communication Studies* 61, no. 1 (February/March 2010).

7 Adam S. Richards, "Predicting Attitude toward Methamphetamine Use: The Role of Antidrug Campaign Exposure and Conversations about Meth in Montana," *Health Communication* 29 (2014).
8 Athena Du Pré, *Communicating about Health: Current Issues and Perspectives*, 4th ed. (New York: Oxford University Press, 2014).
9 Noar et al., "Assessing the Relationship."
10 Du Pré, *Communicating about Health*.
11 Deborah Lupton, "The Pedagogy of Disgust: The Ethical, Moral, and Political Implications of Using Disgust in Public Health Campaigns," *Critical Public Health* 25, no. 1 (2015); Lijiang Shen, "The Effectiveness of Empathy-versus Fear-Arousing Antismoking PSAs," *Health Communication* 26, no. 5 (March 2011).
12 Lupton, "The Pedagogy of Disgust."
13 Kim Witte et al., "Testing the Health Belief Model in a Field Study to Promote Bicycle Safety Helmets," *Communication Research* 20, no. 4 (August 1993), 565.
14 Ibid.
15 Shen, "The Effectiveness of Empathy versus Fear."
16 Du Pré, *Communicating about Health*.
17 Noar et al., "Assessing the Relationship," 42.
18 Shen, "The Effectiveness of Empathy versus Fear."
19 Laura M. Arpan, Young Sun Lee, and Zihan Wang, "Integrating Self-Affirmation with Health Risk Messages: Effects on Message Evaluation and Response," *Health Communication* 32, no. 2 (2017).
20 Lupton, "The Pedagogy of Disgust."
21 Du Pré, *Communicating about Health*, 179.
22 Ibid.
23 Serve Marketing, "New STD Campaign in Omaha Will Make Your Skin Crawl," Serve Marketing. Accessed November 29, 2017, http://servemarketing.org/new-std-campaign-in-omaha-will-make-your-skin-crawl/.
24 Get Checked Omaha, "STDs in Omaha," Get Checked Omaha. Accessed December 29, 2017, www.getcheckedomaha.com/stds-in-omaha/.
25 Women's Fund of Omaha, "Adolescent Health Project," Women's Fund of Omaha. Accessed December 29, 2017, www.omahawomensfund.org/leading-change/adolescent-health-project/.
26 Ibid.
27 Serve Marketing, "New STD Campaign," Serve Marketing.
28 Ibid.
29 Ibid.
30 Robert L. Ivie, "Productive Criticism," *Quarterly Journal of Speech* 81, no. 1 (February 1, 1995); Robert L. Ivie, "Productive Criticism Then and Now," *American Communication Journal* 4, no. 3 (Spring 2001).
31 Ivie, "Productive Criticism," 2.
32 Ivie, "Then and Now," 4.
33 Mark Bonta and John Protevi, *Deleuze and Geophilosophy: A Guide and Glossary* (Edinburgh, Scotland: Edinburgh University Press, 2004), 49.
34 Gregory J. Seigworth and Melissa Gregg, "An Inventory of Shimmers," in *The Affect Theory Reader,* eds. Melissa Gregg and Gregory J. Seigworth (Durham, NC: Duke University Press, 2010).
35 Elena Del Rio, *Deleuze and the Cinemas of Performance: Powers of Affection* (Edinburgh, Scotland: Edinburgh University Press, 2008), 10.
36 Gilles Deleuze, *Difference and Repetition*, trans. Paul Patton (New York: Columbia University Press, 1994), 139.

37 Sara Ahmed, *Cultural Politics of Emotion*, 2nd ed. (New York: Routledge, 2015), 120.
38 Seigworth and Gregg, "An Inventory," 2.
39 Ahmed, *Cultural Politics*, 104.
40 Monica J. Casper and Lisa Jean Moore, *Missing Bodies: The Politics of Visibility* (New York: New York University Press, 2009).
41 Ibid., 4.
42 Ibid., 9–10.
43 Ahmed, *Cultural Politics*, 86.
44 Ibid., 85.
45 Ibid., 86.
46 Lauren B. Wilcox, *Bodies of Violence: Theorizing Embodied Subjects in International Relations* (New York: Oxford University Press, 2015), 85.
47 Gary D. Sherman and Jonathan Haidt, "Cuteness and Disgust: The Humanizing and Dehumanizing Effects of Emotion," *Emotion Review* 3, no. 3 (July 2011).
48 Bieke David and Bunmi O. Olatunji, "The Effect of Digust Conditioning and Disgust Sensitivity on Appraisals of Moral Transgressions," *Personality and Individual Differences* 50, no. 7 (May 2011); E. J. Horberg et al., "Disgust and the Moralization of Purity," *Journal of Personality and Social Psychology* 97, no. 6 (2009); Ibid.
49 Ahmed, *Cultural Politics*, 84.
50 Kristeva, *Powers of Horror*, 4.
51 Ibid., 9–10.
52 Du Pré, *Communicating about Health*, 179.
53 John Berger, *Ways of Seeing* (London, England: Penguin Books, 1972), 51.

Bibliography

Ahmed, Sara. *Cultural Politics of Emotion*. 2nd ed. New York: Routledge, 2015.
———. "Happy Objects." In *The Affect Theory Reader*, edited by Melissa Gregg and Gregory J. Seigworth, 29–51. Durham, NC: Duke University Press, 2010.
Alonso, Leticia Pérez. "Frida Kahlo and the Improper/Unclean: Toward the Condition of Abjection." *Women's Studies* 43 (2014): 407–424.
Arpan, Laura M., Young Sun Lee, and Zihan Wang. "Integrating Self-Affirmation with Health Risk Messages: Effects on Message Evaluation and Response." *Health Communication* 32, no. 2 (2017): 189–199.
Berger, John. *Ways of Seeing*. London, England: Penguin Books, 1972.
Bonta, Mark, and John Protevi. *Deleuze and Geophilosophy: A Guide and Glossary*. Edinburgh, Scotland: Edinburgh University Press, 2004.
Casper, Monica J., and Lisa Jean Moore. *Missing Bodies: The Politics of Visibility*. New York: New York University Press, 2009.
CDC. "2015 STD Surveillance Report." Centers for Disease Control and Prevention. Last Modified October 2016. www.cdc.gov/std/stats15/std-surveillance-2015-print.pdf (Accessed December 3, 2017).
David, Bieke, and Bunmi O. Olatunji. "The Effect of Digust Conditioning and Disgust Sensitivity on Appraisals of Moral Transgressions." *Personality and Individual Differences* 50, no. 7 (May 2011): 1142–1146.
Deleuze, Gilles. *Difference and Repetition*. Translated by Paul Patton. New York: Columbia University Press, 1994.

156   *Jaimee Bodtke and George F. (Guy) McHendry, Jr.*

Deleuze, Gilles, and Félix Guattari. *Anti-Oedipus.* Translated by Robert Hurley, Seem Mark, and Helen R. Lane. Minneapolis: University of Minnesota Press, 1983.

———. *A Thousand Plateaus: Capitalism and Schizophrenia.* Translated by Brian Massumi. Minneapolis: University of Minnesota Press, 1987.

Del Rio, Elena. *Deleuze and the Cinemas of Performance: Powers of Affection.* Edinburgh, Scotland: Edinburgh University Press, 2008.

Du Pré, Athena. *Communicating about Health: Current Issues and Perspectives.* 4th ed. New York: Oxford University Press, 2014.

Get Checked Omaha. "STDs in Omaha." Get Checked Omaha. www.get-checkedomaha.com/stds-in-omaha/ (Accessed December 29, 2017).

Haynes, Melissa. "Regulating Abjection: Disgust, Tolerance, and the Politics of *The Cove.*" *English Studies in Canada* 39, no. 1 (March 2013): 27–50.

Horberg, E. J., Christopher Oveis, Dacher Keltner, and Adam B. Cohen. "Disgust and the Moralization of Purity." *Journal of Personality and Social Psychology* 97, no. 6 (2009): 963–976.

Ivie, Robert L. "Productive Criticism." *Quarterly Journal of Speech* 81, no. 1 (February 1, 1995): 2. Accessed December 29, 2017.

———. "Productive Criticism Then and Now." *American Communication Journal* 4, no. 3 (Spring 2001): 1–4. Accessed December 29, 2017.

Kristeva, Julia. *Powers of Horror: An Essay on Abjection.* New York: Columbia University Press, 1982.

Lupton, Deborah. "The Pedagogy of Disgust: The Ethical, Moral, and Political Implications of Using Disgust in Public Health Campaigns." *Critical Public Health* 25, no. 1 (2015): 4–14.

Middleton, Michael, Aaron Hess, Danielle Endres, and Samantha Senda-Cook. *Participatory Critical Rhetoric: Theoretical and Methodological Foundatings for Studying Rhetoric in Situ.* Lanham, MD: Lexington Books, 2015.

Noar, Seth M., Philip Palmgreen, Rick S. Zimmerman, Mia Liza A. Lustria, and Hung-Yi Lu. "Assessing the Relationship between Perceived Message Sensation Value and Perceived Message Effectiveness: Analysis of PSAs from an Effective Campaign." *Communication Studies* 61, no. 1 (February/March 2010): 21–45.

Owusu-Edusei, K., Jr, H. W. Chesson, T. L. Gift, G. Tao, R. Mahajan, M. C. Ocfemia, and C. K. Kent. "The Estimated Direct Medical Cost of Selected Sexually Transmitted Infections in the United States, 2008." *Sexually Transmitted Diseases* 40, no. 3 (March 2013): 197–201.

Richards, Adam S. "Predicting Attitude toward Methamphetamine Use: The Role of Antidrug Campaign Exposure and Conversations about Meth in Montana." *Health Communication* 29 (2014): 124–136.

Seigworth, Gregory J., and Melissa Gregg. "An Inventory of Shimmers." In *The Affect Theory Reader,* edited by Melissa Gregg and Gregory J. Seigworth, 1–25. Durham, NC: Duke University Press, 2010.

Serve Marketing. "New STD Campaign in Omaha Will Make Your Skin Crawl." Serve Marketing. http://servemarketing.org/new-std-campaign-in-omaha-will-make-your-skin-crawl/ (Accessed November 29, 2017).

Shen, Lijiang. "The Effectiveness of Empathy-versus Fear-Arousing Antismoking PSAs." *Health Communication* 26, no. 5 (March 2011): 404–415.

Sherman, Gary D., and Jonathan Haidt. "Cuteness and Disgust: The Humanizing and Dehumanizing Effects of Emotion." *Emotion Review* 3, no. 3 (July 2011): 245–251.

Wilcox, Lauren B. *Bodies of Violence: Theorizing Embodied Subjects in International Relations*. New York: Oxford University Press, 2015.

Witte, Kim, Daniel Stokols, Philip Ituarte, and Margaret Schneider. "Testing the Health Belief Model in a Field Study to Promote Bicycle Safety Helmets." *Communication Research* 20, no. 4 (August 1993): 564–586.

Women's Fund of Omaha. "Adolescent Health Project." Women's Fund of Omaha. www.omahawomensfund.org/leading-change/adolescent-health-project/ (Accessed December 29, 2017).

11 Aestheticizing the Affective Politics of "If You See Something, Say Something"

Charlotte Kent

In late 2002, the New York City Metropolitan Transit Authority launched the "If You See Something, Say Something" advertisement campaign to raise public awareness about potential terrorist threats in response to the devastating 9/11 attack on the World Trade Center (WTC). In the decade following the campaign release, several artists responded to the campaign by titling works with the slogan. That titular affinity positions each work in the context of the United States' war on terror. A critical evaluation of the conceptual art work by Claire Fontaine, painting by David Lyle, and sculptural installation by Doug Beube must consider the political affect of the nation during this time and address how these art works question the established affective realm of the nation. The following introduction provides a history of the slogan in order to establish its affective influence. Three sections then investigate each art work's critique of the campaign's participation in the war on terror and how each introduces new affective possibilities.

The slogan was conceived the day after the attacks by Allen Kay, chairman and chief executive of Korey Key & Partners, a Manhattan-based advertising agency.[1] A year later, the Metropolitan Transit Authority (MTA) of New York asked him to create a message for the public. By January 2003, the slogan blanketed New York City and its success led to adoption by the Department of Homeland Security (DHS). Nevertheless, many criticized it for "fueling paranoia and fear" across the country.[2]

Terrorism is foremost a psychological weapon. The acts of violence are meant to alter daily behaviors by producing fear, anxiety, and paranoia in the target audience.[3] *The Atlantic* confirms that notion: "19 terrorists, using four jetliners as guided missiles, killed 2,977 people—and enveloped the country in fear."[4] Millions, then billions, of dollars went into improving information and security. Brian Jackson explained that "[f]or terrorists who in part were trying to frighten the country into squandering resources out of sheer panic, the country gave them good reason to feel encouraged."[5] Terrorism succeeds when a fear-response occurs that is beyond the actual potential for experiencing a terrorist act.[6] In other words, terrorism works on an affective level.

Theories of affect have many definitions and approaches, in part because affect rejects a unilateral procedure. By refusing the Cartesian dualism of mind and body, affect theory not only proposes that information is embodied but also that context matters. Affect is the "ongoing force of the social taking form"—not as psychology constructs individual interiorities in conflict and relation with one another, but how society presents an evolving response to events.[7] Though the meaning of art often focuses on psychological, sociopolitical, or other intellectual constructions, Simon O'Sullivan in "The Aesthetics of Affect" reiterates notions expressed by Deleuze and Guattari about how art is "a bundle of affects ... waiting to be reactivated by a spectator or participant."[8] It also poses an ethical imperative to reorder "our selves and our relation to the world."[9] The three art works discussed in this paper activate affect to encourage viewers to reflect on the MTA slogan. When few others question what has become a national slogan, these artists do.

Brian Massumi claims that the media did not provide analysis after the 9/11 attacks, but "affect modulation, affective pick-up from the mythical 'man on the street,' followed by affective amplification."[10] The fear that ordinary citizens expressed became the voice that resonated across media. The National Safety Council puts the odds of being killed by a foreign-born terrorist at 1 in 45,808 (with refugee terrorists and illegal immigrant terrorists even less likely).[11] These odds are minuscule compared to heart disease or cancer (both 1 in 7), diabetes (1 in 53), gun violence (1 in 358), or even walking (1 in 672).[12] Irrational fear does not respond to data and statistics, since it stems from a complex set of personal and social experiences.[13]

Massumi addresses the role of media and public perception in *The Politics of Everyday Fear*, but the topic dates back to Gustave le Bon's *The Crowd, a Study of the Popular Mind* from 1895.[14] Gustave le Bon's work influenced Freud, but was also adopted by Hitler and Mussolini, who used the ideas to cultivate the passions of their nations. Edward Bernays, father of the public relations industry, published *Crystallizing Public Opinion* in 1923, offering principles for corporations and governments to influence desired populations "by utilizing appeals to desire and instincts"—a kind of affect manipulation.[15] Neither text focuses on influencing audiences' critical or intellectual faculties, but rather how organizations can cultivate affect and direct it to a specific end. Herbert I. Schiller published *The Mind Managers* in 1973, criticizing the government for its ongoing public "education" efforts through television, "serving essentially as a marketing instrument" for government and corporations.[16] Thus, for over 100 years, governments and businesses have used media to target affect as a means of managing or manipulating the public.[17]

The way to respond to this targeting of affect is not to deny affect, reaching toward some hyperintellectual, critical discourse with the risk of "falling back on rectitude and right judgment."[18] Righteous attitudes reinforce rigid ideas and divisive positions, creating a space for violence. Massumi suggests an "aesthetic politics" that doesn't simply critique

160   *Charlotte Kent*

cultural affects but engages in affective dynamics "to expand the range of affective potential."[19] As the interactive array of mental processes and felt experiences that influence thought and behavior, affective dynamics inherently broaden the affective spectrum and permit new possibilities. These three art projects present how an aesthetic politics enables a more diverse affective realm than the one offered by the campaign.

I

Claire Fontaine, a Paris-based collective created by Fulvio Carnevale and James Thornhill, titled a work after the MTA campaign slogan, "If You See Something, Say Something." By 2005, the public awareness campaign was familiar to audiences who would then connect the two. This relation discloses a case of affective politics. The MTA campaign message cultivated a sense that everyday items could be dangerous. Things like backpacks, gym bags, and briefcases, if abandoned, were not merely forgotten items by absentminded kids or busy professionals. Exposed electrical wiring wasn't simply shoddy public work. Hooded figures were not expressing a fashion preference, but avoiding observation, and were therefore, questionable. Suggestive targets for people's attention became emblematic of the campaign. The backpack, in particular, was prominently featured as a seemingly innocent item that could be deadly.[20]

In this context, Claire Fontaine exhibited a black leather backpack filled with 15 kilograms (just over 33 pounds) of candy in the autumn of 2005 at Reena Spaulings Fine Art. The backpack is a standard school item akin to the Claire Fontaine notebooks that are popular in schools throughout France and from which the artist collective had taken her name.[21] The backpack does not have any aesthetic alterations; it is simply a leather backpack purchased at a store. As a ready-made, the position in a gallery context transforms it into an art work, just as Marcel Duchamp did with the urinal, *Fountain*, in 1917. Using a ready-made, Claire Fontaine presents audiences with an item full of cultural meaning. Audiences accustomed to the backpack as producing fear, concern, or anxiety are given the affective space to reconsider that reaction, the space to remember that backpacks are not only signs of terrorism but also signs of education. The conflation of terrorism and education is problematic partly for eliminating the critical thinking capacity that an education aims to instill and the aspirations that an education cultivates.[22]

In the language of semiotics, the MTA campaign shifted the signifier "black backpack" from an iconic sign into an indexical sign of terrorism. That is, the backpack is no longer simply a backpack, but suggestive of potential violence. No longer simply a means of carrying school supplies, the backpack points to the dangers of homemade bombs and terrorist activity. Claire Fontaine's creative use of the backpack introduces doubt about the signifiers of terrorism adopted culturally through the public awareness campaign messaging. In so doing, this art work broadens viewers' potential experiences.

This is some of the work that affect does. Affect does not deny the logical structures and meaning-making of language and semiotic analyses, but opens alternative experiences of the world. Claire Fontaine's conceptual piece allows viewers to begin to see black backpacks as they are in each instant of encounter. The world is not only a place of knowledge and judgment but also a space for experiencing. Interpreting the world as a system of signs limits possibilities to those that have already been defined. In other words, observing or creating something new is lost if experience has predetermined meanings. Simon O'Sullivan claims that art's affective function is "to switch our intensive register, to reconnect us with the world" not only by offering representations of it but also by creating a "fissure in representation."[23] Claire Fontaine does not simply offer a backpack as a representation of widespread American fear, but creates a fissure in what backpacks represent. In sum, by broadening potential affective engagement with backpacks, Claire Fontaine creates a crack in a ready-made acceptance of what things mean in the world.

II

Doug Beube's 2008 work "Blast, If You See Something, Say Something" also adopted the MTA slogan as a title. His sculptural work using *Encyclopedia Britannica* introduces questions surrounding knowledge, authority, and power that related to contemporary concerns about the MTA and government. The "If You See Something, Say Something" campaign proposes that the government knows how to handle the information it receives from those who say something. It discourages citizen debate and inquiry in favor of direct reporting to authorities. Affect doesn't reject meaning but operates alongside it to provide alternative experiences and Doug Beube's art work invites viewers to revisit what they are told about the world, by the MTA or any authority (Figure 11.1).

Doug Beube's sculptural object is made of 16 cylindrical "books" of the *Encyclopedia Britannica* that have been rolled like scrolls and wired together. Brown wax seals the top and bottom of the cylindrical books, while "black and red wires clamping onto metal hooks embedded in the top of each cylinder," help create the illusion of "improvised explosive device." The work juxtaposes knowledge and danger.[24] It appears to be a bomb, and yet there is no threat except in a potential explosion of knowledge. The use of encyclopedias for this work addresses some underlying issues with the MTA campaign: how does the MTA support its authority? What references are provided for assessing what to see or say?

The MTA campaign included a hotline for the public to report concerns and incidents, made evident in 2008 when new posters claimed that "1,944 New Yorkers saw something and said something." Inquiries

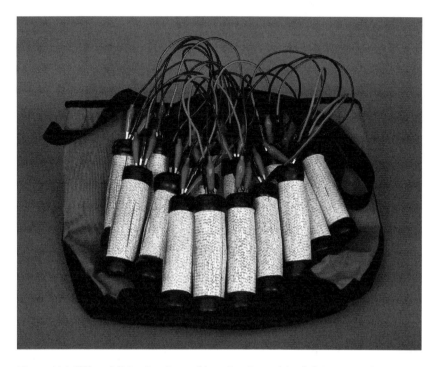

Figure 11.1 "Blast, If You See Something, Say Something" ©Doug Beube (2008).

revealed that the number of New Yorkers claimed in the advertisement had no relation to calls received by the hotline in 2006 (8,999) or 2007 (13,473). Besides some prank calls to the hotline, 816 calls qualified for intelligence investigation in 2006 and 644 in 2007.[25] The numbers, however summed, did not match the advertisement's claim. That kind of confusion, acknowledged by the MTA, led to derision and suspicion. Increased government secrecy during the George W. Bush administration, ongoing terrorist activity nationally and internationally, and frustrations with the ongoing wars in the Middle East reinforced attitudes of doubt toward government authorities. The numbers confusion specifically undermined trust in the MTA campaign and raised questions about whose information was trustworthy.

The *Encyclopedia Britannica* was once every school child's master reference, seen as an objective, democratizing source of knowledge and information, much as Wikipedia is now by eschewing authorities and depending on general population input. Print encyclopedias now derided for their limitations in contrast to the infinite information available online, however, have a history of spreading revolutionary ideas, shattering the status quo. The first encyclopedia compiled by Denis Diderot (published between 1751 and 1766), in principle, shared recent scientific discoveries and new philosophical and aesthetic ideas with all. Though his audience was certainly limited to an educated and reasonably affluent population, the notion that information should be available to any who desired it helped pave the way for revolutions that believed every man should be granted the knowledge and opportunities to determine his own destiny.[26] Though we might not think of encyclopedias as being dangerous, Beube's work questions what references people have for their ideas and how texts become resources for far-removed, violent action.

Using the *Encyclopedia Britannica* also complicates the relationship between education and propaganda. As Bernays explains about the terms in *Crystallizing Public Opinion*: "[t]he advocacy of what we believe is education. The advocacy of what we don't believe is propaganda."[27] The public awareness campaign asks audiences to beware their surroundings and report what they see, not to reflect on the underlying sources for terror, nor to question the terrorist signs identified by the campaign. This discouragement of critical thinking suggests the campaign is less educational in nature and more propagandistic. The inability to explain the campaign claims about the calls to the hotline or the number of prevented attacks led to media shaming and ridicule. Beube explains how the explosion of his encyclopedic IEDs, specifically called *If You See Something, Say Something*, would "strike everyone in the target zone with either wisdom or propaganda," thereby questioning the campaign's position as a trusted authority.[28]

Affect is often misconstrued as mere feelings, but it includes "modes of faculty normally designated as belonging to the mind."[29] Though affect may not have "to do with knowledge or meaning making," thoughtfulness or a desire for knowledge is pertinent to affect.[30] Beube's artwork critiques the MTA's informational campaign, by offering viewers an opportunity to consider what kind of knowledge it disseminates. Through Beube's work, knowledge becomes an affective experience as well as an intellectual one. The choice to trust authority blindly is affective, whereby the culture retreats from inquiry, ignorant of anything beyond the provided messaging. Likewise, accepting intellectual complexities alters affective relations, but that may be necessary before leaping to say something about what one sees.

III

In another case of aesthetic politics, David Lyle's oil on panel painting from 2011 highlights how the MTA campaign created a viewer whose limited knowledge not only perceived objects through a limited scope, but people too. The vigilance encouraged by the MTA campaign isn't necessarily helpful or accurate, because sight is veiled by our beliefs and biases. Anxiety and suspicion of immigrants and strangers has historically been a part of United States culture, despite melting-pot ideals. Brian Michael Jenkins described a "political vigilance that at times borders on paranoia" about newcomers, and

164   *Charlotte Kent*

specified how the nation added "Muslims to the historical company of Free-masons, Catholics, Mormons, Jews, Communists, Irish, Italians, Japanese, and Mexicans" after 9/11.[31] White supremacists, anti-government groups, and various non-Muslim extremists have killed nearly twice the number of people in the United States since September 11, 2001 compared to radical Muslims, reported *The New York Times* in 2015, but young white men have yet to become a feared social group.[32] Lyle's painting startles viewers into questioning what the culture has them identify as potential threats.

Lyle's hyperrealist work portrays five seated Caucasian bus riders placed from the bottom left edge of the painting to the top right. The two men in the upper right-hand corner of the panel are reading newspapers. Their hats and trench coats suggest mid-century American businessmen. A man in a baseball cap and open collar, sitting next to the nearest businessman, peers at his neighbor's newspaper. A tidily coiffed woman wearing a wedding ring, second from the left, has a book in her lap, but is looking down at her open newspaper, the back side of which we see is covered with want ads. Finally, we come to the nearest man. He is wearing a zipped jacket, a striped collar shirt visible beneath it, and is gazing absently in front of him, while holding a bomb with an old-fashioned, double-belled alarm clock. A little over a minute remains before it hits twelve—likely when the bomb will explode. No passenger notices (Figure 11.2).

Though we complain readily in the twenty-first century about every-one's persistent phone gaze, Lyle's work reminds us that people have al-ways found distractions from the boredom of a routine commute and that a more attentive world is a socially constructed nostalgic fantasy. Using black paint and turpentine over a panel covered in white gesso, Lyle re-moves layers of paint to create the complex gray scale effect of a black and white photograph. Using elements of vintage photography cultivates a nostalgia for an earlier, more innocent time, as the dominant culture remembers the 1950s and early 1960s. The sentimental feeling that nostal-gia evokes is ruptured by the subtle presence of the man with the bomb. His presence creates an affective rupture that reminds viewers how visual codes, such as racial familiarity or nostalgic color and lighting, can inhibit our ability to observe carefully and respond accordingly.

The nostalgic color palette and cultural presumptions about Caucasian business people does not prepare viewers to see the man with the ticking bomb, even though the bomb's placement on his lap makes his intentions clear. The MTA campaign emphasized identifying "suspicious" behavior, but media messaging layered this with a focus on certain *populations* rather than behaviors, leading to overt racism.[33] This became evident in calls to the MTA Hotline that often focused on racial groups. Eleven calls in 2017 were about passengers counting on the subway, an act perceived as "om-inous."[34] These passengers were men who "appeared to be Muslim" and whose counting was associated with people boarding and exiting the sub-ways. Investigations discovered that these men were indeed Muslim but

Figure 11.2 "If You See Something, Say Something" ©David Lyle (2011).

were using handheld clicking devices for counting prayers, a modern-day rosary.[35] Lack of knowledge about the devices and an irrational fear of men who "appeared to be Muslim" paved the way for false accusations.

Such racism has been made acceptable by the socially constructed belief that Muslims are likely terrorists. The mass media propagated this message, not the MTA campaign, but the campaign's call for generalized vigilance did not help. Instead of cultivating an acute awareness in public spaces, the slogan allowed audiences to depend on prior beliefs, thereby reinforcing stereotypes. When the majority of domestic terrorism in the United States is perpetrated by far-right extremists without any ties to international terror groups, the media messaging that focused on certain populations created an affect of fear layered with racist anxieties.[36]

Lyle's work skewers the racist notion that Muslims or people of color are the threat. After a terrorist attack, government and citizens seek a target

166   *Charlotte Kent*

to blame and punish. Doing so creates the semblance that danger can be eliminated and control regained. Racism offers an easy solution to generalized or free-floating fear and confusion. Instead of such safety, Lyle's work compels us to remember that anyone can be a terrorist. If anyone can be a terrorist, fear or hate becomes diffuse. There's no focus for the affective intensities of fear, confusion, and anger. Unless someone wants to operate in a paranoiac state of suspicion about everyone, fear must be a response to behavior—not skin tone, nationality, cultural background, age, body size, clothing style, or any other superficial factor. The simplicity of Lyle's painting allows viewers to consider how affective elements like nostalgia can blind us to real dangers.

IV

These artistic efforts question the rhetoric and limited affective responses of the patriotism, vigilance, and caution established by the MTA campaign. Limiting one's affective potential reinforces the efficacy of terrorism. As Siobhan Gorman suggested in *Government Executive*, "the best responses may be to gradually become less afraid of [terrorism]–that is, to prepare for it not only with duct tape but with psychology."[37] The MTA campaign suggests that vigilance can eliminate terrorism, an obviously unrealistic proposition. We can manage risk but not eliminate it. Brian Jackson explains that focusing on risk elimination rather than risk management "undermines efforts to build a society that is resilient to terrorist threats."[38]

Criticism of the government and military is often portrayed as destabilizing security efforts; in 2003, the communications director for the newly formed Department of Homeland Security stressed that, in crisis situations, "the news media's primary responsibility is to disseminate government information, not critique it."[39] Art, on the other hand, has historically critiqued governments and society. Turner's *The Slave Ship* (1840), Picasso's *Guernica* (1937), Rockwell's *The Problem We All Live With* (1964), among many others, addressed government policies and social beliefs. Where the MTA campaign encourages a culture of vigilance, suspicion, and fear, Claire Fontaine, Doug Beube, and David Lyle recommend a more complex experience in relation to terrorism.

These three artworks reveal a wider array of potential affective responses than the rhetoric of the slogan intended. By critiquing the campaign's position, they "expand the range of affective potential" which Massumi desired for a more politically open society.[40] Claire Fontaine reveals how narrowly we perceive threats and the world. Doug Beube opens a space to experience the affective dynamics surrounding knowledge and authority. Lastly, David Lyle offers a clear reminder that cultural assumptions can be false, not only detrimental to social relations but dangerous for safety.

Accepting uncertainty about what we see or think is uncomfortable. A culture that wants to be absolutist will avoid ambiguity and discomfort, but

Aestheticizing the Affective Politics 167

these artists reject the narrow visions of the MTA campaign. Audiences for these art works aren't offered answers about how to fix a society enmeshed in fear and vigilance. The works instead create spaces where audiences can experience new affective relations to the slogan and its culture, and a freedom in thinking and feeling about a world trapped in a war on terror.

Notes

1 Manny Fernandez, "A Phrase for Safety After 9/11 Goes Global," *New York Times*, May 11, 2010, A17, accessed December 21, 2017, www.nytimes.com/2010/05/11/nyregion/11slogan.html. He was partly inspired by the catchiness of the World War II slogan "loose lips sink ships," but knew the content needed to be quite the opposite, since lack of information seemed to be how these men had successfully accomplished the major attack on the United States.

2 Fernandez, "A Phrase for Safety After 9/11 Goes Global," www.nytimes.com/2010/05/11/nyregion/11slogan.html.

3 Curtis D. Boyd, "Terrorism as a Psychological Operation: A Comparative Analysis of the Zionist and the Palestinian Terrorist Campaigns" (Master's Thesis, Naval Post Graduate School, 1994); Robert D. Hanser "Psychological Warfare and Terrorism" *Professional Issues in Criminal Justice* 2, no. 1 (2007): 3–8; Alex Schmid, "Terrorism as Psychological Warfare," *Democracy and Security* 1 (2005): 137–146.

4 Steven Brill, "Is America Any Safer?" *The Atlantic*, September, 2016, www.theatlantic.com/magazine/archive/2016/09/are-we-any-safer/492761/

5 Brian Jackson, "Don't Let Short-Term Urgency Undermine a Long-Term Security Strategy," in *The Long Shadow of 9/11: America's Response to Terrorism*, eds. Brian Michael Jenkins and John Paul Godges (Santa Monica, CA: RAND, 2011), 137.

6 Robert D. Hanser, "Psychological Warfare and Terrorism," *Professional Issues in Criminal Justice* 2, no. 1 (2007): 6.

7 Brian Massumi, *Politics of Affect* (New York, Polity Press, 2015), 205.

8 Simon O'Sullivan, "The Aesthetics of Affect: Thinking Art Beyond Representation," *Angelaki: Journal of Theoretical Humanities* 6, no. 3 (2001): 126.

9 O'Sullivan, "The Aesthetics of Affect: Thinking Art Beyond Representation," 129.

10 Brian Massumi, *Politics of Affect* (New York: Polity Press, 2015), 3.

11 Dave Mosher and Skye Gould, "How Likely Are Foreign Terrorists to Kill Americans?" *Business Insider*, January 31, 2017, www.businessinsider.com/death-risk-statistics-terrorism-disease-accidents-2017-1. A CATO Institute report looking at terrorist activity from 1975 to 2016 found the likelihood of an American dying in a terrorist attack designed by a foreigner to be 1 in 3.6 million. Alex Nowrasteh, "Terrorism and Immigration: A Risk Analysis," *Policy Analysis*, September 13, 2016, no. 798.

12 Mosher and Gould, "How Likely Are Foreign Terrorists to Kill Americans?" They cull data from National Safety Council, National Center for Health Statistics, Alex Nowrasteh at the Cato Institute, Stephen A Nelson at Tulane University, with analyses based on 2013 life expectancy, death statistics, and population.

13 Hanser, "Psychological Warfare and Terrorism," 6.

14 Gustave le Bon, *The Crowd: A Study of the Popular Mind* (Mineola, NY: Dover Publications, 2002). Translator not identified.

15 Edward Bernays, *Crystallizing Public Opinion* (Brooklyn, NY: IG Publishing, 2011).

168   *Charlotte Kent*

16   Herbert L. Schiller, *The Mind Managers* (Boston, MA: Beacon Press, 1973), 42.
17   For more information on the relations between media and persuasion see R. Lance Holbert, "Media Influence as Persuasion," in *The SAGE Handbook of Persuasion: Developments in Theory and Practice*, eds. James Price Dillard and Lijiang Shen (Thousand Oaks, CA: SAGE Publications, 2012), 36–52.
18   Massumi, *Politics of Affect*, 37.
19   Ibid., 36.
20   In 2008, the MTA did an 18 second video about identifying backpacks: www.youtube.com/watch?v=fMqlJbm63QM.
21   The collective selected the name Claire Fontaine to forward a feminine identity where often collectives have been identified as masculine, hence the use of the feminine pronoun.
22   This is not to say that backpacks haven't been used by domestic terrorists: "January 18, 2011, *Spokane, Washington*: Neo-Nazi Kevin William Harpham plants a backpack bomb along the route of a Martin Luther King Day Jr. Day parade; no one is injured because it is spotted and defused." David Neiwert, "Charlottesville Underscores How Home Grown Hate Is Going Unchecked," *Reveal News*, June 21, 2017, updated August 14, 2017, www.revealnews.org/article/home-is-where-the-hate-is/.
23   O'Sullivan, "The Aesthetics of Affect: Thinking Art Beyond Representation," 128.
24   Doug Beube, personal website: www.dougbeube.com/artwork/2160693_Blast_If_You_See_Something_Say_Something.html
25   William Neuman, "A Mystery Tally in New York's 'See Something, Say Something' Posters," *New York Times*, January 7, 2008 B1, www.nytimes.com/2008/01/07/nyregion/07see.html
26   Despite Abigail Adams recommendation to her husband John Adams to "remember the ladies" on March 31, 1776, the American Revolution did not include women in its fight for independence. Throughout Europe, women also wrote about their talents, but independence would not be granted women for another 150 years, so the masculine references here are intentional.
27   Bernays, *Crystallizing Public Opinion*, 200.
28   Doug Beube, personal website: www.dougbeube.com/artwork/2160693_Blast_If_You_See_Something_Say_Something.html
29   Massumi, *Politics of Affect*, 210.
30   O'Sullivan, "The Aesthetics of Affect: Thinking Art Beyond Representation," 126.
31   Brian Michael Jenkins, "The Land of the Fearful, or the Home of the Brave?" in *The Long Shadow of 9/11: America's Response to Terrorism*, eds. Brian Michael Jenkins and John Paul Godges (Santa Monica, CA: RAND, 2011), 206.
32   Scott Shane, "Most U.S. Attacks Are Homegrown and Not Jihadist," *The New York Times*, June 25, 2015, A1, A17 New York Edition, www.nytimes.com/2015/06/25/us/tally-of-attacks-in-us-challenges-perceptions-of-top-terror-threat.html.
33   The Department of Homeland Security now explicitly states that "[f]actors such as race, ethnicity, and/or religious affiliation are not suspicious," on their page dedicated to explaining what qualifies as suspicious activity: www.dhs.gov/see-something-say-something/what-suspicious-activity.
34   Neuman, "A Mystery Tally," B17.
35   Ibid.
36   The Southern Poverty Law Center maintains a chart with the rise and fall of "active antigovernment" groups: www.splcenter.org/active-antigovernment-groups-united-states. The SPLC also tracks hate groups: www.splcenter.org/hate-map.

37 Siobhan Gorman, "Fear Factor: Beyond a Panic-Driven Approach to Home-land Security," *Government Executive*, May 16, 2003, www.govexec.com/defense/2003/05/fear-factor-beyond-a-panic-driven-approach-to-homeland-security/14124/. Gorman offers Israel's cultural encoding of terrorism as an example of how the United States might "simultaneously adjust to the dangers of terrorism and bolster security."

38 Jackson, "Don't Let Short-Term Urgency," 136.

39 Siobhan Gorman, "Fear Factor," www.govexec.com/defense/2003/05/fear-factor-beyond-a-panic-driven-approach-to-homeland-security/14124/.

40 Massumi, *Politics of Affect*, 36.

Bibliography

Bellavita, Christopher. "How Proverbs Damage Homeland Security." *Homeland Security Affairs* 7, Special Issue: *10 Years After: The 9/11 Essays*, September, 2011. www.hsaj.org/articles/62

Bernays, Edward. *Crystallizing Public Opinion*. Brooklyn, NY: IG Publishing, 2011.

Beube, Doug. Personal website: www.dougbeube.com/artwork/2160693_Blast_If_You_See_Something_Say_Something.html

Boyd, Curtis D. "Terrorism as a Psychological Operation: A Comparative Analysis of the Zionist and the Palestinian Terrorist Campaigns." Master's Thesis, Naval Post Graduate School, 1994.

Brill, Steven. "Is America Any Safer?" *The Atlantic*, September, 2016. www.theatlantic.com/magazine/archive/2016/09/are-we-any-safer/492761/

Fernandez, Manny. "A Phrase for Safety After 9/11 Goes Global." *New York Times*, May 11, 2010, A17. www.nytimes.com/2010/05/11/nyregion/11slogan.html (Accessed July 20, 2017).

Gorman, Siobhan. "Fear Factor: Beyond a Panic-Driven Approach to Home-land Security." *Government Executive*, May 16, 2003. www.govexec.com/defense/2003/05/fear-factor-beyond-a-panic-driven-approach-to-homeland-security/14124/.

Gregg, Melissa, and Gregory J. Seigworth, eds. *The Affect Theory Reader*. Durham, NC: Duke University Press, 2010.

Hanser, Robert D. "Psychological Warfare and Terrorism." *Professional Issues in Criminal Justice* 2, no. 1 (2007): 3–8.

Heffernan, Virginia. *Magic and Loss: The Internet as Art*. New York: Simon and Schuster, 2016.

Holbert, R. Lance. "Media Influence as Persuasion." In *The SAGE Handbook of Persuasion: Developments in Theory and Practice*, edited by James Price Dillard and Lijiang Shen, 36–52. Thousand Oaks, CA: SAGE Publications, 2012.

Jackson, Brian. "Don't Let Short-Term Urgency Undermine a Long-Term Security Strategy." In *The Long Shadow of 9/11: America's Response to Terrorism*, edited by Brian Michael Jenkins and John Paul Godges, 133–146. Santa Monica, CA: RAND, 2011.

Jenkins, Brian Michael. "The Land of the Fearful, or the Home of the Brave?" In *The Long Shadow of 9/11: America's Response to Terrorism*, edited by Brian Michael Jenkins and John Paul Godges, 195–208. Santa Monica, CA: RAND, 2011.

le Bon, Gustave. *The Crowd: A Study of the Popular Mind*. Mineola, NY: Dover Publications, 2002. Translator not identified.

170 *Charlotte Kent*

Massumi, Brian. *Politics of Affect*. New York: Polity Press, 2015.

McDonough, Tom. "Unrepresentable Enemies: On the Legacy of Guy Debord and the Situationist International." *Afterall: A Journal of Art, Context and Enquiry* 28 (Autumn/Winter 2011): 42–55.

Mosher, Dave, and Skye Gould. "How Likely Are Foreign Terrorists to Kill Americans?" *Business Insider,* January 31, 2017. www.businessinsider.com/death-risk-statistics-terrorism-disease-accidents-2017-1.

Neiwert, David. "Charlottesville Underscores How Home Grown Hate Is Going Unchecked." *Reveal News,* June 21, 2017, updated August 14, 2017, www.revealnews.org/article/home-is-where-the-hate-is/.

Neuman, William. "A Mystery Tally in New York's 'See Something, Say Something' Posters." *New York Times*, January 7, 2008 B1. www.nytimes.com/2008/01/07/nyregion/07see.html (Accessed July 20, 2017)

Nowrasteh, Alex. "Terrorism and Immigration: A Risk Analysis." *Policy Analysis* 798, September 13, 2016.

O'Haver, Hanson. "How 'If You See Something, Say Something'" Became Our National Motto." *The Washington Post,* September 23, 2016. www.washingtonpost.com/posteverything/wp/2016/09/23/how-if-you-see-something-say-something-became-our-national-motto/?utm_term=.bf30191a55f8 (Accessed July 20, 2017).

O'Sullivan, Simon. "The Aesthetics of Affect: Thinking Art Beyond Representation." *Angelaki: Journal of Theoretical Humanities* 6, no. 3 (2001): 125–135.

Schiller, Herbert L. *The Mind Managers*. Boston, MA: Beacon Press, 1973.

Schmid, Alex. "Terrorism as Psychological Warfare." *Democracy and Security* 1 (2005): 137–146.

Shane, Scott. "Most U.S. Attacks Are Homegrown and Not Jihadist." *The New York Times*, June 25, 2015, A1, A17 New York Edition. www.nytimes.com/2015/06/25/us/tally-of-attacks-in-us-challenges-perceptions-of-top-terror-threat.html (Accessed July 20, 2017).

The Department of Homeland Security. "What is Suspicious Activity?" www.dhs.gov/see-something-say-something/what-suspicious-activity (Accessed March 3, 2018).

The Southern Poverty Law Center. "Active AntiGovernment Groups in the United States." www.splcenter.org/active-antigovernment-groups-united-states. "Hate Map". www.splcenter.org/hate-map (Accessed March 3, 2018).

12 Gratifications from Watching Movies That Make Us Cry

Facilitation of Grief, Parasocial Empathy, and the Grief-comfort Amalgam

Charles (Chuck) F. Aust

Tearjerker films make viewers cry. Some viewers are gratified, saying they loved the movie, report that it was a "good" or "great" film, recommend it to their friends, and might even want to see it again. Examples include *The Notebook, Steel Magnolias, Terms of Endearment, Brian's Song,* and *The Champ,* to name a few. Considering their counterintuitive appeal, intentionally viewing such content has perplexed media effects researchers.[1]

This chapter proposes three mechanisms that could explain this appeal. One is a grief reaction about the loss of a loved one or other significant losses that the film activates in the viewer's mind. Second, viewers obtain comfort and consolation by experiencing a parasocial empathy, in which they perceive that they are recipients of empathy emanating from the experience of the liked and cared-about movie character with whom they have developed a parasocial relationship. Movie content activates this parasocial experience by reminding viewers of their own suffering that is in some way similar to that of the character. Third, spreading activation via rapid cognitive attentional switching, a model from cognitive psychology described below, is implicated in this process. Some viewers experience, along with their crying, comforting feelings associated with some of their own memories. How comforting memories could contribute to the appeal of these films will also be explained. Cumulatively, these mechanisms of grief, parasocial empathy, and spreading activation produce an affective experience I call the grief-comfort amalgam, a powerful effect that leads viewers to deem the overall viewing experience to be gratifying.

But why would viewers deem as "good" or even "great" the movies that make them cry? I propose availability heuristics as one answer. Availability heuristics involves the ease with which ideas come to mind to help us make inferences. This process occurs when we use the memories that are most easily available to make judgments rather than those that are most relevant but that require more cognitive effort to recall and apply. In the case of tearjerkers, the viewers judge that their enjoyment results from the highly

172 *Charles (Chuck) F. Aust*

salient tear-inducing events in the film, the awful things that happened to their beloved character. However, as proposed here, the enjoyment comes not from the film content alone but from the cumulative experience of the grief-comfort amalgam. Availability heuristics could explain why the comforting aspects are outside the awareness of the viewer immediately after the movie. The viewer's thoughts are likely to be focused on the experience of the movie characters portrayed in the just-viewed film, which at that moment is most salient in the viewers' minds and most easily available for recall.

Grieving Is Beneficial and Ultimately Gratifying

Grieving is necessary and beneficial. Grief that is not addressed or that is impeded can be debilitating and hazardous to one's health.[2] Grief counselors recommend specific actions to facilitate the grieving process. Viewing movies that help us grieve a loss is one of the various ways individuals can express emotions associated with their own loss.[3] Films, then, can be powerful triggers of grief. The intervention strategy of the grief therapist includes reactivation of the grieving process.[4] As patients undergo grief therapy, they feel fresh and intense sadness,[5] even if the loss did not occur recently. Part of the value of media content that facilitates grief is that it similarly has the capacity to reactivate emotions related to grieving. A grief reaction to film content could likewise be intense and fresh.

Some people want to grieve, and they intentionally view certain films to help them reflect on their loss, initiate a grief response, and express emotions,[6] while other movie viewers are not seeking or expecting such an experience from the film. Yet the film might trigger a grief reaction in both types of viewer. Some will dislike this experience and continue to resist, while others might find it gratifying because it facilitated unplanned but welcomed expressions of grief.

While the experience of painful emotions associated with grief might be considered unpleasant, viewers report feeling gratified and welcome the experience as emotionally productive and ultimately beneficial.[7] Thus, the grief response to film is welcomed by some viewers as it helps them grieve, whether or not they intentionally exposed themselves to the film for this purpose.

Movie Content Most Likely to Facilitate a Grief Response

At this point, it would be helpful to establish the kind of film content that is likely to trigger expressions of grief and yet be rewarding. There are pivotal moments when the tearjerker film triggers crying in viewers. It occurs when the liked, admired, beloved character in the film suffers pain and loss, and even death. Disposition theory has helped us understand why this is likely to be the pivotal movie material that triggers the grief response.[8] Disposition theory holds that witnessing a character doing agreeable, good things, in the moral judgment of the observer, will foster liking, caring, and friend-like feelings in that observer. As a result, when those characters they like, care about, and admire endure suffering and death, viewers are likely to feel grief.

This does not occur when villains and other characters despised by the viewers are suffering pain and loss. Witnessing those kinds of characters doing disagreeable, bad things in the moral judgment of the observer fosters not grief in the observer but instead disliking, resentment, and enemy-like feelings.[9]

Empathy research provides compelling evidence for these reactions.[10] When viewers hold favorable dispositions toward the film's characters, they respond in a compatible fashion to the good or bad fortunes of those characters. In other words, viewers will be pleased when seeing good fortune happen to liked characters and displeased by the bad fortune endured by those liked characters. The character's joy is the viewer's joy and the character's sorrow is the viewer's sorrow. Conversely, the viewer will be pleased by the misfortune of a disliked character rather than share empathically in the disliked character's sorrow and suffering.

Regarding the present issue of movies generating tears, when our liked and cared-about movie characters suffer loss, some of us are disturbed to the point of tears. We feel empathy toward such characters and co-suffer with them. The unfortunate or tragic circumstances befalling our liked and beloved characters also have the power to remind us of our own similar experiences, a key variable that contributes to the next effect we will explore.

Parasocial Empathy, a Derivative of the Parasocial Relationship

One way we obtain relief from the sad emotions associated with the loss of loved ones or other major losses is to seek out empathic reactions from others. This is one of the powerful comforts that counselors, clergy, and therapists provide. But could it be that film characters, under specific circumstances, can also inadvertently provide empathic comfort? Indeed, a media character can be one of the many sources from which we derive satisfaction of various emotional needs that a friendship provides. One of those needs could be feeling cared about and understood. Some viewers may feel comforted because they perceive that the character reciprocates the empathy the viewers feel for the character. They might sense an emotional kinship when observing a liked character who has suffered in similar ways. This is one of the paradoxical gratifications of tearjerker films.

I call this hedonically positive, or pleasurable, emotional experience "parasocial empathy," and derive it as a logical extension of parasocial

174   *Charles (Chuck) F. Aust*

interaction. In the parasocial interaction, Horton and his collaborators proposed that media consumers develop a quasi-social relationship with certain media characters. In other words, a friendship emerges, at least in the mind of the viewer. And, at an affective level, the viewer does not seem to distinguish between real-life friendship and this mediated, one-sided, simulated friendship.[11] The viewer feels liked and accepted by the media character. And although it is a mediated presentation of a person's presence, that may be enough. The felt truth can be just as gratifying at an empirical truth.

A large volume of research has explored the validity of this parasocial friendship in relation to TV characters, and has generated empirical support for it.[12] It is widely accepted that respondents do develop quasi-social relationships with media characters, and that affective dispositions toward the targeted characters are an integral part of these relationships. Applying parasocial relationship theory to the effect of gratification from tear-jerker films, characters portrayed tend to become sufficiently known to the viewers, so that during the film, those viewers develop an affective disposition (a feeling of like or dislike) toward them.

In real life, people who suffer the same loss, who like and care about each other, and who come together at that time of loss, find comfort in one another's presence as they share the loss and take actions to mutually recognize the loss and its impact on them. Parasocial empathy affords the film viewer a similar sense of comfort and consolation. Although it is a me-diated presentation of a person's presence, the viewer experiences the character as if that character is emotionally available, as if the viewer is with the liked, cared-about film character with whom the viewer shares similar attributes and a similar loss. At pivotal points in a movie, such as when the character is going through an ordeal similar to one that the viewer also has endured, the viewer and character share in co-suffering. Moreover, the greater the perceived similarity between the viewer and character, and the greater the similarity between the misfortune of the character and the viewer, the stronger will be the parasocial empathy felt by the viewer.

As discussed previously, some of our feelings about loss are not acknowl-edged or are acknowledged in awkward and less than empathic ways by others. Our real-life family, friends, and acquaintances, instead of listening and validating our painful feelings, might ignore our feelings, question them, try to change them, try to give us advice about their causes, or listen halfheartedly while they do other tasks. In contrast, as part of the parasocial relationship between viewer and film character, the character represents an unqualified acknowledgement of our own experience and feelings. The movie character does not judge or question our suffering or try to "talk us out of it."

Viewers might feel comfort and consolation at that moment that their own struggle is being recognized, acknowledged, and validated. The trig-gering stimulus for this feeling is the viewer's observation of the movie character's experience, so it is possible that the viewer attributes the acknowledgement to that stimulus, and deems the comforting feelings to be an empathy-like response emanating from the character.

On the face of it, a tragic drama would seem only to make the viewer's emotional condition worse, yet it can eventually provide relief. Parasocial empathy, empathy felt by the viewer when observing a similarly suffering character, is one of the gratifications that makes it worthwhile for viewers to subject themselves to a tragic story that brings them to tears. Another proposed effect involves activation of pleasurable memories in the viewers that are triggered by observing the suffering of the movie character. The next section will explore the mechanism involved to explain how this proposed effect is possible.

Comforting Emotions Temporally Contiguous to the Crying

While exhibiting pain and suffering, the film character might also be modeling perseverance, fidelity to a loved one or a goal, or the stoic forbearance of pain, suffering, and heartache. This could remind viewers of their own perseverance, fidelity, courage, and stamina as they endured suffering and adversity in their own lives, eliciting comforting feelings in them.

What kinds of film events might elicit these comforting feelings? As described previously, the suffering of others might help viewers realize how arduous their own lives have been, how much trauma and loss they have endured. But it can also activate thoughts of how courageous they have been in their endurance of emotional or physical suffering. They might feel proud that they have faced the challenges, taken the risks, and faced their problems instead of retreating from them. They thereby experienced internal rewards, some perhaps quite significant, and some perhaps far-reaching in their positive impact on the viewers' lives or the lives of their loved ones.

They might not have attained these outcomes perfectly, or smoothly, but in their own imperfect way they have endured something painful, and comforting feelings well up within them. Davies captures this well:

> Some of the projects providing the greatest fulfillment demand fearful risks and known costs. Yet people commit themselves cheerfully to intellectually and physically demanding professions, to intense personal relationships, to birthing and raising children, and so on—and they do so not entirely in ignorance of what the future holds in store. Often the hard work, pain, anxiety, and stress are so much a part of the project that it would no longer be the same project were their possibility removed. ... There is not gain without pain, as they say. The deepest satisfactions depend sometimes not just on what was gained but on how hard it was to attain.[13]

Other comforting feelings triggered by the film might include gratitude that the lost loved one was in the viewers' lives, pride for their devotion to the loved one through painful, dreadful circumstances, pride in their ability to "carry on" in spite of the pain and suffering, or relief that the suffering has passed, just to name a few. These pleasurable emotions are triggered in a temporally contiguous fashion with the stimuli that evoke the sadness and crying. Put another way, the viewers' brains are rapidly switching back and forth among thoughts both painful and pleasurable. So while they grieve and feel sorrow, they also feel comfort, consolation, and pride, resulting in a mixture of painful and pleasurable emotions, what I call the grief-comfort amalgam.

The spreading-activation model[14] from cognitive psychology is useful here. According to this model, a stimulus event that refers to a concept activates a node, a cluster of neurons, pertaining to the concept. This activation produces excitation at this node. The excitation at this node then spreads along pathways that connect it to other nodes. This activates peripheral nodes, bringing to consciousness the associated thoughts.

When comforting thoughts occur very close in time to the sorrowful thoughts via spreading activation, and the brain is rapidly switching back and forth between these various activated thoughts, viewers will have difficulty distinguishing between them. The viewer does not realize that their assessment of it as a good cry, rather than a bad cry, derives not from the grieving alone but from the switching back and forth between grief and comforting emotions. However, because of rapid cognitive attentional switching, the thoughts happen in milliseconds. They are fleeting, each occurring very briefly, perhaps some in as little as a fraction of a second.

Experiencing an amalgam of emotions, not just one emotion, could be why it is often so difficult to put a label on a current emotional state. Rapid cognitive attentional switching back and forth among these activated, associated brain pathways gives the viewer the sensation of an amalgamation, not of separate emotions but of a seemingly singular emotion. Inability to distinguish between the emotions and their causes thus results in naming it "a good cry." This amalgamation of emotions might lead viewers to think in a singular way about the crying episode, attributing it to the sad movie content. But there is likely more occurring affectively than just sadness about the plight of the liked and cared-about movie characters and the viewer's own similar suffering. While viewers are reminded of their own loss, they also feel comforting emotions derived from memories of their own courage, perseverance, fidelity to self or others despite the suffering, or ultimate success or relief. We may apply the adjective *bittersweet* to this sensation.[15]

Why Viewers Focus on the Film Rather than on Their Own Thoughts and Feelings

Satisfied viewers of tearjerkers conclude that the movie is gratifying and leaves them in a joyous or peaceful mood. They tend to focus on, and perhaps discuss, the movie character's experience instead of their own memories and emotions activated by the movie. Several factors could explain why the fleeting thoughts and emotions about their own lives escape viewer awareness immediately after the film.

1   Film presentation factors. The viewer's most prominent thoughts are likely to be those associated with the film character, often in painful and distressing circumstances, so the viewer's positive memories and their concomitant pleasurable emotions must compete for attention with the continued presentation of the film events. This, in part, may explain why they do not experience more powerful and sustained pleasurable emotions during the film. The rapid delivery of the film narrative interrupts their ability to reflect on all of these triggered emotions. Instead, their attention is repeatedly drawn back to the vivid sensory experience of the movie.[16] Since these powerful film attributes compete for the viewer's attention, the pleasurable emotions are felt only fleetingly.

2   Attentional switching. Viewers often have difficulty sorting out the various emotions and their causes because they occur so rapidly and in close temporal proximity to the crying. Cognitive attentional switching occurs so rapidly that distinctions regarding the triggers of emotions are very difficult to make.

3   Prominence of the act of crying. The viewer's tears, the lump in the throat, sniffling, puffy eyes, and perhaps even sobbing are so salient that they overwhelm fine cognitive distinctions. Therefore, the viewer fails to notice the concomitant pleasurable or comforting emotions.

4   Distraction because of an inhibition about crying. Additionally, if the viewer is self-conscious about crying in front of others, that preoccupation distracts from a keen awareness of or an ability to sort and reflect on pleasurable emotions they also feel.

So, to recap this section, the continued vivid presentation of the sights and sounds of the film, rapid cognitive attentional switching in the viewer's brain, the overwhelming physical experience of crying, along with possible self-consciousness about crying in front of others present formidable cognitive challenges. Viewers are likely to cognitively attend to or recall the stimuli in the film content that they assume made them cry rather than the activated memories that triggered comforting emotions at the same time as the shedding of tears.

Why the Tearjerker Movie Is Ultimately Judged Enjoyable

When the movie ends and viewers make judgments about how good the film was, the judgment that the movie was gratifying seems a puzzling

178 *Charles (Chuck) F. Aust*

assessment when viewers just witnessed their beloved character suffer greatly and perhaps die. Availability heuristics[17] offers another explanation. This mechanism involves the ease with which ideas come to mind to help us make inferences. This process occurs when we use the thoughts that are most easily available in memory to make judgments, rather than those that are most relevant but require more cognitive effort to recall and apply. We take the cognitive path of least effort. As a result, we sometimes make errors in the conclusions we reach. In the case of tearjerkers, availability heuristics confounds the ability to realize or remember the comforting emotions about oneself that the viewer experienced in close temporal proximity (due to rapid cognitive attentional switching) to the crying about the suffering character. What is most prominent in the mind of the viewer is the character's experience, not the viewer's own life experiences and the fleeting pleasurable emotions that were elicited by memories of the viewer's life experiences.

The most dominant thoughts, because of the power of the images and sounds conveyed by the film, are likely to be of the events the viewer saw the liked character endure. Therefore, the most salient cause the viewer is likely to attribute to the gratification obtained from the viewing experience is what happened to the liked character. Less likely to be recalled by the viewer are the comforting emotions of pride, gratitude, and joy associated with the activated memories about the viewer's own courage, perseverance, and overcoming of adversity, memories that the viewer experienced in such a fleeting manner that those memories do not come to mind again as easily after the film. When viewers are assessing their experience in order to make judgments about the film, they tend to overlook the less obvious but perhaps equally influential gratifications of tearjerkers: comforting emotions elicited by positive memories about their own lives.

Summary

This chapter proposes three mechanisms that explain the appeal of tearjerkers. One is a grief reaction that affords the viewer an opportunity to grieve significant losses that the film content activates in the viewer's mind. Second, viewers obtain comfort and consolation by experiencing parasocial empathy, in which they feel as if they have received empathy by witnessing the liked character endure suffering and loss in some way similar to their own. This is possible because they have developed a parasocial relationship with the suffering character during the film. Movie content activates this parasocial empathy because the viewers are reminded of their own suffering that is in some way similar to that of the character. The viewer might think, "I can relate to this character" or "I've been there too." Third, spreading-activation via rapid cognitive attentional switching is implicated in this process. Some viewers experience—mixed in with their sadness and crying about the suffering of the liked character and their own grief from having suffered similarly—comforting feelings such as pride and gratitude associated with their own positive memories triggered by the movie. The observed suffering of movie characters may activate memories in viewers of how arduous and even traumatic their own lives have been, which elicits a grief response. But such observations also activate thoughts of how courageous viewers have been in their endurance of their own physical and emotional suffering. Suddenly becoming keenly aware of their own recent or perhaps long-term fortitude and perseverance in the face of the struggles, failures, and hardships, as well as the resulting partial or complete successes they have experienced, makes them aware of not just their pain and loss but also their fortitude and triumph over adversity, which could elicit comforting emotions such as pride and gratitude. They might feel proud and relieved that they have faced the challenges, taken the risks, grappled with their problems instead of retreating from them. Or they might suddenly feel a strong sense of gratitude for the love and support of others who helped them in time of trauma or loss. The emotional rewards, some perhaps quite significant, and some perhaps far-reaching in their positive impact on their lives or the lives of loved ones, can produce powerfully comforting effects in the midst of the tears shed about one's own suffering or that of the movie character.

Cumulatively, these mechanisms—grief, parasocial empathy, and spreading activation via rapid cognitive attentional switching—produce an affective experience I call the grief-comfort amalgam. The viewer experiences not one emotion but a mix of emotions, both painful and comforting. The grief-comfort amalgam is a powerful effect that leads viewers to deem the overall viewing experience to be gratifying.

Grief is a universal experience and an emotion that requires healthy expression. Therefore, it is important to understand and value ways to facilitate grieving in order to ameliorate and heal emotions associated with loss. This chapter provides an explanation about one of those valuable ways: tearjerker films. Viewing such films is an opportunity to experience the grief-comfort amalgam, to feel and express valuable emotions, both sad and affirming.

Notes

1　Minet de Wied, Dolf Zillmann, and Virginia Ordman, "The Role of Empathic Distress in the Enjoyment of Cinematic Tragedy." *Poetics* 23 (1994): 91–106; Oliver, M B. "Exploring the Paradox of the Enjoyment of Sad Films." *Human Communication Research* 19 (1993): 315–342.

2　Kenneth R. Mitchell and Herbert Anderson, *All Our Losses, All Our Griefs* (Philadelphia, PA: Westminster Press, 1983); Stephen R. Shuchter, *Dimensions of Grief* (San Francisco, CA: Jossey-Bass, 1986); Ira J. Tanner, *The Gift of Grief: Healing the Pain of Everyday Losses* (New York: Hawthorn, 1976); J. William Worden, *Grief Counseling and Grief Therapy* (New York: Springer, 1982).

180   *Charles (Chuck) F. Aust*

3 William H. Frey and Muriel Langseth, *Crying: The Mystery of Tears* (New York: Winston Press, 1985); Tom Lutz, "*Crying: The Natural and Cultural History of Tears* (New York: Norton, 1999); Ira J. Tanner, *The Gift of Grief: Healing the Pain of Everyday Losses* (New York: Hawthorn, 1976).

4 Kenneth R. Mitchell and Herbert Anderson, *All Our Losses, All Our Griefs* (Philadelphia: Westminster Press, 1983); Stephen R. Shuchter, *Dimensions of Grief* (San Francisco, CA: Jossey-Bass, 1986); J. William Worden, *Grief Counseling and Grief Therapy* (New York: Springer, 1982).

5 J. William Worden, *Grief Counseling and Grief Therapy* (New York: Springer, 1982).

6 William H. Frey and Muriel Langseth, *Crying: The Mystery of Tears* (New York: Winston Press, 1985); Ira J. Tanner, *The Gift of Grief: Healing the Pain of Everyday Losses* (New York: Hawthorn, 1976).

7 William H. Frey and Muriel Langseth, *Crying: The Mystery of Tears* (New York: Winston Press, 1985).

8 Dolf Zillmann, "Mechanisms of Emotional Involvement with Drama," *Poetics* 23 (1994): 33–51.

9 Dolf Zillmann, "The Psychology of Suspense in Dramatic Exposition," in *Suspense: Conceptualizations, Theoretical Analyses, and Empirical Explorations,* eds. Peter Vorderer, Hans J. Wulff, and Mike Friedrichsen (Mahwah, NJ: Erlbaum, 1996), 199–231.

10 Justin Aronfreed, "The Socialization of Altruistic and Sympathetic Behavior: Some Theoretical and Experimental Analyses," in Jacqueline Macaulay and Leonard Berkowitz, eds., *Altruism and Helping Behavior* (New York: Academic, 1970), 103–126; Berger, S. M. "Conditioning through Vicarious Instigation." *Psychological Review* 69, no. 5 (1962): 450–466; Eisenberg, N. and J. Strayer. *Empathy and Its Development* (Cambridge: Cambridge University Press, 1987); Hoffman, M. L. "The Contribution of Empathy to Justice and Moral Judgment," in *Empathy and Its Development,* eds. N. Eisenberg and J. Strayer (Cambridge: Cambridge University Press, 1987), 47–80; E. Stotland, "Exploratory Investigations of Empathy," in *Advances in Experimental Social Psychology,* eds. L. Berkowitz, vol. 4 (New York: Academic Press, 1969), 271–314; Dolf Zillmann, "Affect from Bearing Witness to the Emotions of Others," in *Responding to the Screen: Reception and Reaction Processes,* eds. Jennings Bryant and Dolf Zillmann (Hillsdale, NJ: Erlbaum, 1991), 135–167.

11 Donald Horton and Anselm Strauss, "Interaction in Audience-Participation Shows," *American Journal of Sociology* 62, no. 6 (1957): 579–587; See also Donald Horton and R. Richard Wohl, "Mass Communication and Para-Social Interaction: Observations on Intimacy at a Distance," *Psychiatry* 19 (1956): 215–229.

12 Pekka Isotalus, "Friendship Through Screen," *The Nordicom Review of Nordic Research on Media and Communication* (1995): 59–64; Mark R. Levy, "Watching TV News as Para-Social Interaction" *Journal of Broadcasting* (1979): 69–80.; Elizabeth M. Perse and Rebecca Rubin, "Attribution in Social and Parasocial Relationships," *Communication Research* 23 (1989): 59–77; Rebecca B. Rubin and M. P. McHugh, "Development of Parasocial Interaction Relationships," *Journal of Broadcasting & Electronic Media* 31 (1987): 279–292.

13 Stephen Davies, "Why Listen to Sad Music If It Makes One Feel Sad?" in *Music and Meaning,* ed. Jenefer Robinson (Ithaca, NY: Cornell University Press, 1997), 242–253.

14 Allan M. Collins and Elizabeth F. Loftus, "A Spreading-Activation Theory of Semantic Processing." *Psychological Review* 82, no. 6 (1975): 407–428; Robert S. Wyer, Jr. and Thomas K. Srull, *Memory and Cognition in Its Social Context* (Hillsdale, NJ: Erlbaum, 1989).

15 This dynamic process also explains "tears of joy," how sudden joyful events can also trigger tears: An Olympic athlete winning the gold, a mother giving birth, a father seeing his son or daughter receive their college diploma. In these instances, while thoughts of the tremendous accomplishment elicit joy and pride, the person has brief but sudden recall of other thoughts that are also activated in that moment about sacrifice and suffering related to this joyous event. The Olympic athlete sacrificed friendships, delayed pursuing other milestones, and put aspects of social life on hold for months, maybe years while training, the mother endured physical complications that made the pregnancy extraordinarily difficult, the father worked long hours at a very demanding job to pay for his child's college tuition. An event that brings sudden joy can also elicit painful memories about sacrifice, loss, and deprivation. The emotions that burst forth at that moment are likely to be not one single emotion but an amalgam of both joyous and painful emotions. Grief mixes with joy, a grief-comfort amalgam.

16 Dolf Zillmann, "Affect from Bearing Witness to the Emotions of Others," in Jennings Bryant and Dolf Zillmann, eds., *Responding to the Screen: Reception and Reaction Processes* (Hillsdale, NJ: Erlbaum, 1991), 135–167.

17 Amos Tversky and Daniel Kahneman, "Availability: A Heuristic for Judging Frequency and Probability," *Cognitive Psychology* (1973): 207–232.

Bibliography

Aronfreed, Justin. "The Socialization of Altruistic and Sympathetic Behavior: Some Theoretical and Experimental Analyses." In *Altruism and Helping Behavior,* edited by J. Macaulay and L. Berkowitz, 103–126. New York: Academic, 1970.

Berger, Seymour M. "Conditioning through Vicarious Instigation." *Psychological Review* 69, no. 5 (1962): 450–466.

Collins, Allan M., and Elizabeth F. Loftus. "A Spreading-Activation Theory of Semantic Processing." *Psychological Review* 82, no. 6 (1975): 407–428.

Davies, Stephen. "Why Listen to Sad Music If It Makes One Feel Sad?" In *Music and Meaning,* edited by Jenefer Robinson, 242–253. Ithaca, NY: Cornell University Press, 1997.

de Wied, Minet, Dolf Zillmann, and Virginia Ordman. "The Role of Empathic Distress in the Enjoyment of Cinematic Tragedy." *Poetics* 23 (1994): 91–106.

Eisenberg, Nancy, and Janet Strayer. *Empathy and Its Development.* Cambridge: Cambridge University Press, 1987.

Frey, William H., and Muriel Langseth. *Crying: The Mystery of Tears.* New York: Winston Press, 1985.

Hoffman, Martin L. "The Contribution of Empathy to Justice and Moral Judgment." In *Empathy and Its Development,* edited by Nancy Eisenberg and Janet Strayer, 47–80. Cambridge: Cambridge University Press, 1987.

Horton, Donald, and Anselm Strauss. "Interaction in Audience-Participation Shows." *American Journal of Sociology* 62, no. 6 (1957): 579–587.

Horton, Donald, and R. Richard Wohl. "Mass Communication and Para-Social Interaction: Observations on Intimacy at a Distance." *Psychiatry* 19 (1956): 215–229.

Isotalus, Pekka. "Friendship through Screen." *The Nordicom Review of Nordic Research on Media and Communication* 14 (1995): 59–64.

182 *Charles (Chuck) F. Aust*

Levy, Mark R. "Watching TV News as Para-Social Interaction. *Journal of Broadcasting* 23 (1979): 69–80.

Lutz, Tom. *Crying: The Natural and Cultural History of Tears.* New York: Norton, 1999.

Mitchell, Kenneth R., and Herbert Anderson. *All Our Losses, All Our Griefs.* Philadelphia, PA: Westminster Press, 1983.

Oliver, Mary Beth. "Exploring the Paradox of the Enjoyment of Sad Films." In *Human Communication Research* 19 (1993): 315–342.

Perse, Elizabeth M., and Rebecca Rubin. "Attribution in Social and Parasocial Relationships." *Communication Research* 16 (1989): 59–77.

Rubin, Rebecca B., and Michael P. McHugh. "Development of Parasocial Interaction Relationships." *Journal of Broadcasting & Electronic Media* 31 (1987): 279–292.

Shuchter, Stephen R. *Dimensions of Grief.* San Francisco, CA: Jossey-Bass, 1986.

Stotland, Ezra. "Exploratory Investigations of Empathy." In *Advances in Experimental Social Psychology*, edited by Leonard Berkowitz, 271–314. New York: Academic Press, 1969.

Tanner, Ira J. *The Gift of Grief: Healing the Pain of Everyday Losses.* New York: Hawthorn, 1976.

Tversky Amos, and Daniel Kahneman. "Availability: A Heuristic for Judging Frequency and Probability." *Cognitive Psychology* 5 (1973): 207–232.

Worden, J. William. *Grief Counseling and Grief Therapy.* New York: Springer, 1982.

Wyer, Robert S., and Thomas K. Srull. *Memory and Cognition in Its Social Context.* Hillsdale, NJ: Erlbaum, 1989.

Zillmann, Dolf. "Empathy: Affect from Bearing Witness to the Emotions of Others." In *Responding to the Screen: Reception and Reaction Processes*, edited by Jennings Bryant and Dolf Zillmann, 135–167. Hillsdale, NJ: Erlbaum, 1991.

Zillmann, Dolf. "Mechanisms of Emotional Involvement with Drama." *Poetics* 23 (1994): 33–51.

Zillmann, Dolf. "The Psychology of Suspense in Dramatic Exposition." In *Suspense: Conceptualizations, Theoretical Analyses, and Empirical Explorations*, edited by Peter Vorderer, Hans Jurgen Wulff, and Mike Friedrichsen, 199–231. Hillsdale, NJ: Erlbaum, 1996.

Part IV

Affect in 2016 U.S. Presidential Election

13 The Circulation of Rage
Memes and Donald Trump's Presidential Campaign

Jeffrey St. Onge

Donald Trump's rise to the presidency was historically improbable. Though Trump invoked a style of populism dating back to nineteenth-century America, positioning himself as an angry outsider with limitless contempt for the political establishment, he was the first such candidate to actually win the office.[1] A great deal has been written about Trump's political rise, and many note the unorthodox nature of his campaign, which relied heavily on Twitter as opposed to more traditional forms of political advertising.[2] Trump eschewed virtually all conventional wisdom of presidential campaigns, appealing directly to voters through social media and a busy schedule of heavily attended campaign rallies and media appearances. Further, he seemed to have no concern for discursive norms of the campaign trail. Though it was certainly not the only factor in his victory, Trump clearly struck a nerve with an electorate eager for some kind of change from the status quo of American politics.

Crucially, Trump both drew on and cultivated a widespread sense of anger and rage that seemed to define 2016 in the United States. Jennifer Finney Boylan called it the "year of the angry voter," noting that "it's vitriol itself, rather than any particular strategy for the future, that's propelling the electorate."[3] 2016 was similarly called the "year of anger," the "age of anger," and the "year of populist anger" in other publications.[4] As Tammy Webber and Emily Swanson reported in April of that year, "Almost 8 in 10 Americans say they're dissatisfied or angry with the way the federal government is working …. Republicans are far more likely to be angry … and those Republicans are much more supportive of Donald Trump."[5] The country was thus overcome with anger toward the status quo, and Trump became an avatar for the rage that defined the political landscape. He drew upon the general feeling of the populace and drove it to new levels with a seemingly endless supply of vitriol to deliver to any political figure or institution, friend or foe.

Anger and rage were key ingredients of Trump's success, functioning as primary warrants for his larger stated goal of "making America great again." As Jonah Berger and Katherine L. Milkman observed in a study of viral messaging, high-arousal emotions—including anger—are more likely than low-arousal emotions (e.g., sadness) to be shared on social media.[6]

The Trump campaign seized on this axiom of viral marketing, and future campaigns by mainstream and outsider candidates are likely to do so as well.[7] Anger and rage spread throughout the populace like a disease, infecting the larger body politic and shaping the political conversation in dramatic ways. Social media helped to create perfect conditions for anger and rage to grow by encouraging the instant sharing of information, often in echo chambers where opinions are not challenged and alternative viewpoints are not offered. It provided a welcoming landscape for calculated propaganda designed to spread resentment and distrust of the status quo.[8] Furthermore, social media was Trump's primary interface with the electorate, and his tweets not only circulated in the digital realm but were picked up and debated endlessly on cable news. As Trump himself stated in an interview, "I doubt I would be here if it weren't for social media …. Tweeting is like a typewriter—when I put it out, you put it immediately on your show. When somebody says something about me, I am able to go bing, bing, bing and I take care of it. The other way, I would never be able to get the word out."[9] Thus, he was able to draw upon, influence, and communicate with an angry populace on a daily basis through a social matrix of new and traditional communication channels. To understand Trump, then, scholars should consider the role of media in fostering and expanding affectual dimensions of political attitudes, in this case, anger and rage.

Affect theory provides one way to understand how anger/rage[10] shaped and influenced political discourse surrounding the 2016 election. Anna Gibbs describes affect as a *contagion*, noting that "contagious epidemics now potentially occur on a global scale and, thanks to electronic media, with incredible rapidity."[11] In the social realm, contagions replicate via mimetic communication, a process that connects "heterogeneous networks of media and conversation," including arguments, statements, images, and objects.[12] In other words, mimetic communication is the process of imitation between and among individuals, often unconsciously performed, where affect plays a central role.[13] Communication via digital replication across various networks is thus informed by an affective dimension.

The affective dimension of mimetic communication shapes democratic culture by influencing how information is consumed and shared. As Gibbs argues, mimetic communication is responsible for "the making—and breaking—of social bonds, [which] form the basis for a sense of 'belonging,' and, ultimately, of the polis, as what forms the affective basis of political orders."[14] Put differently, the mimetic circulation of affect (in this case, anger/rage) helps to construct and give shape to political culture, which in a democracy is constantly shifting and changing. An epidemiological view of mimetic communication can provide insight into the processes by which ideas replicate and dimensions of affect spread. By focusing on the process of mimetic communication, it is possible to better understand how anger/rage infected the populace in ways sufficient to reject politics-as-usual in favor of the apocalyptic view offered by Trump.

Affect Theory, Memes, and Democracy

Many discussions of affect theory begin with the work of psychologist Silvan Tomkins, who outlined the fundamental role of affect in human relations.[15] Humans, Tomkins noted, learn through affect. If a baby sees a parent smile, it is likely that the baby will also smile; fear, sadness, and other emotions work in similar ways. Affect is one way humans form bonds and learn to relate to others as friends or enemies, and it orients us to the world, providing a means to understand ideas, interpretations, and instructions for action.[16] Human communication is fundamentally imitative—we learn to speak from others; ideas, slogans, and other forms of communication replicate throughout society to become linguistic conventions and rhetorical commonplaces.[17] These conventions shape the practice of democracy in a given time by defining norms of political discourse and thought.

A culture saturated with social media provides a fertile ground for affect contagions to spread and replicate; a primary vehicle for this replication is the meme. The term "meme" was coined by biologist Richard Dawkins in his 1976 book *The Selfish Gene.* In the book, Dawkins describes the process of cultural evolution, which, like biological evolution, works through the reproduction of concepts and ideas and concerns the evolution of knowledge. In his own words, Dawkins created the term (which has roots in the Greek *mimema*) out of the need for "a noun that conveys the idea of a unit of cultural transmission, or a unit of *imitation*."[18] He defines it through example, including "tunes, ideas, catch-phrases, clothes fashions, ways of making pots or of building arches."[19] Dawkins intentionally draws a comparison to *genes*: "Just as genes propagate themselves in the gene pool by leaping from body to body via sperms or eggs, so memes propagate themselves in the meme pool by leaping from brain to brain via a process which, in the broad sense, can be called imitation."[20] Limor Shifman sharpens Dawkins' definition: "Memes may be best understood as cultural information that passes along from person to person, yet gradually scales into a shared social phenomenon. Although they spread on a micro basis, memes' impact is on the macro: they shape the mindsets, forms of behavior, and actions of social groups."[21] Like genes, the diffusion of memes involves a process of competition and selection. As Shifman notes, "Memes vary greatly in their degree of fitness, that is, their level of adaptiveness to the sociocultural environment in which they propagate."[22] Condensed pieces of cultural information expressed in image form are ubiquitous because they respond in some way to the culture in which they are situated. Thus, a successful meme can be read as a marker of conventional wisdom, or as a way to gain a deeper understanding of the culture in which it has flourished. At the same time, memes help to spread, define, and shape the norms of thought and action in society.

Memes played a critical part in shaping political discussion leading up to the 2016 presidential election. As noted in an article for the news magazine *The Conversation,* "Election memes reflected the political narrative of Hillary

188 *Jeffrey St. Onge*

Clinton's inauthenticity and corruption, and Donald Trump's capacity to understand and connect to his followers."[23] The authors cite Trump's "directness" of speech, which helped him to become "a mascot of anti-political-correctness for groups such as the alt-right, an online far-right movement housed in forums like Reddit and its hostile brother 4chan."[24] These internet forums have become "echo chambers for many far-right ideologies: nationalism, pro-guns, anti-feminism, anti-Semitism, anti-multiculturalism and white supremacy. And they quickly became bases of Trump fandom."[25] These various subcultures, existing primarily online, found in Trump a figure who shared disdain for mainstream notions of decorum and political correctness. Trump then functioned as a lynchpin of sorts, connecting through mediated networks a coalition loosely defined as the "alt-right."

Trump's direct and unfiltered speech fit neatly into the vast linkages of internet communities deeply engaged in "meme culture," where the meme has become a weaponized form of argument and a key discursive element unifying various groups. As Schifman argues, "Shared slogans that travel easily across large and diverse populations are essential to stimulating thousands or millions of people to take up a cause."[26] Memes, in addition to helping to form (if sometimes fleeting) group identities, function rhetorically in political movements by directing that group identity toward action. As Francis Heylighen and Klaas Chielens explain, "The transmission of cultural traits ... in many ways resembles the spread of an infectious disease: the carrier of a certain idea, behavior or attitude directly or indirectly communicates this idea to another person, who now also becomes a carrier, ready to 'infect' further people."[27] Functioning as a "thought contagion," a successful meme "spreads like an epidemic, infecting the whole of the population, in order to end up as a stable, endemic component of that population's culture."[28] Memes help create a shared set of attitudes—in this case, the attitudes embraced by the Trump campaign—and provide members of a community ways to act on those attitudes (i.e., voting for Trump).

The Trump campaign was aware of the power of memes, going as far as hiring a "technological director" deeply engaged in what journalist Ben Schreckinger called "the Great Meme War," a term to describe "the decentralized efforts of a swarm of anonymous internet nerds to harass Trump's detractors and flood the Web with pro-Trump, anti-Hillary Clinton propaganda. Their weapons of choice were memes .... a mass of pro-Trump iconography as powerful as the Obama 'Hope' poster and far more adaptable."[29] Strategist Steve Bannon and Social Media Director Dan Scavino monitored internet sites such as 4chan and Reddit for memes that could prove effective against Clinton and other political enemies, and Trump himself would often retweet controversial memes.

Perhaps the most well-known meme of the Trump campaign is that of Pepe the Frog, a green, animated creature first created by Matt Furie for the comic book *Boy's Club*. The nonpolitical cartoon figure was picked up by members of the alt-right and became an avatar of sorts for the whole movement, circulating widely on internet message boards supportive of Trump.[30] Pepe later appeared in a tweet by Donald Trump, Jr. as part of a movie parody poster titled "The Deplorables" and was later tweeted by candidate Trump himself, with Pepe altered to look like Trump, wearing a similar suit and sporting a similar haircut.[31] Pepe the Frog became a mascot of sorts for a large segment of Trump supporters, and Trump's inclusion of the cartoon frog in a tweet let them know that he was, in fact, connected to that community. The Trump family legitimized the meme and imbued it with new power by sharing it with large audiences on social media. It became a simple image to connote the various strains of populism supporting and supported by Trump.

Memes dominated much of social media during the 2016 election, and the overwhelming tilt was in favor of Trump and against Clinton. In addition to the proliferation of Pepe the Frog, Trump supporters spread a number of memes related to the following subjects: Clinton's email scandal; billionaire George Soros' alleged shadowy control of the Democratic Party; the mainstream media as a shill for Clinton (e.g., CNN: the "Clinton News Network"); "Pizzagate" (the conspiracy that a Washington, D.C. pizza place was the site of a child prostitution ring run by the Clintons); the theme of "drain the swamp" (a common metaphor used by Trump about status quo politics); Clinton's alleged rigging of the election; and the trope of "cucks" (or, individuals who are essentially being taken advantage of by liberalism without realizing it).[32] Collectively, these memes saturated the mediated environment, spreading anger/rage like a contagion through message boards, social media posts, and, often, the mainstream media. Taken individually, they may seem harmless or mildly concerning. Taken together, they reflect a culture of anger/rage growing exponentially and being actively fostered in the mediated public sphere.

Perhaps the best illustration of the confluence between candidate Trump and the social meme network is the image of Trump's "rage face." This image, so popular that it has spawned the creation of a meme generator for anyone to use,[33] features Trump in a state of anger, seemingly in the middle of screaming. His index finger is extended, pointing upward, his face is clenched, and his teeth are exposed. It makes plain that his anger is motivating his run for office. As a simple image of one person's face, though, it transmits feeling more readily than it does any type of argument or political position. Facial responses are a fundamental and primordial instance of affect transmission.[34] As Gibbs argues, "it is very difficult not to respond to a spontaneous smile with a spontaneous smile of one's own, and one's own smile provides sufficient feedback to our own bodies to activate the physiological and neurological aspects of joy."[35] As with joy, the obvious anger/rage in one's face can trigger similar responses in others. Trump's face, contorted into an extreme embodiment of rage, functions to spread a sense of anger through the populace, and the circulation of this meme likely has varying effects. The political right may be motivated to support Trump's campaign; conversely, the political left may be motivated to fight

190 *Jeffrey St. Onge*

against it. In both cases, however, the affectual dimension of anger/rage animates political discussion and decision-making.

Crucially, memes do not advance precise or complete logical arguments, but rather function as a mixture of argument and attitude about a subject. As Davi Johnson argues, memes are characterized by their "apparent slipperiness or ambiguity," and the ambiguity of a meme "ultimately aids its evolutionary survival and replication."[36] Memes related to the Trump campaign typically carried both specific argumentation (i.e., Hillary Clinton is "crooked") and more general feelings of anger/rage about contemporary political life. As such, the anger/rage inherent in Trump memes registered both analytically (as one confronts the meaning of the images) and uncritically (as one feels the emotional response produced by the affect contagion). Political information, filtered through this affectual dimension, was imbued with the anti-establishment logic of the Trump campaign, and thus, provided a warrant for his argument to "make America great again."

Conclusion

Memes should be considered not as an aberration of political culture but rather as a now-standard means of political influence and argumentation. As easily replicable (and shareable) mini-arguments, memes circulate not only ideas but also feelings, giving shape to group identities and the emotional forces that animate them. In the case of Trump, memes helped to spread anger/rage about any number of targets—Hillary Clinton, Barack Obama, the mainstream media, immigrants, "freeloaders," trade agreements, Hollywood elites, etc.,—and functioned to make an improbable candidacy a successful expression of frustration toward the status quo. That Trump's candidacy was based in anger/rage helped to create ideal conditions for memes and viral images to circulate, which contributed to a feedback loop of anxiety and distrust toward mainstream political thought.

Digital campaigns will get more, rather than less, sophisticated, and as such, it is necessary to understand the various ways digital media contribute to the larger discourse in terms of both feeling and argument. Memes are a key element of the contemporary political ecosystem, and scholars require a better understanding of how they impact the rhetorical operations of democratic culture. As Kenneth Burke argues, language—particularly the rhetorical energy within it—motivates individuals to form attitudes about the world.[37] That is, communication "defines situations for individuals."[38] As social media becomes the primary interface between citizens and the public sphere, memes and other viral media will have increased influence over the formation of political attitudes and the construction of political campaigns. They are part of the language of contemporary politics. Thus, analyses of democracy that seek to understand the contours of political debate and the shape and scope of political culture have to contend with the digital public sphere that encompasses not only mainstream social media like Facebook and Twitter, but shadowy networks, message boards, and even foreign entities that utilize the rapid efficiency and affective power of social media to influence political outcomes abroad.

As scholars continue to study the role of affect in political culture, it may be useful to consider memes and viral images as defining features of the *sensus communis*. They are not solely contributors to public argument and discussion but also influential contagions that color the way information is processed and analyzed. It is likely the case, after all, that many people are motivated to vote by feeling rather than by strict logical analysis of policies or candidates. In the case of Trump, memes and viral images function to reflect, build, and spread a sense of deep anger/rage that justified and supported his populist candidacy. A deeper understanding of the constitutive nature of memes in relation to the public sphere can provide further insight into political movements that are otherwise difficult to comprehend.

Notes

1 John M. Judis, "All the Rage," *New Republic,* September 19, 2016, https://newrepublic.com/article/136327/all-rage-sanders-trump-populism.

2 See, for example, Robert E. Denton, Jr., ed., *Studies of Communication in the 2016 Presidential Campaign* (New York: Rowman & Littlefield, 2017); Jeanine E. Kraybill, ed., *Unconventional, Partisan, and Polarizing Rhetoric: How the 2016 Election Shaped the Way Candidates Strategize, Engage, and Communicate* (New York: Rowman & Littlefield, 2017).

3 Jennifer Finney Boylan, "The Year of the Angry Voter," *New York Times,* February 10, 2016, www.nytimes.com/2016/02/11/opinion/the-year-of-the-angry-voter.html.

4 Paul Moss, "2016: The Year of Anger," *BBC News,* December 31, 2016, www.bbc.com/news/world-38460516; Pankaj Mishra, "Welcome to the Age of Anger," *Guardian,* December 8, 2016, www.theguardian.com/politics/2016/dec/08/welcome-age-anger-brexit-trump; Walter Shapiro, "Big Money Backlash Has Turned 2016 into Year of Populist Anger," *Brennan Center for Justice,* January 26, 2016, www.brennancenter.org/blog/big-money-backlash-has-turned-2016-year-populist-anger. See also, Michel Martin, "This Year, Anger Is All the Rage in Politics. Why?" *NPR: All Things Considered,* February 7, 2016, www.npr.org/2016/02/07/465934702/this-year-anger-is-all-the-rage-in-politics-why.

5 Tammy Webber and Emily Swanson, "Americans May Be Happy with Their Friends and Finances, but the Federal Government Is Making Them See Red," *US-News,* April 18, 2016, www.usnews.com/news/politics/articles/2016-04-18/poll-americans-angry-with-federal-government-happy-at-home.

6 Jonah Berger and Katherine L. Milkman, "What Makes Online Content Viral?" *Journal of Marketing Research* 49, no. 2 (2012): 192–205. https://doi.org/10.1509/jmr.10.0353.

7 Andrew Marentz, "Trump and the Truth: The Viral Candidate," *The New Yorker,* November 4, 2016, www.newyorker.com/news/news-desk/trump-and-the-truth-the-viral-candidate.

8 Katharine Viner, "How Technology Disrupted the Truth," *The Guardian,* July 12, 2016, www.theguardian.com/media/2016/jul/12/how-technology-disrupted-the-truth.

9 Chris Baynes, "Donald Trump Says He Would Not Be President without Twitter," *Independent,* October 22, 2017, www.independent.co.uk/news/

192 *Jeffrey St. Onge*

world/americas/us-politics/donald-trump-tweets-twitter-social-media-facebook-instagram-fox-business-network-would-not-be-a8013491.html.

10 For the remainder of this essay, I will refer to anger and rage interchangeably. I draw the anger/rage affect category from Silvan Tomkins, who in his groundbreaking research on affect and human relations included it as one of the seven key dimensions of affect. For a simplified explanation, see "Nine Affects, Present at Birth, Combine with Life Experience to Form Emotion and Personality," The Tomkins Institute, accessed December 15, 2017, www.tomkins.org/what-tomkins-said/introduction/nine-affects-present-at-birth-combine-to-form-emotion-mood-and-personality/.

11 Anna Gibbs, "After Affect: Sympathy, Synchrony, and Mimetic Communication," in *The Affect Theory Reader*, eds.Melissa Gregg and Gregory J. Seigworth (Durham, NC: Duke University Press, 2010), 186.

12 Gibbs, "After Affect," 187.

13 Ibid.

14 Ibid., 191.

15 See especially, Silvan S. Tomkins, *Affect Imagery Consciousness Volume III. The Negative Affects: Anger and Fear* (New York: Springer, 1991).

16 Anna Gibbs, "Disaffected," *Continuum: Journal of Media & Cultural Studies* 16, no. 3 (2002): 339. doi:10.1080/1030431022000018690.

17 Gibbs, "After Affect," 192.

18 Richard Dawkins, *The Selfish Gene* (Oxford: Oxford University Press, 1990), 192. Emphasis in original.

19 Ibid.

20 Ibid.

21 Limor Shifman, "Memes in a Digital World: Reconciling with a Conceptual Troublemaker," *Journal of Computer-Mediated Communication* 18, no. 3 (2013): 364–365. doi:10.1111/jcc4.12013.

22 Shifman, "Memes," 365. See also, Robert Aunger, *Darwinizing Culture: The Status of Memetics as a Science* (Oxford: Oxford University Press, 2000), 1–24.

23 Rodney Taveira and Emma Balfour, "How Donald Trump Won the 2016 Meme Wars," *The Conversation,* November 29, 2016, https://theconversation.com/how-donald-trump-won-the-2016-meme-wars-68580.

24 Ibid.

25 Ibid.

26 Limor Shiffman, *Memes in Digital Culture* (Boston, MA: MIT Press, 2013), 128.

27 Francis Heylighen and Klaas Chielens, "Cultural Evolution and Memetics," in *Encyclopedia of Complexity and System Science*, ed. Robert A. Meyers (New York: Springer-Verlag), 2.

28 Heylighen and Chielens, "Cultural Evolution," 2–3.

29 Ibid.

30 "Pepe the Frog," The Anti-Defamation League, accessed December 15, 2017, www.adl.org/education/references/hate-symbols/pepe-the-frog.

31 Jessica Roy, "How 'Pepe the Frog' Went from Harmless to Hate Symbol," *Los Angeles Times*, October 11, 2016, www.latimes.com/politics/la-na-pol-pepe-the-frog-hate-symbol-20161011-snap-htmlstory.html. The "deplorables" title refers a statement Hillary Clinton made about Trump's supporters; this statement was seized upon and employed by the Trump campaign as a means of connecting various figures supportive of his campaign.

32 For a helpful list of common meme types, see Aja Romano, "The 2016 Culture War, as Illustrated by the Alt-Right," *Vox,* December 30, 2016, www.vox.com/culture/2016/12/30/13572256/2016-trump-culture-war-alt-right-meme. It has now come to light that Russian operatives were behind

many memes, working in large "troll armies" to shape the outcome of the election toward ends favorable to Russian interests. See, for example, Scott Shane, "The Fake Americans Russia Created to Influence the Election," *New York Times,* September 7, 2017, www.nytimes.com/2017/09/07/us/politics/russia-facebook-twitter-election.html.

33 "Trump Rage Face Meme Generator," *IMGFLIP,* accessed December 15, 2017, https://imgflip.com/memegenerator/60940003/Trump-Rage-Face.

34 Gibbs, "After Affect," 191.

35 Ibid.

36 Davi Johnson, "Mapping the Meme: A Geographical Approach to Materialist Rhetorical Criticism," *Communication and Critical/Cultural Studies* 4, no. 1 (2007): 42. doi:10.1080/14791420601138286.

37 Kenneth Burke, *The Philosophy of Literary Form* (Berkeley: University of California Press, 1974), 292–304.

38 Donald G. Ellis, *Transforming Conflict: Communication and Ethnopolitical Conflict* (New York: Rowman & Littlefield, 2006), 19.

Bibliography

The Anti-Defamation League. "Pepe the Frog." www.adl.org/education/references/hate-symbols/pepe-the-frog (Accessed December 15, 2017).

Aunger, Robert. *Darwinizing Culture: The Status of Memetics as a Science.* Oxford: Oxford University Press, 2000.

Baynes, Chris. "Donald Trump Says He Would Not Be President without Twitter." *Independent,* October 22, 2017. www.independent.co.uk/news/world/americas/us-politics/donald-trump-tweets-twitter-social-media-facebook-instagram-fox-business-network-would-not-be-a8013491.html.

Berger, Jonah, and Katherine L. Milkman. "What Makes Online Content Viral?" *Journal of Marketing Research* 49, no. 2 (2012): 192–205. https://doi.org/10.1509/jmr.10.0353.

Boylan, Jennifer Finney. "The Year of the Angry Voter." *New York Times,* February 10, 2016. www.nytimes.com/2016/02/11/opinion/the-year-of-the-angry-voter.html.

Burke, Kenneth. The *Philosophy of Literary Form.* Berkeley: University of California Press, 1974.

Dawkins, Richard. *The Selfish Gene.* Oxford: Oxford University Press, 1990.

Denton, Jr., Robert E, ed. *Studies of Communication in the 2016 Presidential Campaign.* New York: Rowman & Littlefield, 2017.

Ellis, Donald G. *Transforming Conflict: Communication and Ethnopolitical Conflict.* New York: Rowman & Littlefield, 2006.

Gibbs, Anna. "Disaffected." *Continuum: Journal of Media & Cultural Studies* 16, no. 3 (2002): 335–341. doi:10.1080/1030431022000018690.

Gibbs, Anna. "After Affect: Sympathy, Synchrony, and Mimetic Communication." In *The Affect Theory Reader,* edited by Melissa Gregg and Gregory J. Seigworth, 186–205. Durham, NC: Duke University Press, 2010.

Heylighen, Francis, and Klaas Chielens. "Cultural Evolution and Memetics." In *Encyclopedia of Complexity and System Science,* edited by Robert A. Meyers, 1–27. New York: Springer Verlag, 2008.

Johnson, Davi. "Mapping the Meme: A Geographical Approach to Materialist Rhetorical Criticism." *Communication and Critical/Cultural Studies* 4, no. 1 (2007): 27–50. doi:10.1080/14791420601138286.

194 *Jeffrey St. Onge*

Judis, John M. "All the Rage." *New Republic,* September 19, 2016. https://newrepublic.com/article/136327/all-rage-sanders-trump-populism.

Kraybill, Jeanine E, ed. *Unconventional, Partisan, and Polarizing Rhetoric: How the 2016 Election Shaped the Way Candidates Strategize, Engage, and Communicate.* New York: Rowman & Littlefield, 2017.

Marentz, Andrew. "Trump and the Truth: The Viral Candidate." *The New Yorker,* November 4, 2016. www.newyorker.com/news/news-desk/trump-and-the-truth-the-viral-candidate.

Martin, Michel. "This Year, Anger Is All the Rage in Politics. Why?" *NPR: All Things Considered,* February 7, 2016. www.npr.org/2016/02/07/465934702/this-year-anger-is-all-the-rage-in-politics-why.

Mishra, Pankaj. "Welcome to the Age of Anger." *Guardian,* December 8, 2016. www.theguardian.com/politics/2016/dec/08/welcome-age-anger-brexit-trump.

Moss, Paul. "2016: The Year of Anger." *BBC News,* December 31, 2016. www.bbc.com/news/world-38460516.

Romano, Aja. "The 2016 Culture War, as Illustrated by the Alt-Right." *Vox,* December 30, 2016. www.vox.com/culture/2016/12/30/13572256/2016-trump-culture-war-alt-right-meme.

Roy, Jessica. "How 'Pepe the Frog' Went from Harmless to Hate Symbol." *Los Angeles Times,* October 11, 2016. www.latimes.com/politics/la-na-pol-pepe-the-frog-hate-symbol 20161011-snap-htmlstory.html.

Shane, Scott. "The Fake Americans Russia Created to Influence the Election." *New York Times,* September 7, 2017. www.nytimes.com/2017/09/07/us/politics/russia-facebook-twitter-election.html.

Shapiro, Walter. "Big Money Backlash Has Turned 2016 into Year of Populist Anger." *Brennan Center for Justice,* January 26, 2016. www.brennancenter.org/blog/big-money-backlash-has-turned-2016-year-populist-anger.

Shiffman, Limor. *Memes in Digital Culture.* Boston, MA: MIT Press, 2013.

Shifman, Limor. "Memes in a Digital World: Reconciling with a Conceptual Troublemaker." *Journal of Computer-Mediated Communication* 18, no. 3 (2013): 362–377. doi:10.1111/jcc4.12013.

Taveira, Rodney, and Emma Balfour. "How Donald Trump Won the 2016 Meme Wars." *The Conversation,* November 29, 2016. https://theconversation.com/how-donald-trump-won-the-2016-meme-wars-68580.

The Tomkins Institute. "Nine Affects, Present at Birth, Combine with Life Experience to Form Emotion and Personality." www.tomkins.org/what-tomkins-said/introduction/nine-affects-present-at-birth-combine-to-form-emotion-mood-and-personality/ (Accessed December 15, 2017).

Tomkins, Silvan S. *Affect Imagery Consciousness Volume III. The Negative Affects: Anger and Fear.* New York: Springer, 1991.

Viner, Katharine. "How Technology Disrupted the Truth." *The Guardian,* July 12, 2016. www.theguardian.com/media/2016/jul/12/how-technology-disrupted-the-truth.

Webber, Tammy, and Emily Swanson. "Americans May Be Happy with Their Friends and Finances, but the Federal Government Is Making Them See Red." *USNews,* April 18, 2016. www.usnews.com/news/politics/articles/2016-04-18/poll-americans-angry-with-federal-government-happy-at-home.

14 Feelings Trump Facts

Affect and the Rhetoric of Donald Trump

Lucy J. Miller

In a July 22, 2016 interview, *CNN*'s Alisyn Camerota pressed former Speaker of the House Newt Gingrich on the facts of the FBI crime statistics that disproved Donald Trump's repeated references to the rise in violent crime in America during his 2016 Republican National Convention acceptance speech. Gingrich replied, "As a political candidate, I'll go with how people feel, and I'll let you go with the theoreticians." Gingrich's claim that a politician should care more about the feelings of the people than the facts of "theoreticians" is emblematic of the discourse surrounding the 2016 Republican National Convention and the presidential campaign as a whole. This privileging of feelings over facts can be seen clearly in Donald Trump's rhetoric on the campaign trail and as president. In his speeches, Trump seeks to prompt feelings of fear or anger in his audience and then use those feelings to drive them away from his opponents and toward himself. Trump prompts certain feelings in his audience in order to achieve his goal of maintaining the White, patriarchal, neoliberal status quo that enabled his presidency,[1] and he does not allow the facts of a situation to interfere with the effectiveness of his emotional appeals.

Trump's privileging of feelings over facts contradicts the claims made by some scholars that increased access to information renders other forms of persuasion unnecessary. In "Rhetoric, Legal Advocacy, and Legal Reasoning," Richard Posner offers information costs as a concept through which scholars can determine when a speaker can persuade solely through supplying information and when they must employ rhetoric, which Posner limits to "using signals of one sort or another to enhance the credibility of the speaker's arguments."[2] When information costs are high, meaning that the information itself is either hard to find or difficult to understand without expert knowledge, rhetoric can be useful in supporting an expert's efforts to communicate with a less knowledgeable audience;[3] when they are low, rhetoric is unnecessary because the information can persuade on its own.[4] James Arnt Aune has roundly critiqued Posner's lack of understanding of rhetoric and human communication,[5] and Chaïm Perelman firmly places the empirical, reason-based knowledge Posner labels information within the sphere of rhetoric.[6] Even if we take Posner's concept as it is, though, it is still unable to accurately explain the rhetorical situation surrounding Donald Trump's candidacy and presidency. Information costs are currently extremely low with the average citizen having access, through the internet and other sources, to seemingly unlimited information. Such extremely low information costs, according to Posner, should mean that information dominates. Instead, Newt Gingrich argues that how people feel matters more than the actual facts. Low information costs have made information alone virtually useless.

The inability for facts and information to persuade on their own is a prominent feature of the current rhetorical situation in American politics. Donald Trump's use of emotional appeals seems perfectly suited for this rhetorical situation, but a closer analysis of his use of emotional appeals reveals that he is using them to reinforce the status quo rather than as the populist outsider he is often portrayed as. Affect and emotion are useful concepts for analyzing the current rhetorical situation, and several scholars have identified distinctions between the two concepts, with affect referring to our often unconscious responses to stimuli and emotion referring to our public communication of our responses that are shaped by our relationships with others and reflective of cultural ideologies.[7] However, theorizing the distinctions between affect and emotion is not the purpose of this chapter, so the more generic term of "feelings" will be used throughout to cover both concepts. "Emotional appeals" will be used to refer to efforts to persuade an audience through feelings. What is most important from a rhetorical perspective is that feelings have been recognized since Aristotle as motivating an audience to respond to a persuasive argument.[8] Feelings have played various roles in public life,[9] and rhetorical criticism provides a means for analyzing these roles as reflective of both cultural ideologies and relationships among individuals and groups.

At issue is not the use of emotional appeals per se. The issue with Trump's use of emotional appeals is that he is uninterested in whether or not they are supported by facts. In this chapter, I use Brigitte Bargetz's political grammar of feelings to analyze how Trump models for his audience the privileging of feelings over facts in order to maintain the current status quo.[10] Bargetz distinguishes between "*feeling politics*" and "a politics *of* feelings."[11] By feeling politics, Bargetz is interested in the historical, hierarchical power relations that are reflected in our feelings.[12] A politics of feelings, on the other hand, emphasizes "that power and politics work through feelings" by focusing on how feelings "are produced within specific normative frames."[13] In analyzing Donald Trump's rhetoric, I am interested in the politics of feelings that are found in his privileging of feelings over facts, as seen in two of his speeches: his July 21, 2016 address at the Republican National Convention and his Inaugural Address on January 20, 2017. Trump prompts feelings of fear and anger in his audience in order to position himself as the sole individual capable of remedying the situation that has led to those feelings. The facts are irrelevant to his project of re-centering white, patriarchal neoliberalism in American politics and society. He works through the feelings of his audience to constitute his political power. In our attempts to respond to Trump's rhetoric, we might try to upend this era of feelings over facts by redoubling our focus on facts, but facts without feelings ring hollow. Emma Gonzalez's speech on February 18, 2018 in the aftermath of the shooting at Marjory Stoneman Douglas High School that left 17 dead provides an example of how to resist the felt politics expected of the victims of gun violence, allowing her to make powerful claims about the failures of our current political system through her own experience as a survivor of a mass shooting. To understand Trump's use of emotional appeals and how to respond, we first need to consider the role feelings play in Trumpism as an ideology.

The Role of Feelings in Trumpism

Feelings are at the heart of Trumpism, an ideology defined by individual success, a leadership style that gives complete credit to the person at the top, and the belief that winning means that your actions are correct.[14] Trump wants his audience to be afraid and angry about the changes in the nation and feel that their position of power is tenuous.[15] The fear and anger that is a key component of Trumpism is directed at the idea that "the country itself is changing in ways that many citizens neither requested nor endorsed."[16] Emotional appeals are particularly successful in what Christian Fuchs calls the "age of post-truth" in which expertise and knowledge are no longer trusted and ideological arguments prevail.[17] Trump found a home in this new age dating back to his perpetuation of the Birther conspiracy against President Obama that was grounded in fears of the other.[18] During his campaign for president and upon assuming office, Trump continued his appeals to fear, anger, and hatred in his promises to make the country great again.[19] Fear involves a turning away from an unfamiliar other in anticipation of injury,[20] while anger and hate involve a similar turning away, but the other in this case is intimately familiar to the individual.[21] In his frequent uses of emotional appeals based on feelings of fear and anger, Trump seeks to turn his audience away from his opponents and toward himself. He wants his audience to be afraid of and angry toward others and to love him. Love involves an idealization of the object of the feeling that allows the individual to think better of themselves through the association.[22] Through their love for Trump, his supporters are able to see an idealized version of themselves. As a national figure, though, Trump cannot fulfill the promise of returning the feeling found in love, so this failed response perpetuates the feeling of love toward Trump as his supporters cling to the hope that he will one day return their feelings.[23] Trump's support will continue so long as his audience responds to the fear and anger he directs toward his opponents and the love he directs toward himself.

Donald Trump's emotional appeals work for many of his supporters because they position him as authentic, giving the impression "that

198 *Lucy J. Miller*

they have direct access to his very real emotions."[24] He is able to use the authenticity attributed to him by his supporters to deflect criticism of his more offensive and dangerous statements. After his latest racist, sexist, or xenophobic outburst, such as calling for a ban on Muslim immigration or claiming that Megyn Kelly could not effectively moderate a debate because she had blood "coming out of her wherever," his supporters are able to claim to know the real, authentic Trump behind the façade created for the media.[25] Trump is also able to deflect criticism because he has inculcated in his supporters the belief that winning is the only thing that matters by drawing on his public persona as a ruthless businessman, entrepreneur, and reality show host willing to make the tough decisions necessary for success.[26] While Trump's emotional appeals may serve as nothing more than a strategy to win at all costs, a fuller understanding of how they are constructed might decrease their effectiveness in the future.

"I am Your Voice": Emotional Appeals in the Rhetoric of Donald Trump

Fear, anger, hate, and love are the primary feelings prompted by Donald Trump in the speeches under analysis in this chapter. He paints a picture in his speeches of an America in decline and ruin, prompting the feelings of fear, anger, and hate in his audience. These feelings are then transformed into emotional appeals that seek to persuade the audience to fear and hate Trump's opponents as the causes of the problems facing the nation. The love his audience feels for Trump seeks to persuade them that he is the only one who can restore order and fix the problems.

In his speech at the Republican National Convention, Trump says, "I will present the facts plainly and honestly. We cannot afford to be so politically correct anymore." He then proceeds to present a set of "facts" that were quickly disputed, from the level of violence in this country to the number of border crossings from Mexico. He is unconcerned with the accuracy of his statements because they represent the larger facts that he wants his audience to agree with: traditional America is under attack, and we do not talk about it because we are trying to be politically correct. He prompts feelings of fear and anger in his audience through the loss of their vision of what America should be.

This prompting of fear and anger can also be seen in Trump's reference to "American carnage" in his Inaugural Address.

> But for too many of our citizens, a different reality exists: mothers and children trapped in poverty in our inner cities; rusted-out factories scattered like tombstones across the landscape of our nation; an education system, flush with cash, but which leaves our young and beautiful students deprived of knowledge; and the crime and gangs

and drugs that have stolen too many lives and robbed our country of so much unrealized potential. This American carnage stops right here and stops right now.

Whether or not he has facts to back up his claim that the current state of the nation can be accurately described as carnage is irrelevant because Trump wants his audience to feel that it is true. In his Inaugural Address and Republican National Convention speech, he also provides his audience with targets to direct their feelings toward, from the Washington establishment that "protected itself, but not the citizens of our country" to Hillary Clinton who has a legacy of "death, destruction, and weakness." Trump's statements scapegoat his opponents as the only causes of the nation's problems. Kenneth Burke writes of the use of the scapegoat as "delegat[ing] the personal burden to an external bearer" and "attributing one's own vices or temptations to the delegated vessel."[27] Trump directs the fear and anger of his audience toward his enemies as a means of pushing America's responsibilities and failures onto someone else, regardless of whether the facts support scapegoating this individual or group. The destruction of the nation is not the responsibility of real Americans but outsiders, international opponents, and the elite establishment. Real Americans can be comforted by having Donald Trump to fight for them.

After prompting feelings of fear and anger in his audience and giving them objects for those feelings, Trump wants to restore their hope if they will only believe in him. In his Inaugural Address, Trump makes a promise to his audience, saying, "I will fight for you with every breath in my body – and I will never, ever let you down. America will start winning again, winning like never before." If you sustain your love and support for Trump, he will never fail you, even if he cannot return your affection directly.[28] Trump's desire for his audience to invest him with their love and affection can be found in his continued use of his campaign promise to make America great again. In his Republican National Convention speech, Trump says to his audience, "To all Americans tonight, in all our cities and towns, I make this promise: we will make America strong again. We will make America proud again. We will make America safe again. And we will make America great again." Trump's slogan serves as a promise that fulfills the support his audience has for him, with its enthymematic structure, not stating part of the argument that the audience supplies, allowing the audience to fill in any time in which they think America was formerly great.[29] Being vague on the time period in which America was great allows Trump to reap the benefits of his audience's feelings toward the idea of America's greatness without being challenged on facts that question that greatness, such as the treatment of minority groups and women. Trump's privileging of feelings over facts has turned his audience's feelings of fear and anger into a political movement of the supposed forgotten Americans. He ends his Inaugural Address by speaking directly to those who feel forgotten, saying, "So to all Americans, in every city near and far, small and large, from mountain to mountain, and from ocean to ocean, hear these words: You will never be ignored again." Trump hears the cries of fear and anger from his audience, feelings he helped stoke through his rhetoric, and he will not ignore them. In actuality, since his audience is made up mostly of members of dominant groups, they are hardly ignored or forgotten, but Trump's rhetoric allows them to ignore this fact in favor of their feelings. Trump's audience enacts the felt politics that are prompted by his rhetoric, but we need to resist any effort that seeks to persuade us that our feelings matter more than the truth of a situation by combining facts with feelings in order to once again allow feelings to perform their proper role of moving us to action in response to a well-reasoned argument. Emma Gonazalez's speech on February 18, 2018 provides us with a model of how to resist the felt politics of a situation.

"We Call BS": Emma Gonzalez's Message on Gun Violence

Emma Gonzalez begins her speech in response to the mass shooting in Parkland, Florida with an acknowledgment of the feelings expected of victims of gun violence, saying, "Every single person up here today, all these people should be home grieving. But instead we are up here standing together because if all our government and president can do is send thoughts and prayers, then it's time for victims to be the change that we need to see." The felt politics of gun violence tell us that all we can do is offer our thoughts and prayers to the victims who should be so overcome with grief that they are unable to take public action. Gonzalez resists the expectations of the felt politics of the rhetorical situation in order to deliver a message on gun violence rooted in facts and her emotional experience as a survivor. You do not have to have direct experience in order to resist the felt politics of a situation, but Gonzalez's speech demonstrates the power that experience can have.

Gonzalez raises the issue of the ease with which the Parkland shooter obtained a firearm by stating the facts of Florida's policies on guns, saying, "We certainly do not understand why it should be harder to make plans with friends on weekends than to buy an automatic or semi-automatic weapon. In Florida, to buy a gun you do not need a permit, you do not need a gun license, and once you buy it, you do not need to register it. You do not need a permit to carry a concealed rifle or shotgun. You can buy as many guns as you want at one time." The ease with which you can obtain a gun in Florida is contrasted with the difficulty teenagers have making plans for the weekend, what the survivors would have been able to focus on if their school had not been the target of a mass shooting. The triviality of teenage life, which could be used to undermine the ethos of Gonzalez as a speaker, is contrasted with the ease of getting a gun, thus turning it into the truly trivial activity. Gonzalez's argument is ultimately to reform gun policy to make purchasing a gun anything but trivial.

She then points out a website that tracks mass shootings, and while there is nothing about the title that suggests it is only about America, she asks, "yet does it need to address that?" She lists the facts of the low levels of gun violence and mass shootings in other countries to answer her question. The facts show that such a website would only need to track gun violence in America because it is relatively nonexistent in places like Australia, Canada, and Japan.

Having shown that gun violence is a uniquely American issue, Gonzalez then builds to the emotional high point of her speech when she demands that politicians do something to address the problem, saying, "Politicians who sit in their gilded House and Senate seats funded by the NRA telling us nothing could have been done to prevent this, we call BS … They say no laws could have been able to prevent the hundreds of senseless trage-dies that have occurred. We call BS. That us kids don't know what we're talking about, that we're too young to understand how the government works. We call BS." Gonzalez uses her anger and grief as a victim of gun violence to demand change. By being willing to speak up in public as a victim of gun violence and combing facts with emotional appeals to per-suade her audience to support gun control, Gonzalez serves as a model for how to resist the felt politics of the current rhetorical situation.

Conclusion

Trump wants to prompt a felt politics of anger and fear in his audience at their traditional place of power being reduced while disregarding facts that undermine that position, such as the fact that immigrants from the countries that are included in his travel ban have committed zero acts of terrorism in the United States or that the crime rate in this country has been declining since the early 1990s. His successful use of this strategy to win the presidency in 2016 may encourage us to respond by seeking to break up his coalition by appealing to the same individuals through messages that treat their feelings as valid regardless of the facts. Instead of maintaining the status quo that positions the white, patriarchal, neolib-eral citizen as of singular importance,[30] we must ensure that all voices are heard and that the needs of all citizens are not ignored in order to appease the feelings of the dominant group. Gonzalez serves as an example of a better way to resist the felt politics of the current political environ-ment by supporting emotional appeals with facts. Hopefully, her example makes her dream for the future come true when she says, "We are going to be the kids you read about in textbooks. Not because we're going to be another statistic about mass shooting in America, but because, just as

202 *Lucy J. Miller*

David said, we are going to be the last mass shooting. Just like *Tinker v. Des Moines*, we are going to change the law." Trump's centering of the feelings of the status quo can only be countered by tapping into the resistant passion of those who want to see true change in this nation.

Notes

1 While individual actions taken by the Trump administration, such as tariffs being placed on imports of steel and aluminum, may not fit with the goals of a neoliberal approach to free-market capitalism, the system as a whole that Trump is trying to preserve is still neoliberal.
2 Richard A. Posner, "Rhetoric, Legal Advocacy, and Legal Reasoning," in *Overcoming Law* (Cambridge, MA: Harvard University Press, 1995), 500.
3 Ibid., 503.
4 Ibid., 514.
5 James Arnt Aune, *Selling the Free Market: The Rhetoric of Economic Correctness* (New York: The Guilford Press, 2001), 52–55.
6 Chaïm Perelman, *The Realm of Rhetoric*, trans. by William Kluback (Notre Dame, IN: University of Notre Dame Press, 1982), 5.
7 Marco Abel, *Violent Affect: Literature, Cinema, and Critique after Representation* (Lincoln: University of Nebraska Press, 2007), 6; Sara Ahmed, *The Cultural Politics of Emotion*, 2nd ed. (New York: Routledge, 2015), 10–12; Dana L. Cloud and Kathleen Eaton Feyh, "Reason in Revolt: Emotional Fidelity and Working Class Standpoint in the 'Internationale,'" *Rhetoric Society Quarterly* 45, no. 4 (2015): 303; Daniel M. Gross, *The Secret History of Emotion: From Aristotle's Rhetoric to Modern Brain Science* (Chicago, IL: The University of Chicago Press, 2006), 2–3; Robert Perinbanayagam, *The Rhetoric of Emotions: A Dramatistic Exploration* (New Brunswick, NJ: Transaction Publishers, 2016), 19; Silvan S. Tomkins, *Affect, Imagery, Consciousness Volume I: The Positive Affects* (New York: Springer Publishing Company, 1962), 22.
8 Aristotle, *On Rhetoric: A Theory of Civic Discourse*, trans. by George A. Kennedy (New York: Oxford University Press, 1991), 38–39.
9 Murali Balaji, "Racializing Pity: The Haiti Earthquake and the Plight of 'Others,'" *Critical Studies in Media Communication* 28, no. 1 (2011): 56; Caitlin Bruce, "The Balaclava as Affect Generator: Free Pussy Riot Protests and Transnational Iconicity," *Communication and Critical/Cultural Studies* 12, no. 1 (2015): 49; Erin J. Rand, "An Inflammatory Fag and a Queer Form: Larry Kramer, Polemics, and Rhetorical Agency," *Quarterly Journal of Speech* 94, no. 3 (2008): 297–298; Raka Shome, "'Global Motherhood': The Transnational Intimacies of White Femininity," *Critical Studies in Media Communication* 28, no. 5 (2011): 392; Bradford Vivian, "Neoliberal Epideictic: Rhetorical Form and Commemorative Politics on September 11, 2002," *Quarterly Journal of Speech* 92, no. 1 (2006): 15; Isaac West, "Reviving Rage," *Quarterly Journal of Speech* 98, no. 1 (2012): 100; Emily Winderman, "S(anger) Goes Postal in *The Woman Rebel*: Angry Rhetoric as a Collectivizing Moral Emotion," *Rhetoric & Public Affairs* 17, no. 3 (2014): 390.
10 Brigitte Bargetz, "Mapping Affect: Challenges of (Un)timely Politics," in *Timing of Affect: Epistemologies, Aesthetics, Politics*, eds. Marie-Luise Angerer, Bernd Bösel, and Michaela Ott (Berlin: Diaphanes, 2014), 293.
11 Ibid., 293.
12 Ibid., 299.
13 Ibid.

14 Christian Fuchs, "Donald Trump: A Critical Theory-Perspective on Authoritarian Capitalism," *tripleC* 15, no. 1 (2017): 66.
15 Paul Elliott Johnson, "The Art of Masculine Victimhood: Donald Trump's Demagoguery," *Women's Studies in Communication* 40, no. 3 (2017): 241.
16 Samuel Goldman, "Fusionism Once and Future," *Modern Age* 59, no. 2 (2017): 71.
17 Fuchs, "Donald Trump," 54.
18 Vincent N. Pham, "Our Foreign President Barack Obama: The Racial Logics of Birther Discourses," *Journal of International and Intercultural Communication* 8, no. 2 (2015): 98–99.
19 Patrick J. Deneen. "The Ghost of Conservatism Past," *Modern Age* 59, no. 2 (2017): 29.
20 Ahmed, "Cultural Politics," 65.
21 Ibid., 51.
22 Ibid., 128.
23 Ibid., 131.
24 Eric Guthey, "Don't Misunderestimate the Donald (Like We Did)," *Television & New Media* 17, no. 7 (2016): 668.
25 Mark Andrejevic, "The *Jouissance* of Trump," *Television & New Media* 17, no. 7 (2016): 652–653.
26 Greg Elmer and Paula Todd, "Don't Be a Loser: Or How Trump Turned the Republican Primaries into an Episode of *The Apprentice*," *Television & New Media* 17, no. 7 (2016): 661.
27 Kenneth Burke, *The Philosophy of Literary Form: Studies in Symbolic Action*, 3rd ed. (Berkeley: University of California Press, 1973), 45.
28 Ahmed, "Cultural Politics," 131.
29 Craig R. Smith, "Ronald Reagan's Rhetorical Re-Invention of Conservatism," *Quarterly Journal of Speech* 103, no. 1–2 (2017): 54.
30 Kristan Poirot, "Violence and White Heteronormative Citizenship," *Women's Studies in Communication* 40, no. 4 (2017): 323.

Bibliography

Abel, Marco. *Violent Affect: Literature, Cinema, and Critique after Representation.* Lincoln: University of Nebraska Press, 2007.

Ahmed, Sara. *The Cultural Politics of Emotion.* 2nd ed. New York: Routledge, 2015.

Andrejevic, Mark. "The *Jouissance* of Trump." *Television & New Media* 17, no. 7 (2016): 651–655.

Aristotle, *On Rhetoric: A Theory of Civic Discourse.* Translated by George A. Kennedy. New York: Oxford University Press, 1991.

Aune, James Arnt. *Selling the Free Market: The Rhetoric of Economic Correctness.* New York: The Guilford Press, 2001.

Balaji, Murali. "Racializing Pity: The Haiti Earthquake and the Plight of 'Others.'" *Critical Studies in Media Communication* 28, no. 1 (2011): 50–67.

Bargetz, Brigitte. "Mapping Affect: Challenges of (Un)timely Politics." In *Timing of Affect: Epistemologies, Aesthetics, Politics*, edited by Marie-Luise Angerer, Bernd Bösel, and Michaela Ott, 289–302. Berlin: Diaphanes, 2014.

Bruce, Caitlin. "The Balaclava as Affect Generator: Free Pussy Riot Protests and Transnational Iconicity." *Communication and Critical/Cultural Studies* 12, no. 1 (2015): 42–62.

Burke, Kenneth. *The Philosophy of Literary Form: Studies in Symbolic Action*. 3rd ed. Berkeley: University of California Press, 1973.

Cloud, Dana L., and Kathleen Eaton Feyh. "Reason in Revolt: Emotional Fidelity and Working Class Standpoint in the 'Internationale.'" *Rhetoric Society Quarterly* 45, no. 4 (2015): 300–323.

Deneen, Patrick J. "The Ghost of Conservatism Past." *Modern Age* 59, no. 2 (2017): 23–32.

Elmer, Greg, and Paula Todd. "Don't Be a Loser: Or How Trump Turned the Republican Primaries into an Episode of *The Apprentice*." *Television & New Media* 17, no. 7 (2016): 660–662.

Fuchs, Christian. "Donald Trump: A Critical Theory-Perspective on Authoritarian Capitalism." *tripleC* 15, no. 1 (2017): 1–72.

Goldman, Samuel. "Fusionism Once and Future." *Modern Age* 59, no. 2 (2017): 65–74.

Gross, Daniel M. *The Secret History of Emotion: From Aristotle's Rhetoric to Modern Brain Science*. Chicago, IL: The University of Chicago Press, 2006.

Guthey, Eric. "Don't Misunderestimate the Donald (Like We Did)." *Television & New Media* 17, no. 7 (2016): 667–670.

Johnson, Paul Elliott. "The Art of Masculine Victimhood: Donald Trump's Demagoguery." *Women's Studies in Communication* 40, no. 3 (2017): 229–250.

Perinbanayagam, Robert. *The Rhetoric of Emotions: A Dramatistic Exploration*. New Brunswick, NJ: Transaction Publishers, 2016.

Perelman, Chaïm. *The Realm of Rhetoric*. Translated by William Kluback. Notre Dame, IN: University of Notre Dame Press, 1982.

Pham, Vincent N. "Our Foreign President Barack Obama: The Racial Logics of Birther Discourses." *Journal of International and Intercultural Communication* 8, no. 2 (2015): 86–107.

Poirot, Kristan. "Violence and White Heteronormative Citizenship." *Women's Studies in Communication* 40, no. 4 (2017): 321–324.

Posner, Richard A. "Rhetoric, Legal Advocacy, and Legal Reasoning." In *Overcoming Law*. Cambridge, MA: Harvard University Press, 1995, 498–530.

Rand, Erin J. "An Inflammatory Fag and a Queer Form: Larry Kramer, Polemics, and Rhetorical Agency." *Quarterly Journal of Speech* 94, no. 3 (2008): 297–319.

Shome, Raka. "'Global Motherhood': The Transnational Intimacies of White Femininity." *Critical Studies in Media Communication* 28, no. 5 (2011): 388–406.

Smith, Craig R. "Ronald Reagan's Rhetorical Re-Invention of Conservatism." *Quarterly Journal of Speech* 103, no. 1–2 (2017): 33–65.

Tomkins, Silvan S. *Affect, Imagery, Consciousness Volume I: The Positive Affects*. New York: Springer Publishing Company, 1962.

Vivian, Bradford. "Neoliberal Epideictic: Rhetorical Form and Commemorative Politics on September 11, 2002." *Quarterly Journal of Speech* 92, no. 1 (2006): 1–26.

West, Isaac. "Reviving Rage." *Quarterly Journal of Speech* 98, no. 1 (2012): 97–102.

Winderman, Emily. "S(anger) Goes Postal in *The Woman Rebel*: Angry Rhetoric as a Collectivizing Moral Emotion." *Rhetoric & Public Affairs* 17, no. 3 (2014): 381–420.

15 Affect, Aesthetics, and Attention

The Digital Spread of Fake News Across the Political Spectrum

Kayla Keener

There has been a growing attention to the influence of fake news, understood here as "hoax-based stories that perpetuate hearsay, rumors, and misinformation."[1] Within the 2016 U.S. election cycle, fake stories and sites were overwhelmingly believed to be accurate[2] and received up to 159 million visits during the month of the election, with the most widely shared stories during the election being not only fake, but pro-Trump.[3] This chapter will examine how specific instances of fake news concerning the 2016 U.S. election and Donald Trump's presidency have circulated through digital media and popular discourse, with an eye to the ways that fake news is consumed, spread, and believed by individuals on *all* points of the ideological spectrum. With its rise during the 2016 election cycle, fake news has been framed as an issue limited to conservative circles, but this chapter argues that liberals as well as conservatives are susceptible to the tactics of fake news—despite conservatives being unevenly targeted.[4] Fake news is able to deceive consumers across partisan lines by specifically targeting preexisting fears and beliefs, mimicking the aesthetics of mainstream news websites, and circulating through social media. These factors, paired with an overall lack of attention to the particulars of a story,[5] contribute to fake news' appearance of legitimacy and ability to mislead consumers.

This analysis of the contributing factors to the rise of fake news, as seen in the run-up-to, and aftermath of, the 2016 U.S. presidential election and into the presidency of Donald Trump, is framed by a theorization of the central role affect plays in the virality of certain stories. Understood as a precognitive embodied response to stimuli, affect functions here as the bodily manifestation of confirmation bias, or the tendency to interpret new evidence as confirmation of one's existing beliefs, as well as a response to the perceived threat presented by the content of fake news stories, and which is predicated on a pervasive sense of anxiety within contemporary politics. This chapter will end with an examination of recent and proposed changes to digital platforms, framed within Mark Andrejevic's identification of a contemporaneous infoglut,[6] or an excessive supply of information, to think through what it means to engage with digital information in a time of exceptional divisiveness and extreme fracturing of worldviews. Ultimately, fake news confirms what individuals already believe and uses affective responses to further its reach and garner more clicks and ad revenue, to deleterious ends, including contributing to the rise of a post-truth political mediascape that must be curbed in order to realign reality with empirical, not felt, facts.

The New Mediascape

Jürgen Habermas argues that the contemporary political public sphere is dominated by mediated communication that discourages deliberative debate through unequal forms of power, and an unregulated system of dispersal. Habermas notes that the growth of digital media forms "interfere[s] with the normative requirement that *relevant* issues, *required* information, and *appropriate* contributions be mobilized."[7] As the public is presented with an onslaught of information online, it becomes less clear not only what is credible or fake, but what constitutes pertinent information that should be considered in political debate, elections, or policy. In this way, news creators (and curators) demonstrate media power by determining what is of importance through what they choose to present to the public. This power of selection becomes problematic with the rise of fake news, as these sites are indistinguishable from credible news, and all information potentially seems equally relevant, or credible. A Fake news exploits the unregulated digital information onslaught that drives people to self-select, or filter, their news consumption.

The inability for people to differentiate between relevant, credible, and fake news stories and sites is heightened within the contemporary attention economy, a term developed by Richard Lanham to demonstrate how economic exchanges have changed in the West from focuses on goods, to trades in information, and, more than information, in the attention necessary to consume information.[8] Attention is a scarce resource to be competed for, not through the development of more appealing goods, but through the aesthetics of style.[9] The style, of news sites here, has become the substance of what is purchased and consumed. For fake news, this means that its aesthetic features must meet certain stylistic standards in order to garner attention. In this way, fake news sites attempt to adhere to the conventions of mainstream news style, while their headlines make purchase through outlandish, attention-seeking claims.

As attention is competed for, more information with more sensational stylistic attractors are developed, creating an infoglut within digital spaces,[10] which has amplified the self-selection of information that affirms individuals' preexisting confirmation biases. This cycle of consuming information that reinforces worldviews contributes to the development of filter bubbles, where because of algorithm and shared social circles, people see things that they tend to agree with, while minimizing contact or experience with those that they don't.[11]

Within this new mediascape, fake news is immune to ideological debunking or fact checking, since various sites operate in isolation, not in contestation with one another. Instead, affective attachments and felt realities, or a 'gut reaction' to the news with which one comes into contact, become viable alternatives to empirically based discourse.[12] Fake news and other ideologically inflected news sites and stories modulate affect by leveraging the affective responses that certain stories garner by "feeling right."[13] This is further visible in Brian Massumi's conception of affective facts, or felt realities, where something "will have been real because it was *felt* to be real".[14] Acting as a form of affective confirmation bias, affective facts manifest themselves in the unfalsifiable felt reality of a story that is immune to fact checking. Affective facts function as a form of common sense, which "feels coherent" and "becomes intuitive."[15] To this end, it is not necessary for fake news, or media ideologues, to control the dominant narrative of a given story, or the empirical facts of the matter, so long as a story can modulate affect and present "alternative facts" as viable potentials that adequately reflect preexisting worldviews and resonate affectively.

The following section will explore the ways that fake news sites develop stylistic modes that conform to mainstream news standards as a way to confer legitimacy onto these sites and stories, and thus further affirm the affective reactions to their false claims. Stylistic factors, taken with the affective facts that affirm biases, function in tandem to legitimize the appearance of fake news, and reify the hyperpartisan beliefs and fears that it promotes for monetary and political gain.

The Visuality and Virality of Fake News

Fake news assumes the appearance of mainstream news sites, which makes it possible for consumers to treat it as they would other media. Traditional news sites typically share a basic format, with a menu bar across the top of their main page, followed by a headline, and then a list of top stories often divided by category, and all accompanied by photos. Fake news sites tend to mimic this format, with key differences that belie their lack of empiricism or sustainability as a news project. Their URL usually mimics mainstream sites (24newsflash.com, buzzfeedusa.com), but often come from a blogging host site like Wordpress (70news.wordpress.com), which anyone can cheaply purchase and promote.[16] Fake news sites may often include only one main story (which the site was created to promote) and stories often include grammatical errors, falsified or uncorroborated information, and a general lack of evidence.[17] These sites also tend to be crowded with various forms of advertisements, much more than a mainstream news website (which often have no advertisements) because the primary motivator behind these sites, aside from pushing an ideological agenda, is to be profitable.[18] Yet, the aesthetics of fake news sites is only secondary to the content of the individual headlines.

The headlines of fake news stories are key in affirming felt realities and confirmation biases of readers. Fake, as well as credible, news stories are often shared across social media platforms without being clicked on or read entirely, with consumers depending on the affective affirmation of a headline to denote its truth capacity.[19] In other words, if the headline feels true, as an affective fact, then it can be accepted as a felt reality without (much) inspection. To this end, fake news headlines typically have a strong ideological leaning that can easily reach and resonate with a particular audience. Headlines from one fake news conglomerate include: "City in Michigan First to Fully Implement Sharia Law" and "Trump to Limit All Intelligence Briefings to 140 Characters."[20] These headlines are believable to those who have an immediate, affective reaction that the claim *feels* right, or *could* be right, while they are unbelievable to those who are not already inclined to agree with the statement. Since the websites these stories stem from often fail to fully recreate the aesthetics of mainstream news and offer no verified information, fake news creators depend on the affirmation of bias and lack of attention to the details of a story or its origin in order for their misinformation to spread, or become viral.

In addition to a reliance on the affective affirmation of a headline, fake news creators depend on the assumed reliability of social networks to ensure their stories reach a wide audience, as sharing becomes a substitute for evidence. Facebook in particular has played a central role in the spread of fake news, with users clicking, sharing and commenting on fake news and hyperpartisan sites 8,711,000 times in the final three months before the election, while users only interacted with stories from 19 major news websites curated on Facebook a total of 7,367,000 times during the same period.[21] Facebook and social networking sites in general are a key source of information for consumers not only through the sharing of sources but also through their curated news platforms, such as Facebook Instant Articles, which is similar to the Apple News app. These platforms standardize the design features of all stories and sites they curate, making one's ability to differentiate between the credibility of sources nearly impossible, unless they visit the original site— through a web browser, *not* these curating platforms—and investigate.[22] The combination of these factors—the design aesthetics of fake news sites, their spreadability across social media platforms, and the homogenization of their design alongside credible sources—detracts from an individual's capacity to investigate claims or use context clues to determine a source's validity and collapses all forms of information into potential fact. Paired with these stories' intent to affirm extant biases and fears, fake news functions as a powerful political tool within the post-truth mediascape.

The following are only two of countless examples exhibiting fake news' vast digital and real world reach that is manifested through these stories' ability to garner affective responses and create hysteria. In particular, the viral fake news story known as "Pizzagate" demonstrates the powerful mobilization of negative affects and manipulation of preexisting fears through the circulation of fake news in both the virtual and real worlds. It is representative of a post-truth political moment where facts have been unseated by beliefs and felt realities that play on anxieties and fears as a way to legitimate alternative narratives and promote ideological agendas.

Immediately following the release of the now infamous Access Hollywood tapes featuring Donald Trump making lewd comments toward women, WikiLeaks released the emails of John Podesta (then Chairman of Hillary Clinton's presidential campaign) on October 7th, 2016.[23] On October 30th, 2016, someone tweeting under the handle @DavidGoldbergNY cited rumors that the new emails "point to a pedophilia ring and @HillaryClinton is at the center".[24] The hashtag #pizzagate first appeared on Twitter on November 7th, 2016, and would be tweeted and retweeted between hundreds and thousands of times each day over the next several weeks.[25] The theory that the pizza restaurant Comet Ping Pong, located in a wealthy neighborhood of Washington, D.C., was a hub for a ring of child sex-traffickers, led by Hillary Clinton and John Podesta—among other influential Washington figures—was circulated through Reddit, Twitter, Facebook, fake news sites, and vitriol-spewing punditry pages such as the far-right leaning Alex Jones's Infowars.[26]

At the height of this hysteria, threats came into the restaurant online and over the phone, with as many as 150 calls per day[27] and five #pizzagate Twitter posts per minute.[28] Likewise, employees, patrons, and business neighbors of Comet Ping Pong received similar threats and accusations of involvement in the alleged sex trafficking ring.[29] Finally, the affective tension coalesced in the form of Edgar Welch's act of charging on to the premises, determined to save the children. On Sunday, December 4th, 2016, armed with several loaded guns, Welch fired shots into the building and attempted to find the nonexistent helpless victims, while employees fled the scene.[30] Welch quickly surrendered himself to police after he realized there was nothing to find.[31] Shortly after Welch pleaded guilty to a series of charges relating to the incident, several dozen people gathered outside the White House to demand an investigation into the Pizzagate rumors.[32]

Pizzagate was made possible through the fake news story's ability to travel across social media platforms and through seemingly trustworthy sources, while affirming the worldviews of voters who were already suspicious of Hillary Clinton and fearful of her seemingly inevitable presidency. The hysteria of Pizzagate was built on preexisting formations of misogyny—including a distrust of Clinton's lack of traditional femininity,[33] national panic about child sexual abuse,[34] and a distrust of the Washington, D.C. political scene. The creators and spreaders depended on this outlandish story's ability to resonate with voters who would be more susceptible to accepting it as fact because it aligned with established fears and *felt* right, *not* because it presented compelling evidence or came from a trustworthy site. While the initial creator of this particular story remains unknown, it is a significant example of the virality of fake news as it stoked the fears of many conservative voters, and circulated throughout social media and into the ranks of the Trump administration.[35]

While the majority of fake news spread during the election targeted fears about the assumed erosion of traditional values under a possible Clinton presidency, fake news stories spread following Trump's surprise election have worked on liberals' fears regarding the erosion of the federal government's legitimacy. One story that gained traction across social media and mainstream news circles began circulating less than one month after Trump's inauguration. On Wednesday, February 1st, 2017, a panel discussion was convened by the Bipartisan Policy Center about the role of Russia and Turkey in the fight against ISIS in Syria.[36] During the discussion, the vice president of the American Foreign Policy Council, Ilan Berman, noted that the Kremlin had issued a detailed readout of the recent phone conversation between President Trump and President Putin, while the White House had not. Berman then suggested that the readout was never released because White House staffers had turned off the tape recorder, despite admittedly having no knowledge about the actual circumstances of the call.[37] Liberal websites soon began running headlines claiming that Trump had indeed failed to record the conversation, and had done something suspicious on the call itself as well.[38] The story soon went viral on Facebook and Twitter, generating over 70,000 retweets.[39]

This viral story was able to gain traction because it confirmed liberals' biases regarding Trump's inability to govern, as well as growing suspicion of his, and his staff's, collusion with Russians throughout the presidential campaign, and indeed into his presidency. The story functioned as an affective fact more than an empirical fact predicated on credible evidence; while it remains unclear whether such calls between state leaders are to be recorded, the White House did in fact issue a brief readout of the call, which was pointed out by conservative websites shortly after the story began to spread.[40] Yet this information, and Berman's own admission that his claim was conjecture,[41] did nothing to stop the spread of the story as many consumers were already inclined to believe it because it felt right and aligned with their preexisting beliefs.

Each of these stories, and countless others like them, are able to become viral phenomena because they leverage and confirm specific biases through emotional appeals to consumers. Suggestions within mainstream media that liberals spread fake news as a knowing joke while conservatives actually believe such falsities[42] place these ambiguously identified groups in a false binary that positions liberals as inherently able to differentiate fact from fiction and engage reason over emotion, with conservatives as more vulnerable to emotional appeals and attention grabbing headlines. In reality, consumers across the ideological spectrum are susceptible to the tactics of fake news that capitalize on existing fears and anxieties that have only grown within the post-truth political moment and associated attention-based economy. To this end, the aesthetics of fake news sites, though key in providing a sense of legitimacy to their promoted stories, is only secondary to the stories' and headlines' ability to produce an immediate, affective reaction from consumers that further solidifies their ideological position and reifies the political divide.

Reconciling the New Mediascape

Fake news creators compete for consumers' limited attention within the new attention economy, which is complicated by a glut of information. In order to secure attention, clicks and shares, creators craft fake news sites to mimic the aesthetics of mainstream and credible news sources, but importantly rely on catchy and ideologically motivated headlines to garner an affective response that coincides with preexisting confirmation biases. Paired with these design features and platforms that collapse all websites into a uniform format, fake news creators also depend on the wide reach and presumed reliability of consumers' social networks to spread their stories to particular demographics.

In order to combat the spread and impact of fake news, changes are being made in the digital realm to how people may experience fake news and be exposed to information. In July of 2017, Facebook announced policy updates tied to the Facebook Journalism Project that could potentially curb the spread of fake news on the platform.[43] The changes include limiting fake news creators' access to buying ads, testing ways for people to report fake stories, and limiting the link preview editing capabilities to people who are the article's publisher.[44] It is unclear what the impact of these changes will be, and they are merely one necessary step in changing how people interact with information online. Research published following the 2016 election found that fake news stories and credible claims are equally likely to go viral on Facebook when consumers lack the time, attention, and skills necessary to differentiate between relevant sources.[45] This lack of adequate time and media literacy skills in the face of an infoglut points toward the necessity of limiting the onslaught of information that is thrust at the public, particularly in social media settings, while developing media literacy tools that target fake news and generally unreliable sources. Such changes and restructuring in how consumers access and share information are key to limiting the development of not only fake news, but the advent of the post-truth political mediascape as a whole.

Notes

1 Paul Mihailidis and Samantha Viotty, "Spreadable Spectacle in Digital Culture," *American Behavioral Scientist* 61, no. 4 (2017): 441–454.
2 Craig Silverman and Jeremy Singer-Vine, "Most Americans Who See Fake News Believe It, New Survey Says," *BuzzFeed News*, December 6, 2016.

3 Ibid.
4 Hunt Allcott and Matthew Gentzkow, "Social Media and Fake News in the 2016 Election," *Journal of Economic Perspectives* 31, no. 2 (Spring 2017): 211–236.
5 Richard Lanham, *The Economics of Attention: Style and Substance in the Age of Information* (Chicago, IL: University of Chicago Press, 2007).
6 Mark Andrejevic, *Infoglut: How the Digital Era Is Changing the Way We Think about Information* (New York: Routledge, 2013).
7 Jürgen Habermas, "Political Communication in Media Society: Does Democracy Still Enjoy an Epistemic Dimension? The Impact of Normative Theory on Empirical Research," *Communication Theory* 16 (2006): 418.
8 Lanham.
9 Ibid., xi.
10 Andrejevic.
11 Eli Pariser, *The Filter Bubble: How the Personalized Web Is Changing What We Read and How We Think* (London: Penguin Books, 2012).
12 Andrejevic, 60.
13 Ibid., 155.
14 Brian Massumi, "The Future Birth of the Affective Fact: The Political Ontology of Threat," in *The Affect Theory Reader*, ed. Melissa Gregg and Greg Seigworth (Durham, NC: Duke University Press, 2010), 53.
15 Ben Anderson, "Neoliberal Affects," *Progress in Human Geography* 40, no. 6 (2015): 5.
16 Kyle Chayka, "Facebook and Google Makes Lies as Pretty as Truth: How AMP and Instant Articles Camouflage Fake News," *The Verge*, December 6, 2016.
17 James Titcomb and James Carson, "Fake News: What Exactly Is It – And Can It Really Swing an Election?" *Telegraph*, November 14, 2017.
18 See Laura Sydell, "We Tracked Down a Fake-News Creator in the Suburbs. Here's What We Learned," *NPR*, November 23, 2016; Samantha Subramanian, "Inside the Macedonian Fake-News Complex," *Wired*, February 15, 2017.
19 See Xiaoyan Qui, Diego Oliveira, Alireza Shirazi, Alessandro Flammini, and Filippo Menczer, "Limited Individual Attention and Online Virality of Low-Quality Information," *Nature Human Behaviour* 1 (2017).
20 Zack Crockett, "How the 'King of Fake News' Built His Empire," *The Hustle*, November 7, 2017.
21 Craig Silverman, "This Analysis Shows How Viral Fake Election News Stories Outperformed Real News on Facebook," *BuzzFeed News*, November 16, 2016.
22 Chayka.
23 Aaron Sharockman, "It's True: WikiLeaks Dumped Podesta Emails Hour after Trump Video Surfaced," *Politifact*, December 18, 2016.
24 Marc Fisher, John Woodrow Cox, and Peter Hermann, "Pizzagate: From Rumor to Hashtag, to Gunfire in D.C." *The Washington Post*, December 6, 2016.
25 Fisher, Cox and Hermann.
26 Ibid.
27 Ibid.
28 Cecilia Kang, "Fake News Onslaught Targets Pizzeria as Nest of Child-Trafficking," *The New York Times*, November 21, 2016.
29 Andrew Breiner, "Pizzagate Explained: Everything You Want to Know about the Comet Ping Pong Pizzeria Conspiracy Theory but Are Too Afraid to Search for on Reddit," *Salon*, December 10, 2016.

Affect, Aesthetics, and Attention 213

30 See Breiner; Faiz Siddiqui and Susan Svrluga, "N.C. Man Told Police He Went to D.C. Pizzeria with Gun to Investigate Conspiracy Theory," *The Washington Post*, December 5, 2016.
31 Breiner.
32 Michael Miller, "Protestors Outside White House Demand 'Pizzagate' Investigation," *The Washington Post*, March 25, 2017.
33 See Hannah Groch-Begley, "A Comprehensive Guide to Sexist Attacks on Hillary Clinton from the 2008 Campaign," *Media Matters for America*, February 5, 2016.
34 See Roger Lancaster, *Sex Panic and the Punitive State* (Oakland: University of California Press, 2011).
35 See Faiz Siddiqui and Susan Svrluga about how former National Security Advisor Michael Flynn shared the viral story on social media.
36 "Enemies or Partners? Russia and Turkey in Syria," *Bipartisan Policy Center*, February 1, 2017.
37 Craig Silverman, "How Liberal Websites Pushed a Dubious Claim That Trump 'Turned Off' a Recorder for His Call with Putin," *BuzzFeed News*, February 6, 2017.
38 Ibid.
39 Ibid.
40 Ibid.
41 Ibid.
42 See Mike Pearl, "Let's Take a Look at Some Anti-Trump Fake News," *Vice News*, December 2, 2017.
43 Daniel Funke, "Facebook Releases an Update on Its Project to Combat Fake News and Support Journalists," *Poynter*, July 20, 2017.
44 See Daniel Funke; Christine Schmidt, "Facebook's Busy Week: What Link Ownership, Instant Articles Subscriptions, and 6 Months of Its Journalism Project Add Up to," *Nieman Lab*, July 20, 2017.
45 Xiaoyan Qui, Diego Oliveira, Alireza Shirazi, Alessandro Flammini, and Filippo Menczer.

Bibliography

Allcott, Hunt, and Matthew Gentzkow. "Social Media and Fake News in the 2016 Election." *Journal of Economic Perspectives* 31, no. 2 (Spring 2017): 211–236.
Anderson, Ben. "Neoliberal Affects." *Progress in Human Geography* 40, no. 6 (2015): 5.
Andrejevic, Mark. *Infoglut: How the Digital Era Is Changing the Way We Think about Information*. New York: Routledge, 2013.
Bipartisan Policy Center. "Enemies or Partners? Russia and Turkey in Syria." February 1, 2017.
Breiner, Andrew. "Pizzagate Explained: Everything You Want to Know about the Comet Ping Pong Pizzeria Conspiracy Theory but Are Too Afraid to Search for on Reddit." *Salon*, December 10, 2016.
Chayka, Kyle. "Facebook and Google Makes Lies as Pretty as Truth: How AMP and Instant Articles Camouflage Fake News." *The Verge*, December 6, 2016.
Crockett, Zack. "How the 'King of Fake News' Built His Empire." *The Hustle*, November 7, 2017.
Fisher, Marc, John Woodrow Cox, and Peter Hermann. "Pizzagate: From Rumor to Hashtag, to Gunfire in D.C." *The Washington Post*, December 6, 2016.

Funke, Daniel. "Facebook Releases an Update on Its Project to Combat Fake News and Support Journalists." *Poynter*, July 20, 2017.

Habermas, Jürgen. "Political Communication in Media Society: Does Democracy Still Enjoy an Epistemic Dimension? The Impact of Normative Theory on Empirical Research." *Communication Theory* 16 (2006): 418.

Kang, Cecilia. "Fake News Onslaught Targets Pizzeria as Nest of Child-Trafficking." *The New York Times*, November 21, 2016.

Lanham, Richard. *The Economics of Attention: Style and Substance in the Age of Information*. Chicago, IL: University of Chicago Press, 2007.

Massumi, Brian. "The Future Birth of the Affective Fact: The Political Ontology of Threat." In *The Affect Theory Reader*, edited by Melissa Gregg and Greg Seigworth, 53. Durham, NC: Duke University Press, 2010.

Mihailidis, Paul, and Samantha Viotty. "Spreadable Spectacle in Digital Culture." *American Behavioral Scientist* 61, no. 4 (2017): 1–14.

Miller, Michael. "Protestors Outside White House Demand 'Pizzagate' Investigation." *The Washington Post*, March 25, 2017.

Pariser, Eli. *The Filter Bubble: How the Personalized Web Is Changing What We Read and How We Think*. London: Penguin Books, 2012.

Qui, Xiaoyan, Diego Oliveira, Alireza Shirazi, Alessandro Flammini, and Filippo Menczer. "Limited Individual Attention and Online Virality of Low-Quality Information." *Nature Human Behaviour* 1 (2017): 1–22.

Sharockman, Aaron. "It's True: WikiLeaks Dumped Podesta Emails Hour after Trump Video Surfaced." *Politifact*, December 18, 2016.

Siddiqui, Faiz, and Susan Svrluga. "N.C. Man Told Police He Went to D.C. Pizzeria with Gun to Investigate Conspiracy Theory." *The Washington Post*, December 5, 2016.

Silverman, Craig. "This Analysis Shows How Viral Fake Election News Stories Outperformed Real News on Facebook." *BuzzFeed News*, November 16, 2016.

———. "How Liberal Websites Pushed a Dubious Claim That Trump 'Turned Off' a Recorder for His Call with Putin." *BuzzFeed News*, February 6, 2017.

Silverman, Craig, and Jeremy Singer-Vine. "Most Americans Who See Fake News Believe It, New Survey Says." *BuzzFeed News*, December 6, 2016.

Titcomb, James, and James Carson. "Fake News: What Exactly Is It – And Can It Really Swing an Election?" *Telegraph*, November 14, 2017.

16 Meta-Sexist Discourses and Affective Polarization in the 2018 U.S. Presidential Campaign

Jamie Capuzza

In her first interview since losing the 2016 election, Hillary Clinton affirmed misogyny contributed to her election loss.[1] Indeed, gender played a significant role throughout the campaign, not only because for the first time in the nation's history a woman ran on a major political party's ticket but also because her opponent ran on a campaign of unhinged misogyny surpassed perhaps only by his bombastic anti-immigrant, anti-Muslim, anti-media outbursts. Gender politics permeated the campaign from start to finish. Clinton announced her bid for the presidency in May 2015 talking about her mother, abortion, and the importance of telling daughters that they, too, could be president. After conceding the election, Clinton tweeted, "To all the little girls watching ... never doubt that you are valuable and powerful & deserving of every chance & opportunity in the world."[2] Trump, characterized as a pussy-grabbing womanizer, threatened punishment for women who opt for abortions and suggested a working wife was problematic.[3] Voters were exposed to a barrage of sexist and misogynist messages ranging from sexist jokes to advertisements that sexually objectified women, from sexual harassment to pornification of women candidates and their families.[4]

This was not Clinton's first loss. If we take a cultural and historical approach, we recognize that many voters already made up their mind about Clinton before the campaign. She lived in the public spotlight for decades as First Lady, a U.S. senator, Secretary of State, and a 2012 presidential hopeful. She'd been a public victim of sexism for just as long.[5] Trump's discourse and the response to it brought to mind years of sexism Clinton endured, as well as that of many other women politicians. The electorate negotiated the meaning of these exchanges and the role they play in political communication drawing upon both affect and reason. In this regard, "Hillary Hate" not only influenced her electability but also raised larger questions about cultural assumptions related to femininity, women's place in society, feminism, and gendered power relations in general.

How we talk about sexism and misogyny matters. Though these dialogues are often difficult, they are the primary means by which gender oppression is acknowledged and challenged. Tanya Romaniuk termed dialogues such as these "meta-sexist discourse," and she described them as follows:

> At the first level, some action is produced that is interpretable as possibly sexist, an action that may be produced *in situ* or prior to the present interaction. At the second level, an accusation or claim of sexism is made that treats the action as sexist. Finally, at the third level, people may engage in talk about that accusation or claim of sexism. This third level is what is meant by "meta-sexist" talk.[6]

I extend this definition to include misogynist discourses as well. Meta-sexist discourses deserve scholarly attention because such research allows us to explore which claims of sexism and misogyny are introduced into public discourse and how these claims are framed and debated, as well as how we evaluate and respond to them.

The goals of this chapter are to advance understanding of meta-sexist discourse and to illustrate the usefulness of affect theory in doing so. Sexist and misogynist discourses are both grounded in and have the potential to evoke strong affective and emotional responses. Misogyny, by definition, is grounded in hatred and distrust of women and femininity. Sexism is often grounded in fear, anger, and feelings related to entitlement. Targets of sexism and misogyny experience a range of negative affects and emotions such as shame, humiliation, outrage, and resolve. Thus, affect theory can play a productive role in an analysis of meta-sexist discourse.

Affective Intelligence

This chapter draws upon two affective theories, affective intelligence and affective polarization, and does so recognizing the impact of culture on affect. Affective rhetoric is a key component of political communication. The theory of affective intelligence, from the perspective of political science and neuroscience, acknowledges that the nature and quality of human reasoning, including political judgments, lie in the experience of emotion. Affective intelligence challenges conventional Western scholarship for its emphasis on rationality and the dualism between emotion and reason. Because humans are never solely feeling creatures or solely thinking creatures, the false dichotomy between emotion and reason is eschewed. Politics, after all, is as much about winning hearts as it is minds. To be sure, this false dichotomy has served patriarchal ends; a basic feminist critique of Western philosophy calls into question the argument that reason must control the passions. One means of supporting the gender binary and barring women from public life has been to stereotype them as "overly emotional" while stereotyping men as the logical and rational half of the species more suitable for public power.

Focusing specifically on enthusiasm, anger, and anxiety in a political context, Neuman and his colleagues developed the theory of affective intelligence to describe and explain a dual system of cognitive processing information including the dispositional system and surveillance.[7] The dispositional system is akin to personality traits and mood. The surveillance system relates to how people evaluate the importance of issues, events, and public figures when making political judgments and explains how we focus our conscious state on explicit considerations on the best courses of action. For example, when a woman political candidate is victimized by sexism or misogyny, or when others witness that exchange, the dispositional system provides for a visceral reaction prior to cognitively processing the message sufficiently to label it "sexist" or "misogynist" or to decide how to respond, if at all, at the surveillance level.

It is important to contemplate how the interaction between affect and reason transpires within a particular cultural context. Patriarchal culture depends on objectification, harassment, and intimidation, all of which influence how emotions are experienced. The relentless and cumulative effect of gender oppression results in deeply embedded feelings of shame, self-doubt, and fear, and for those people who experience a feminist consciousness-raising, potentially anger or resolve. The lived experience of sexism and misogyny, as well as feminist consciousness-raising, operates within a cultural context. When sexism or misogyny are experienced or witnessed, a complex interaction between affect and reason begins, and while the interaction may not be culturally determined, it is nonetheless influenced by the patriarchal cultural context.

Affective Polarization

Affective polarization, as described by political scientists, is a theory that describes and explains the hostility felt by partisans toward members of opposing political parties and favoritism felt toward their own party members. Acknowledging that party affiliation is built on both affective and cognitive foundations, partisan political identities are reinforced through feelings of interconnectedness. Partisans differentiate themselves from out-group members by displaying positive feelings toward fellow party members and negative feelings toward the opposition.

According to the Pew Research Center, there is a growing intensity of dislike for the opposing political party in recent years. For decades, the American National Election Studies (ANES) have asked voters to rate their feelings toward their own party and other parties using a "feeling thermometer" on a scale of 1–100, where one is the most negative or "cold" rating and 100 the most positive or "warm" feeling. The average rating for Trump among Democrats was 11 and the average rating for Clinton among Republicans was 12. Eighty-seven percent of both Democrats and

218 *Jamie Capuzza*

Republicans report that the opposing party makes them feel frustrated, fearful, or angry. In contrast, Americans' feelings about their own political parties have changed very little. Democrats rate their own party at 76 and Republicans average a rating of 68. Seventy-three percent of Democrats and 64% of Republicans say their own parties make them feel hopeful, but far fewer say they feel enthusiasm or pride.[8]

More often than not, political debates characterized by affective polarization are based less in logical appeals than affect. This phenomenon shapes collective solidarities within the electorate. According to Steven Webster and Alan Abramowitz, "Rising affective polarization is a product of group loyalties that are activated by campaign rhetoric and partisan news coverage … There is no question that affective polarization has increased substantially within the American public over the past several decades".[9] To be sure, emotions ran high in the 2016 presidential campaign, which was often described as emotionally draining and overwrought. An American Psychological Association survey revealed 55%–59% of Americans felt the election was a "very or somewhat significant source of stress".[10]

Certainly, the media play an important role in both reflecting and affecting the electorate's emotional state. The increase in partisan media has exacerbated affective polarization. In particular, social media increased affective polarization in that users tend to construct homogeneous networks insulating themselves from opposing points of view that can lead to closed-mindedness creating political echo chambers.[11]

Affective Rhetoric, Politics, and Twitter

The primary texts for this analysis of meta-sexist discourse will be drawn from the Twitter accounts of Trump and Clinton, of their political parties, and of their supporters. Twitter is frequently used and is now perceived to be a necessary and legitimate communication channel for politicians. Moreover, tweets are a constructive choice for this investigation because Twitter provides a rapid, open-ended network for stimulation and intensification of affect and emotions. Sarah Gilmore and Samantha Warren maintained that the disembodied nature of online communication, the illusion of privacy, and anonymity carry the potential for greater emotional expression.[12] Furthermore, research indicated that Twitter messages that feature a higher degree of emotionality generate more retweets, potentially increasing affective energy and synergy.[13]

In 2016, both the Clinton and Trump campaigns utilized a variety of social media platforms, including Twitter, Facebook, YouTube, and Instagram. Additionally, the Clinton campaign incorporated Pinterest to its overall strategy knowing that this platform is used heavily by American women. The Twitter strategies of the two presidential campaigns differed in that the Trump campaign was more willing to engage with the public and take the risk of retweeting content it did not control, while the Clinton campaign was more guarded. Trump incorporated user-generated content as sources of his tweets significantly more often while three-quarters of Clinton's tweets were original content generated by her team. Clinton and Trump also differed in message content. Clinton's tweets focused primarily on issues, campaign-related activities and endorsements. Trump's tweets focused primarily on endorsements, attacks on others, and campaign-related activities. More men than women followed Trump on Twitter. According to a Bloomberg analysis of his social media account, women comprised only 19% of Trump's 27.6 million Twitter followers. Overall, Trump was discussed in tweets far more often than Clinton.[14]

With this conceptual framework and background in place, this chapter will explore the role affective rhetoric played in meta-sexist discourses in the 2016 presidential campaign and its relation to affective polarization. It would be nearly impossible to inventory the extent of the campaign's sexist vitriol, but three incidents stand out as particularly egregious and suffice as case studies for this chapter, including the Twitter war on former Fox News anchor Megyn Kelly, the infamous *Access Hollywood* video, and the debate insult of Clinton as a "nasty woman." Even though the latter was the only event directly aimed at Clinton, all of these cases influenced how Clinton was perceived, particularly as a woman candidate. Furthermore, people looked to Clinton for meta-sexist commentary about Trump's misogyny.

Blood Coming Out Her Wherever

The contentious feud between Trump and Kelly constituted an important example of meta-sexist discourse within this political campaign. Trump's misogyny, a long-established topic of public debate and media coverage, emerged again shortly after the announcement of his candidacy. While moderating the first Republican debate in August 2015, Kelly asked Trump to respond to the accusation, "you've called women you don't like 'fat pigs,' 'dogs,' 'slobs.'" Trump dismissed her during the debate, but later tweeted: "I really enjoyed the debate tonight even though the @FoxNewstrio, especially @megynkelly, was not very good or professional!" and "Wow, @megynkelly really bombed tonight. People are going wild on twitter! Funny to watch."[15] Tweeting he "enjoyed" the debate and framing the exchange as "funny" invited Trump supporters to associate positive feelings with him, and describing Kelly's performance as "bombing" invited supporters to associate negative feelings toward Kelly, thus deflecting and alleviating affective energy that may have generated cause for concern regarding the impact of the exchange on his candidacy.

Within days, Trump exacerbated the incident and intensified affect by stating on *CNN Tonight*, "when you meet her you realize she's not very tough and she's not very sharp. She gets out there and she starts asking me all sorts of ridiculous questions, and you could see there was blood coming out of her eyes, blood coming out of her ... wherever."[16] This exchange began a highly emotional vendetta against Kelly that continued many months, primarily on Twitter. Trump supporters took to Twitter attacking Kelly as follows, "MEGYN KELLY THE MEDIA POLE DANCER!!" and "@megynkelly put on your big girl pants ... if you can't take it ... Don't dish it out!"[17] In this manner, Trump's supporters magnified his incendiary remarks on Twitter strengthening affective attachments that fueled political polarization.

As Trump's emotional taunts flared, the campaign was forced to respond, engaging in meta-sexist discourse strategically by employing the voices of Republican women, in particular. Daughter Ivanka Trump responded, "I've certainly thought that certain things should be toned down" and Counselor to the President Kellyanne Conway offered up Trump's record of employing women as evidence that Trump wasn't sexist.[18]

Clinton and her supporters joined this meta-sexist discourse and did so primarily by discussing affect and emotion. Clinton described the comments about Kelly as "overboard, offensive, outrageous."[19] Clinton's public display of affect became a political statement. Appealing to the audience's affective intelligence, Clinton invited the electorate to make a political judgment about Trump based on the experience of emotion. Her comments framed this exchange as a case of sexism and established as a matter of public debate whether or not such discourse is appropriate for a presidential candidate, and she suggested that outrage was an appropriate public response. Furthermore, Clinton used the exchange to call into question Trump's strategy of fomenting an emotional frenzy within his base as follows: "It's all entertainment–I think he's having the time of his life, being up on the stage, saying whatever he wants to say, getting people excited."[20]

Clinton also used the Trump/Kelly exchange to reinforce her own public pro-woman image and created positive affect among her supporters by complimenting Kelly as a "superb journalist."[21] Clinton extended her pro-woman stance by using the exchange to underscore her support of women's reproductive rights. In the three days following the "blood coming out her wherever" comment, Clinton and the Democratic National Committee (DNC) tweeted responses seven times, six of which specifically provided support for Planned Parenthood and reproductive rights. Clinton's team strategically underscored their pride in standing with Planned Parenthood and incorporated fear appeals emphasizing the Republican Party's "assault on women's health."[22] In this regard, public expression of emotions such as pride and fear became an important component of meta-sexist discourse and contributed to affective polarization among reproductive rights opponents and proponents.

Clinton's characterization of the Trump/Kelly exchange as sexist also functioned to create a social space for others to participate in meta-sexist discourse, and in so doing, to share similar affective energy. Her followers tweeted messages such as: "Ms @megynkelly, I might not agree w u on much but #THANKYOU for the #Trump question! He answered like the #sexist he is" and "Potential Leader of the Free World Spends Night Harassing Woman on Twitter."[23] Such comments reaffirmed gut-level impressions of Trump as sexist that contributed to affective solidarity and political polarization.

Furthermore, the Trump/Kelly exchange was an opportunity for the Clinton campaign and the media to establish a pattern of behavior. This exchange quickly became linked to previous comments of a similarly sexist nature from Trump's past. The opposition built an inductive argument claiming this altercation was indicative of a larger pattern of behavior. For example, the media incorporated Trump's previous description of his opponent, Carly Fiorina, into the fray as follows, "Look at that face. Would anyone vote for that? Can you imagine that, the face of our next president? I mean, she's a woman, and I'm not supposed to say bad things, but really, folks, come on. Are we serious?"[24] Bringing up such incidents intensified affect among the electorate.

The circulation of negative affective energy within meta-sexist discourses also can be illustrated by two campaign videos posted to Twitter. Shortly after the "blood coming out her wherever" comment, a pro-Clinton super PAC, Priorities USA Action, released two videos. The first advertisement, "Speak," featured women and one man lip-syncing Trump's sexist comments starting with those directed at Kelly, moving on to other sexist comments, and ending with a narrator asking: "Does Donald Trump speak for you?" The second advertisement, "Respect," began with Trump claiming no one respected women more than he did, but then showcased the Kelly insult, his promises to defund Planned Parenthood, and his claim there should be some form of punishment for women seeking abortions.[25] Clinton and her supporters, drawing upon affective intelligence, claimed that the Trump/Kelly exchange was not a one-time slip of the tongue under the pressure of a televised presidential debate, but rather an indication of Trump's perspective on women, which they should fear. The Democratic base was invited to drawn upon both affect and reason to increase interconnectedness with their party and negative evaluations of the opposing party.

Trump continued this meta-sexist dialogue responding to Clinton's characterization of his exchange with Kelly by denigrating his opponent, a strategy he employed throughout the campaign. Trump responded to Clinton's characterization as follows: "She is a woman, she is playing the woman card left and right. Frankly, if she didn't, she would do very poorly. If she were a man and she was the way she is, she would get virtually no votes."[26] In this regard, Trump's denigration tapped into his base's negative affect. He increased affective polarization by deflecting accusations of sexism as "playing the gender card" and calling into question Clinton's

222 *Jamie Capuzza*

qualifications. Clinton resisted the gender-baiting. Instead of going on the defense, she responded with wit and affirmed her feminist identity by saying, "deal me in."

In summary, the now infamous "blood coming out her wherever" remark garnered politically advantageous emotional responses for Clinton, and served as an example of affective intelligence in that voters made political judgments about both candidates within the experience of these emotions. Moreover, the circulation of negative affect related to outrage, offense, and fear stimulated collective solidarity among Clinton supporters, intensifying affective polarization on both sides of the campaign.

Grab Them by the Pussy

A second illustration of meta-sexist discourse is the now infamous *Access Hollywood* video documenting Trump pronouncing, "I just start kissing them. I don't even wait. And when you're a star, they let you do it. You can do anything ... Grab them by the pussy."[27] CNN's Anderson Cooper later asked Trump during a subsequent debate if the nominee understood that the actions he described constituted sexual assault, to which Trump contented, "No. This was locker room talk. I have great respect for women. Nobody has more."[28] Eventually Trump issued an apology, but only after public pressure to do so.

The *Access Hollywood* video, met with unified shock and horror, circulated negative affect for weeks. Many Republican leaders retracted their support for Trump's candidacy and several political strategists were convinced the leaked video would be the end of his campaign. House Speaker Paul Ryan said that the video "sickened" him and withdrew an invitation for Trump to appear with him in Wisconsin. Senator Mitch McConnell said, "As the father of three daughters, I strongly believe that Trump needs to apologize directly to women and girls everywhere, and take full responsibility for the utter lack of respect for women shown in his comments on that tape."[29] Republican opponent Jeb Bush commented, "As the grandfather of two precious girls, I find that no apology can excuse away Donald Trump's reprehensible comments degrading women." Marco Rubio tweeted, "Donald's comments were vulgar, egregious & impossible to justify. No one should ever talk about any woman in those terms, even in private," and Scott Walker tweeted, "Inexcusable. Trump's comments are inexcusable."[30] Even wife Melania released a statement, describing her husband's words as "unacceptable and offensive."[31] These examples illustrate the level of negative affect generated by the video even within the Republican Party.

Yet, many Trump supporters favored his brand of hegemonic masculinity, taking to Twitter to deflect the firestorm of controversy. Some defenders engaged in meta-sexist discourse with tweets such as "lol don't all guys talk about banging chicks? I mean women do the same. I don't understand the big deal" and "dear media, What @billclinton has done to women is a lot worse than what @realDonaldTrump has said about women," or "Trust me! None of us Trump Supporting females are offended by Trump's private locker room talk! Non issue!"[32] In this example of affective polarization, supporters laughed off accusations of sexual assault, rekindled negative affect associated with the Bill Clinton/Lewinsky scandal, and denied feeling offended.

As would be expected, the Clinton campaign joined the meta-sexist discourse. Clinton invited her supporters to trust their affective intelligence concluding Trump's words were sexist. To further confirm this interpretation and to encourage women's outrage in particular, the campaign retweeted President Obama acknowledging, "A woman who expresses her emotions oftentimes is questioned … it is part of the subtle - and not so subtle - biases that we have."[33] Clinton urged the electorate to make the political judgment that Trump was unfit for office based on their affective response to the video. Clinton issued a formal statement linked to her Twitter account asserting, "What we all saw and heard on Friday was Donald talking about women, what he thinks about women, what he does to women."[34] In a separate tweet that included a direct link to the *Access Hollywood* tape, Clinton declared, "Women have the power to stop Trump."[35] Clinton amplified negative affect associated with Trump such as outrage while simultaneously magnifying positive affect with herself evoking feelings of empowerment. The Clinton campaign also used the controversy as a fund-raising opportunity with a tweet that read, "Chip in to make sure Donald Trump never becomes president" and included a video of little girls engaged in typical daily activities with recordings of Trump uttering various misogynist remarks as the voice-over.[36] This video further circulated negative affect potentially increasing both campaign donations and affective polarization.

Clinton's supporters extended the meta-sexist discourse. The DNC issued several tweets, all of which included a direct link to the *Access Hollywood* video, asking voters to judge Trump unfit for office. For example, "Yesterday we heard Donald Trump say some truly degrading things about women. The saddest part? We weren't surprised."[37] Clinton's running mate, Senator Tim Kaine, interjected the video "makes me sick to my stomach" and Senator Cory Booker tweeted a link to an emotionally rousing video of him speaking on Clinton's behalf at a campaign rally.[38]

Much the same as the Trump/Kelly exchange, the *Access Hollywood* video elicited politically advantageous public emotions for Clinton and served as an example of affective intelligence in that voters were called upon to make political judgments about Trump within the experience of these emotions. Moreover, the circulation of negative affect related to sexism and misogyny stimulated affective solidarities on both sides, escalating political polarization.

224 *Jamie Capuzza*

Nasty Woman

Trump's insult of Clinton as a "nasty woman" serves as the last instance of meta-sexist discourse for this chapter. During the final presidential debate, Trump leaned into the microphone interrupting Clinton, one of 48 times he did so that night, to call her a "nasty woman."[39] Again, Clinton refused to succumb to gender-baiting, instead she deftly completed her argument unflustered. Trump's insult exploited existing disdain for Clinton among his base.

However, his insult resonated with many women voters who resented his effort at gender policing or, for that matter, any man's attempt to define what is and is not appropriate behavior for a woman. The public response was quick and emotionally intense forging an affective solidarity among feminists and Clinton supporters. "Nasty woman" became a rallying call on Twitter before the debate even ended. The hashtag "#NastyWoman" posted humorous memes, photographs, and videos scorning Trump. Numerous tweets appropriated the insult, typified by examples such as "'Such a Nasty Woman' is my new battle cry," "'Such a nasty woman.' My mouth fell open. I'm utterly shocked that a boorish misogynist of this caliber is on that stage," and "You know what a #NastyWoman is good at? Voting."[40]

While earlier examples of Trump's misogyny initially stimulated affective energy related to shock and disbelief for many onlookers, by this point in the campaign, such discourse no longer took anyone by surprise. The initial response in this case differed from previous cases in that it was no longer necessary to frame the comment as sexist or to illustrate an appropriate public affective response would be one of offense. Instead, the response of Clinton supporters turned immediately to mocking. Within days, "Nasty Women" merchandise was available and Clinton herself appropriated the insult mocking Trump's misogyny by posting a photograph of herself holding up a "Nasty Woman" t-shirt to her Twitter account.

Clinton's and the DNC's Twitter accounts posted ten messages in the three days that followed the insult. Clinton's first tweets emphasized her experience and Trump's inexperience, "I'm happy to compare my 30 years of experience with your 30 years." One of her first tweets included a video of her pro-women remarks highlighting excerpts of her speech "Women's Rights are Human Rights" delivered to the United Nations while First Lady.[41] Appealing to affective intelligence, the video was designed to provide a stark contrast between her pro-woman position and Trump's misogyny. The association of positive affect with her and negative affect with him provided her base with a rationale rooted in both affect and logic to vote for Clinton and/or against Trump.

The meta-sexist dialogue expanded to include Senator Elizabeth Warren asserting at a campaign rally, "And nasty women have really had it with guys like you. Get this Donald, nasty women are tough, nasty women are smart, and nasty women vote." Representative Jim Himes, sarcastically noted, "Women who disagree with you aren't 'nasty'. In this case, they are what is known as 'right'." Highlighting Trump's contradictions, Senator Barbara Boxer tweeted, "It's especially hard to reconcile Trump's remark with a claim he made earlier the night that 'no one has more respect for women than I do.'"[42] Daughter Chelsea Clinton, when asked to respond during an interview, described her feelings as, "So it just makes me sad that that is part of our presidential election season."[43]

As for the Republican response, few from the GOP came to Trump's aid after the debate. Conservative radio host Mark Levin's argument there was nothing sexist about the remark proved largely ineffectual. Congressman Brian Babin's defense, "Sometimes a lady needs to be told when she's being nasty," did little to stop the onslaught of protest.[44] However, Trump's impulsivity did find favor among his Twitter followers who posted messages such as, "Are you going to let #hillary Bully you? I didn't think so. #RedNationRising @VoteMAGA #Women4Trump are Strong!" and "Amen @realdonaldtrump #God give you strength today #MAGA # Women4Trump It's a war between good & evil now," and "@MELANIATRUMP you are not alone in defending your husband! MILLIONS of #Women4Trump are standing with you defending him!"[45]

Akin to the previous two cases, this incident further illustrated the affective nature of meta-sexist discourse during this campaign, especially on Twitter. The electorate was asked to base political decisions on their own experiences of emotions, and upon the candidates' public display of affect and that of their base. Such political communication contributed to polarization by associating positive affect with one candidate and negative affect with his or her opponent.

Conclusions

The focus on gender throughout the campaign dramatically changed how the nation will discuss sexism and misogyny well into the future. Both men and women, Republican and Democrat, participated in the meta-sexist discourse of the campaign. Both sides negotiated which emotions were appropriate to feel, when they should feel them, toward whom, and how they should be publically expressed in the face of sexism. The three cases presented in this chapter, the Trump/Kelly exchange, the *Access Hollywood* video, and the "nasty woman" debate insult, illustrated that sexism and misogyny did not go unchallenged; it rather elicited a powerful affective response. Furthermore, these cases allow us to recognize that the nature and quality of human reasoning, including political judgments, lie in the experience of emotion as the theory of affective intelligence claims.

Moreover, this meta-sexist discourse functioned in a variety of ways including, most noteworthy for the purposes of this chapter, affective polarization. Trump tapped into long existing contempt for Clinton specifically, and into distrust of women in general. In so doing, Trump was able

226 *Jamie Capuzza*

to reify misogyny, motivate his base, and reinforce feelings of interconnectedness among his followers and negative feelings toward his opponent. The more hostile voters were toward women, the more likely they were to support Trump indicating sexism galvanized his base.[46] Clinton legitimated existing feelings of shame, humiliation, fear, and anger associated with sexism and misogyny. In so doing, Clinton was able to motivate her base reinforcing feelings of interconnectedness among her followers, emboldening feminist voices, and reinforcing negative feelings toward her opponent. These feelings later manifested as the Women's March, a protest of approximately 5 million people across all seven continents.

It is noteworthy that Trump's incendiary remarks and responses to them accumulated affective value on Twitter. Both candidates were able to generate affective intensity via this social media platform. Trump supporters utilized Twitter to show their disdain of Clinton and enthusiasm for Trump's candidacy even when his misogyny was challenged by his own party and the Clinton campaign. Clinton supporters utilized Twitter to challenge misogyny. The public exposure to others' emotions on Twitter, including shock, anger, outrage, and fear, increased the intensity of commitment to feminist ideals as well as enthusiasm and pride in the possibility of the nation's first woman president. In both campaigns, Twitter played a dramatic role in the affective polarization of the electorate.

Notes

1 Aaron Blacke, "Hillary Clinton Adds Misogyny- and More – To the List of Things She Blames for Her 2016 Loss," *The Washington Post*, May 2, 2017, www.washingtonpost.com/news/the-fix/wp/2017/05/02/hillary-clinton-adds-misogyny-and-more-to-the-list-of-reasons-she-lost/?utm_term=.fb8717b7aa2c.

2 Hillary Clinton, Twitter post, November 9, 2016, 12:51 p.m., https://twitter.com/hillaryclinton/status/796394920051441664?lang=en.

3 "Transcript: Donald Trump's Taped Comments about Women," *The New York Times*, October 8, 2016, www.nytimes.com/2016/10/08/us/donald-trump-tape-transcript.html; Kitty Bennett and Thomas Kaplan, "Trump's Call on Abortions Rattles G.O.P.," *The New York Times*, March 31, 2016, A1; Claire Cohen, "Donald Trump Sexism Tracker: Every Offensive Comment in One Place," *The Telegraph*, July 14, 2017, www.telegraph.co.uk/women/politics/donald-trump-sexism-tracker-every-offensive-comment-in-one-place/.

4 Examples of sexism in the 2016 presidential campaign can be found in articles such as: Margaret Talbot, "That's What He Said," *The New Yorker*, October 24, 2016, 92 no. 34, 19; Peter Beinart, "Fear of a Female President," *The Atlantic*, October 2016, www.theatlantic.com/magazine/archive/2016/10/fear-of-a-female-president/497564/; "What Does the US Election Say about Misogyny," *The Guardian*, November 9, 2016, www.theguardian.com/commentisfree/2016/nov/09/us-election-result-misogyny-america-panel-woman; Karrin Vasby Anderson, "'Rhymes with Blunt': Pornification and U.S. Political Culture," *Rhetoric and Public Affairs* 14, no. 2 (2011): 327.

5 Examples of sexism against Hillary Rodham Clinton as First Lady, U.S. Senator, Secretary of State, and as presidential candidate in 2008 and 2016 are too

numerous to document ranging from 1992 Republican characterizations of her as an overbearing, ambitious, radical feminist working wife unsuitable for the office of First Lady, to hecklers yelling, "Iron my shirt," to buttons that read "Trump that bitch" to political cartoons depicting her violating gender norms. For a comprehensive historic overview of sexism against Clinton, see Susan Bordo, *The Destruction of Hillary Clinton* (New York: Melville House Publishing, 2017).

6 Tanya Romaniuk, "Talking about Sexism: Meta-Sexist Talk in Presidential Politics," *Journal of Language and Social Psychology* 34, no. 4 (2015): 446.

7 W. Russell Neuman, George E. Marcus, Ann Crigler, and Michael MacKuen, *The Affect Effect: Dynamics of Emotion in Political Thinking and Behavior* (Chicago, IL: University of Chicago Press, 2007); George E. Marcus, W. Russell Neuman, and Michael MacKuen, *Affective Intelligence and Political Judgment* (Chicago, IL: University of Chicago Press, 2000).

8 The Pew Research Center, "Partisanship and Political Animosity in 2016," June 22, 2016, www.people-press.org/2016/06/22/partisanship-and-political-animosity-in-2016/; Shanto Iyengar, Gaurav Sood and Yphtach Lelkes, "Affect, Not Ideology a Social Identity Perspective on Polarization," *Public Opinion Quarterly* 76, no. 3 (2012): 405; Patrick Miller and Pamela Johnston Conover, "Red and Blue States of Mind: Partisan Hostility and Voting in the United States," *Political Research Quarterly* 68, no. 2 (2008): 225; Alan Abramowitz, *The Disappearing Center: Engaged Citizens, Polarization, and American Democracy* (New Haven, CT: Yale University Press, 2010).

9 Steven Webster and Alan Abromowitz, "The Ideological Foundation of Affective Polarization in the U.S. Electorate," *American Politics Research* 45, no. 4 (2017): 623.

10 American Psychological Association, "Stress in America: U.S. Presidential Election," October 13, 2016, www.apa.org/news/press/releases/stress/2016/presidential-election.pdf.

11 Rachel Neo, "Favoritism or Animosity? Examining How SNS Network Homogeneity Influences Vote Choice via Affective Mechanisms," *International Journal of Public Opinion Research* 28, no. 4 (2016): 461; Shanto Iyengar and Kyu S. Hahn, "Red Media, Blue Media: Evidence of Ideological Selectivity in Media Use," *Journal of Communication* 59, no. 1 (2009): 19; Mathew Levendusky, "Why Do Partisan Media Polarize Voters?" *American Journal of Political Science* 57, (2013): 611.

12 Sarah Gilmore and Samantha Warren, "Emotion Online: Experiences of Teaching in a Virtual Learning Environment," *Human Relations* 60, no. 4 (2007): 581.

13 Linh Dang-Xuan, Stefan Stieglitz, Jennifer Waldarsch and Christopher Neuberger, "An Investigation of Influentials and the Role of Sentiment in Political Communication on Twitter during Election Periods," *Information, Communication & Society* 16, no. 5 (2013): 795.

14 Jayeon Lee and Young-shin Lim, "Gendered Campaign Tweets: The Cases of Hillary Clinton and Donald Trump," *Public Relations Review* 42, (2016): 849; Gunn Enli, "Twitter as Arena for the Authentic Outsider: Exploring the Social Media Campaigns of Trump and Clinton in the 2016 US Presidential Election," *European Journal of Communication* 32, no. 1 (2017): 50.

15 Donald J. Trump, Twitter post, August 7, 2015, 12:53 a.m., https://twitter.com/realdonaldtrump/status/629561051982495744?lang=en; Donald J. Trump, Twitter post, August 7, 2015, 12:40 a.m., www.google.com/search?client=safari&rls=en&q=Wow,+@megynkelly+really+bombed+tonight.+People+are+going+wild+on+twitter!+Funny+to+watch&ie=UTF-8&oe=UTF-8.

16 Holly Yan, "Donald Trump's 'Blood' Comment about Megyn Kelly Draws Outrage," *CNN*, August 8, 2015, www.cnn.com/2015/08/08/politics/donald-trump-cnn-megyn-kelly-comment/index.html.

228 *Jamie Capuzza*

17 Trump Loyal!! @Apipwhisperer, Twitter post, August 7, 2015, https://twitter. com/Apipwhisperer; covfefe_jana, Twitter post, August 6, 2015, https://twitter. com/search?q=%E2%80%9C%40megynkelly%20put%20on%20your%20 big%20girl%20pants.%20.%20.%20.%20if%20you%20can%E2%80%99t%20 take%20it%20.%20.%20.%20Don%E2%80%99t%20dish%20it%20 out!&src=typd.
18 "Ivanka Trump Responds to 'Disturbing' Accusations about Her Father," *CBS News*, May 18, 2016, www.cbsnews.com/news/ivanka-trump-defends-donald-new-york-times-article-attacks-against-women-business-working-woman/; "Media Reaction to Megyn Kelly's Interview with Donald Trump," *Fox News*, May 18, 2016.
19 Sarah Begley, "Hillary Clinton Calls Trump Remarks 'Overboard, Offensive, Outrageous'," *Time*, August 10, 2015, http://time.com/3991549/ hillary-clinton-trump-megyn-kelly/.
20 Andrew Rafferty and Monica Alba, "Hillary Clinton on Donald Trump: 'It's All Entertainment'," *NBC News,* August 11, 2015, www.nbcnews. com/politics/hillary-clinton/hillary-clinton-donald-trump-it-s-all-entertainment-n407371.
21 Hadas Gold, "Hillary Clinton: Megyn Kelly Is a 'Superb Journalist'," *Politico,* April 5, 2016, www.politico.com/blogs/on-media/2016/04/hillary-clinton-megyn-kelly-is-a-superb-journalist-221581
22 Hillary Clinton, Twitter post, August 6, 2015, 7:37 p.m., https://twitter. com/hillaryclinton/status/629481461486370816.
23 Rae, Twitter post, August 7, 2015, 11:43 a.m., https://twitter.com/ RaeRaesTravels/status/629724477916598276.
24 Adam Lusher, "Donald Trump: All the Sexist Things He Said," *Independent,* October 9, 2016, www.independent.co.uk/news/world/americas/us-elections/ donald-trump-sexist-quotes-comments-tweets-grab-them-by-the-pussy-when-star-you-can-do-anything-a7353006.html.
25 Priorities USA, "Speak," May 16, 2016, https://youtu.be/JekzM26TF3Q; Priorities USA, "Respect," May 16, 2016, https://youtu.be/IkeLYDZdPSc
26 Alan Rappeport, "Trump Defends His Comment That Clinton Would Lose as a Man," *The New York Times*, April 26, 2016, A13.
27 Transcript: Donald Trump's Taped Comments about Women," *The New York Times*, October 8, 2016, www.nytimes.com/2016/10/08/us/donald-trump-tape-transcript.html.
28 Daniella Diaz, "Three Times Trump Defended His 'Locker Room Talk'," *CNN*, October 9, 2016, www.cnn.com/2016/10/09/politics/donald-trump-locker-room-talk-presidential-debate-2016-election/index.html.
29 Transcript: Donald Trump's Taped Comments about Women," *The New York Times*, October 8, 2016, www.nytimes.com/2016/10/08/us/donald-trump-tape-transcript.html.
30 Jeb Bush, Twitter post, October 7, 2016, 4:05 p.m., https://twitter.com/ jebbush/status/784530223605903360?lang=en; Marco Rubio, Twitter post, October 7, 2016, 6:29 p.m., https://twitter.com/marcorubio/status/784566 254271094788?lang=en.
31 Lynn Sweet, "Melania Trump: Donald Trump's Words 'Unacceptable and Offensive," *The Chicago Sun Times*, October 8, 2016, https://chicago.suntimes.com/ news/melania-trump-donald-trumps-words-unacceptable-and-offensive/.
32 Ms.BloodyButcher, Twitter post, October 7, 2016, https://twitter.com/search? q=%20lol%20don%27t%20all%20guys%20talk%20about%20banging%20 chicks%3F%20I%20mean%20women%20do%20the%20same.% 20I%20don%27t%20understand%20the%20big%20deal.%20%23Women 4Trump&src=typd; Phatzs, Twitter post, October 7, 2016, https://twitter.com/

search?q=dear%20media%2C%20What%20%40billclinton%20has%20
done%20to%20women%20is%20a%20lot%20worse%20than%20what%20
%40realDonaldTrump%20has%20said%20about%20women&src=
typd; I Voted Trump Dianna, Twitter post, October 7, 2016, https://twit-
ter.com/search?q=21.%09%20I%20Voted%20Trump%20Dianna%20
%40elvisinoregon%20%207%20Oct%202016&src=typd.

33 Hillary Clinton, Twitter post, October 7, 2016, 1:02 p.m., https://twitter.
com/hillaryclinton/status/784483939977158656?lang=en.

34 Amanda Hoover, "Hillary Clinton: Donald Trump's Lewd Comments
about Women Represent 'Exactly Who He Is'," Boston.com, October 9,
2016, www.boston.com/news/politics/2016/10/09/hillary-clinton-donald-
trumps-lewd-comments-about-women-represent-exactly-who-he-is.

35 Hillary Clinton, Twitter post, October 7, 2016, 4:54 p.m., https://twitter.
com/hillaryclinton/status/784542470847631360?lang=en.

36 Hillary Clinton, Twitter post, October 8, 2016, 7:13 a.m., https://twitter.
com/hillaryclinton/status/784758605937455104?lang=en.

37 The Democrats, Twitter post, October 8, 2016, 8:01 a.m., https://twitter.
com/thedemocrats/status/784770620668116992.

38 Alexander Burbs, Maggie Haberman, and Jonathan Martin, "Donald Trump
Apology Caps Day of Outrage Over Lewd Tape," The New York Times, October 7, 2016, https://nyti.ms/2dG9VYn.

39 David Johnson and Chris Wilson, "Donald Trump's 'Nasty Woman'" Comment Was 1 of His 48 Interruptions at the Presidential Debate," Time, October
20, 2016, http://time.com/4538271/donald-trump-nasty-woman-interruption-
presidential-debate/.

40 Jessica Samakow, "32 Tweets That Will Make You Damn Proud to Be a
Nasty Woman," Huffington Post, October 19, 2016, www.huffingtonpost.
com/entry/32-tweets-that-will-make-you-damn-proud-to-be-a-nasty-
woman_us_58083374e4b0180a36e8f59d.

41 Hillary Clinton, Twitter post, October 19, 2016, 9:46 p.m., https://twitter.
com/hillaryclinton/status/788964498401071104?lang=en.

42 Alana Horowitz Satlin, "Congressman Shuts Down Trump 'Nasty Woman'
Remark with One Simple Observation," Huffington Post, October 20, 2016,
www.huffingtonpost.com/entry/trump-clinton-debate-nasty-woman-jim-
hines_us_580898dbe4b0180a36e96474.

43 "Chelsea Clinton on 'Nasty Woman' Remark and More from Final Debate," "The
Talk," MSN, October 11, 2016, www.msn.com/en-us/travel/tripideas/the-
talk-chelsea-clinton-on-nasty-woman-remark-and-more-from-final-debate/
vp-AAjckdt.

44 Grace Guarnieri, "Texas Republican Hits Hillary Clinton: 'Sometimes a Lady
Needs to Be Told When She's Being Nasty'," Salon, October 21, 2016, www.
salon.com/2016/10/21/texas-republican-hits-hillary-clinton-sometimes-a-
lady-needs-to-be-told-when-shes-being-nasty/.

45 Deplorable ET, Twitter post, October 19, 2016, https://twitter.com/search?
q=are%20you%20going%20to%20let%20Hillary%20bully%20you%20I%20
didn%27t%20think%20so&src=typd&lang=en; Goladygo, Twitter post, November 3, 2016, https://twitter.com/search?q=%40realdonaldtrump%20%23
God%20give%20you%20strength%20today%20%23MAGA%20%23Wo-
men4Trump%20It%27s%20a%20war%20between%20good%20%26%20
evil%20now%2C&src=typd&lang=en; Lori Hendry, Twitter post, October
17, 2016, https://twitter.com/search?q=you%20are%20not%20alone%20in%
20defending%20your%20husband!%20%20MILLIONS%20of%20
%23Women4Trump%20are%20standing%20with%20you%20defending
%20him!"&src=typd&lang=en.

230 *Jamie Capuzza*

46 Brian Schaffner, Matthew MacWilliams, and Tatishe Nteta, "Explaining White Polarization in the 2016 Vote for the President: The Sobering Role of Racism and Sexism (Presentation: Conference on the U.S. Elections of 2016: Domestic and International Aspects, Herzliya, Israel, January 8–9, 2017); Carly Wayne, Nicholas Valentino, and Marzia Oceno, "How Sexism Drives Support for Donald Trump," *The Washington Post,* October 23, 2016, www.washingtonpost.com/news/monkey-cage/wp/2016/10/23/how-sexism-drives-support-for-donald-trump/?utm_term=.577111eb8d0b; Kate Ratliff, Liz Redford, John Conway and Colin Tucker Smith, "Engendering Support: Hostile Sexism Predicts Voting for Donald Trump over Hillary Clinton in the 2016 U.S. Presidential Election," *Group Processes & Intergroup Relations,* December 29, 2017, https://doi.org/10.1177/1368430217741203.

Bibliography

Abramowitz, Alan. *The Disappearing Center: Engaged Citizens, Polarization, and American Democracy.* New Haven, CT: Yale University Press, 2010.

American Psychological Association. "Stress in America: U.S. Presidential Election." October 13, 2016. www.apa.org/news/press/releases/stress/2016/presidential-election.pdf.

Anderson, Karrin Vasby. "'Rhymes with Blunt': Pornification and U.S. Political Culture." *Rhetoric and Public Affairs* 14, no. 2 (2011): 327–368.

Begley, Sarah. "Hillary Clinton Calls Trump Remarks 'Overboard, Offensive, Outrageous'." *Time,* August 10, 2015. http://time.com/3991549/hillary-clinton-trump-megyn-kelly/.

Beinart, Peter. "Fear of a Female President." *The Atlantic,* October 2016. www.theatlantic.com/magazine/archive/2016/10/fear-of-a-female-president/497564/.

Bennett, Kitty, and Thomas Kaplan. "Opinion Trump's Views on Abortion and Women." *The New York Times,* March 31, 2016. www.nytimes.com/2016/04/01/opinion/trumps-views-on-abortion-and-women.html.

Blake, Aaron. "Analysis Hillary Clinton Adds Misogyny – and More – to the List of Things She Blames for Her 2016 Loss." *The Washington Post,* May 2, 2017. www.washingtonpost.com/news/the-fix/wp/2017/05/02/hillary-clinton-adds-misogyny-and-more-to-the-list-of-reasons-she-lost/?utm_term=.fb8717b7aa2c.

Bordo, Susan. *The Destruction of Hillary Clinton.* New York: Melville House Publishing, 2017.

Burbs, Alexander, Maggie Haberman, and Jonathan Martin. "Donald Trump Apology Caps Day of Outrage over Lewd Tape." *The New York Times,* October 7, 2016. https://nyti.ms/2dG9VYn.

Bush, Jeb. *Twitter,* October 7, 2016. https://twitter.com/jebbush/status/784530223605903360?lang=en.

"Chelsea Clinton on 'Nasty Woman' Remark and More from Final Debate." "The Talk," *MSN,* October 11, 2016. www.msn.com/en-us/travel/tripideas/the-talk-chelsea-clinton-on-nasty-woman-remark-and-more-from-final-debate/vp-AAjckdt.

Clinton, Hillary. *Twitter,* November 9, 2016. https://twitter.com/hillaryclinton/status/796394920051441664?lang=en

Clinton, Hillary. *Twitter,* October 7, 2016. https://twitter.com/hillaryclinton/status/784483939977158656?lang=en.

Clinton, Hillary. *Twitter*, August 6, 2015. https://twitter.com/hillaryclinton/status/629481461486370816.

Clinton, Hillary. *Twitter*, October 7, 2016. https://twitter.com/hillaryclinton/status/784542470847631360?lang=en.

Clinton, Hillary. *Twitter*, October 8, 2016. https://twitter.com/hillaryclinton/status/784758605937455104?lang=en.

Clinton, Hillary. *Twitter*, October 19, 2016. https://twitter.com/hillaryclinton/status/788964498401071104?lang=en.

Cohen, Claire. "Donald Trump Sexism Tracker: Every Offensive Comment in One Place." *The Telegraph*. July 14, 2017. www.telegraph.co.uk/women/politics/donald-trump-sexism-tracker-every-offensive-comment-in-one-place/.

Covfefe_jana. *Twitter*, August 6, 2015. https://twitter.com/search?q=%E2%80%9C%40megynkelly%20put%20on%20your%20big%20girl%20pants.%20.%20.%20.%20if%20you%20can%E2%80%99t%20take%20it%20.%20.%20.%20Don%E2%80%99t%20dish%20it%20out!&src=typd.

Dang-Xuan, Linh, Stefan Stieglitz, Jennifer Waldarsch, and Christopher Neuberger. "An Investigation of Influentials and the Role of Sentiment in Political Communication on Twitter during Election Periods." *Information, Communication & Society* 16, no. 5 (2013): 795–825.

Deplorable ET, *Twitter*, October 19, 2016. https://twitter.com/search?q=are%20you%20going%20to%20let%20Hillary%20bully%20you%20I%20didn%27t%20think%20so&src=typd&lang=en; Goladygo, Twitter post, November 3, 2016.

Diaz, Daniella. "Three Times Trump Defended His 'Locker Room Talk'." *CNN*, October 9, 2016. www.cnn.com/2016/10/09/politics/donald-trump-locker-room-talk-presidential-debate-2016-election/index.html.

Enli, Gunn. "Twitter as Arena for the Authentic Outsider: Exploring the Social Media Campaigns of Trump and Clinton in the 2016 US Presidential Election." *European Journal of Communication* 32, no. 1 (2017): 50–61.

Gilmore, Sarah, and Samantha Warren. "Emotion Online: Experiences of Teaching in a Virtual Learning Environment." *Human Relations* 60, no. 4 (2007): 581–608.

Goladygo, *Twitter*, November 3, 2016. https://twitter.com/search?q=%40realdonaldtrump%20%23God%20give%20you%20strength%20today%20%23MAGA%20%23Women4Trump%20It%27s%20a%20war%20between%20good%20%26%20evil%20now%2C&src=typd&lang=en; Lori Hendry, Twitter post, October 17, 2016.

Gold, Hadas. "Hillary Clinton: Megyn Kelly Is a 'Superb Journalist'." *Politico*, April 5, 2016. www.politico.com/blogs/on-media/2016/04/hillary-clinton-megyn-kelly-is-a-superb-journalist-221581.

Guarnieri, Grace. "Texas Republican Hits Hillary Clinton: 'Sometimes a Lady Needs to Be Told When She's Being Nasty.'" *Salon*, October 21, 2016. www.salon.com/2016/10/21/texas-republican-hits-hillary-clinton-sometimes-a-lady-needs-to-be-told-when-shes-being-nasty/.

Hoover, Amanda. "Hillary Clinton: Donald Trump's Lewd Comments about Women Represent 'Exactly Who He Is'." Boston.com, October 9, 2016. www.boston.com/news/politics/2016/10/09/hillary-clinton-donald-trumps-lewd-comments-about-women-represent-exactly-who-he-is.

Horowitz Satlin, Alana. "Congressman Shuts Down Trump 'Nasty Woman' Remark with One Simple Observation." *Huffington Post*, October 20, 2016. www.

232 *Jamie Capuzza*

huffingtonpost.com/entry/trump-clinton-debate-nasty-woman-jim-hines_us_580898dbe4b0180a36e96474.

"Ivanka Trump Responds to 'Disturbing' Accusations about Her Father." *CBS News*, May 18, 2016. www.cbsnews.com/news/ivanka-trump-defends-donald-new-york-times-article-attacks-against-women-business-working-woman/.

I Voted Trump Dianna, *Twitter*, October 7, 2016. https://twitter.com/search?q=21.%09%20I%20Voted%20Trump%20Dianna%20%40elvisinoregon%20%207%20Oct%202016&src=typd.

Iyengar, Shanto, Gaurav Sood, and Yphtach Lelkes. "Affect, Not Ideology a Social Identity Perspective on Polarization." *Public Opinion Quarterly* 76, no. 3 (2012): 405–431. doi:10.1093/poq/nfs038.

Iyengar, Shanto, and Kyu S. Hahn. "Red Media, Blue Media: Evidence of Ideological Selectivity in Media Use." *Journal of Communication* 59, no. 1 (2009): 19–39.

Johnson, David, and Chris Wilson. "Donald Trump's 'Nasty Woman" Comment Was 1 of His 48 Interruptions at the Presidential Debate." *Time*, October 20, 2016. http://time.com/4538271/donald-trump-nasty-woman-interruption-presidential-debate/.

Lee, Jayeon, and Young-shin Lim. "Gendered Campaign Tweets: The Cases of Hillary Clinton and Donald Trump." *Public Relations Review* 42 (2016): 849–855.

Levendusky, Mathew. "Why Do Partisan Media Polarize Voters?" *American Journal of Political Science* 57 (2013): 611–623.

Lori Hendry, *Twitter*, October 17, 2016. https://twitter.com/search?q=you%20are%20not%20alone%20in%20defending%20your%20husband!%20%20MILLIONS%20of%20%23Women4Trump%20are%20standing%20with%20you%20defending%20him!"&src=typd&lang=en.

Lusher, Adam. "Donald Trump: All the Sexist Things He Said." *Independent*, October 9, 2016. www.independent.co.uk/news/world/americas/us-elections/donald-trump-sexist-quotes-comments-tweets-grab-them-by-the-pussy-when-star-you-can-do-anything-a7353006.html.

Marcus, George E., W. Russell Neuman, and Michael MacKuen. *Affective Intelligence and Political Judgment*. Chicago, IL: University of Chicago Press, 2000.

"Media Reaction to Megyn Kelly's Interview with Donald Trump, *Fox News*, May 18, 2016.

Miller, Patrick, and Pamela Johnston Conover. "Red and Blue States of Mind: Partisan Hostility and Voting in the United States." *Political Research Quarterly* 68, no. 2 (2008): 225–239. doi.org/10.1177/1065912915577208.

Ms.BloodyButcher, *Twitter*, October 7, 2016. https://twitter.com/search?q=%20lol%20don%27t%20all%20guys%20talk%20about%20banging%20chicks%3F%20I%20mean%20women%20do%20the%20same.%20I%20don%27t%20understand%20the%20big%20deal.%20%23Women4Trump&src=typd.

Neo, Rachel. "Favoritism or Animosity? Examining How SNS Network Homogeneity Influences Vote Choice via Affective Mechanisms." *International Journal of Public Opinion Research* 28, no. 4 (2016): 461–483. doi.org/10.1093/ijpor/edv035.

Neuman, W. Russell, Marcus, George E., Crigler, Ann, and MacKuen, Michael. *The Affect Effect: Dynamics of Emotion in Political Thinking and Behavior*. Chicago, IL: University of Chicago Press, 2007.

Pew Research Center. "Partisanship and Political Animosity in 2016." June 22, 2016. www.people-press.org/2016/06/22/partisanship-and-political-animosity-in-2016/.

Phatzs. *Twitter*, October 7, 2016. https://twitter.com/search?q=dear%20media%2C%20What%20%40billclinton%20has%20done%20to%20women%20is%20a%20lot%20worse%20than%20what%20%40realDonaldTrump%20has%20said%20about%20women&src=typd.

Priorities USA. "Respect," May 16, 2016. https://youtu.be/IkeLYDZdPSc.

Priorities USA. "Speak," May 16, 2016. www.youtube.com/watch?v=JekzM26TF3Q.

Priorities USA, "Speak," May 16, 2016. https://youtu.be/JekzM26TF3Q.

Rae. *Twitter*, August 7, 2015, 11:43 a.m. https://twitter.com/RaeRaesTravels/status/629724477916598276.

Rafferty, Andrew, and Monica Alba. "Hillary Clinton on Donald Trump: 'It's All Entertainment'." *NBC News*, August 11, 2015. www.nbcnews.com/politics/hillary-clinton/hillary-clinton-donald-trump-it-s-all-entertainment-n407371.

Rappeport, Alan. "Trump Defends His Comment that Clinton Would Lose as a Man." *The New York Times*, April 26, 2016, A13.

Ratliff, Kate, Liz Redford, John Conway, and Colin Tucker Smith. "Engendering Support: Hostile Sexism Predicts Voting for Donald Trump over Hillary Clinton in the 2016 U.S. Presidential Election." *Group Processes & Intergroup Relations*, December 29, 2017. doi.org/10.1177/1368430217741203.

Romaniuk, Tanya. "Talking About Sexism: Meta-Sexist Talk in Presidential Politics." *Journal of Language and Social Psychology* 34, no. 4 (2015): 446–463.

Rubio, Marco. *Twitter*, October 7, 2016. https://twitter.com/marcorubio/status/784566254271094788?lang=en.

Samakow, Jessica. "32 Tweets That Will Make You Damn Proud to Be a Nasty Woman." *Huffington Post*, October 19, 2016. www.huffingtonpost.com/entry/32-tweets-that-will-make-you-damn-proud-to-be-a-nasty-woman_us_58083374e4b0180a36e8f59d.

Schaffner, Brian, Matthew MacWilliams, and Tatishe Nteta. "Explaining White Polarization in the 2016 Vote for the President: The Sobering Role of Racism and Sexism (Presentation: Conference on the U.S. Elections of 2016: Domestic and International Aspects, Herzliya, Israel, January 8–9, 2017).

Sweet, Lynn. "Melania Trump: Donald Trump's Words 'Unacceptable and Offensive." *The Chicago Sun Times*, October 8, 2016. https://chicago.suntimes.com/news/melania-trump-donald-trumps-words-unacceptable-and-offensive/.

Talbot, Margaret. "That's What He Said." *The New Yorker*, October 24, 2016.

The Democrats. *Twitter*, October 8, 2016. https://twitter.com/thedemocrats/status/784770620668116992.

"Transcript: Donald Trump's Taped Comments about Women." *The New York Times*, October 8, 2016. www.nytimes.com/2016/10/08/us/donald-trump-tape-transcript.html.

Trump, Donald J. Twitter, August 7, 2015. https://twitter.com/realdonaldtrump/status/629561051982495744?lang=en.

Trump, Donald J. Twitter, August 7, 2015. www.google.com/search?client=safari&rls=en&q=Wow,+@megynkelly+really+bombed+tonight.+People+are+going+wild+on+twitter!+Funny+to+watch&ie=UTF-8&oe=UTF-8.

Trump Loyal!! @Apipwhisperer, Twitter, August 7, 2015. https://twitter.com/Apipwhisperer.

Wayne, Carly, Nicholas Valentino, and Marzia Oceno. "How Sexism Drives Support for Donald Trump." *The Washington Post*, October 23, 2016. www.washingtonpost.com/news/monkey-cage/wp/2016/10/23/how-sexism-drives-support-for-donald-trump/?utm_term=.577111eb8d0b.

234 *Jamie Capuzza*

Webster, Steven, and Alan Abromowitz. "The Ideological Foundation of Affective Polarization in the U.S. Electorate." *American Politics Research* 45, no. 4 (2017): 623–624.

"What Does the US Election Say about Misogyny." *The Guardian,* November 9, 2016. www.theguardian.com/commentisfree/2016/nov/09/us-election-result-misogyny-america-panel-woman.

Yan, Holly. "Donald Trump's 'Blood' Comment about Megyn Kelly Draws Outrage." *CNN,* August 8, 2015. www.cnn.com/2015/08/08/politics/donald-trump-cnn-megyn-kelly-comment/index.html.

Index

abject/abjection 8, 144, 146, 148–52
Access Hollywood tapes 209, 219,
  222–23, 225
advertising/advertisement 70, 74–5,
  136, 138, 145–46, 158, 185
aesthetic(s) 9–10, 61–3, 159–60, 163,
  205–06, 208, 211
affect: theories of 17–18, 25, 34, 45–6,
  56, 61, 106, 108–09, 113, 158, 186–87,
  216; definition of 21, 23–5, 37, 39–40,
  50, 70, 94–5, 108; circulation of 8,
  22–3, 115, 186; emotion and 10, 37,
  44, 98; discursive dimension of 23
affect/emotion distinction 7, 34–5, 41,
  49–51
affective appeal(s) 6–7, 70, 135–36, 140
affective resonance 115
affective rhetoric 8, 70, 148, 150;
  definition of 71–2; significance of 74–6
affective turn/turn to affect 7, 35, 37,
  48, 51
affective: bias 3, 4; cogitation 63–4;
  culture(s) 95, 97–101; intelligence
  216–17; neuroscience 24;
  polarization 217–19
agency 23, 58, 60, 82; denial of 151
Ahmed, Sarah 23, 95–8, 101, 109–10,
  112, 116, 148–49, 152
alexithymia 4–6
alt-right 188
anger 1–2, 5, 8–9, 18, 43, 45–7, 49–50,
  58, 69, 74, 115–21, 166, 185–86,
  189–91, 195–201, 216–17, 226
anti-Muslim 8, 116–17, 119–20, 122, 215
anti-terrorism campaign 8
anxiety 5, 8, 22, 47, 82, 86, 115–17, 121,
  145, 158, 160, 163, 175, 190, 205, 217
appetite 3, 21, 22, 57
archetype/archetypal 8, 62, 133–37,
  139, 140

argumentation 6, 7, 44, 69, 70–2,
  74–6, 190
Aristotle/Aristotelian: 18–22, 57–8,
  196; *Rhetoric* 6, 18–20, 69–70;
  Nicomachean Ethics 19–20; topology
  of the soul 19; *logos* 57, 69 *see also*
  logic/logical appeals/logos; *pathos*
  17–19, 69–70, 196
attention economy/*Economics of
  Attention* 4, 206, 211
Augustine 59–60

basic emotions 26
Bathroom Bill, *see* North Carolina
  House Bill 2
Bernays, Edward 159, 163
Beube, Doug 158, 161–63, 166
Brennan, Teresa 58–9
Burke, Kenneth 57, 71, 190, 199

Cambridge Analytica 2
Cassirer, Ernst 57
Cicero, Marcus Tullius 58, 61, 69
Claire Fontaine 160–61, 166
Clinton, Hillary 2, 10, 188–90, 199,
  209–10, 215, 217–26
Clough, Patricia 37–8, 48, 96
Condit, Celeste 27
core emotion 26
cultural narrative 95, 98–101
cultural studies 1, 6, 7, 17, 20, 26–7, 39,
  115–16, 148

Darwin, Charles/Darwinian 17, 25–6;
  *The Expression of Emotions in Man and
  Animals* 25
Dawkins, Richard 187
decision-making 3, 4, 5, 19, 137, 190
Deleuze, Gilles/ Deleuzian 17, 20,
  22–4, 27, 39, 96, 148, 159

236 *Index*

design/design aesthetics 1, 4, 144, 150, 208
desire 6, 18, 21–4, 37, 44, 60–1, 70–2, 74, 82, 86, 108, 113, 118, 149, 152, 159, 163
discursive regimes 23–4, 27
discursive turn 7, 35, 37–8, 44, 48–9, 51
disgust 8, 45, 50, 69, 108, 119, 144–46, 148–53
disposition theory 172–73
doxa 84, 95, 98–9, 101

Eco, Umberto 135–6, 138
Ekman, Paul 17, 26, 45
embodied cognition 22
embodied reason 22
emotion 2–7, 17–27, 34–45, 47–51, 69, 71–6, 82, 85, 97–8, 101, 107–09, 113, 115–19, 148, 172–73, 175; definitions of 18, 24, 39–40, 50, 96; appeals to 1, 3, 70, 144–45, 195–96, 198, 201, 210 *see also* pathos
emotional-material rhetoric 27
emotional: embodiment 25; logic 19
empathy 5, 171, 173–75, 178–79
enthymeme 6, 71
envy 37, 49–50, 58
ethos 69, 138, 201

Facebook 191, 208–11, 218
fake news 9, 205–06, 208–11
fear 1, 2, 5, 8–9, 18, 45–7, 49–50, 60, 74, 86, 93, 99–100, 106, 108–09, 111–13, 115–22, 144–45, 152–53, 158–61, 165–67, 187, 196–201, 205, 207–10, 216–17, 220–22, 226
feminism/feminist 48, 107, 215–17, 222, 224, 226
Foucault, Michel 23–4, 41
Frank, Adam 44–6, 48
Freud, Sigmund/Freudian 20, 22, 24, 46–8, 159

Gibbs, Anna 27, 186, 189
Gonzalez, Emma 9, 197, 200–01
Grant, Ulysses 8, 133–37, 139–40
grief 117, 171–73, 176, 178–79, 200–01
Grossberg, Lawrence 23–4, 27
Guattari, Felix 17, 20, 22–4, 27, 96, 159

Habermas, Jürgen 206
Haidt, Johnathan 56
hate 1, 59, 116, 120, 166, 197–98

hate crimes 106, 109, 115, 118
Hawhee, Debra 27
HB2 *see* North Carolina House Bill 2

ideology 8, 24, 44, 76, 93–5, 97, 99, 101, 118, 197
Information Deficit Model 3
intertextual frames 136, 138
Islamophobia 83, 116, 119, 120

James-Lange theory of emotion 25 *see also* theories of emotion
James, William 20, 25
jealousy 34–8, 47, 49

Kelly, Megyn 198, 219–21, 223, 225

Lacan, Jacques/Lacanian 20, 22, 24, 47
Lange, Carl 25
Lanham, Richard 22, 206
Lee, Robert 8, 81, 93, 99, 101, 133–40
LGBTQ 95, 107, 109–13
logos/logical appeal 6, 57, 69, 72, 218
Lyle, David 163–66

Marcuse, Herbert 62–4
mass media 1, 7, 8, 44, 70, 75–6, 94, 165
Massumi, Brian 9, 24, 27, 34, 37–8, 48, 49–51, 82, 93, 96, 108, 121, 159, 166, 207; "The Autonomy of Affect" 39–44
memes 138, 187–91, 224
meta-sexist discourse 215–19, 223–26
mimetic communication 186
misogyny 2, 10, 208, 215–16
moral interpretation of affect 58–61
moral reasoning 4, 5, 56

neuroscience 1, 3, 6–7, 17, 20, 24–6, 51, 115, 215
North Carolina's House Bill 2 106–08, 110–13
nostalgia 7, 81–7, 138, 164, 166
Nussbaum, Martha 20

Obama, Barack 3, 100, 188, 190, 197, 223
objectification 58, 217
Olbrechts-Tyteca, Lucy 7, 70

panopticism 24
parasocial 9, 171, 173–75, 178–79

passion 21–2, 51, 71–2, 118, 159, 202, 216
pathos 17–19, 69, 72
Perelman, Chäim 7, 70, 195
persuasion 1, 3, 6, 10, 60, 69–72, 74–6, 94, 115–16, 144, 195
pity 18, 20, 69
Pizzagate 189, 209
Plato 18–20, 97–9, 115
pleasure 18, 19, 21, 138, 151–53
political grammar of feelings 196
politics of feeling 196
post-structuralist 48
Post-truth 8, 9, 119–22, 197, 206, 208–09, 211, 220
pride 58, 60, 74, 176, 179, 218, 226
productive criticism 144, 148–50, 153
prototypical emotional episode 25
psychoanalysis 22, 46–8
Psychoanalysis in Context 46–8
psychographics 135
public health campaign 8–9, 143–50

Queer bodies 109–10, 112
Queer theory 39, 107

rage 9, 18, 45, 116, 118, 185–86, 189–91
rationality 38, 59, 60

reason-emotion dichotomy/binary 21, 115
Romantic Interpretation of affect 61–4

Schaefer, Donovan 56, 116
Sedgwick, Eve 44–6, 48, 108, 111
sexism 2, 10, 215–17, 220–21, 223, 225–26
shame 8, 45–6, 50, 106, 108–11, 113
social constructionist 35, 48
Social stigma 144–46
Spinoza, Benedict/Spinozan 17, 20–4, 39, 49–50, 96
spreading-activation model 176

tearjerker 9, 171–74, 176–78
theology 59–61, 64
thymos 6
Tomkins, Silvan 3, 26, 43–7, 50, 108–09, 187
topos/topoi 84, 86
Toulmin, Stephen 7, 70
Trump, Donald 1–2, 8–10, 82, 86, 93, 95, 98–100, 119–20, 185–86, 188–91, 195–202, 205, 208–10, 215, 217–26
Twitter 81–2, 186, 191, 209–10, 218–26

White nationalism 7, 81–7

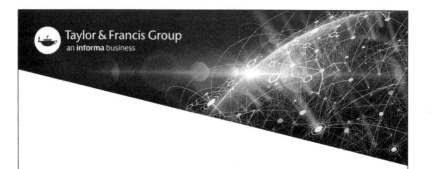